Preface

Welcome to "Internet of Things." The Internet of Things (IoT) is more than just a buzzword; it's a transformative force that's reshaping the way we interact with the world around us. From smart homes that anticipate our needs to industrial processes optimized for efficiency, the IoT has woven itself into the fabric of our daily lives and industries, promising a future of unprecedented connectivity and convenience.

This book, "Internet of Things," is your comprehensive guide to understanding, developing for, and thriving in this exciting and dynamic field. Whether you're a curious newcomer, a seasoned developer, or a business leader seeking to harness the potential of IoT, this book has something to offer you. The journey through the pages of this book will take you from the fundamentals of IoT, exploring its history and core concepts, to diving deep into the technologies and protocols that power it. You'll discover the myriad of applications where IoT is making a difference, from smart homes and healthcare to agriculture and smart cities.

We'll explore the critical issues surrounding IoT, such as data security and privacy, and equip you with the knowledge to navigate these challenges effectively. Through hands-on examples and practical advice, you'll gain the skills needed to develop IoT solutions, whether you're building a simple home automation project or a complex industrial system. But this book isn't just about the nuts and bolts of IoT; it's also about the bigger picture.

We'll examine the ethical and social implications of a world where everything is connected, discussing the responsible development and deployment of IoT technologies. As you delve into the Chapters that follow, you'll find a wealth of information, insights, and inspiration to fuel your IoT journey. This book is a testament to the incredible possibilities that emerge when our physical world meets the digital realm, and we hope it serves as a valuable resource on your quest to master the Internet of Things.

The IoT landscape is evolving rapidly, and it's an exciting time to be a part of this technological revolution. So, let's embark on this journey together and explore the limitless potential of the Internet of Things.

Table of Contents

Chapter 1: Introduction to the Internet of Things

What is the Internet of Things?

Internet of Things (IoT) in essence connects everyday devices to the Internet and allows them to communicate with us, with anyone and computer systems. These objects or "things" are equipped with sensors, processors and communication technologies that allow them to store and exchange information.

The way it works is as follows:

Sensors and Devices: The Internet of Things starts with the things around us. These devices can be anything from household appliances (like a heater or refrigerator), to industrial machinery (like manufacturing robots) or personal equipment (like fitness trackers or smart watches). These products are equipped with sensors such as small probes that can detect information such as temperature, motion, light, humidity or location.

Data Collection: These sensors are constantly collecting data. For example, a smart thermostat can measure the temperature in your home, and a fitness tracker can track your heart rate and daily steps.

InternetConnection: IoT devices have a way to connect to the Internet. This connection can be made via WiFi, cellular, Bluetooth or other means. This allows them to send the recorded data to other devices or to the cloud (a remote location on the Internet).

Data Transmission: The collected data is sent over the Internet to a central location or to another device. This can be your smartphone, computer or a private cloud server.

Data Analysis: Data can be analyzed when it reaches its target. This analysis can reveal important information or patterns. For example, your smart fridge can analyze data to alert you when your inventory is running low.

Automation and Control: The Internet of Things also enables automation and control. You can use your smartphone to control smart home appliances such as lights, thermostats or meters. Industrial IoT systems can adjust production processes based on real-time data from sensors.

Applications: The possibilities of the Internet of Things are vast. It is used in many applications such as medicine, agriculture, transportation and business smart buildings and devices. For example, it can help doctors monitor patients' health, farmers optimize irrigation based on soil moisture data, or improve transport efficiency by tracking vehicles and managing routes.

Security and Privacy: Security and privacy is a major concern as all this information is shared. Securing IoT systems is critical to protecting data and the devices themselves.

In fact, IoT brings physical devices to the digital world by connecting them to the internet. It creates a network of smart data storage devices that can make our lives easier, more efficient and more informed.

IoT and Digitization

IoT (Internet of Things) and digitization are two interconnected concepts that have significantly reshaped industries and daily life. IoT encompasses a network of smart devices equipped with sensors and connectivity, enabling them to collect and share data over the internet. This data, often generated in real-time, drives automation, enhances efficiency, and finds applications in smart homes, healthcare, agriculture, transportation, and industry. However, IoT's success relies on digitization, the process of converting Analog information, processes, and objects into digital formats. Digitization facilitates the transformation of data collected by IoT devices into digital form, allowing for storage, analysis, and data-driven decision-making. This digital transformation is characterized by streamlined processes, automation, improved accessibility, and enhanced customer experiences. Together, IoT and digitization form a powerful duo, with IoT generating valuable data for digitization processes to unlock new possibilities, efficiencies, and insights across various domains.

IoT Devices Vs Computers

Aspect	Traditional Computers	Internet of Things
Purpose and Function	General-purpose computing	Specialized data collection or control
Connectivity	Primarily wired or Wi-Fi	Various protocols (Wi-Fi, Bluetooth, Cellular, etc.)
Size and Form Factor	Diverse form factors	Compact and embedded in objects or environments
Processing Power	Powerful processors	Limited processing power
User Interaction	User interfaces (keyboard, mouse, touchscreen)	Limited or remote user interaction
Lifecycle and Deployment	Broad range of applications	Specific applications and environments

Historical Evolution

Birth of the Web: Everything starts with the web. Back within the 1960s, the web was made as a way for computers to conversation to each other. It was like building a mammoth phone framework for computers.

Early Concepts: Within the 1980s and 1990s, intelligent people begun considering approximately interfacing more than fair computers. They envisioned interfacing all sorts of regular things, like machines and contraptions, to the web. This was the exceptionally starting of the IoT thought.

RFID Labels: Within the early 2000s, Radio-Frequency Recognizable proof (RFID) labels came into play. These are modest chips that can be joined to things and utilized to track them. They were like infant steps toward making regular objects "keen."

Smartphones and Remote Web: The genuine enchantment happened when smartphones got to be well known around the mid-2000s. These phones had capable computers interior them and may interface to the web wirelessly. Individuals might control things like their music, cameras, and indeed domestic indoor regulators from their phones.

Sensors All over: Around the same time, sensors begun getting littler, cheaper, and more effective. This implied that ordinary things like streetlights, cars, and indeed waste cans may have sensors interior them to gather information.

Savvy Homes: By the late 2000s and early 2010s, companies started making keen domestic gadgets like indoor regulators, light bulbs, and doorbells. These contraptions may interface to the web and be controlled from your phone. It was the starting of the smart domestic transformation.

Mechanical IoT: Within the mechanical world, IoT was utilized to form industrial facilities and businesses more productive. Machines and hardware begun talking to each other to optimize generation and diminish downtime.

Development and Challenges: IoT kept developing, and by the 2010s, it was all around us. We had smartwatches, associated cars, and indeed wearable wellness trackers. But alongside all the cool stuff, individuals begun stressing around protection and security since so much information was being collected.

Future Conceivable outcomes: Nowadays, IoT could be a huge bargain. We will control our homes remotely, screen our wellbeing with wearable gadgets, and indeed have self-driving cars on the skyline. Long-standing time might bring indeed more energizing employments of IoT, from shrewd cities to progressed healthcare.

In straightforward terms, IoT is like turning regular objects into savvy, associated gadgets that make our lives simpler and more helpful. It all begun with the web and the thought of things talking to each other. Over a long time, innovation advanced, making it conceivable for our things to gotten to be more astute and more associated than ever some time recently.

Key Concepts and Definitions

Here are a few key concepts and definitions within the Web of Things (IoT):

IoT Device: An IoT gadget may be a physical question or thing equipped with sensors, actuators, and network innovation that permits it to gather and trade information over the web. Cases incorporate keen indoor regulators, wellness trackers, and mechanical sensors.

Sensors: Sensors are components inside IoT gadgets that can distinguish and degree physical or natural properties such as temperature, stickiness, movement, light, and more. They are capable for collecting information from the device's environment.

Actuators: Actuators are components that empower IoT gadgets to perform activities or assignments based on informational gotten. For case, a savvy entryway bolt can be an actuator that locks or opens the entryway remotely.

Network: Network alludes to the implies by which IoT gadgets communicate with each other or with central frameworks. Common network choices incorporate Wi-Fi, cellular networks, Bluetooth, Zigbee, and LoRaWAN.

IoT Stage: An IoT stage may be a program system or benefit that gives instruments and foundation for overseeing and analysing IoT information. It frequently incorporates information capacity, handling, security, and gadget administration highlights.

Data Analytics: Information analytics in IoT includes analysing and deriving insights from the endless sum of information created by IoT devices. This may incorporate real-time checking, prescient examination, and information visualization to create educated choices.

Edge Computing: Edge computing could be a concept where information handling and investigation happen closer to the IoT gadgets themselves, instead of in a centralized cloud. This diminishes inactivity and can improve real-time decision-making.

Cloud Computing: Cloud computing includes putting away and handling IoT information on inaccessible servers facilitated on the web. Cloud stages offer versatility and openness for overseeing expansive volumes of IoT information.

Interoperability: Interoperability alludes to the capacity of distinctive IoT gadgets and frameworks to work together consistently. Standardization and common conventions are basic for accomplishing interoperability.

Security: Security is basic in IoT to ensure gadgets, information, and systems from cyberattacks. It incorporates measures such as encryption, verification, and get to control to guarantee the privacy and judgment of IoT frameworks.

Protection: Protection concerns the security of individuals' individual information collected by IoT gadgets. Controls and approaches frequently administer how IoT data can be utilized and shared to protect users' security.

IoT Biological system: The IoT biological system includes all the interconnected components, counting gadgets, systems, stages, and applications, that collectively empower IoT usefulness and administrations.

Savvy Domestic: A savvy domestic may be a private environment prepared with IoT gadgets that upgrade mechanization, vitality effectiveness, security, and comfort. Illustrations incorporate shrewd lighting, indoor regulators, and voice-controlled collaborators.

Industrial IoT (IIOT): IIOT centres on the application of IoT innovation in mechanical settings to progress fabricating forms, screen gear, and optimize supply chains.

5G and IoT: The fifth-generation (5G) cellular organize plays a pivotal part in supporting the enormous network and low-latency requirements of IoT applications.

IoT Functional blocks

Here are the key IoT functional blocks:

IoT Devices: Physical sensors and objects that collect data.

Connectivity: Communication protocols for device networking.

Data Processing: Handling, filtering, and analysis of data.

Data Storage: Storage solutions for collected data.

Security: Measures to protect devices and data.

Device Management: Provisioning, configuration, and monitoring.

IoT Applications: End-user software for specific services.

User Interfaces: Interfaces for human interaction.

Cloud Computing: Scalable infrastructure for data processing.

Edge and Fog Computing: Local data processing.

Networking Infrastructure: Networking components.

Scalability and Orchestration: Resource management.

Monitoring and Management: Systemhealthinsights.

APIs and Integration: Interconnectingcomponents.

IoT Architecture

This is a 4 layered architecture that enables IoT systems to collect, communicate, process, and present data efficiently while ensuring user accessibility and security.

Sensing Layer: Collects data from sensors and actuators, measuring physical parameters like temperature and humidity. Devices are connected through wired or wireless protocols.

Network Layer: Provides communication between IoT devices and the internet. Uses technologies like WIFI, Bluetooth, Zigbee, and cellular networks. May include gateways and security measures like encryption.

Data Processing Layer: Receives and processes data from IoT devices. Utilizes data management systems, analytics platforms, and machine learning to extract insights. Examples include data lakes for raw data storage.

Application Layer: Interacts with end-users, offering user-friendly interfaces (e.g., mobile apps, web portals) to control IoT devices. Middleware services enable device communication, while advanced analytics provide meaningful insights.

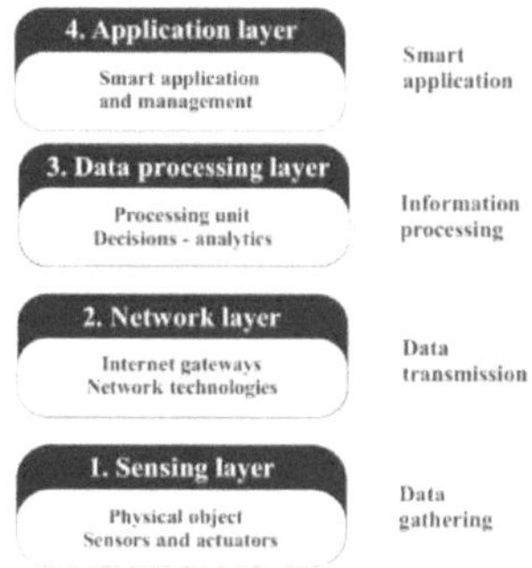

Levels of IoT

IoT (Internet of Things) systems can be categorized into various levels based on their complexity and functionality. These levels help us understand the different components and capabilities of IoT systems. Here are some common levels of IoT systems:

Level 1: Device-Level IoT System:

Description: This is the foundational level where IoT systems start. It consists of individual devices or sensors that can connect to the internet or a network to collect data. These devices are typically simple and transmit data to a central server or cloud platform for processing.

Components:

IoT Devices/Sensors: Physical sensors or devices that collect data, such as temperature sensors, motion detectors, or basic smart home devices.

Communication Protocols: Basic communication protocols like Wi-Fi, Bluetooth, Zigbee, or cellular connectivity are used for data transmission.

Data Transmission: Data collected by the devices is transmitted to a central location for storage and further analysis.

Use Cases: Examples include smart thermostats, fitness trackers, and basic environmental monitoring systems.

Complexity: Level 1 systems are simple, lacking advanced features like real-time analytics or complex automation.

Level 2: Connectivity and Data Processing:

Description: At this level, IoT systems become more capable by adding data processing capabilities closer to the devices themselves. This can include edge computing devices or gateways that preprocess data before sending it to the cloud.

Components:

IoT Devices/Sensors: Physical sensors or devices that collect data, such as temperature sensors, motion detectors, or basic smart home devices.

Edge Computing/Gateway Devices: Devices that can process data locally, reducing latency and bandwidth requirements.

Communication Protocols: Basic communication protocols like Wi-Fi, Bluetooth, Zigbee, or cellular connectivity are used for data transmission.

Data Transmission: Data is processed locally before being transmitted to a central server or cloud.

Use Cases: Industrial automation, real-time monitoring, and remote asset management are examples where Level 2 IoT systems shine.

Complexity: Increased compared to Level 1 due to edge computing capabilities.

Level 3: Data Analytics and Intelligence:

Description: Level 3 systems focus on data analytics and intelligence. They use advanced data processing techniques, including machine learning and AI algorithms, to extract meaningful insights from the collected data.

Components:

IoT Devices/Sensors: Physical sensors or devices that collect data, such as temperature sensors, motion detectors, or basic smart home devices.

Edge Computing/Gateway Devices: Enhanced with more advanced processing capabilities.

Communication Protocols: Basic communication protocols like Wi-Fi, Bluetooth, Zigbee, or cellular connectivity are used for data transmission.

Data Transmission: Data is processed locally and sent to the cloud, where advanced analytics and AI models generate actionable insights.
Use Cases: Predictive maintenance, smart cities, and healthcare monitoring systems benefit from Level 3 IoT capabilities.
Complexity: Considerably higher due to the integration of data analytics and AI.
Level 4: Integration with Enterprise Systems:
Description: Level 4 systems integrate IoT data with existing enterprise systems such as ERP (Enterprise Resource Planning) or CRM (Customer Relationship Management) to provide a unified view of operations.
Components:
IoT Devices/Sensors: Physical sensors or devices that collect data, such as temperature sensors, motion detectors, or basic smart home devices.
Edge Computing/Gateway Devices: Enhanced for robust data processing.
Communication Protocols: Basic communication protocols like Wi-Fi, Bluetooth, Zigbee, or cellular connectivity are used for data transmission.
Data Transmission: Data is sent to the cloud, integrated with enterprise systems for business process optimization.
Use Cases: Supply chain optimization, logistics, and facility management are examples where Level 4 IoT systems excel.
Complexity: High due to the need for seamless integration with existing enterprise infrastructure.
5. Level 5: AI-Driven Autonomous Systems:
Description: The highest level of IoT systems involves fully autonomous systems that use AI for decision-making and control. These systems can take actions without human intervention.
Components:
IoT Devices/Sensors: Physical sensors or devices that collect data, such as temperature sensors, motion detectors, or basic smart home devices.
Edge Computing/Gateway Devices: Advanced AI capabilities.
Communication Protocols: Basic communication protocols like Wi-Fi, Bluetooth, Zigbee, or cellular connectivity are used for data transmission.
Data Transmission: Data is processed and used to make real-time decisions and control devices autonomously.
Use Cases: Autonomous vehicles, smart grids, and advanced robotics are examples of Level 5 IoT systems.
Complexity: Extremely high due to the reliance on AI for decision-making.
Each level represents a progression in IoT system capabilities, with higher levels offering more advanced features and greater complexity to support a wider range of applications and services.

Characteristics of IoT

The environment and traffic characteristics of IoT (Internet of Things) refer to the conditions and patterns of data transmission and communication that are typical in IoT applications. These characteristics are important to consider when designing and deploying IoT systems.

Environment Characteristics of IoT:

1.Heterogeneous Environment: IoT devices can operate in diverse and heterogeneous environments. Some devices may be located indoors, while others are outdoors. They can be exposed to various conditions such as extreme temperatures, humidity, dust, or corrosive substances. Designing IoT devices that can withstand and function in different environments is crucial.

Harsh Conditions Some IoT applications, such as industrial IoT (IIoT) or agricultural IoT, may expose devices to harsh conditions like high-vibration environments, chemical exposure, or underwater deployment. Specialized ruggedized IoT devices are needed for such scenarios.

Urban and Rural Environments: IoT applications are deployed in both urban and rural settings. Urban environments often have dense wireless networks and interference, while rural areas may have limited connectivity and longer communication ranges. IoT solutions need to adapt to these variations.

Indoor vs. Outdoor: IoT devices can be deployed indoors, outdoors, or in transitional spaces. Each environment may have different signal propagation characteristics, which affect wireless communication. Indoor environments, for example, may have more obstacles like walls and floors, while outdoor environments may have more line-of-sight.

Traffic Characteristics of IoT:

Low Data Rate: Many IoT devices generate and transmit small amounts of data at low data rates. This includes sensor data such as temperature, humidity, or motion detection. The low data rate nature of IoT traffic helps conserve power and bandwidth.

Intermittent Traffic: IoT devices often transmit data intermittently based on specific events or triggers. For example, a motion sensor will only send data when motion is detected. This intermittent traffic pattern is in contrast to continuous data streams seen in some other communication systems.

Asymmetric Traffic: IoT traffic can be highly asymmetric, with devices sending data more frequently than they receive. This is common in scenarios where sensors collect data and transmit it to a central hub or cloud server.

Bursty Traffic: Some IoT applications, like surveillance cameras, may generate bursty traffic, where there are short periods of intense data transmission followed by long periods of inactivity.

Many-to-One Traffic: In many IoT deployments, multiple IoT devices transmit data to a single central node or cloud server. This many-to-one traffic pattern requires efficient aggregation and management of data to avoid bottlenecks.

Latency Sensitivity: While some IoT applications can tolerate latency, others, such as autonomous vehicles or industrial automation, are highly sensitive to delay. Ensuring low latency in data transmission is critical in such cases.

Scalability: IoT deployments often involve a large number of devices, which can lead to scalability challenges in managing and processing the incoming data streams.

Understanding these environment and traffic characteristics is essential for designing IoT systems that are robust, efficient, and capable of meeting the specific requirements of different applications. IoT solutions need to be adaptable to various environmental conditions and traffic patterns to ensure successful deployment and operation.

"5A" and "3I" characteristics -The **"5A" and "3I"** characteristics are often used to describe the key attributes or dimensions of the Internet of Things (IoT) ecosystems. These characteristics help in understanding the fundamental

5A Characteristics of IoT

Anytime: IoT enables connectivity and data exchange between devices and systems at any time. Devices can communicate and share data in real-time, regardless of the time of day or night.

Anywhere: IoT devices can be located anywhere, whether it's in a remote field, a factory floor, a home, or a vehicle. They can communicate from diverse physical locations and environments.

Anyone: IoT systems are accessible to anyone with the appropriate permissions. Users, whether they are individuals or organizations, can access and interact with IoT devices and data as authorized.

Anything: IoT connects a wide variety of "things" or objects, including sensors, actuators, appliances, vehicles, industrial machines, and more. These things can range from simple to complex, and IoT facilitates their communication and interaction.

Any Network: IoT devices can connect to different types of networks, such as cellular networks, Wi-Fi, Bluetooth, LPWAN (Low-Power Wide-Area Network), and even satellite networks. The flexibility in network connectivity is a hallmark of IoT.

3I Characteristics of IoT:

Intelligence: IoT systems often incorporate intelligence through data analytics, machine learning, and artificial intelligence. They can process and analyse the vast amount of data generated by IoT devices to derive insights, make decisions, and trigger actions autonomously.

Interconnectivity: Interconnectivity is at the core of IoT. Devices within an IoT ecosystem are connected to each other and to central platforms or the cloud. This interconnectivity allows data to flow seamlessly between devices and systems, enabling coordination and automation.

Instrumentation: IoT relies on sensors and other data-capturing instruments to collect information from the physical world. These sensors can measure various attributes such as temperature, humidity, location, motion, and more. Instrumentation is critical for the data-driven nature of IoT.

These characteristics collectively define the essence of IoT, emphasizing its ubiquity, accessibility, diversity, and the ability to add intelligence to everyday objects and systems. Understanding these characteristics is essential for designing, implementing, and harnessing the full potential of IoT solutions in various industries and applications.

Identity Management in IoT

Identity management in the Internet of Things (IoT) refers to the processes and techniques used to establish and manage the identities of IoT devices, users, and entities within an IoT ecosystem. It plays a crucial role in ensuring the security, privacy, and trustworthiness of IoT deployments. Identity management in IoT involves uniquely identifying and authenticating devices and users, granting appropriate access permissions, and managing their interactions within the IoT network. Here are two identity management techniques commonly used in IoT:

Device-centric identity management and hybrid identity management are two approaches to managing identities and access control in IoT (Internet of Things) ecosystems. They have distinct characteristics and are suited to different use cases. Here's a comparison of these two approaches:

Device-Centric Identity Management:

Focus: Device-centric identity management primarily revolves around authenticating and authorizing IoT devices themselves. Each device is assigned a unique identity, typically in the form of a digital certificate or token, which is used for secure communication and access control.

Security: This approach prioritizes device security and prevents unauthorized devices from accessing the network or resources. It is well-suited for applications where device-to-device trust is essential, such as industrial IoT and critical infrastructure.

Scalability: Device-centric identity management can be challenging to scale for environments with a large number of devices, as each device needs its own certificate or identity token. Managing a vast number of device identities can become complex.

Use Cases: It is commonly used in scenarios where device security and authentication are critical, such as smart grids, manufacturing processes, and remote infrastructure monitoring.

Examples: Public Key Infrastructure (PKI), X.509 certificates, and device authentication protocols like OAuth 2.0 for IoT are examples of device-centric identity management.

Hybrid Identity Management:

Focus: Hybrid identity management combines both device-centric and user-centric identity management approaches. It considers the identities of both devices and users. In this approach, devices and users are granted access based on their respective identities.

Security: It offers a balance between device and user security. While it ensures the trustworthiness of devices, it also takes into account the roles and permissions of users interacting with these devices and the data generated by them.

Scalability: Hybrid identity management is more scalable than purely device-centric approaches because it allows for a flexible integration of user identities and access control policies.

Use Cases: It is well-suited for IoT applications that involve user interaction and control alongside device-to-device communication. Examples include smart homes, healthcare IoT, and smart city solutions.

Examples: Solutions like Azure IoT Hub, AWS IoT, and Google Cloud IoT offer hybrid identity management features that allow both device and user identities to be managed and integrated.

In summary, device-centric identity management is primarily concerned with securing and managing IoT devices themselves, making it suitable for environments where device trust is paramount. On the other hand, hybrid identity management takes a more comprehensive approach, considering both device and user identities, making it flexible for IoT applications that involve user interaction and access control alongside device communication. The choice between these approaches depends on the specific requirements and security considerations of the IoT use case in question.

Device Authentication and Authorization:

Device authentication and authorization are fundamental techniques in IoT identity management. They involve verifying the identity of IoT devices and determining what actions they are allowed to perform within the network. Two common techniques for device authentication and authorization are:

Digital Certificates: In this approach, each IoT device is equipped with a digital certificate that contains its unique identifier (e.g., device ID or serial number) and a public key. When a device connects to the IoT network, it presents its certificate to a trusted authentication server. The server uses the certificate to verify the device's identity and grant appropriate access privileges. Digital certificates provide a strong level of security and are widely used in IoT deployments.

OAuth (Open Authorization): OAuth is a protocol that allows IoT devices to access resources on behalf of users or other devices without revealing their credentials (such as passwords). In OAuth-based identity management, devices obtain access tokens from an authorization server after user consent or device registration. These tokens are used to access specific resources or perform actions within the IoT network. OAuth is often used in scenarios where fine-grained access control is required, such as granting access to specific APIs or services.

Role-Based Access Control (RBAC):

Role-Based Access Control is a technique used to manage the permissions and access rights of users and devices based on their roles and responsibilities within the IoT system. In IoT deployments, RBAC helps ensure that entities (devices or users) are granted appropriate access privileges. Here's how RBAC works in IoT:

Roles and Permissions: IoT systems define various roles that entities can assume, such as administrator, device owner, or guest. Each role is associated with a set of permissions that determine what actions the entity is allowed to perform. For example, an administrator role may have full access to manage devices, while a guest role may only have read-only access.

Assignment of Roles: When a device or user joins the IoT network, the identity management system assigns them a specific role based on their attributes, credentials, or user profiles. This assignment is typically done during the registration process.

Access Control Policies: Access control policies define which roles are allowed to perform specific actions or access particular resources within the IoT network. For instance, a policy might specify that only devices with the "sensor" role can read data from a temperature sensor.

By implementing these identity management techniques, IoT systems can control access, protect sensitive data, and ensure that only authorized entities interact with the network. Effective identity management is essential for maintaining the security and integrity of IoT ecosystems, especially as the number of connected devices continues to grow.

Challenges of IoT

The Internet of Things (IoT) presents numerous challenges across various domains, including technology, security, privacy, and scalability. Here are some of the key challenges associated with IoT:

Security and Privacy:

Data Security: Protecting data generated by IoT devices from unauthorized access and tampering.

Device Security: Ensuring the security of IoT devices themselves to prevent them from being compromised and used for malicious purposes.

Privacy Concerns: Managing the privacy of individuals whose data is collected by IoT devices, including issues related to data consent and ownership.

Interoperability:

Ensuring that diverse IoT devices and systems can communicate and work together seamlessly, often in heterogeneous environments.

Scalability:

As the number of IoT devices continues to grow, managing the scalability of IoT networks, data storage, and processing becomes a significant challenge.

Reliability and Quality of Service (QoS):

Maintaining consistent performance and reliability of IoT systems, especially in critical applications like healthcare and industrial automation.

Energy Efficiency:

Many IoT devices are battery-powered or have limited power sources. Ensuring energy-efficient operation and optimizing power consumption is crucial.

Network Connectivity:

IoT devices may be deployed in areas with limited or unreliable network connectivity, making it challenging to establish and maintain connections.

Data Management and Analytics:

Handling and analysing the vast amounts of data generated by IoT devices and turning it into actionable insights can be daunting.

Standards and Protocols:

The lack of universal IoT standards can hinder interoperability and lead to fragmentation within the IoT ecosystem.

Regulatory and Legal Issues:

Adhering to regulations related to data privacy, security, and device certification can be complex and costly.

Device Lifecycle Management:

Managing the entire lifecycle of IoT devices, from provisioning and updates to decommissioning and disposal, can be challenging at scale.

Environmental Impact:

The proliferation of IoT devices and the associated energy consumption can have environmental implications, raising concerns about sustainability.

Cost:

The cost of deploying, maintaining, and managing IoT infrastructure and devices can be a barrier to adoption, especially for smaller organizations.

Human Factors:

Ensuring that users can effectively interact with and benefit from IoT devices and systems, including addressing issues related to user interfaces and user experience.

Addressing these challenges requires collaboration among various stakeholders, including technology providers, policymakers, and industry experts, to develop solutions that make IoT more secure, efficient, and reliable.

IoT devices

IoT Devices are a critical component of the IoT ecosystem. They enable the collection of real-world data, facilitate automation, and enhance our ability to monitor and control devices remotely. These devices are characterized by their ability to connect to the internet or other networks, gather data from their surroundings, and often execute actions based on that data. IoT devices have applications across various domains, including smart homes, healthcare, agriculture, industrial automation, and more. Their proliferation continues to drive innovation and improve efficiency in numerous industries.

List of Ten IoT Devices

Smart Thermostat: Smart thermostats, like the Nest Thermostat, can automatically adjust your home's temperature based on your preferences and occupancy. They help save energy and increase comfort.

Fitness Tracker: Devices like Fitbit monitor your physical activity, heart rate, and sleep patterns. They sync data with your smartphone or computer to help you track and improve your fitness.

Smart Lock: Smart locks, such as August Smart Lock, allow you to control access to your home remotely. You can lock or unlock doors using a smartphone app and provide temporary access to guests.

Connected Car Diagnostic Device: These devices, like the OBD-II port plug, monitor your car's performance, diagnose

Smart Smoke Detector: Smart smoke detectors, like the Nest Protect, not only sound alarms but also send alerts to your phone in case of a fire, enabling faster response and safety.

Smart Refrigerator: IoT-enabled refrigerators, such as Samsung Family Hub, can track food inventory, suggest recipes based on available ingredients, and display a calendar or weather information.

Industrial IoT Sensors: These sensors are used in manufacturing and industrial settings to monitor equipment performance, predict maintenance needs, and optimize operations, ensuring efficiency and reducing downtime.

Smart Agriculture Sensors: IoT devices in agriculture measure soil moisture, temperature, and other variables to help farmers optimize irrigation, crop health, and yield.

Wearable Health Monitors: Devices like Apple Watch and ECG monitors can continuously track vital signs, send health alerts, and share data with healthcare providers for remote monitoring.

Smart Lighting System: IoT-based lighting systems, like Philips Hue, enable you to control the brightness and color of lights via a smartphone app, voice commands, or automation routines, saving energy and enhancing ambiance.

These IoT devices represent just a fraction of the diverse range of connected devices available today. They illustrate the versatility and potential impact of IoT technology in our daily lives and various industries, making processes more efficient, convenient, and intelligent.

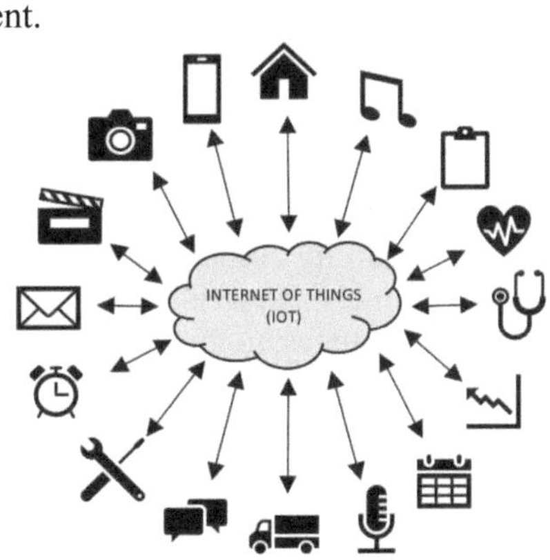

Interoperability of IoT Devices

Interoperability of IoT Devices refers to the ability of different IoT devices, systems, or platforms to seamlessly communicate, work together, and share data, regardless of their manufacturer, communication protocols, or underlying technologies. Achieving interoperability is essential for the successful deployment and scalability of IoT solutions. Here are key aspects of IoT device interoperability:

Standardized Protocols: Standard communication protocols such as MQTT, CoAP, and HTTP facilitate device interoperability by providing a common language for devices to exchange data. These protocols enable devices from various manufacturers to communicate without compatibility issues.

IoT Standards and Frameworks: Industry-specific standards and IoT frameworks, like OCF (Open Connectivity Foundation), oneM2M, and Thread, promote interoperability by defining common rules and practices for IoT devices.

IoT Ecosystems: Some companies and organizations create IoT ecosystems that ensure interoperability within their product lines. For example, the Apple HomeKit ecosystem ensures that compatible smart devices can work together seamlessly within the Apple ecosystem.

APIs (Application Programming Interfaces): APIs provide a standardized way for devices and applications to interact. IoT devices with well-documented APIs can be easily integrated into existing systems and applications.

Middleware and Edge Computing: Middleware solutions and edge computing platforms can bridge the gap between devices with different protocols by translating and normalizing data, enabling them to work together.

IoT Gateways: Gateways act as intermediaries between IoT devices and the cloud or other systems. They can **convert** data from various devices into a common format for processing and analysis, enhancing interoperability.

Interoperability Testing: Rigorous testing, certification programs, and compliance checks ensure that IoT devices meet interoperability standards, improving their compatibility with other devices.

Semantic Interoperability: Beyond technical compatibility, semantic interoperability focuses on ensuring that devices understand and interpret data consistently. Semantic standards like JSON-LD and RDF enable devices to share meaningful data.

Cloud-to-Cloud Integration: Cloud-based IoT platforms often provide tools for integrating and managing diverse devices and systems. These platforms facilitate interoperability by acting as intermediaries for data exchange.

Vendor Collaboration: Collaboration among IoT device manufacturers and technology providers can lead to the development of open standards and best practices that promote interoperability across the industry.

Role controller in IoT system

In an IoT (Internet of Things) system, a controller service plays a crucial role in managing and controlling various aspects of the IoT devices and the overall system. Here are some key functions and roles of a controller service in an IoT system:

Device Management: Controller services are responsible for managing IoT devices within the network. This includes device registration, configuration, provisioning, and maintenance. It ensures that all devices are properly connected and functioning as expected.

Data Collection and Aggregation: IoT systems generate a vast amount of data from connected devices. Controller services collect data from these devices, aggregate it, and prepare it for further processing or analysis. This can involve data filtering, compression, and formatting.

Command and Control: Controller services enable centralized control of IoT devices. They facilitate the sending of commands to devices to perform specific actions or change their configurations. This is essential for tasks like firmware updates, remote troubleshooting, and real-time adjustments.

Security Management: Security is a critical concern in IoT systems. Controller services often include security features like authentication, authorization, and encryption to protect data and devices from unauthorized access or malicious activities.

Monitoring and Alerts: Controller services monitor the health and status of IoT devices. They can detect anomalies, failures, or unusual behaviour and trigger alerts or notifications to administrators or other systems. This proactive monitoring helps in maintaining the reliability of the IoT network.

Data Routing and Forwarding: IoT systems may involve multiple data sources and destinations. Controller services handle the routing and forwarding of data between devices and applications, ensuring that data reaches the right endpoints efficiently.

Scalability and Load Balancing: As IoT networks grow, controller services ensure that the system can scale to accommodate a larger number of devices and data traffic. Load balancing techniques may be employed to distribute workloads effectively.

Integration with Cloud and Backend Systems: IoT systems often integrate with cloud platforms and backend systems for data storage, analysis, and further processing. Controller services facilitate this integration by managing the communication and data exchange between IoT devices and cloud services.

Energy Management: In battery-powered IoT devices, controller services may play a role in optimizing energy consumption. They can schedule device operations and manage power-saving modes to extend the battery life of these devices.

Device Lifecycle Management: IoT systems typically have devices with varying lifecycles. Controller services handle device provisioning, de-provisioning, and retirement when devices are no longer in use.

Overall, a controller service acts as a central hub that orchestrates and manages the various components of an IoT system, ensuring that it operates efficiently, securely, and in accordance with the desired functionalities and goals of the IoT deployment.

Scale of Use of IoT Devices in Contemporary Times

The scale of IoT device use continues to evolve, and the numbers have likely increased further since then. Here are some key points regarding the scale of IoT device use in contemporary times:

Explosive Growth: IoT adoption has seen explosive growth, with billions of devices connected to the internet. The proliferation of IoT devices is driven by advancements in technology, falling hardware costs, and the increasing recognition of IoT's potential across industries.

Industry Adoption: IoT devices are used extensively in industries such as manufacturing, healthcare, agriculture, logistics, energy, and smart cities. They are employed for various applications, including asset tracking, predictive maintenance, remote monitoring, and automation.

Smart Homes: IoT devices have found their way into homes worldwide, creating smart homes equipped with connected thermostats, lighting systems, security cameras, voice assistants, and more. These devices offer convenience, energy savings, and enhanced security.

Agriculture: Agriculture has seen a significant uptake of IoT for precision farming. IoT sensors and devices are used to monitor soil conditions, weather, crop health, and livestock, leading to more efficient farming practices.

Healthcare: The healthcare sector relies on IoT for remote patient monitoring, wearable health devices, medication adherence solutions, and smart medical equipment. IoT has the potential to improve patient outcomes and reduce healthcare costs.

Smart Cities: Municipalities around the world are deploying IoT solutions for smart city initiatives. These include smart streetlights, waste management, traffic monitoring, and environmental sensors to enhance urban living and sustainability.

Industrial IoT (IIoT): IIoT is transforming manufacturing and industrial processes. IoT devices embedded in machines and equipment enable predictive maintenance, real-time quality control, and supply chain optimization.

Transportation: IoT devices are integral to modern transportation systems. Fleet management solutions use IoT for vehicle tracking, route optimization, and fuel efficiency. Autonomous vehicles also rely on IoT technology.

Energy Management: IoT devices are used to monitor and manage energy consumption in commercial and residential buildings, optimizing energy usage and reducing costs.

Retail: In the retail sector, IoT devices are used for inventory management, customer tracking, and personalized shopping experiences. Retailers leverage IoT for supply chain visibility and improved operations.

Environmental Monitoring: IoT sensors are employed to monitor air and water quality, weather conditions, and natural disasters, aiding in early warning systems and environmental conservation efforts.

Consumer Electronic: IoT is integrated into an array of consumer electronics, including smart TVs, wearable fitness trackers, smart appliances, and home entertainment systems.

The scale of IoT device usage is vast and continually expanding. As more industries recognize the value of IoT for improving efficiency, reducing costs, and enhancing services, the adoption of IoT devices is expected to continue its upward trajectory. Furthermore, advancements in 5G connectivity, edge computing, and AI are likely to further accelerate the proliferation of IoT in contemporary times and beyond.

Key Components of IoT

A block diagram of an IoT (Internet of Things) device illustrates the key components and their interconnections within the device. IoT devices can vary widely in complexity and functionality, but a typical block diagram might include the following elements:

Microcontroller/Processor Unit: This is the brain of the IoT device. It controls the device's operation, processes data, and manages communications. Common choices include microcontrollers like Arduino, Raspberry Pi, or specialized IoT-focused chips.

Sensors: Sensors are the input devices that collect data from the device's environment. They can include various types such as temperature sensors, humidity sensors, light sensors, motion sensors, gas sensors, or any other sensor relevant to the device's purpose.

Actuators: Actuators are output devices that perform actions based on commands received from the microcontroller. Examples include motors, relays, solenoids, or LEDs.

Communication Module: The communication module enables the device to connect to a network, typically the internet or a local network. This module may include Wi-Fi, cellular, Ethernet, Bluetooth, LoRa, Zigbee, or other wireless or wired communication interfaces.

Power Supply: The power supply block provides the necessary electrical power to operate the device. It may include a battery, power management circuitry, and voltage regulation components.
Memory: Memory components, such as flash memory or EEPROM, are used to store data, program code, and configuration settings.
Control and Processing Unit: This block includes components like microcontrollers or digital signal processors (DSPs) that manage the data from sensors, execute control algorithms, and interface with the communication module.
User Interface (Optional): Some IoT devices may include user interfaces like buttons, touchscreens, or displays to interact with users or provide status information.
Security Features: Security is a critical aspect of IoT devices. This block may include hardware security modules (HSMs), secure elements, or encryption/decryption components to protect data and device integrity.
Clock/Timer: A clock or timer unit helps with time-based operations and scheduling tasks within the IoT device.
Antenna: If the device uses wireless communication, it will have an antenna to transmit and receive data wirelessly.
I/O Ports: Input/output ports are used for connecting sensors, actuators, and external peripherals to the device. These ports provide physical connections for data exchange.
Environmental Housing (Optional): In some cases, especially for outdoor or rugged IoT devices, an environmental housing or enclosure may be included to protect the device from environmental factors like moisture, dust, or extreme temperatures.
Debugging/Programming Interface (Optional): For development and debugging purposes, IoT devices may have a dedicated interface for programming and troubleshooting.
Firmware/Software: This represents the embedded software or firmware that runs on the microcontroller, controlling the device's behaviour, data processing, and communication.

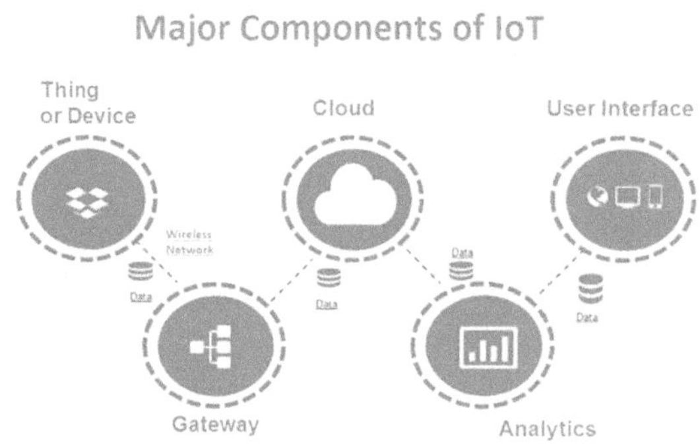

Features of IoT

The Internet of Things (IoT) enables value creation in various industries and applications by leveraging connected devices and sensors to collect, transmit, and analyse data. Here are some key features of value creation using IoT:
Data Collection: IoT devices can collect vast amounts of data from various sources, including sensors, cameras, and user interactions, providing valuable insights into operations, environments, and behaviours.
Real-time Monitoring: IoT allows for real-time monitoring of processes, assets, and systems, enabling immediate response to anomalies, failures, or opportunities for optimization.
Predictive Maintenance: IoT data can be used to predict when equipment or machinery is likely to fail, allowing for proactive maintenance and reducing downtime and repair costs.
Improved Efficiency: IoT can optimize resource usage, such as energy, water, and raw materials, leading to cost savings and reduced environmental impact.
Enhanced Customer Experience: IoT applications can personalize and improve customer experiences by offering smart and connected products and services.
Supply Chain Visibility: IoT sensors can track the movement and condition of goods throughout the supply chain, providing transparency and reducing losses due to theft, damage, or spoilage.
Healthcare Monitoring: In healthcare, IoT devices can monitor patient vitals, medication adherence, and even enable remote consultations, improving patient care and reducing healthcare costs.
Smart Agriculture: IoT sensors and devices can optimize farming practices by monitoring soil conditions, weather, and crop health, leading to increased yields and sustainability.

Smart Cities: IoT can enhance urban living through smart traffic management, waste management, public safety, and energy-efficient infrastructure.

Asset Tracking: IoT enables the tracking and management of assets in industries like logistics, helping businesses locate and optimize the use of valuable equipment.

Energy Management: IoT can optimize energy consumption in buildings and industrial facilities by adjusting lighting, heating, and cooling based on occupancy and environmental conditions.

Environmental Monitoring: IoT can be used to monitor and analyse environmental factors like air quality, water quality, and pollution levels, aiding in sustainability efforts.

Fleet Management: For transportation and logistics companies, IoT helps track vehicle location, performance, and driver behaviour, leading to improved safety and efficiency.

Security and Surveillance: IoT-based security systems can provide real-time monitoring and alerts for intrusion detection, fire safety, and video surveillance.

Data Analytics and AI: IoT data can be analysed using advanced analytics and artificial intelligence algorithms to derive actionable insights and make informed decisions.

Remote Control: IoT devices can be remotely controlled and managed, allowing for automation and control of processes and equipment from anywhere.

Scalability: IoT solutions can easily scale to accommodate a growing number of devices and data sources, making them suitable for both small-scale applications and large enterprises.

Customization: IoT solutions can be tailored to specific industry needs and use cases, providing flexibility in designing applications that create value.

Cost Reduction: While there are upfront costs associated with IoT deployment, long-term benefits often include cost savings through increased efficiency, reduced maintenance, and better resource management.

Competitive Advantage: Embracing IoT can give businesses a competitive edge by offering innovative products and services, improving customer satisfaction, and staying ahead of market trends.

These features demonstrate the diverse range of opportunities for value creation through the implementation of IoT technologies across various industries and domains.

Implementation of IoT

The Internet of Things (IoT) can be implemented using various technologies, including programmable logic controllers (PLC). PLCs are commonly used in industrial automation and control systems, and when integrated with IoT technology, they can enable efficient monitoring, control, and data collection in industrial and manufacturing settings. Here's an overview of how IoT can be implemented using PLC technology:

PLC Basics: PLCs are specialized industrial computers designed to control machinery and processes. They can read input signals from sensors, process the data, and control output devices like motors, valves, and actuators based on a set of predefined logic instructions.

IoT Integration with PLCs: To enable IoT capabilities, PLCs are equipped with communication modules or protocols that allow them to connect to the internet or a local network. These modules may include Ethernet ports, Wi-Fi adapters, or support for industrial communication protocols like MQTT, OPC UA, or Modbus.

Sensor Integration: IoT-enabled PLCs can be connected to a wide range of sensors and devices, such as temperature sensors, pressure sensors, flow meters, and more. These sensors collect data from the physical environment.

Data Collection and Monitoring: PLCs collect data from sensors in real-time and can transmit this data to centralized systems or cloud platforms via the internet. This data can include information about process variables, machine status, and environmental conditions.

Cloud Connectivity: PLCs can use IoT protocols to securely transmit data to cloud-based platforms, where the data is stored and made accessible to authorized users. Cloud platforms can provide data analytics, visualization, and storage capabilities.

Remote Monitoring and Control: IoT-enabled PLCs allow for remote monitoring and control of industrial processes and equipment. Authorized personnel can access real-time data and make adjustments or troubleshoot issues remotely using web interfaces or mobile applications.

Data Analytics: IoT data collected from PLCs can be analysed to identify trends, anomalies, and opportunities for optimization. Advanced analytics can help improve process efficiency, reduce downtime, and enhance overall performance.

Predictive Maintenance: By analysing data from PLCs and connected sensors, predictive maintenance models can be developed. These models can predict when equipment is likely to fail, allowing for proactive maintenance to prevent costly unplanned downtime.

Energy Management: IoT-enabled PLCs can monitor energy consumption in industrial facilities, helping organizations optimize energy usage and reduce costs.

Security: Implementing security measures is crucial when integrating IoT with PLCs to protect against cyber threats and unauthorized access. This includes securing communication channels, using encryption, and implementing access control mechanisms.

Scalability: IoT-enabled PLC solutions can scale to accommodate additional sensors, devices, and processes as a business grows or evolves.

Overall, integrating IoT technology with PLCs enhances industrial automation and control by providing real-time data, remote access, and advanced analytics capabilities. It improves operational efficiency, reduces downtime, and supports data-driven decision-making in industrial and manufacturing environments.

Industrial IoT, Infrastructure IoT, and IoMT

Industrial IoT (IIoT): Industrial IoT, often referred to as IIoT, is a subset of the broader IoT landscape focused specifically on applications within industrial sectors such as manufacturing, energy, agriculture, and logistics. It involves the use of IoT technologies to enhance industrial processes, monitor equipment, improve efficiency, and gather real-time data for decision-making.

Key Characteristics of IIoT:

Machine-to-Machine Communication: IIoT facilitates communication between machines, sensors, and control systems. This enables automated processes and data exchange without human intervention.

Predictive Maintenance: Sensors and analytics in IIoT systems can predict when equipment is likely to fail, allowing for proactive maintenance, reducing downtime, and extending the lifespan of machinery.

Quality Control: IIoT can monitor and control production processes to ensure product quality, consistency, and compliance with industry standards.

Energy Management: IIoT helps industries optimize energy consumption by monitoring and controlling energy-intensive processes and equipment.

Supply Chain Optimization: IIoT can provide real-time visibility into the supply chain, improving inventory management, logistics, and distribution.

Infrastructure IoT: Infrastructure IoT, sometimes referred to as IIoT (Industrial Infrastructure IoT), focuses on applying IoT technology to critical infrastructure sectors such as transportation, utilities, and smart cities. It aims to enhance the efficiency, safety, and sustainability of infrastructure systems.

Key Characteristics of Infrastructure IoT:

Smart Transportation: IoT sensors and data analytics can be used to monitor traffic, optimize public transportation, and improve road safety through real-time data collection.

Smart Grids: IoT enables utility companies to build smart grids that monitor electricity consumption, detect outages, and optimize distribution, leading to improved reliability and efficiency.

Smart Cities: IoT technologies are applied to urban environments to enhance services like waste management, energy usage, and public safety.

Environmental Monitoring: Infrastructure IoT includes monitoring systems to assess air and water quality, detect pollution, and respond to environmental emergencies.

Internet of Military Things (IoMT): The Internet of Military Things (IoMT) is a specialized category of IoT tailored to military applications. It involves the use of IoT devices and technologies to enhance military capabilities, improve situational awareness, and optimize logistics and operations.

Key Characteristics of Internet of Military Things (IoMT):

Situational Awareness: IoMT provides real-time data from sensors, drones, and other devices to enhance military situational awareness, aiding decision-making in the field.

Logistics and Asset Tracking: IoMT can be used to track military assets, supplies, and equipment, ensuring they are where they are needed when they are needed.

Communication and Connectivity: IoMT includes secure communication networks for military personnel and equipment, even in remote or hostile environments.

Unmanned Systems: Drones and unmanned vehicles are key components of IoMT, providing reconnaissance, surveillance, and even autonomous operations.

Cybersecurity: Given the sensitive nature of military operations, IoMT includes robust cybersecurity measures to protect data and prevent unauthorized access.

It's important to note that each of these categories—IIoT, Infrastructure IoT, and IoMT—has unique challenges and considerations regarding security, scalability, and regulatory compliance, given their specific application domains.

As technology continues to advance, these categories of IoT will play increasingly significant roles in improving efficiency, safety, and capabilities across various sectors.

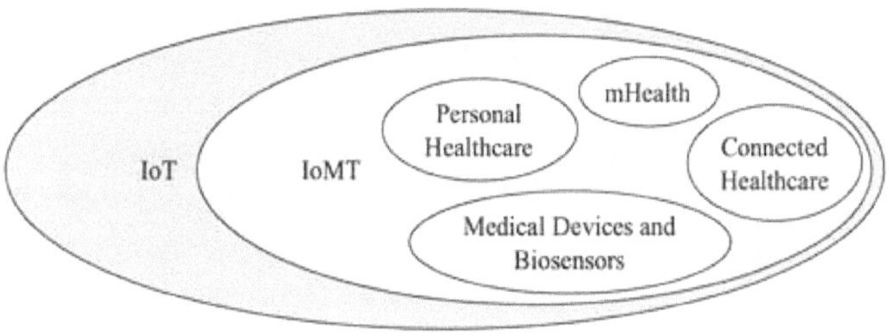

Benefits of IoT

The Internet of Things (IoT) offers a wide range of benefits across various industries and aspects of daily life. Here are some key advantages of IoT:

Efficiency Improvement: IoT enables automation and optimization of processes, reducing manual intervention and human errors. This leads to increased operational efficiency and cost savings.

Data-Driven Decision-Making: IoT devices collect vast amounts of data from the physical world. This data can be analysed to gain insights, make informed decisions, and identify trends or patterns.

Cost Reduction: Through predictive maintenance and resource optimization, IoT helps organizations reduce maintenance costs, minimize energy consumption, and extend the lifespan of equipment.

Enhanced Safety: In industries like manufacturing, healthcare, and transportation, IoT applications improve safety by monitoring critical parameters, alerting to potential hazards, and enabling quicker emergency responses.

Improved Quality of Life: In smart homes, IoT devices enhance comfort, convenience, and security. Smart thermostats, lighting systems, and security cameras are examples of IoT devices that improve quality of life.

Environmental Benefits: IoT contributes to sustainability efforts by enabling more efficient resource usage. Smart agriculture reduces water consumption, while smart cities optimize energy usage and reduce pollution.

Healthcare Advancements: IoT in healthcare facilitates remote patient monitoring, medication adherence tracking, and wearable health devices, leading to better healthcare outcomes and reduced hospitalizations.

Supply Chain Optimization: IoT provides real-time visibility into the supply chain, tracking products, monitoring conditions, and reducing losses due to spoilage or theft.

Smart Cities: IoT technologies help create smart cities with efficient transportation systems, intelligent waste management, and enhanced public services, leading to improved urban living.

Asset Tracking: IoT enables real-time tracking of assets, such as vehicles, equipment, and inventory, optimizing logistics and reducing losses.

Consumer Convenience: IoT applications in consumer products, like voice assistants and wearable devices, offer convenience and personalized experiences.

Predictive Maintenance: IoT sensors can predict equipment failures before they occur, reducing downtime and costly repairs.

Remote Monitoring: Remote monitoring of devices, infrastructure, and environments is made possible through IoT, improving overall system reliability.

Energy Management: IoT helps manage energy consumption by controlling lighting, heating, and cooling based on occupancy and environmental conditions.

Market Insights: IoT data provides valuable market insights and consumer behavior analysis, assisting businesses in making informed marketing and product development decisions.

Agricultural Productivity: IoT applications in agriculture enable precise irrigation, crop monitoring, and livestock management, leading to higher yields and resource conservation.

Asset Utilization: Organizations can optimize asset utilization by tracking how assets are used and allocating resources more effectively.

Competitive Advantage: Adopting IoT can provide a competitive edge by offering innovative services, improving customer experiences, and responding quickly to market changes.

Global Connectivity: IoT enables remote access and control of devices and systems from anywhere in the world, expanding the reach of businesses and services.

Customization: IoT allows for the customization of products and services based on individual preferences and needs.

Overall, IoT has the potential to transform industries, enhance daily life, and drive innovation by harnessing the power of connected devices and data analytics. Its benefits extend to improving efficiency, safety, sustainability, and the quality of services across various sectors.

Exercise

Exercise 1 – MCQ

1. What does IoT mean?
a) Internet Technology
b) Internet of Things
c) Internet of Transmission
d) Internet of Telecommunication
2. Which of the following best describes the Internet of Things?
a) A global network of interconnected supercomputers
b) A network of interconnected physical devices capable of exchanging data
c) Advanced technology
d) A new type of Internet browser

Exercise 2 – True/ False

1. IoT devices communicate with each other using Internet Protocol (IP).
2. Internet of Things, refers to everyday products and devices that are connected to the Internet and allow them to store and exchange information.

Exercise 3 – Fill in the blanks

1. The Internet of Things is a network that connects ___________ devices to communicate and share information.
2. The Internet of Things relies on sensors and ___________ to collect and transmit data from the physical world.

Exercise 4 – Match case

Match the following terms with their meanings:
1. Sensor
2. IoT
3. Cloud Computing
Meanings:
a) A network of interconnected physical objects and devices.
b) A device that detects and measures physical properties or environmental conditions.
c) A technology that enables remote data storage and processing.

Exercise 5 – One word answer

1. Which technology enables communication between IoT devices in close proximity.
2. What type of network uses a low-power, wide-area communication protocol for long-range IoT applications?

Exercise 6 – Small answer

1. What is the primary purpose of IoT-enabled sensors in smart agriculture?
2. Give an example of a common IoT device used in smart homes.

Exercise 7 – Long answer

1. Explain the concept of IoT.
2. Explain three real-world examples of how IoT technology is being used to improve various aspects of daily life.

Answer:

Exercise 1.
1. b) Internet of Things
2. b) A network of interconnected physical devices capable of exchanging information
Exercise 2.
1. True
2 True
Exercise 3
1. Objects
2. Actuator
Exercise 4.
1. Sensor – b)
2. IoT – a)

3. Cloud Computing – c)
Exercise 5.
1. Bluetooth
2. LoRaWAN

Previous Year Questions

1. List various levels of IoT system and explain Level 1 IoT system with diagram. (SPPU B.Tech. 2015)
2. List different IoT enabling technologies which play a key-role and explain any of them. (Anna University M.Tech. 2018)
3. List any six IoT devices available in market. (Anna University M.Tech. 2018)
4. Explain in detail IoT Architecture with neat diagram. (SPPU B.Tech. 2017)
5. Explain Environment, Traffic characteristics of IoT (SPPU B.Tech. 2017)
6. What is Identity management in Internet of Things? Explain any 2 Identity management techniques of Internet of Things. (SPPU 2017)
7. What are the challenges of IoT? (SPPU B.Tech. 2022)
8. What is the top most layer in IoT architecture? (SPPU B.Tech. 2022)
9. What is the role of controller service in an IoT system? (SPPU B.Tech. 2017)
10. Write a short note on 5A and 3I characteristics of IoT. (Anna University B.Tech. 2018)
11. Draw and explain block diagram of an IoT device. (Anna University B.Tech. 2018)
12 Compare device centric identity management and hybrid identity management in IoT. (Uttar Pradesh University B.Tech. 2021-22)
13. Illustrate sources of the IoT with example. (Uttar Pradesh university B.Tech. 2021-22)
14. What is Identity management in Internet of Things? Explain any 2 Identity management techniques of Internet of Things. (Uttar Pradesh university B.Tech. 2018- 19)
15. What are different challenges of IoT (Uttar Pradesh university Btech2018-19)
16. Explain different characteristics of IoT. (Uttar Pradesh university B.Tech. 2018-19)
17. Explain in detail access control and message integrity of Internet of Things. (Uttar Pradesh university B.Tech. 2018)
18. Define internet of things. (Uttar Pradesh university B.Tech. 2021-22)
19. List features of value creation using IoT. (Uttar Pradesh university B.Tech. 2021-22)
20. Explain about Internet of Thing using PLC technology. (Uttar Pradesh university B.Tech. 2018-19)
21. Explain layered IOT architecture using a figure. (Uttar Pradesh university B.Tech. 2018-19)
22. What is IoT? Explain: Things in IoT. (SPPU B.Tech. 2019)
23. What is Internet of Things (IoT)? What are the characteristics? Also explain industrial IoT, infrastructure IoT and internet of military categories of IoT. things (IoMT) (IGNOU MCA 2022)
24. What is IOT? (Chaudhary Charan Singh University B. Tech 2017)
25. Define Internet of things and briefly explain its characteristics. (Mumbai University 2017)
26.Give in brief overview of Internet of Things (IOT) (Chaudhary Charan Singh University B. Tech 2017)
27. Explain IOT architecture with help of a diagram. (Chaudhary Charan Singh University B. Tech 2017)
28. Explain 4 stages of IoT architecture. (RTU B.Tech. 2022)
29. What is the scale of use of IoT devices in contemporary times. (RTU B.Tech. 2022)
30. What is the top most layer in IoT architecture? (RTU B.Tech. 2022)
31. What are the challenges of IoT? (RTU B.Tech. 2022)
32. Describe in detail with suitable example CoAP and MQTT protocols used in application Layer. (Mumbai University)
33. Define various levels of IoT systems and explain Level 1 and Level 2 with suitable diagram. (Mumbai University)

ONLINE RESOURCES

Link: https://forms.gle/rt7UncVr4PanLaMf7

QR Code

Link: https://www.youtube.com/playlist?list=PLzlh_31VWEFq_veknwWqAPPP6-VBBTjWz

QR Code

Chapter 2: IoT Technologies and Components

Baseline Technologies of IoT

The Internet of Things (IoT) relies on a range of baseline technologies that enable devices and sensors to communicate, collect data, and interact with each other and the cloud. These foundational technologies provide the infrastructure for IoT applications. Here are some of the key baseline technologies of IoT:

Wireless Communication Protocols:

Wi-Fi: Wi-Fi provides high-speed, local area wireless connectivity and is commonly used in IoT devices for data transmission within homes and offices.

Bluetooth: Bluetooth is suitable for short-range communication between devices, such as smartphones and IoT sensors.

Zigbee: Zigbee is a low-power, low-data-rate protocol designed for IoT applications like home automation and industrial control.

Z-Wave: Z-Wave is another low-power protocol often used in smart home devices for reliable and low-latency communication.

LoRa (Long Range): LoRa is designed for long-range, low-power communication and is commonly used in IoT applications like smart agriculture and smart cities.

Narrowband IoT (NB-IoT): NB-IoT is a cellular-based technology that provides wide-area coverage with low power consumption, making it suitable for IoT deployments in remote areas.

Sensors and Actuators: Sensors collect data from the physical world, including temperature, humidity, light, motion, and more. Actuators are devices that can perform actions based on commands, such as turning on a light or locking a door.

Microcontrollers and Embedded Systems: Microcontrollers are the "brains" of IoT devices, controlling their operations and processing data. They often have low power consumption to extend device battery life.

Cloud Computing: Cloud platforms like AWS IoT, Azure IoT, and Google Cloud IoT provide services for device management, data storage, analytics, and machine learning. IoT devices send data to the cloud for processing and storage.

Edge Computing: Edge computing involves processing data closer to where it's generated (at the "edge" of the network), reducing latency and the need for constant cloud connectivity. Edge devices, such as gateways and edge servers, play a crucial role in this approach.

Data Analytics and Machine Learning: IoT generates vast amounts of data. Analytics and machine learning techniques are used to extract insights, detect anomalies, and make predictions based on this data.

Security: Security is paramount in IoT to protect devices and data from cyberattacks. Technologies such as encryption, authentication, and secure boot are essential for IoT security.

Protocols for Device Communication: Protocols like MQTT (Message Queuing Telemetry Transport), CoAP (Constrained Application Protocol), HTTP, and WebSocket enable devices to communicate with each other and with cloud platforms.

IoT Operating Systems: Specialized operating systems for IoT, like Free RTOS, RIOT OS, and Mbed OS, are designed to run efficiently on resource-constrained IoT devices.

Power Management: IoT devices often run on batteries or have limited power sources. Power management technologies help optimize energy consumption for extended battery life.

Network Infrastructure: IoT relies on the existing network infrastructure, including the internet, cellular networks, and wireless LANs, to transmit data.

Standards and Interoperability: Standards like MQTT, CoAP, and the Thread protocol help ensure interoperability between different IoT devices and systems.

These baseline technologies form the foundation for IoT applications across various industries and domains. IoT development often involves integrating these technologies into cohesive solutions that meet specific use case requirements, whether it's in smart homes, industrial automation, healthcare, or any other IoT application area.

IoT Enablers and Connectivity Layers

IoT (Internet of Things) enablers and connectivity layers play a pivotal role in enabling the seamless integration of a diverse range of devices, sensors, and systems in IoT ecosystems. These layers provide the foundation for IoT communication, data exchange, and device management. Here's an overview of IoT enablers and connectivity layers:

IoT Enablers:

IoT enablers are fundamental technologies, protocols, and components that enable the deployment and functionality of IoT systems. They serve as the building blocks for IoT applications. Key IoT enablers include:

Wireless Communication Technologies: These encompass various wireless standards such as Wi-Fi, Bluetooth, Zigbee, Z-Wave, LoRaWAN, Sigfox, and cellular networks (2G/3G/4G/5G). Each technology offers different ranges, data rates, and power consumption profiles, making them suitable for specific IoT use cases.

Sensor Technologies: Sensors are essential for collecting data from the physical world. IoT enablers include a wide range of sensors such as temperature sensors, motion sensors, humidity sensors, GPS receivers, accelerometers, and more. These sensors convert physical phenomena into digital data.

Embedded Systems: IoT devices are typically built using embedded systems, which consist of microcontrollers, microprocessors, memory, and interfaces. Embedded systems enable device control, data processing, and communication capabilities.

Data Protocols: Data protocols like MQTT (Message Queuing Telemetry Transport), CoAP (Constrained Application Protocol), HTTP (Hypertext Transfer Protocol), and AMQP (Advanced Message Queuing Protocol) facilitate data exchange between IoT devices and cloud or edge systems.

Security Mechanisms: IoT enablers include security features such as encryption, authentication, access control, and secure boot processes to protect IoT devices and data from threats.

Edge Computing: Edge computing platforms and devices enable local data processing, real-time analytics, and decision-making at the network edge. This reduces latency and bandwidth requirements.

Cloud Services: Cloud platforms offer scalable storage, data processing, and analytics capabilities. They serve as the backend infrastructure for managing and analysing IoT data.

IoT Connectivity Layers:

IoT connectivity layers define the communication infrastructure that connects IoT devices to each other and to the broader network, enabling data exchange and control. These layers ensure seamless and reliable communication across diverse IoT ecosystems. Key IoT connectivity layers include:

Device Connectivity: This layer includes the physical and wireless connectivity technologies (e.g., Wi-Fi, cellular, LPWAN) that enable IoT devices to connect to local networks or the internet. It encompasses device protocols and drivers.

Network Connectivity: Network connectivity layer manages the routing, addressing, and data transmission within local area networks (LANs), wide area networks (WANs), and the internet. It ensures devices can communicate across networks.

Edge Connectivity: Edge connectivity involves communication and data exchange between IoT devices and edge computing platforms or gateways. It facilitates local data processing and aggregation before transmitting data to the cloud.

Cloud Connectivity: Cloud connectivity enables data transmission between edge or device endpoints and cloud-based services. It ensures secure and reliable data transfer to cloud platforms for storage and further processing.

Application Connectivity: This layer connects IoT applications, services, and user interfaces to the IoT ecosystem. It enables users to interact with and control IoT devices and access real-time data and analytics.

Device Management Connectivity: Device management connectivity supports remote device management and monitoring. It allows for firmware updates, configuration changes, and troubleshooting of IoT devices.

Security Connectivity: Security connectivity ensures that communication between devices, networks, and cloud services is protected. It includes encryption, authentication, and security protocols to safeguard data and devices.

IoT Protocols and Standards: IoT connectivity relies on communication protocols and standards like MQTT, CoAP, IPv6, WebSocket's, and HTTP/HTTPS. These protocols define how devices and systems interact within the IoT ecosystem.

The effective integration and management of these enablers and connectivity layers are essential for the success of IoT deployments. They enable IoT applications to operate reliably, securely, and efficiently, driving innovation and solving real-world challenges across industries.

Need of Analog / Digital Conversion.

The need for Analog-to-digital conversion (ADC) and digital-to-Analog conversion (DAC) arises from the fundamental difference between Analog and digital signals and the requirements of modern electronic systems. Here's why these conversions are essential:

Digital Processing and Communication:

Representation: Digital systems, including computers and microcontrollers, primarily work with digital signals (0s and 1s). To process and communicate with Analog signals, such as those from sensors or audio sources, they need to convert them into digital form (ADC).

Processing Power: Digital signal processing (DSP) techniques are powerful and flexible, enabling various operations like filtering, compression, encryption, and analysis. ADC enables Analog data to be processed using these techniques.

Compatibility: Digital data is well-suited for transmission over long distances and across different devices. Converting Analog signals to digital allows for efficient data transmission, storage, and sharing.

Accuracy and Precision:

Quantization: ADC provides a means to quantize continuous Analog signals into discrete digital values. This quantization process allows for precise representation and measurement of Analog data, reducing errors associated with continuous signals.

Signal Conditioning: Digital representation allows for accurate signal conditioning, filtering, and calibration, which are crucial in applications like instrumentation and industrial control.

Noise Immunity:

Noise Rejection: Digital signals are less susceptible to noise and interference during transmission and processing compared to Analog signals. ADC helps convert Analog signals into digital form, where they can be robustly processed and transmitted without significant degradation.

Storage and Memory:

Data Storage: Digital data is easily stored and retrieved in memory devices like hard drives, flash storage, and RAM. ADC enables Analog data to be digitized and stored efficiently, facilitating data analysis and retrieval.

Compatibility with Digital Devices:

Modern Devices: Many devices and systems are inherently digital, including computers, smartphones, and digital communication networks. ADC and DAC are essential for interfacing Analog sensors, actuators, and audio devices with these digital systems.

Signal Reproduction:

Output Devices: In various applications, such as audio systems and control systems, it's necessary to convert digital signals back to Analog form (DAC) to interact with the physical world, driving speakers, motors, or other Analog devices.

Signal Processing and Analysis:

Digital Signal Processing (DSP): DSP techniques, such as filtering, modulation, and Fourier analysis, are commonly used for signal manipulation and analysis. These techniques require digital input data, which ADC provides.

Flexibility and Programmability:

Programmable Processing: Digital signals can be easily processed and manipulated using software. ADC and DAC allow for the programmable control and processing of signals, enabling adaptable and versatile systems.

Integration and Miniaturization:

Integration: Modern electronics often require miniaturization and integration of multiple functions into a single chip or system. ADC and DAC can be integrated into such systems, enabling compact and feature-rich devices.

In summary, the need for Analog-to-digital conversion (ADC) and digital-to-Analog conversion (DAC) arises from the compatibility, precision, noise immunity, and processing capabilities of digital systems. These conversions enable Analog data to be effectively processed, stored, transmitted, and interfaced with modern digital devices and systems, making them essential in various fields, including telecommunications, instrumentation, audio processing, and control systems.

The Core IoT Functional Stack

Layer 1 – Things: Sensors and Actuators Layer

The Sensors and Actuators Layer is a fundamental component of the Internet of Things (IoT) architecture. This layer is responsible for interfacing with the physical world, capturing data from sensors, and enabling actions through actuators. It plays a crucial role in sensing the environment, collecting data, and initiating responses in IoT systems. Here's an overview of the Sensors and Actuators Layer:

Sensors:

Purpose: Sensors are devices or components that detect physical changes or conditions in the environment and convert them into electrical signals or data that can be processed by IoT systems.

Types: Various types of sensors exist, including temperature sensors, humidity sensors, motion detectors, light sensors, pressure sensors, proximity sensors, and many more.

Functions: Sensors continuously monitor and measure physical parameters, providing real-time data to IoT applications. They are the "input" devices of the IoT ecosystem.

Actuators:

Purpose: Actuators are devices that perform physical actions or control mechanisms based on commands received from IoT systems or applications.

Types: Actuators come in different forms, such as motors, servos, relays, solenoids, valves, and switches, each suited for specific actions.

Functions: Actuators enable IoT systems to interact with the physical world by executing actions in response to data or commands. For example, actuators can control lights, motors, locks, valves, or other devices.

Sensor Interface:

Purpose: The sensor interface includes hardware and software components that connect sensors to the IoT network or gateway.

Components: Analog-to-digital converters (ADCs), sensor drivers, communication protocols (e.g., I2C, SPI, UART), and sensor hubs.

Functions: The interface facilitates data collection from sensors, digitizes Analog signals, and prepares the data for transmission to the IoT platform or edge devices.

Actuator Control:

Purpose: Actuator control mechanisms manage the activation and control of actuators in response to commands from IoT applications or systems.

Components: Microcontrollers, drivers, and actuators themselves.

Functions: Actuator control ensures that actions are executed accurately and in a controlled manner based on the instructions received.

Data Preprocessing:

Purpose: Data preprocessing involves filtering, aggregating, and contextualizing sensor data before it is transmitted to higher layers of the IoT architecture.

Functions: Preprocessing helps reduce data volume, eliminate noise, and enhance the quality of data before it is sent to the IoT platform, saving bandwidth and processing resources.

Power Management:

Purpose: Power management components and strategies optimize the energy usage of sensors and actuators, especially in battery-operated IoT devices.

Functions: Power management prolongs the lifespan of IoT devices by minimizing energy consumption during data collection and actuation processes.

Communication Protocols:

Purpose: Communication protocols enable sensors and actuators to transmit data and receive commands from IoT gateways, edge devices, or the cloud.

Types: Common communication protocols include Wi-Fi, Bluetooth, Zigbee, LoRaWAN, MQTT, CoAP, and others.

Functions: These protocols ensure reliable and efficient data exchange between sensors, actuators, and other components within the IoT ecosystem.

The Sensors and Actuators Layer forms the foundation of IoT systems, enabling them to interact with the physical world and collect data from the environment. This layer's design and components must be chosen carefully to meet the specific requirements of IoT applications, including factors like data accuracy, real-time responsiveness, power efficiency, and scalability.

Layer 2 – Communications Network Layer

The Communications Network Layer, often referred to as the Network Layer, is a critical component of the Internet of Things (IoT) architecture. It plays a central role in enabling communication between IoT devices, gateways, and the broader network infrastructure. The primary purpose of the Communications Network Layer is to manage the transmission of data within the IoT ecosystem efficiently and reliably. Here's an overview of theCommunications Network Layer:

Connectivity:

Purpose: Establish and maintain connections between IoT devices and the network, enabling data exchange.

Functions:

Device Discovery: Identifying and registering new IoT devices on the network.

Connection Establishment: Establishing and managing communication links between devices and gateways.

Network Topology: Defining the structure of the IoT network, including star, mesh, or hierarchical topologies.

Communication Protocols:

Purpose: Specify the rules and conventions for data transmission, ensuring devices can understand and exchange information.

Functions:

Data Encapsulation: Structuring data for transmission, including headers, metadata, and payload.

Error Handling: Detecting and correcting transmission errors to ensure data integrity.

Message Routing: Determining the path and destination for data packets within the network.

Quality of Service (QoS): Managing data priorities, latency requirements, and reliability levels.

IoT Gateways:
Purpose: IoT gateways act as intermediaries between IoT devices and the broader network, translating and forwarding data to the appropriate destinations.
Functions:
Protocol Translation: Converting data between IoT device-specific protocols and network protocols (e.g., MQTT to HTTP).
Aggregation: Collecting data from multiple devices, performing preprocessing, and transmitting it to the cloud or data centre.
Security: Enhancing security by implementing firewalls, access control, and encryption.
Network Addressing and Routing:
Purpose: Ensure that data packets are routed to the correct destination within the IoT network.
Functions:
IP Address Assignment: Assigning unique IP addresses to IoT devices for identification.
Routing Tables: Maintaining routing tables that define the path for data packets.
Dynamic Routing: Adapting routing paths based on network conditions and device availability.
Communication Mediums:
Purpose: Define the physical and wireless mediums through which data is transmitted.
Functions:
Wired Communication: Utilizing Ethernet, Fiber Optics, or other wired technologies for reliable and high-speed communication.
Wireless Communication: Leveraging wireless technologies like Wi-Fi, Bluetooth, Zigbee, LoRa, and cellular networks to connect devices.
Network Security:
Purpose: Protect IoT communication from unauthorized access, data breaches, and cyber threats.
Functions:
Authentication: Verifying the identity of IoT devices and gateways.
Encryption: Encrypting data in transit to ensure confidentiality.
Access Control: Restricting access to network resources based on permissions and policies.
Intrusion Detection: Monitoring for unusual or malicious network activity.
Network Scalability:
Purpose: Ensure that the IoT network can accommodate a growing number of devices and data traffic.
Functions:
Load Balancing: Distributing network traffic evenly across resources to prevent congestion.
Network Design: Creating a scalable network architecture that can expand as needed.
The Communications Network Layer is responsible for creating a robust and efficient communication infrastructure for IoT devices, enabling them to transmit data reliably and securely. It plays a pivotal role in facilitating the exchange of information between IoT devices, gateways, edge computing resources, and cloud platforms, making it a foundational component of IoT ecosystems.
The Communications Network Layer in IoT typically consists of several sublayers, each responsible for specific functions and tasks. Here's an overview of the sublayers you mentioned:
Access Network Sublayer:
Purpose: The Access Network Sublayer focuses on connecting IoT devices to the network infrastructure, managing device connectivity, and handling the last-mile communication.
Functions:
Device Connectivity: Establish connections between IoT devices and the network.
Communication Protocols: Define the rules for data transmission within the access network.
Access Points and Gateways: Manage entry points for devices and protocol translation.
Wireless and Wired Connectivity: Support various connectivity technologies.
Network Security: Ensure secure access for devices.
Scalability and Manageability: Enable network growth and device management.
Gateways and Backhaul Sublayer:
Purpose: This sublayer deals with intermediate points that collect data from IoT devices and transmit it to the core network or the cloud. It often involves gateways and backhaul communication.
Functions:
Data Aggregation: Collect data from multiple devices in a local area.
Protocol Translation: Translate data between device-specific protocols and network protocols.

Connection Management: Maintain connections between IoT devices and the broader network.
Backhaul Communication: Transmit aggregated data to the core network or cloud.
Load Balancing: Distribute data traffic effectively.
Security: Implement security measures for data in transit.
Network Transport Sublayer:
Purpose: The Network Transport Sublayer is responsible for ensuring reliable end-to-end data transmission within the network, managing data packets, and addressing routing challenges.
Functions:
Data Packet Routing: Determine the optimal path for data packets to reach their destination.
Quality of Service (QoS): Prioritize data packets based on application requirements.
Error Detection and Correction: Detect and manage transmission errors.
Data Packet Fragmentation and Reassembly: Divide data into smaller packets for transmission and reassemble them at the destination.
IoT Network Management Sublayer:
Purpose: The IoT Network Management Sublayer focuses on the overall management, monitoring, and control of the IoT network.
Functions:
Device Lifecycle Management: Handle device provisioning, configuration, and maintenance.
Security Management: Implement security policies, access controls, and threat detection.
Performance Monitoring: Continuously monitor network performance and device health.
Data Analytics: Analyse network data for insights and optimizations.
Network Troubleshooting: Identify and address network issues and anomalies.
Scalability Planning: Prepare for network growth and expansion.
These sublayers work together to form a comprehensive network infrastructure that facilitates communication between IoT devices, gateways, edge computing resources, and cloud platforms. They ensure the efficient and secure transmission of data, manage network resources, and enable scalability and manageability in IoTdeployments. The specific functions and technologies involved in each sublayer may vary depending on the IoT application and network architecture.
Layer 3 – Applications and Analytics Layer
The Applications and Analytics Layer is a critical component within the Internet of Things (IoT) architecture, situated above the Communications Network Layer and the Middleware Layer. This layer focuses on processing and deriving actionable insights from the data collected by IoT devices, ultimately delivering value to end-users or organizations. Here's an overview of the Applications and Analytics Layer:
Data Processing and Transformation:
Purpose: Process raw data collected from IoT devices and transform it into a usable format for analysis.
Functions:
Data Aggregation: Combine data from multiple sources to create a comprehensive dataset.
Data Cleansing: Remove outliers, errors, and inconsistencies from the data.
Data Normalization: Standardize data units, formats, and scales for consistent analysis.
Real-time Data Analysis:
Purpose: Perform immediate analysis of IoT data to support real-time decision-making and actions.
Functions:
Complex Event Processing (CEP): Detect and respond to critical events or patterns in real time.
Alerting and Notifications: Generate alerts and notifications based on predefined conditions.
Predictive Analytics: Use machine learning algorithms to predict future events or trends.
Batch Data Processing:
Purpose: Analyse large volumes of historical data to identify long-term trends, patterns, and insights.
Functions:
Data Warehousing: Store historical data in a structured manner for analysis.
Batch Analytics: Run scheduled or ad-hoc batch analytics jobs to extract insights.
Reporting and Dashboarding: Create reports and dashboards to visualize historical data.
Machine Learning and AI:
Purpose: Employ machine learning and artificial intelligence techniques to extract valuable insights, make predictions, and automate decision-making.
Functions:
Predictive Maintenance: Predict when equipment or devices require maintenance.

Anomaly Detection: Identify unusual patterns or deviations in data.
Personalization: Customize user experiences and recommendations based on data analysis.
Natural Language Processing (NLP): Analyse text data for sentiment analysis or content understanding.
Visualization and User Interfaces:
Purpose: Present data and insights to end-users in an understandable and actionable format.
Functions:
Interactive Dashboards: Create visual dashboards with charts, graphs, and widgets.
Data Visualization Tools: Utilize tools like Tableau, Power BI, or custom applications.
User-Friendly Interfaces: Design intuitive user interfaces for configuring and interacting with IoT systems.
Integration with External Systems:
Purpose: Enable seamless integration between IoT data and external systems, such as ERP (Enterprise Resource Planning) systems, CRM (Customer Relationship Management) systems, or third-party services.
Functions:
API Integration: Develop APIs to allow external systems to access and utilize IoT data.
Data Exchange Protocols: Use standard data exchange protocols like REST or MQTT.
Business Process Automation: Automate workflows and actions based on IoT data.
Business Logic and Rules Engine:
Purpose: Implement business rules and logic that guide decision-making and actions based on IoT data.
Functions:
Rule-Based Systems: Define rules to trigger specific actions or alerts.
Workflow Automation: Automate processes based on predefined business logic.
Event-Driven Architecture: Enable real-time responses to specific events or conditions.
User and Stakeholder Engagement:
Purpose: Engage with end-users, stakeholders, and decision-makers to ensure that IoT insights lead to meaningful actions and outcomes.
Functions:
User Feedback Loops: Collect and incorporate user feedback for continuous improvement.
Reporting and Insights Sharing: Share reports and insights with relevant stakeholders.
Decision Support Systems: Provide tools and information to aid decision-makers.
The Applications and Analytics Layer is where the value of IoT data is unlocked. It leverages data processing, analytics, visualization, and integration capabilities to turn raw data into actionable insights. These insights can inform real-time decision-making, drive process optimizations, and create new business opportunities, making this layer a crucial component of any IoT ecosystem.

Analytics and Control Applications

Analytics and Control Applications:
Analytics Applications: Analytics applications in IoT are primarily focused on processing and analysing data generated by IoT devices. These applications use various data analysis techniques, including machine learning and statistical methods, to derive insights, patterns, and trends from the data. The goal is to provide valuable information to users, organizations, or systems for decision-making or optimization.
Control Applications: Control applications, on the other hand, are designed to take actions or make decisions based on the insights derived from analytics. They use the analysed data to control devices, systems, or processes in real time. For example, predictive maintenance systems can use analytics to predict equipment failures and trigger maintenance actions automatically.

Data and Network Analytics:

Data Analytics: Data analytics focuses on analysing the data generated by IoT devices themselves. It involves processing and interpreting the sensor data, telemetry, and other information collected from the IoT devices. Data analytics helps extract meaningful insights from the raw data, enabling informed decision-making and optimizations.
Network Analytics: Network analytics, on the other hand, is concerned with monitoring and analysing the performance and health of the communication network that connects IoT devices. It involves tracking data traffic, network congestion, latency, security threats, and overall network efficiency. Network analytics ensures reliable and efficient data transmission within the IoT ecosystem.

Data Analytics and Business Benefits:

Data Analytics: Data analytics focuses on the technical aspects of processing and analysing data. It involves data cleansing, transformation, statistical analysis, machine learning, and visualization. The primary goal is to extract insights, detect patterns, and generate actionable information from the data.

Business Benefits: Business benefits refer to the tangible advantages and value that organizations or users gain from data analytics. These benefits can include improved operational efficiency, cost savings, enhanced decision-making, predictive maintenance, personalized services, and competitive advantages. The ultimate goal of data analytics is to translate data insights into meaningful business outcomes.

Sensor Technology

Sensor technology plays an important role in the Internet of Things (IoT) ecosystem. It acts as the eyes and ears of I oT devices, enabling them to collect and understand data from the physical world. These sensors are essential tools f or IoT applications to collect real-world data and enable data-driven decision making and automation.

Below are the details of IoT sensor technology:

What are sensors in IoT?

A sensor is a device or module that can detect and measure an object or environment. They are equipped with the ca pability to convert physical phenomena, such as temperature, light, humidity, motion, or sound, into electrical signal s that can be processed by IoT devices.

Types of Sensors in IoT:

There is a wide range of sensors used in IoT applications, including but not limited to:

Temperature Sensors: Measure temperature variations.

Proximity Sensors: Detect the presence or absence of nearby objects.

Light Sensors: Measure light intensity.

Humidity Sensors: Monitor moisture levels in the environment.

Motion Sensors: Detect movement or changes in position.

Pressure Sensors: Measure pressure changes.

Gas Sensors: Detect the presence and concentration of gases.

Sound Sensors (Microphones): Capture sound and audio data.

Image and Video Sensors (Cameras): Capture images and videos.

Biometric Sensors: Measure physiological or behavioral characteristics for security and identification purposes

Role of Sensors in IoT:

Sensors act as data collectors, capturing information from the physical world. This data is then transmitted to IoT de vices or platforms, where it can be processed, analyzed, and acted upon.

Sensors enable IoT applications to monitor and respond to changes in the environment, enabling smart homes, smart cities, industrial automation, healthcare monitoring, and more.

They facilitate realtime tracking, predictive maintenance, and automation, improving efficiency and reducing human intervention.

Characteristics and Specifications of sensors:

The characteristics and specifications of sensors are essential for understanding their capabilities and choosing the right sensor for a specific use case. Here are some key characteristics and specifications of sensors:

SensingRange:

Definition: The range over which a sensor can accurately detect and measure a specific physical quantity (e.g., temperature, pressure, distance).

Example: A temperature sensor may have a range of -40°C to 150°C.

Sensitivity:

Definition: Sensitivity refers to how responsive a sensor is to changes in the measured quantity. It quantifies the change in sensor output for a given change in the input.

Example: A light sensor with high sensitivity can detect slight changes in light intensity.

Resolution:

Definition: Resolution is the smallest detectable change in the measured quantity that a sensor can distinguish.

Example:A digital thermometer with a resolution of 0.1°C can detect temperature changes as small as 0.1°C.

Accuracy:

Definition: Accuracy indicates how closely the sensor's measurements align with the true value of the physical quantity being measured.

Example: An accurate pressure sensor provides measurements that are very close to the actual pressure.

Precision:

Definition: Precision relates to the repeatability and consistency of sensor measurements. It measures how closely repeated measurements match each other.

Example:A precise scale consistently provides the same weight measurement for the same object.

Linearity:

Definition: Linearity assesses how well the sensor's output corresponds to changes in the input quantity across its entire range.

Example:A linear position sensor produces a proportional change in voltage or current for a proportional change in distance.

Hysteresis:

Definition: Hysteresis refers to the variation in sensor output when the input quantity changes along a specific path, compared to when it changes along the reverse path.

Example:A pressure sensor may exhibit hysteresis when pressure is increased and then decreased.

Response Time:

Definition: Response time measures how quickly a sensor can detect and react to changes in the measured quantity.

Example: A fast-response temperature sensor can provide a new temperature reading within milliseconds.

Environmental Conditions:

Operating Conditions: Sensors may have specific requirements for temperature, humidity, pressure, and other environmental factors during operation.

Storage Conditions: Manufacturers specify temperature and humidity conditions for storing sensors when not in use.

Output Type:

Analog: Analog sensors provide continuous output signals (e.g., voltage, current) that vary proportionally with **the** measured quantity.

Digital: Digital sensors provide discrete, quantized readings that are typically in digital format (e.g., binary values).

Power Requirements:

Voltage: Sensors may require a specific voltage supply for operation.

Power Consumption: Sensors consume power, and their power requirementsimpact battery life in portable devices.

Calibration:

Sensors may require periodic calibration to maintain accuracy and compensate for drift or aging.

Interfacing:

Sensors may use different interfaces (e.g., I2C, SPI, analog voltage) for connecting to microcontrollers or data acquisitionsystems.

Size and Form Factor:

The physical size and shape of a sensor are important considerations, especially in space-constrained applications.

Cost:

The cost of a sensor can vary widely based on its capabilities, accuracy, and features.

Durability and Lifespan:

The expected lifespan of a sensor and its resistance to environmental factors such as moisture, dust, and vibrations are crucial for long-term applications.

Understanding these characteristics and specifications is essential for selecting the right sensor for a particular application, ensuring accurate and reliable measurements, and meeting the specific requirements of the system or device in which the sensor will be used.

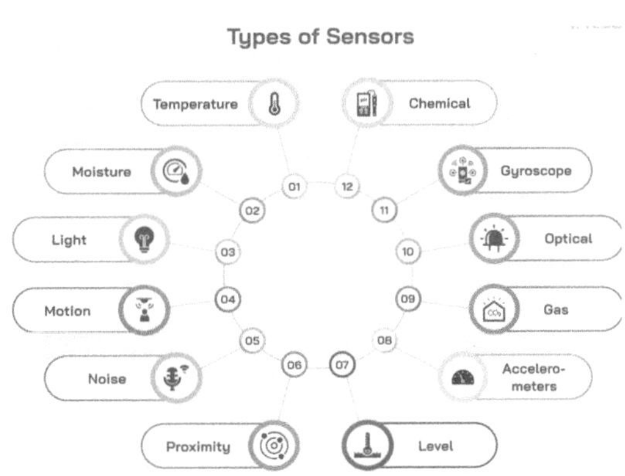

Communication Protocols:
Sensors often communicate with IoT devices and platforms using various communication protocols, including Wi-Fi, Bluetooth, Zigbee, LoRaWAN, and cellular networks, depending on the application's requirements and constraint s.
Power Efficiency:
Most IoT sensors are designed to be energy efficient as they always run on batteries or low power sources. Energy-saving sensors can work for a long time without the need for frequent battery replacement.
Data Processing at the Edge:
Some IoT applications require instant decision making based on sensor data. Edge computes the data process locally on IoT devices or gateways, enabling real-time responses without sending data to central cloud servers.
Data Security and Privacy:
Data security and privacy are important as sensors collect data from the physical world. It is important to encrypt dat a in transit and at rest and use appropriate authentication methods.
Challenges and decisions:
Sensor technologies in the Internet of Things face challenges such as sensor calibration, accuracy, interoperability an d scalability. Choosing the right sensor for a particular IoT application and ensuring data transfer and processing is c rucial.
In a nutshell, sensor technology is an essential part of the Internet of Things, allowing IoT devices to collect real-world data, monitor the environment, and respond to changes. Advances in technology continue to drive innovation i n the Internet of Things, enabling smarter, more flexible and more efficient production across industries.

Connectivity Protocols

Connectivity Protocols in the Internet of Things (IoT) is essential to enable communication between IoT devices, sensors, and the underlying network or cloud platform. These laws determine how data is transferred so that devices can exchange data efficiently and securely in a standardized manner. Here is some of the connections available for IoT:
Wi-Fi (Wireless Fidelity):
Description: Wi-Fi is a widely used wireless networking technology that allows IoT devices to connect to the Internet and local networks. It provides high flexibility and is suitable for applications where power consumption is not important.
Use Examples: Home Automation, Smart Office, Industrial Automation and Consumer IoT Devices.
Bluetooth:
Description: Bluetooth is a short-range wireless communication protocol used to connect nearby IoT devices. Bluetooth Low Energy (BLE) is the most energy efficient technology used in IoT applications.
Use Examples: Wearables, Healthcare Devices, Proximity Based Apps and Smart Home Appliances.
Zigbee:
Description: Zigbee is a low power, low data rate wireless communication protocol designed for IoT and home energy use. It uses a mesh network that allows devices to create a self-healing network.
Use Cases: Smart Lighting, Home Energy Management, Industrial Automation and Building Automation.
Z-Wave:
Description: Z-Wave is a wireless communication protocol designed for smart home applications. It operates in the frequency range below 1 GHz, providing good service and low power consumption.
Use Cases: Smart Home Devices, Security Systems and Home Automation.
LoRaWAN (Long Range Wide Area Network):
Description: LoRaWAN is a long range, low power wireless protocol designed for IoT applications requiring service in the region. It is suitable for applications where equipment is spread over a large area.
Use Examples: Smart Agriculture, Asset Tracking, Environmental Monitoring and Smart Cities.
NB-IoT (Narrowband Internet of Things):
Description: NB-IoT is a cellular communication standard designed for low power, wide area IoT Design for network deployment. It provides good service and access by operating in a licensed frequency band.
Use Examples: Service Measurement, Smart Cities, Remote Monitoring and Asset Tracking.
MQTT (Message Queue Telemetry Transport):
Description: MQTT is a simple publish-subscribe messaging protocol used for IoT communication. It is designed for efficient data transmission and is suitable for situations with low bandwidth and reliability.

Use Examples: IoT data telemetry, real-time monitoring and industrial automation.

CoAP (Constrained Application Protocol):

Description: CoAP is a lightweight, efficient protocol designed for constrained applications with limited resources. Designed for applications where overhead is low and simplicity is key.

Use Cases: Smart Grid, Wearable Devices and Sensor Networks.

HTTP/HTTPS:

Description: Hypertext Transfer Protocol (HTTP) and its secure type (HTTPS) are used for IoT communication, especially when the device needs to interact with web services and cloud platforms.

Use Examples: Web connected devices, cloud-based IoT solutions and IoT applications with RESTful APIs.

Choosing the appropriate network protocol for an IoT application depends on many factors, such as energy consumption, data rate, security and the specific data requirements used. Many IoT deployments can use a combination of technologies to meet different communication needs.

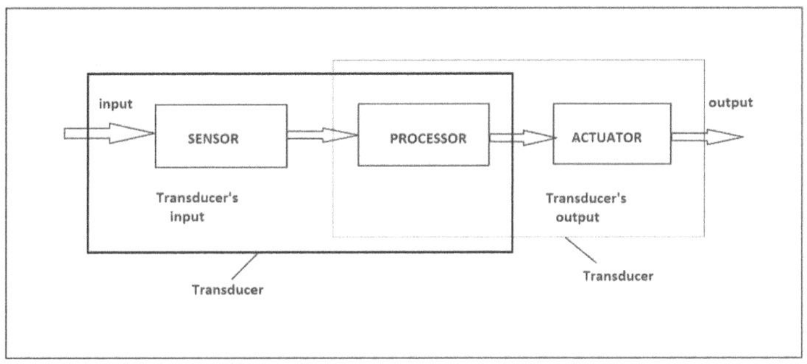

Data Storage and Processing

Data storage and processing in the Internet of Things (IoT) are key components that enable IoT applications to collect, manage, analyse and deliver useful insights from massive amounts of data from connected devices and sensors. Details on storage and operation in IoT are:

Data Collection:

IoT devices and sensors are constantly collecting data from the physical world. This information can be temperature, humidity, location, movement, photos, videos, etc. may contain information.

The sensors send the collected data to the central point via various communication methods, often referred to as data reception or data gateway protocols.

Health Data:

Data from IoT devices are entered into the central system or cloud platform for processing and storage.

Content consumption often uses chatbots, IoT platforms or edge gateways to retrieve, retrieve and store data. Pre-process data before storing.

Data Storage:

Different solutions can be used depending on the application to store IoT data

Data Connection:

When data documents created by relationships need to be stored and queried.

NoSQL Database: For processing large databases of unstructured or semi-structured data such as text and logs.

Time Series Database: Designed to manage time series data common in IoT applications.

Storage: Used to store binaries, images, videos and data created by IoT devices.

Data Processing:

Data processing includes analysing, transforming and gaining insights from IoT data. This can be done through batch processing, stream processing, or a combination of the two:

Batch Processing: Analyse large datasets on a schedule to generate report alert, historical analysis, and insight.

Stream function: Create real-time or near-real-time data streams from sensors for immediate action or alert.

Data processing will include computational complexity (CEP), machine learning, data enrichment and data cleansing.

Edge Processing:

In some IoT scenarios, data processing takes place at the edge, near the IoT device. Edge computing processes data locally, reducing latency and bandwidth usage.

devices and gateways often perform intensive analysis, filtering and decision-making algorithms.

Data Visualization and Reporting:
All IoT data can be visualized via dashboards and reports. Visualization tools help users interpret data and make informed decisions.
The reporting process can automatically generate reports and reports based on predefined criteria.
Data Security and Privacy:
Data security is very important in the Internet of Things. Measures such as encryption, access control, and secure communication protect data from unauthorized access and modification.
Privacy concerns should be considered, especially when dealing with sensitive personal or corporate information.
Scalability and Resource Efficiency:
IoT data storage and solutions should scale seamlessly as the number of connected devices and data volumes increase.
Resource efficient and distributed systems help solve scalability issues.
Cloud-based on-premises solutions:
Organizations can choose between cloud-based IoT platforms and on-premises solutions based on costs such as cost, documentation and housing arrangements.
Data storage and retention:
The IoT data storage policy defines how long data should be retained and when it should be retained or removed. Compatibility and application will determine these requirements.
Storage and efficiency are key to exploiting the full potential of IoT applications. They enable real-time monitoring, predictive maintenance, decision making and advice, ultimately promoting efficiency and innovation across the enterprise.

Security Considerations

Determining the security of the Internet of Things (IoT) is important because of the increasing number of connected devices and possible interactions with them. Protecting the IoT ecosystem from vulnerabilities and threats is critical to ensuring data privacy, device integrity, and reliability of IoT applications. Security considerations in IoT include:
Device Authentication and Authorization:
IoT devices must identify themselves to the networks and services they interact with. Strong authentication mechanisms such as digital certificates or biometrics can be used.
Permissions ensure that devices can only access resources and information for which they are authorized.
Secure communication:
Data sent between IoT devices, gateways and cloud platforms must be encrypted using protocols such as TLS/SSL. Encrypted communication prevents eavesdropping and data tampering.
Enabling mutual authentication between devices and servers adds an extra layer of security.
Firmware and software updates:
Device must support firmware and software updates for security areas. Developers are required to release security updates on a regular basis.
Members should be notified of updates and encouraged to use them quickly.
Access Control and Segmentation:
Use powerful controls to restrict access to devices and networks. Network segmentation can separate IoT devices from the core infrastructure.
Use minimum order policy to limit device permissions.
Physical Security:
Physical access to IoT devices should be limited to authorized personnel only. Tamper-proof and tamper-resistant design helps detect and prevent physical attacks.
Protect storage and handling equipment from theft or tampering during manufacture or export.
Data Encryption and Privacy:
Data stored on IoT devices and transmitted over the network needs to be encrypted. Protect sensitive information and keep information private.
Data anonymity and mitigation should be used to collect necessary data to reduce privacy risk.
Secure Boot and Device ID:
Follow the secure boot process to ensure the boot state is properly recognized. This prevents unauthorized firmware updates.
Provides unique identification of devices to prevent fraud and enable device-to-device communication.
Network Security:

Network infrastructure (such as routers, gateways and access points) should be properly maintained. Eliminate unnecessary ports and services to reduce traffic.

Intrusion detection and prevention can help detect and respond to network threats.

Monitoring and Logging:

Performs monitoring and logging of operational equipment and network connections. Check for suspicious or unauthorized behaviour reports.

Use the alarm system to report the security situation to the authorities.

Compliance with standards and standards:

Comply with industry-specific regulations and standards such as ISO/IEC 27001, NIST and GDPR to ensure security and privacy are adhered to.

Regular security audits and assessments can help identify vulnerabilities and ensure compliance.

Supply Chain Security:

Secure the entire supply chain from production to distribution. Check the integrity of products and software between devices.

Build trust by reviewing the security practices of third-party vendors and service providers.

Incident Response Plan:

Create an incident response plan to address a security breach or vulnerability in a timely manner. Define roles and responsibilities for security solutions.

Constantly test and update your emergency response plan to keep up with changes.

IoT security is an ongoing process that requires collaboration between manufacturers, developers, network administrators and end users. Keeping up with emerging threats and security best practices is critical to mitigating risk and increasing the strength of the IoT ecosystem.

Steps of IoT Networking

IoT (Internet of Things) networking is a critical aspect of building and managing IoT ecosystems. It involves connecting a multitude of devices, sensors, and systems to enable data exchange and control. Here are the fundamental steps and basics of IoT networking:

Device Connection:

Device Onboarding: Add IoT devices to the network by configuring network settings and security credentials.

Connectivity Protocols: Choose appropriate communication protocols such as Wi-Fi, Bluetooth, Zigbee, LoRa, or cellular to connect devices.

Network Infrastructure:

Networking Architecture: Design the network architecture, considering factors like topology, scalability, and latency requirements.

Network Components: Include routers, switches, access points, gateways, and network cables as needed.

Data Transmission:

Data Protocols: Select data transfer protocols like MQTT, CoAP, HTTP, or custom protocols for transmitting data between devices and servers.

Data Security: Implement encryption and authentication mechanisms to secure data in transit.

Cloud Integration:

Cloud Platforms: Integrate IoT devices with cloud platforms like AWS IoT, Azure IoT, or Google Cloud IoT Core for data storage, processing, and analytics.

APIs and SDKs: Use provided APIs and SDKs to facilitate communication between devices and cloud services.

Edge Computing:

Edge Devices: Deploy edge computing devices like gateways or edge servers to perform data processing and analytics closer to IoT devices, reducing latency.

Local Data Storage: Store essential data locally forimmediate access and decision-making.

IoT Security:

Access Control: Enforce access controls to ensure only authorized devices can connect to the network.

Data Encryption: Encrypt data at rest and in transit to protect sensitive information.

Security Updates: Regularly update device firmware and software to patch vulnerabilities.

Scalability:

Plan for Growth: Design the network to accommodate a growing number of IoT devices and increased data traffic.

Load Balancing: Implement load balancing strategies to distribute traffic evenly across network resources.

Data Management:

Data Storage: Determine where and how IoT data will be stored, whether in cloud databases, on-premises servers, or distributed file systems.
Data Retention: Establish data retention policies to manage and clean up historical data.
Monitoring and Management:
Network Monitoring: Deploy monitoring tools to track device health, network performance, and security.
Remote Management: Enable remote device management, including firmware updates and configuration changes.
Analytics and Insights:
Data Analytics: Analyse IoT data to gain insights, detect anomalies, and make informed decisions.
Visualization: Create dashboards and reports for visualizing IoT data and key performance indicators.
Compliance and Regulations:
Compliance: Ensure that your IoT network and devices comply with relevant industry standards and data privacy regulations.

Networking Components in IoT

IoT networking relies on several key components and technologies to facilitate communication and data exchange. These components include:
IoT Devices: These are the physical sensors, actuators, and devices that collect data and interact with the physical world.
Network Protocols: Various communication protocols like MQTT, CoAP, HTTP, and others are used to transmit data between devices and the network.
Gateways: Gateways act as intermediaries between IoT devices and the wider network infrastructure, facilitating protocol translation and data aggregation.
Connectivity Technologies: IoT networks can use different connectivity technologies, including Wi-Fi, Bluetooth, Zigbee, LoRa, cellular (2G/3G/4G/5G), and wired Ethernet.
Cloud Services: Cloud platforms provide scalable storage, processing, and analytics capabilities for IoT data.
Edge Computing Devices: Edge servers or gateways perform data processing and analytics closer to IoT devices to reduce latency and enhance real-time decision-making.
Security Mechanisms: IoT security features include access controls, encryption, authentication, and security patches to protect devices and data.
Network Infrastructure: This includes routers, switches, access points, and cables that form the physical and logical foundation of the network.
Monitoring and Management Tools: Tools and software for monitoring device health, network performance, and remote management of IoT devices.
Data Storage and Databases: Storage solutions like cloud databases, NoSQL databases, or distributed file systems for storing IoT data.
Analytics Tools: Data analytics tools and platforms for extracting insights and patterns from IoT data.
Compliance and Regulations: Adherence to industry-specific regulations and standards, such as GDPR for data privacy.
These components work together to create a robust and scalable IoT networking environment capable of supporting diverse IoT applications and use cases.

Networking Components

Networking components in the context of computer networks and IoT (Internet of Things) play crucial roles in facilitating data communication, connectivity, and overall network functionality. Here are key networking components:
Devices:
IoT Devices: These include sensors, actuators, smart appliances, wearables, and various IoT endpoints that collect data or control physical processes.
Network Devices: Traditional network devices such as computers, smartphones, servers, and routers are also part of the ecosystem.
Communication Protocols:
IoT Protocols: IoT communication protocols like MQTT, CoAP, HTTP, and AMQP are designed for efficient data exchange between IoT devices and networks.
Network Protocols: Networking protocols like TCP/IP, Ethernet, Wi-Fi, and Bluetooth enable data transmission and routing within networks.
Gateways:

IoT Gateways: These act as intermediaries between IoT devices and the broader network, translating between IoT-specific protocols and standard network protocols.

Network Gateways: In traditional networks, gateways connect different networks or network segments and provide protocol translation if needed.

Connectivity Technologies:

Wireless: Technologies like Wi-Fi, Bluetooth, Zigbee, LoRaWAN, and cellular (2G/3G/4G/5G) provide wireless connectivity for IoT devices.

Wired: Ethernet is a common wired connectivity option used in both IoT and traditional network environments.

Network Infrastructure:

Switches: Ethernet switches are used to connect devices within a local area network (LAN).

Routers: Routers are responsible for routing data between different networks or subnets.

Access Points: In wireless networks, access points provide connectivity to Wi-Fi or other wireless devices.

Cabling: Ethernet cables, fibre-optic cables, and other physical mediums connect devices to the network.

Network Services:

DNS (Domain Name System): Converts domain names into IP addresses, allowing users to access websites and services by name.

DHCP (Dynamic Host Configuration Protocol): Assigns IP addresses dynamically to devices on a network.

Firewalls: Protect networks by filtering and controlling incoming and outgoing traffic.

Load Balancers: Distribute network traffic across multiple servers to optimize performance and ensure high availability.

Security Mechanisms:

Firewalls: Protect networks by filtering and controlling incoming and outgoing traffic.

Intrusion Detection and Prevention Systems (IDPS): Monitor networks for suspicious activitiesand take actions to prevent security breaches.

Access Control: Enforces permissions and authentication for network resources.

VPN (Virtual Private Network): Provides secure, encrypted communication over public networks.

Monitoring and Management Tools:

Network Monitoring Tools: Software and hardware solutions for monitoring network health, performance, and security.

Configuration Management Tools: Tools to manage and configure network devices.

Cloud Services:

IoT Cloud Platforms: Cloud platforms like AWS IoT, Azure IoT, and Google Cloud IoT Core provide scalable storage, processing, and analytics for IoT data.

Traditional Cloud Services: General-purpose cloud platforms like Amazon Web Services (AWS) and Microsoft Azure support various network-related services.

Edge Computing Devices:

Edge Servers: Devices located closer to IoT endpoints or users that perform data processing, analytics, and decision-making at the network edge.

Data Storage and Databases:

IoT Data Stores: Databases and data storage solutions to manage and store IoT data, including NoSQL databases, time-series databases, and cloud-based data stores.

Traditional Data Storage: In traditional networks, data storage includes file servers, database servers, and cloud-based storage solutions.

Compliance and Regulations:

Security Standards: Adherence to industry-specific security standards and best practices to ensure network and data security.

Data Privacy Regulations: Compliance with data protection regulations such as GDPR for personal data handling.

These networking components collectively form the infrastructure and ecosystem that enable data communication, connectivity, and the functioning of both IoT networks and traditional computer networks. Their proper configuration and integration are essential for network reliability, security, and performance.

Network Topologies

Network topologies refer to the arrangement or layout of devices and connections in a computer network. Different topologies offer various advantages and disadvantages in terms of cost, scalability, reliability, and ease of management. Here are some common network topologies:

Star Topology:
Description: In a star topology, all devices connect to a central hub or switch. The central hub acts as a distribution point for data traffic.
Advantages: Easy to set up and manage, if one connection fails, it doesn't affect other devices, suitable for small to medium-sized networks.
Disadvantages: Dependent on the central hub; if it fails, the entire network can be disrupted.
Bus Topology:
Description: In a bus topology, all devices share a single communication line or cable. Data is broadcast to all devices on the network.
Advantages: Simple and inexpensive to install, suitable for small networks with minimal data traffic.
Disadvantages: If the main cable fails, the entire network is affected, performance decreases as more devices are added.
Ring Topology:
Description: In a ring topology, each device connects to exactly two other devices, forming a closed loop. **Data** travels in one direction around the ring.
Advantages: Equal access to resources, no central point of failure.
Disadvantages: Difficult to install and reconfigure, failure of one device can disrupt the entire network.
Mesh Topology:
Description: In a mesh topology, every device is connected to every other device. This results in redundant paths for data transmission.
Advantages: High redundancy, fault tolerance, no single point of failure.
Disadvantages: Expensive to implement and maintain, complex cabling and configuration.
Hybrid Topology:
Description: A hybrid topology combines two or more different topologies. For example, connecting star topologies with a central hub forms a hybrid topology.
Advantages: Offers a balance of features from different topologies, can be tailored to meet specific network requirements.
Disadvantages: Can be complex to design and manage, cost may be higher depending on the components used.
Tree (Hierarchical) Topology:
Description: A tree topology combines multiple star topologies into a single network. It includes a central hub with branches extending to additional hubs or switches.
Advantages: Scalable, suitable for larger networks, allows for better organization of devices.
Disadvantages: Failure of the central hub can disrupt entire branches, can become complex to manage in large networks.
Point-to-Point Topology:
Description: Each device is directly connected to another device. This topology is common in WAN (Wide Area Network) connections.
Advantages: Simple and efficient for connecting two devices, minimal interference from other devices.
Disadvantages: Limited to connecting only two devices, not suitable for larger networks.
Daisy Chain Topology:
Description: Devices are connected in a linear fashion, like links in a chain. Data travels sequentially from one device to the next.
Advantages: Simple and easy to install for a small number of devices.
Disadvantages: Susceptible to failure if one device in the chain fails, may require significant reconfiguration when adding or removing devices.

The choice of network topology depends on factors such as the network's size, intended use, scalability requirements, budget constraints, and the need for redundancy and fault tolerance. Different topologies are suitable for different scenarios, and hybrid topologies are often used to achieve specific objectives.

Sensor Network

A sensor network is a collection of interconnected sensors that collaborate to monitor and gather data from the physical world. These networks are commonly used in various applications, including environmental monitoring, surveillance, industrial automation, and more. The basic components of a sensor network include:

Sensors: Sensors are the primary components of the network responsible for data collection. They can measure various physical parameters such as temperature, humidity, light, pressure, motion, and more. Sensors are often specialized for specific tasks and can be deployed in large numbers to cover a wide area.

Sensor Nodes: A sensor node is a fundamental building block of a sensor network. It typically includes one or more sensors, a processing unit (microcontroller or microprocessor), memory for data storage, and communication interfaces. Sensor nodes are responsible for collecting data, processing it if needed, and transmitting it to other nodes or a central location.

Communication Interfaces: Sensor nodes need to communicate with each other or with a central base station. They may use wired or wireless communication interfaces depending on the application. Common wireless technologies include Wi-Fi, Zigbee, Bluetooth, LoRa, and cellular networks. The choice of communication technology depends on factors like range, power consumption, and data rate requirements.

Data Processing Unit: Sensor nodes often include microcontrollers or microprocessors to perform basic data processing tasks. This can involve data filtering, aggregation, or even running simple algorithms on the collected data before transmitting it. Processing at the node level can reduce the amount of data transmitted and conserve power.

Power Source: Sensor nodes require a power source to operate. This can be in the form of batteries, energy harvesting systems (such as solar panels or kinetic energy harvesters), or even wired power sources in some cases. Power efficiency is crucial, as many sensor nodes are deployed in remote or inaccessible locations.

Memory: Sensor nodes have memory to store collected data temporarily or for buffering before transmission. Memory is also used to store program code and configuration settings for the node.

Networking Protocol: Sensor networks use networking protocols to enable communication between nodes. These protocols define how data is transmitted, how nodes discover each other, and how they handle issues like routing and data integrity. Common sensor network protocols include Zigbee, MQTT, CoAP, and IEEE 802.15.4.

Gateway or Base Station: In many sensor networks, there is a central point of data aggregation called a gateway or base station. This device collects data from multiple sensor nodes, processes it if necessary, and may transmit it to a higher-level network or the internet. Gateways often have more processing power and storage capacity than individual sensor nodes.

Management and Control Software: Sensor networks often require software for managing and controlling the nodes. This includes tasks like node configuration, software updates, and monitoring the health of the network. Network management software helps ensure the reliability and efficiency of the sensor network.

User Interface and Applications: Finally, the data collected by the sensor network is typically usedfor specific applications. User interfaces and applications are developed to visualize, analyse, and make decisions based on the sensor data. These can range from simple dashboards to complex data analytics and decision support systems.

These basic components work together to create a functional sensor network that can monitor, collect, and transmit data from the physical world to enable various applications and services. The design and configuration of these components can vary significantly depending on the specific requirements of the sensor network application.

Zigbee

Zigbee is a wireless communication protocol widely used in the field of home automation, industrial control systems, and sensor networks. Its architecture is designed to support low-power, short-range, and reliable communication among a variety of devices.

Zigbee Network Topology:

Zigbee networks typically use a mesh network topology. In this topology, devices, also known as nodes, are interconnected, allowing them to relay data to one another. This redundancy enhances network reliability, as data can find multiple paths to reach its destination.

Zigbee Devices:

Zigbee networks consist of various types of devices:

Coordinator: The network coordinator initiates and manages the network. There is always one coordinator in a Zigbee network.

Router: Routers extend the network's coverage by forwarding data between devices. They play a crucial role in expanding the network's reach.

End Device: End devices are often battery-powered and communicate with routers or the coordinator. They are usually sensors or actuators.

Zigbee Layers:

The Zigbee architecture is organized into layers, each responsible for specific functions:

Application Layer: This top layer handles application-specific tasks, defining how devices interact with each other. Zigbee application profiles specify the communication rules for various applications, such as lighting control or home automation.
Network Layer: The network layer is responsible for managing device addressing, routing, and data forwarding within the network. It ensures data reliability and optimal path selection.
MAC (Media Access Control) Layer: This layer controls access to the physical radio channel, managing data transmission and reception. It handles aspects like channel selection and data framing.
PHY (Physical) Layer: The PHY layer manages the actual radio communication, including modulation and transmission power. It ensures that data is transmitted and received correctly over the wireless medium.

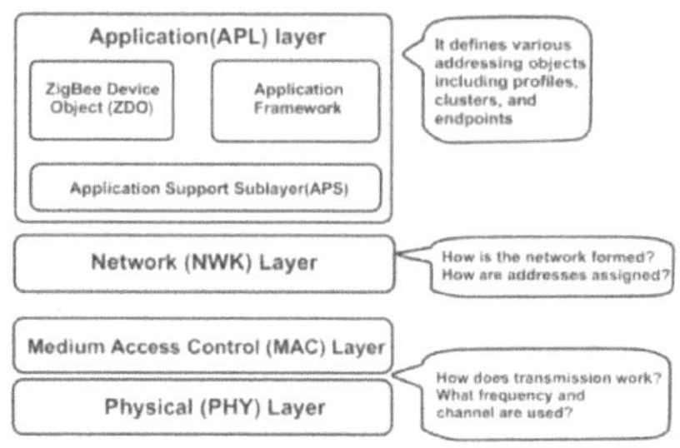

Zigbee Communication:
Devices in a Zigbee network communicate using predefined channels in the 2.4 GHz ISM (Industrial, Scientific, and Medical) band or other frequency bands, depending on regional regulations. Communication is organized into small data frames, making it efficient for low-power devices. Devices can send data directly to each other or use routing via routers to reach distant destinations.
Security: Zigbee networks prioritize security, employing encryption, authentication, and access control mechanisms to protect data. Each device in the network has a unique network key, and data can be encrypted end-to-end, safeguarding against unauthorized access.
Zigbee Alliance:
The Zigbee Alliance is a consortium of companies that develop and maintain the Zigbee standard. They work together to ensure interoperability and evolve the protocol to meet the needs of various industries and applications.
In summary, Zigbee is a wireless communication protocol with a robust architecture designed for low-power, short-range, and reliable networking. Its mesh topology, layered structure, and emphasis on security make it well-suited for applications such as home automation, industrial control, and sensor networks.
RFID (Radio-Frequency Identification) Sensors
RFID sensors represent a specialized branch of RFID technology, harnessing radio-frequency signals to remotely identify and track objects, assets, or individuals. With its efficiency, precision, and versatility, RFID technology has garnered widespread adoption across diverse industries. RFID sensors encompass three fundamental components:
RFID Tags: These are compact, passive devices that store data and can be affixed to or integrated within objects. RFID tags come in various forms, including passive, active, and semi-passive. Passive tags draw power from RFID readers' transmitted signals and then transmit data, while active tags possess their own power sources, allowing for longer signal transmission distances.
RFID Readers: RFID readers emit radio-frequency signals and capture data from RFID tags. These readers can be handheld, fixed, or integrated into other systems. When a reader emits a signal, nearby RFID tags respond by transmitting their stored data.
Data Processing Software: This software interprets the data acquired by RFID readers, facilitating organizations' ability to make informed decisions based on the collected information.
Diverse Applications of RFID Sensors: RFID sensors find utility across a spectrum of industries:
Retail: RFID sensors serve in inventory management and theft prevention. Retailers can swiftly scan items on shelves, monitor stock levels, and reduce the necessity for manual stock checks.
Logistics and Supply Chain: RFID tracking ensures the seamless flow of goods within supply chains. It enables real-time tracking of shipments, reduces errors, and enhances overall logistics efficiency.

Healthcare: RFID sensors aid in managing patient records, monitoring medical equipment, and enhancing medication administration. Additionally, they play a pivotal role in asset tracking within healthcare facilities.

Manufacturing: RFID sensors are indispensable for quality control, tracking work-in-progress, and overseeing the inventory of raw materials and finished products within manufacturing plants.

Transportation: RFID sensors contribute to toll collection, vehicle identification, and smart parking systems. They are also instrumental in tracking and managing assets within the transportation sector.

Agriculture and Livestock: In agriculture, RFID tags are employed for tracking livestock, monitoring crop conditions, and managing farm resources and equipment.

Access Control and Security: RFID sensors enable secure access control systems within buildings and facilities. They find application in employee ID badges and regulating access to restricted areas.

Waste Management: RFID sensors are employed to track waste containers and optimize waste collection routes, resulting in cost savings and reduced environmental impact.

Advantages of RFID Sensors:

Efficiency: RFID sensors facilitate rapid and automated data capture, diminishing the necessity for manual data input.

Accuracy: They provide precise, real-time information, reducing errors and bolstering decision-making.

Versatility: RFID sensors are adaptable across diverse environments and scenarios.

Cost Efficiency: Streamlined operations, reduced labour costs, and improved inventory management contribute to cost efficiency.

Security: RFID technology can furnish authentication and encryption for secure data transmission.

RFID sensors continue to evolve in tandem with technological advancements, incorporating features such as environmental monitoring, temperature tracking, and other data-capturing capabilities. As industries increasingly pivot toward data-driven decision-making, RFID sensors are poised to play a pivotal role in process optimization and efficiency enhancement.

Challenges and issues

RFID (Radio Frequency Identification) offer various benefits, such as improved asset tracking, inventory management, and supply chain visibility. However, they also come with several challenges and issues that organizations must address when implementing RFID technology. Here are some of the key challenges and issues associated with RFID sensors:

Cost: RFID technology, including tags, readers, and infrastructure, can be relatively expensive, especially for large-scale deployments. The initial investment can be a significant barrier for some organizations.

Interference: RFID signals can be subject to interference from other electronic devices or metal objects, leading to read errors or reduced performance. Proper tag placement and frequency selection are essential to mitigate interference.

Tag Collision: In environments with a high density of RFID tags, multiple tags may respond simultaneously when a reader initiates a query, causing signal collisions. This can result in missed reads and data inaccuracies.

Read Range: The read range of RFID tags varies depending on the type of RFID technology used. Achieving the desired read range for specific applications can be challenging and may require careful consideration of tag selection and reader placement.

Data Privacy and Security: RFID sensors can raise concerns about data privacy and security. Unauthorized access to RFID data can lead to privacy breaches or counterfeiting issues. Encryption and access control mechanisms are necessary to address these concerns.

Standardization: Different industries and regions may have varying RFID standards and frequencies, leading to compatibility issues when deploying RFID systems across borders or in diverse environments. Standardization efforts aim to address this challenge.

Power Source: Passive RFID tags rely on energy harvested from reader signals, which limits their range and functionality. Battery-powered active tags offer longer read ranges but require periodic battery replacement or recharging.

Tag Durability and Environment: RFID tags may be exposed to harsh environmental conditions, such as extreme temperatures or moisture. Ensuring tag durability and performance in such conditions is crucial.

Integration with Existing Systems: Integrating RFID systems with existing IT infrastructure, such as inventory management or enterprise resource planning (ERP) systems, can be complex and require custom software development.

Tag Orientation and Placement: The orientation and placement of RFID tags on objects can affect their readability. Ensuring consistent tag placement and orientation is essential for reliable data capture.

Scalability: As organizations expand their RFID deployments, scalability becomes an issue. Ensuring that the system can handle a growing number of tags and readers while maintaining performance is a challenge.

Regulatory Compliance: RFID deployments must comply with regulations and standards related to radio frequency emissions and data privacy, which can vary by region and industry.

Return on Investment (ROI): Measuring the ROI of RFID implementations can be challenging, as it depends on factors like cost reduction, improved efficiency, and increased revenue, which may not always be easy to quantify.

Addressing these challenges and issues requires careful planning, testing, and ongoing management. Organizations should conduct thorough feasibility studies and consider the specific requirements of their RFID applications to ensure successful deployments.

NFC (Near Field Communication) in IoT

Near Field Communication (NFC) is a short-range wireless technology that has gained significant traction in the Internet of Things (IoT) ecosystem due to its ability to provide seamless and secure communication between devices. NFC technology is primarily known for enabling contactless payments and access control, but its applications in IoT go far beyond these use cases. In this article, we will explore how NFC is integrated into IoT solutions and the benefits it offers. **How NFC Works:**

NFC is a form of radio-frequency identification (RFID) technology that operates over short distances, typically within a range of a few centimetres. It uses electromagnetic induction to establish communication between two NFC-enabled devices, one acting as an initiator (e.g., a smartphone or reader) and the other as a target (e.g., an NFC tag or sensor). NFC operates in two modes:

Active Mode (Peer-to-Peer): In this mode, two NFC devices, such as smartphones or tablets, can establish a two-way communication link to exchange data. This is commonly used for tasks like sharing files, pairing Bluetooth devices, or initiating payment transactions.

Passive Mode (Reader-Writer): In passive mode, one NFC device (the reader or writer) interacts with an NFC tag or passive device (the target) to read or write data. Passive NFC devices are often used in IoT applications, as they are low-cost and energy-efficient.

Integration of NFC in IoT:

NFC technology is being integrated into IoT devices and systems in various ways:

Smart Asset Tracking: NFC tags are attached to assets (e.g., equipment, tools, or inventory items) to enable real-time tracking. When a mobile device equipped with NFC reads these tags, it can retrieve information about the asset's status, location, or maintenance history.

Access Control and Security: NFC is widely used for access control systems, allowing users to unlock doors or gates by simply tapping an NFC-enabled card or smartphone on a reader. This technology enhances security and traceability in IoT-based access control solutions.

Inventory Management: NFC tags can be placed on products in a retail store or in a warehouse to streamline inventory management. Scanning these tags with an NFC-enabled device updates inventory records and triggers reordering when stock levels are low.

Smart Packaging: NFC tags embedded in product packaging enable consumers to access information about the product, verify authenticity, and even reorder the item with a simple tap of their smartphone. This enhances the consumer experience and helps combat counterfeiting.

Healthcare: NFC-enabled medical devices and wearable health trackers can securely transmit patient data to healthcare providers, ensuring timely and accurate monitoring of vital signs and treatment adherence.

Benefits of NFC in IoT:

Simplicity and User-Friendly: NFC is easy to use, as it requires no pairing or complex setup. A simple tap is all it takes to establish a connection, making it user-friendly for consumers and businesses alike.

Security: NFC offers built-in security features, including data encryption and authentication, making it a secure choice for IoT applications.

Low Power Consumption: Passive NFC devices, such as NFC tags, operate with minimal power consumption, making them suitable for battery-powered IoT devices.

Cost-Effective: NFC tags are relatively inexpensive, which makes them an attractive option for applications that require widespread deployment.

Compatibility: NFC technology is widely supported by smartphones and tablets, ensuring broad compatibility and accessibility.

In conclusion, NFC technology plays a pivotal role in the growth of the Internet of Things, enhancing connectivity, security, and user experience in various IoT applications. Its simplicity, security features, and low power consumption make it an excellent choice for IoT deployments, particularly in scenarios where short-range, contactless communication is essential. As the IoT ecosystem continues to expand, we can expect to see even more innovative uses of NFC technology in various industries.

Far Field Communication in IoT

While Near Field Communication (NFC) is ideal for short-range communication, Far Field Communication (FFC) technologies are designed to bridge the gap for long-range connectivity in the Internet of Things (IoT). FFC encompasses various wireless technologies that enable devices to communicate over greater distances, typically extending from several meters to several kilometres. In this article, we will explore the importance and applications of FFC in the IoT landscape.

Types of Far Field Communication Technologies:

Wi-Fi: Wi-Fi is one of the most prevalent FFC technologies in IoT. It provides wireless internet connectivity over a local area, allowing devices to communicate over a range of several meters to hundreds of meters, depending on the Wi-Fi standard used (e.g., Wi-Fi 6).

Bluetooth: Bluetooth, while often associated with short-range communication, also supports long-range modes, such as Bluetooth Low Energy (BLE) with extended range. BLE's longer-range capabilities make it suitable for IoT applications where devices need to communicate over larger distances.

Cellular Networks: Cellular networks, including 4G LTE and emerging 5G, provide extensive coverage and long-range communication capabilities. IoT devices equipped with cellular connectivity can transmit data over vast areas, making them suitable for remote monitoring and tracking applications.

PWAN (Low-Power Wide-Area Network): LPWAN technologies like LoRaWAN and NB-IoT are specifically designed for long-range, low-power communication. They can transmit data over several kilometres, making them ideal for IoT applications like smart cities, agriculture, and asset tracking.

Applications of Far Field Communication in IoT:

Smart Agriculture: In agriculture, FFC technologies enable farmers to monitor and control equipment, collect data from sensors deployed in fields, and receive real-time weather information over long distances. This helps optimize crop yields and resource utilization.

Smart Cities: FFC is instrumental in creating connected urban environments. IoT devices using FFC can monitor traffic, control street lighting, manage waste collection, and enable efficient utility management over extensive citywide areas.

Asset Tracking: Industries like logistics and supply chain management rely on FFC to track the location and condition of goods and assets across long distances. This improves inventory management and reduces the risk of theft or loss.

Environmental Monitoring:FFC technologies are used in environmental applications to collect data from sensors placed in remote or challenging-to-reach locations, such as forests, oceans, or remote industrial sites. This data helps researchers and authorities make informed decisions.

Remote Healthcare: In rural or remote areas, FFC-enabled IoT devices can transmit vital health data from patients to healthcare providers over long distances, enabling remote monitoring and telemedicine services.

Benefits of Far Field Communication in IoT:

Long-Range Connectivity: FFC technologies overcome the limitations of short-range communication, allowing IoT devices to connect and communicate over extended distances.

Scalability: FFC is scalable, making it suitable for large-scale IoT deployments that cover vast geographic areas, such as smart cities or agricultural networks.

Reliability: Cellular networks and LPWAN technologies offer high reliability and connectivity even in remote or challenging environments.

Global Coverage: Cellular networks provide global coverage, ensuring connectivity for IoT devices across borders and regions.

Low Power Options: Some FFC technologies, like LPWAN, are designed for low power consumption, extending device battery life and reducing maintenance requirements.

In conclusion, Far Field Communication (FFC) technologies play a pivotal role in expanding the capabilities and reach of the Internet of Things. They enable long-range communication and connectivity, making it possible to deploy IoT solutions in a wide range of applications that require extensive coverage, from smart cities to remote environmental monitoring. As FFC technologies continue to evolve and become more accessible, we can expect to see even more innovative and impactful IoT applications in the future.

Actuators

Actuators are essential components in the Internet of Things (IoT) ecosystem, playing a crucial role in converting digital commands or signals into physical actions or changes in the physical environment. They are the counterparts to sensors, which collect data from the physical world, while actuators enable IoT systems to interact with and control physical objects and processes. Here is a detailed overview of actuators in IoT:

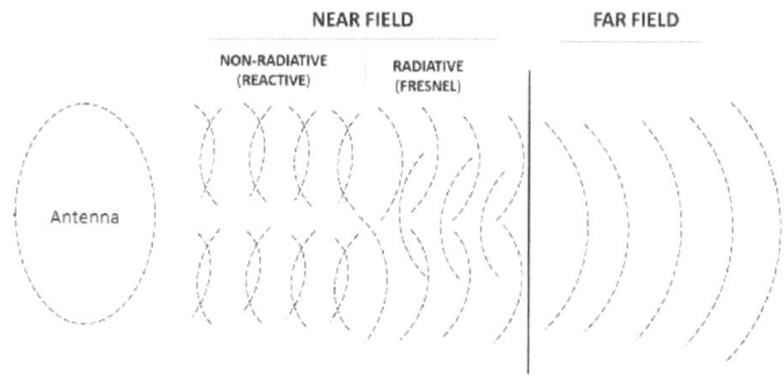

Classification and specification of IoT

Actuators are devices that convert energy into mechanical motion to perform various tasks, such as moving, controlling, or adjusting mechanical systems. The characteristics and specifications of actuators are important for selecting the right one for a particular application. Here are key characteristics and specifications of actuators:

Type of Actuation:

Electric Actuators: Operate using electrical energy and are available in various types, including linear actuators, rotary actuators, and solenoids. They offer precise control and are commonly used in automation and robotics.

Pneumatic Actuators: Use compressed air to produce motion. They are known for their quick response and are often used in applications requiring rapid and adjustable movements.

Hydraulic Actuators: Employ pressurized hydraulic fluid to generate motion. They are capable of delivering high force and are commonly found in heavy-duty industrial applications.

Mechanical Actuators: Rely on mechanical components like gears, cams, levers, and screws to produce motion. They are simple and reliable but may lack the precision of other types.

Motion Type:

Linear Actuators: Produce linear motion, moving along a straight path, often in the form of extending or retracting a rod or shaft.

Rotary Actuators: Generate rotational motion, rotating an output shaft or wheel. Some rotary actuators can provide limited linear motion as well.

Multi-Axis Actuators: Combine both linear and rotary motion capabilities within a single device.

Force and Torque:

Force: The maximum force that an actuator can exert, typically measured in Newtons (N) or pounds-force (lbf). It represents the actuator's strength or pushing/pulling capability.

Torque: The rotational force that an actuator can apply, usually measured in Newton-meters (Nm) or pound-feet (lb-ft). Torque is relevant for rotary actuators.

Speed:

Speed: The rate at which an actuator can move or rotate, typically measured in units like millimetres per second (mm/s), meters per second (m/s), or revolutions per minute (RPM).

Stroke or Travel:

Stroke (Linear Actuators): The maximum distance over which a linear actuator can extend or retract, often measured in millimetres (mm) or inches (in).

Rotation Angle (Rotary Actuators): The maximum angle through which a rotary actuator can rotate.

Precision and Accuracy:

Precision: The ability of an actuator to position or move with a high degree of accuracy and repeatability.

Resolution: The smallest step or increment by which an actuator can move or rotate.

Operating Environment:

Environmental Conditions: Actuators may have specific requirements for temperature, humidity, exposure to dust, or corrosive substances.

Enclosure Rating: An IP (Ingress Protection) rating indicates the level of protection against dust and moisture.

Control Interface:

Control Signals: Actuators can be controlled using various signal types, including analog voltage, current, or digital signals.

Communication Protocols: Some actuators can be controlled and monitored using communication protocols like Modbus, CAN (Controller Area Network), or industrial Ethernet.

Power Supply:

Voltage: The required voltage level for the actuator to operate.

Power Consumption: The amount of electrical or pneumatic power consumed by the actuator during operation.

Mounting and Installation:

Mounting Type: The method used to attach the actuator to the application, such as flange mounting, base mounting, or wall mounting.

Dimensions: The physical size and shape of the actuator, including its form factor and weight.

Maintenance and Lifespan:

Maintenance Requirements: Information about maintenance tasks, lubrication, and component replacement.

Lifespan: The expected operational life of the actuator under normal conditions.

Safety and Redundancy:

Safety Features: Some actuators may include safety features like emergency stop mechanisms or overload protection.

Redundancy: In critical applications, redundant actuators may be used to ensure continued operation in case of a failure.

Cost: The cost of the actuator, including the purchase price, installation costs, and potential maintenance expenses.

Understanding these characteristics and specifications is crucial when selecting actuators for specific applications to ensure they meet the requirements for force, speed, precision, environmental conditions, and control methods while considering factors such as cost and safety. Actuators are integral components in various industries, including manufacturing, robotics, aerospace, automotive, and more.

Functions and Applications:

Control and Automation: Actuators are used to control various devices and processes in IoT, such as opening and closing valves, adjusting motor speeds, and positioning equipment. In industrial automation, they control manufacturing processes and machinery.

Robotics: Actuators are essential in robots to provide motion to limbs, grippers, and other parts. They enable robots to interact with and manipulate objects in the physical world.

Environmental Control: Actuators are used in HVAC (Heating, Ventilation, and Air Conditioning) systems to regulate temperature, humidity, and airflow in buildings and smart homes.

Smart Lighting: Actuators control the on/off and dimming functions of smart lighting systems in homes, offices, and cities.

Automotive: In connected vehicles, actuators control functions like engine components, brakes, and steering, contributing to vehicle safety and efficiency.

Healthcare: In medical IoT, actuators are used in devices like insulin pumps and prosthetics to deliver precise doses or manipulate mechanical parts.

Agriculture: In smart agriculture, actuators control irrigation systems, crop harvesting equipment, and drones used for precision agriculture.

Consumer Electronics: In IoT-connected appliances, actuators enable features like automatic door locks, motorized window blinds, and adjustable furniture.

Challenges and Considerations:

Power Efficiency: IoT devices often run on battery power, so actuator designs must consider power efficiency to prolong battery life.

Latency: Some IoT applications require low-latency responses from actuators. Real-time control of critical systems, such as autonomous vehicles, demands minimal delay in actuator response.

Reliability: Actuators in industrial IoT settings must be highly reliable to prevent costly downtime and safety hazards.

Security: Securing actuators is essential to prevent unauthorized access and tampering. Compromised actuators can have serious consequences, especially in critical infrastructure.

Integration: Actuators must seamlessly integrate with IoT platforms, protocols, and control systems to ensure smooth operation and compatibility.

IoT Actuator Control:

IoT actuators are typically controlled remotely through IoT platforms or edge devices. Commands can be sent via wired or wireless connections, including Wi-Fi, Bluetooth, Zigbee, LoRa, or cellular networks.

Actuator control commands can be initiated by humans through mobile apps, web interfaces, or voice assistants, or they can be generated automatically based on sensor data or predefined rules and algorithms.

Future Trends:

Miniaturization: Actuators are becoming smaller and more compact, allowing their integration into tiny IoT devices and wearables.

Enhanced Materials: Advances in materials science are leading to more efficient, durable, and reliable actuators.

Edge Processing: Edge computing enables more localized actuator control, reducing latency and dependence on centralized cloud platforms.

AI Integration: Machine learning and AI algorithms are being used to optimize actuator control and decision-making in IoT systems.

In summary, actuators are integral components of the Internet of Things, enabling physical interactions and control in a wide range of applications. Their design, efficiency, and reliability are critical considerations in the development of IoT systems, contributing to improved automation, convenience, and efficiency in various industries and domains.

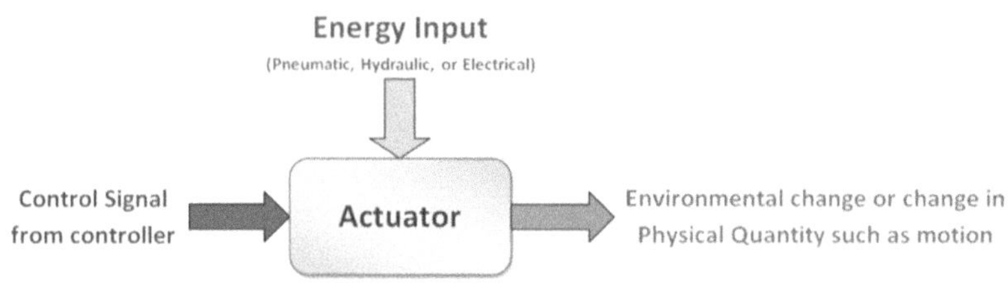

Figure- Block diagram of an actuator

IoT Processors: Powering the Brains of the Internet of Things

In the world of the Internet of Things (IoT), where countless devices are connected and communicating, the choice of processors is critical. IoT processors serve as the computational brains behind IoT devices, determining their performance, power efficiency, and capabilities. In this article, we will explore IoT processors, their key characteristics, and their role in shaping the IoT landscape.

What are IoT Processors?

IoT processors, often referred to as microcontrollers (MCUs) or system-on-chip (SoC) devices, are specialized semiconductor chips designed to handle the computing tasks of IoT devices. Unlike traditional desktop or server processors, IoT processors are optimized for low power consumption, cost-effectiveness, and integration of various hardware components.

Key Characteristics of IoT Processors:

Low Power Consumption: One of the most critical features of IoT processors is their ability to operate on minimal power. IoT devices are often battery-powered or have limited access to power sources, making power efficiency a top priority. Processors in this category are designed to enter low-power states when idle and efficiently manage power consumption during active operation.

Small Form Factor: IoT devices come in various sizes and form factors, and their processors must be compact and integrate multiple functions into a single chip. IoT processors typically combine CPU cores, memory, connectivity interfaces (such as Wi-Fi, Bluetooth, or LoRa), and sometimes even hardware accelerators for specific tasks like encryption or signal processing.

Cost-Efficiency: IoT deployments often involve a large number of devices, so cost-effectiveness is crucial. IoT processors are designed to provide the necessary computational power without breaking the budget.

Real-Time Capabilities: Many IoT applications require real-time processing, such as monitoring and controlling industrial equipment, autonomous vehicles, or robotics. IoT processors are equipped to handle these tasks with minimal latency.

Security Features: Security is a significant concern in IoT, as many devices handle sensitive data. IoT processors often include hardware security features like secure boot, hardware-based encryption, and trusted execution environments to protect data and firmware from unauthorized access.

Types of IoT Processors:
General-Purpose MCUs: These processors are versatile and can be used in a wide range of IoT applications. They are typically based on Arm Cortex-M cores and are known for their low power consumption and cost-effectiveness.
Application-Specific MCUs: Some IoT devices have unique requirements that demand specialized processors. For example, a device with advanced image processing capabilities might use an MCU with a dedicated image signal processor.
Wireless Connectivity MCUs: These processors are optimized for wireless communication protocols such as Wi-Fi, Bluetooth, Zigbee, or LoRa. They are commonly used in IoT devices that rely heavily on wireless connectivity.
ASICs and FPGAs: In some cases, custom-designed Application-Specific Integrated Circuits (ASICs) or Field-Programmable Gate Arrays (FPGAs) are used for highly specialized IoT applications where standard MCUs may not suffice.
Future Trends in IoT Processors:
AI and Machine Learning Acceleration: As IoT devices become more intelligent, there is a growing need for IoT processors with hardware acceleration for AI and machine learning workloads, enabling on-device inferencing and decision-making.
Edge Computing: IoT processors will continue to evolve to support edge computing capabilities, allowing devices to process data locally and reduce the need for constant cloud connectivity.
Enhanced Security: Given the increasing concerns about IoT security, processors will incorporate more advanced security features to protect devices and data.
5G Integration: As 5G networks become more widespread, IoT processors will integrate 5G modem capabilities to enable high-speed, low-latency connectivity.
In conclusion, IoT processors are the unsung heroes behind the IoT revolution, powering the devices that are transforming industries, homes, and cities. Their ability to balance power efficiency, cost-effectiveness, and functionality makes them essential components in the ever-expanding ecosystem of connected devices. As IoT continues to grow and diversify, we can expect IoT processors to evolve further, enabling even more sophisticated and capable IoT applications.

IoT Testing Tool

Testing is a critical aspect of ensuring the reliability, security, and performance of IoT (Internet of Things) systems. There are various IoT testing tools and frameworks available that cater to different aspects of IoT development and deployment. Here are some popular IoT testing tools as of my last knowledge update in September 2021:
IoTIFY: IoTIFY is a cloud-based testing tool that allows you to simulate IoT devices and networks. It helps developers and testers evaluate how their applications and devices behave under different network conditions, including various protocols and packet loss scenarios.
Eclipse IoT Packages: Eclipse IoT provides a collection of open-source projects and packages that are useful for IoT testing. Some of these projects include Eclipse Paho (for MQTT testing), Eclipse Mosquito (an MQTT broker), and Eclipse Californium (for CoAP testing).
Postman: Postman is a versatile API testing tool that can be used to test RESTful APIs, which are commonly used in IoT for communication between devices and servers. It allows you to create and automate API tests and monitor their performance.
Jenkins: Jenkins is a widely used automation server that can be configured to automate the testing and deployment of IoT applications. It is especially useful for continuous integration and continuous deployment (CI/CD) pipelines in IoT development.
JMeter: Apache JMeter is a popular open-source tool for performance testing. It can be used to simulate the behaviour of IoT devices and applications under load, helping to identify bottlenecks and performance issues.
Wireshark: Wireshark is a network protocol analyser that can capture and inspect network traffic. It is useful for debugging and analysing the communication between IoT devices and the network.
Mongoose IoT: Mongoose IoT offers a range of tools and services for testing and managing IoT devices and applications. It includes a lightweight IoT operating system (Mongoose OS) and a cloud-based IoT platform.
Robot Framework: Robot Framework is a generic test automation framework that can be extended for IoT testing. It supports both RESTful API testing and keyword-driven testing, making it versatile for IoT testing scenarios.
Testbeds and Emulators: Some IoT platforms and hardware manufacturers provide testbeds and emulators specific to their IoT devices and platforms. These tools allow developers to simulate real-world IoT environments for testing purposes.
Security Testing Tools: For IoT security testing, tools like OWASP IoT Project and IoT Inspector can help identify vulnerabilities and weaknesses in IoT applications and devices.

Types of Testing in IoT

Testing in IoT (Internet of Things) is crucial to ensure the reliability, security, and performance of IoT devices and applications. There are several types of testing specific to IoT, each with its own focus and objectives. Here's a list and explanation of some common types of testing in IoT:

Functional Testing:

Objective: To verify that IoT devices and applications perform their intended functions correctly.

Description: This testing involves checking if devices can collect, process, and transmit data as expected. It also ensures that applications can control and interact with IoT devices effectively.

Compatibility Testing:

Objective: To ensure that IoT devices, protocols, and applications work seamlessly together across different platforms and environments.

Description: Compatibility testing assesses the interoperability of IoT components, such as devices, gateways, and cloud platforms, to confirm they can communicate and function together.

Performance Testing:

Objective: To evaluate the responsiveness, scalability, and efficiency of IoT systems under various loads and conditions.

Description: Performance testing involves assessing the speed, resource utilization, and responsiveness of IoT devices and applications. It helps identify bottlenecks and optimize system performance.

Security Testing:

Objective: To identify vulnerabilities and weaknesses in IoT devices and applications to mitigate security risks.

Description: Security testing examines IoT systems for potential security threats, including data breaches, unauthorized access, and device tampering. It involves penetration testing, vulnerability scanning, and code analysis.

Reliability and Availability Testing:

Objective: To assess the stability and uptime of IoT devices and systems.

Description: This testing aims to determine the reliability of IoT devices by monitoring their performance over extended periods. Availability testing checks if devices are accessible when needed.

Usability Testing:

Objective: To evaluate the user-friendliness and user experience (UX) of IoT applications and interfaces.

Description: Usability testing assesses how easily users can interact with IoT applications, set up devices, and access data. It helps improve the overall user experience.

Interoperability Testing:

Objective: To verify that IoT devices can communicate and function with other devices, networks, and platforms.

Description: Interoperability testing ensures that IoT devices adhere to communication protocols and standards, enabling them to work seamlessly with other devices and ecosystems.

Scalability Testing:

Objective: To evaluate how well IoT systems can handle increasing numbers of devices, data, and users.

Description: Scalability testing simulates growth scenarios to assess whether IoT systems can scale resources, such as servers and databases, to accommodate higher demands

Compliance and Regulatory Testing:

Objective: To ensure that IoT products comply with industry standards, regulations, and certifications.

Description: Compliance testing verifies that IoT devices and applications meet legal and industry-specific requirements, such as safety, electromagnetic compatibility (EMC), and data privacy regulations.

Firmware and Over-the-Air (OTA) Update Testing:

Objective: To validate the correctness and reliability of firmware updates delivered remotely to IoT devices.

Description: Firmware and OTA update testing assesses the process of delivering and applying software updates to IoT devices, ensuring that updates don't introduce issues or vulnerabilities.

Each type of testing plays a vital role in ensuring the overall quality and reliability of IoT solutions. The choice of testing types depends on the specific requirements, use cases, and goals of the IoT project.

IoT Framework

An IoT (Internet of Things) framework is a structured approach or architecture that provides a foundation for building, managing, and scaling IoT solutions. It encompasses various components, protocols, and layers necessary to enable seamless communication, data processing, and device management within the IoT ecosystem. Here are the key elements of an IoT framework:

Device Layer:

IoT Devices: The physical devices or sensors that collect data, such as temperature sensors, cameras, or wearables.
Connectivity: Protocols and technologies for device connectivity, including Wi-Fi, Bluetooth, Zigbee, LoRa, and cellular networks.
Device Management: Tools for provisioning, configuring, and managing IoT devices throughout their lifecycle.
Communication Layer:
IoT Protocols: Standardized communication protocols like MQTT, CoAP, and HTTP that enable devices to send data to gateways or the cloud.
Gateways: Intermediate devices that aggregate data from multiple IoT devices, preprocess it, and transmit it to the cloud.
Edge Computing: Local data processing and analytics at the edge of the network to reduce latency and bandwidth usage.
Cloud and Data Layer:
Cloud Platforms: Cloud-based services for data storage, processing, and analysis, such as AWS IoT, Azure IoT, or Google Cloud IoT Core.
Big Data and Analytics: Tools for extracting insights from large volumes of IoT data, including machine learning and data visualization.
Data Security: Protocols and measures to secure data in transit and at rest, including encryption and access control.
Application Layer:
IoT Applications: Custom or third-party applications that provide specific functionalities or services based on IoT data.
APIs: Application Programming Interfaces for integrating IoT data into existing systems or third-party applications.
User Interfaces: Dashboards and user interfaces for monitoring and controlling IoT devices and systems.
Security and Privacy:
Identity and Access Management: Authentication and authorization mechanisms to ensure only authorized users and devices access IoT resources.
Security Standards: Compliance with security standards and best practices to protect against cyber threats and data breaches.
Privacy Controls: Measures to protect user data and comply with data privacy regulations like GDPR.
Scalability and Interoperability:
Scalability: The ability to handle a growing number of devices and data without compromising performance.
Interoperability: Compatibility with a wide range of devices, protocols, and platforms to ensure seamless communication and integration.
Device Lifecycle Management:
Device Onboarding: The process of adding new devices to the IoT network securely.
Firmware Updates: Mechanisms for remotely updating device firmware and software.
Monitoring and Maintenance: Continuous monitoring of device health and performance, along with maintenance tasks.
Regulatory Compliance:
Ensuring compliance with industry-specific regulations, standards, and certifications relevant to IoT deployments.

An IoT framework provides a structured approach to designing, implementing, and managing IoT solutions, fostering interoperability, security, and scalability. It serves as a blueprint for creating robust and efficient IoT ecosystems that can address a wide range of use cases across industries.

IoT Operating Systems

Internet of Things (IoT) operating systems, often referred to as IoT OS or IoT firmware, are specialized software platforms designed to run on IoT devices. These operating systems play a crucial role in managing the hardware resources, facilitating communication, and executing applications or firmware specific to IoT devices. Here's a detailed overview of IoT operating systems:

Key Features and Characteristics of IoT Operating Systems:
Resource Efficiency: IoT devices often have limited processing power, memory, and storage. IoT operating systems are optimized for resource-constrained environments, ensuring efficient utilization of available hardware.
Real-time Capability: Some IoT applications require real-time processing, such as sensor data collection or control systems. Real-time operating systems (RTOS) are commonly used in such cases to meet stringent timing requirements.

Low Power Consumption: Many IoT devices operate on battery power or have power constraints. IoT OSs are designed to minimize power consumption by efficiently managing sleep modes and power states.

Security: IoT devices are susceptible to security threats. IoT operating systems incorporate security features like encryption, secure boot, and access control to protect devices and data.

Connectivity: IoT devices need to communicate with other devices, edge gateways, or cloud services. IoT OSs provide networking and communication stacks to support various protocols like Wi-Fi, Bluetooth, Zigbee, LoRa, and cellular.

Device Management: IoT operating systems often include tools and protocols for device management, enabling tasks like remote configuration, firmware updates, and monitoring.

Scalability: IoT deployments can vary from a handful of devices to thousands or even millions. Scalable IoT OSs can handle varying device counts and workloads.

Interoperability: To promote interoperability between devices from different manufacturers, some IoT OSs adhere to industry standards and open-source protocols.

Popular IoT Operating Systems:

Free RTOS: A widely used open-source real-time operating system for microcontrollers, Free RTOS is known for its small footprint and energy efficiency. It supports various architectures and communication protocols.

mbed OS: Developed by Arm, mbed OS is designed for IoT devices with Arm-based microcontrollers. It provides a rich set of features, including connectivity, security, and device management.

Contiki: An open-source IoT operating system, Contiki is known for its low memory footprint. It is highly suitable for resource-constrained devices and supports various networking protocols.

RIOT OS: RIOT is an open-source IoT operating system designed for low-power and memory-constrained devices. It is particularly well-suited for IoT applications like sensor networks.

Zephyr Project: Zephyr is a Linux Foundation project that offers a scalable, real-time operating system for IoT devices. It supports a wide range of hardware platforms and communication protocols.

Tiny OS: Tiny OS is designed for wireless sensor networks (WSNs) and is known for its small size and energy efficiency. It is commonly used in academic and research settings.

Windows 10 IoT Core: Microsoft's IoT operating system, Windows 10 IoT Core, targets devices with more significant processing power. It provides support for Windows applications and services on IoT devices.

Factors to Consider When Choosing an IoT Operating System:

Device Constraints: Consider the hardware limitations of your IoT devices, such as CPU power, memory, and storage, and choose an OS that matches those constraints.

Connectivity Requirements: Determine the communication protocols and connectivity options required for your IoT application.

Security Needs: Assess the level of security required for your IoT devices and select an OS with appropriate security features.

Scalability: Consider the scalability requirements of your IoT solution, especially if you plan to expand your deployment.

Community and Support: Evaluate the availability of a developer community and support resources for the chosen IoT OS.

Licensing: Be aware of licensing terms, especially for commercial IoT OSs, and ensure they align with your project's budget and goals.

IoT operating systems are a critical component of IoT solutions, and choosing the right one is essential to ensure the efficiency, reliability, and security of your IoT devices and applications.

Connection between IoT and Sensors in the Commercial Enterprise

The connection between IoT (Internet of Things) and sensors in the commercial enterprise is fundamental and transformative. IoT relies heavily on sensors as the primary data source to monitor, collect, and transmit information about the physical world. Here's how IoT and sensors are interlinked and their significance in commercial enterprises:

Sensor Data Collection: IoT involves the deployment of various sensors, such as temperature sensors, humidity sensors, motion detectors, cameras, RFID tags, and more, throughout commercial environments. These sensors continuously collect data on various parameters.

Data Transmission: Sensors transmit the data they collect to IoT devices or gateways through wired or wireless connections. This data can include information about environmental conditions, equipment status, energy consumption, and more.

Data Aggregation: IoT gateways or devices aggregate the data from multiple sensors, often in real-time, and send it to cloud-based platforms or on-premises servers for processing and analysis.

Data Analysis and Insights: IoT platforms analyse the sensor data to derive meaningful insights. Machine learning and data analytics techniques are often employed to identify patterns, anomalies, and trends in the data.

Real-Time Monitoring: Commercial enterprises can use IoT applications to monitor operations and assets in real-time. For example, temperature sensors in a cold storage facility can provide continuous monitoring, triggering alerts if temperatures exceed safe limits.

Predictive Maintenance: IoT and sensor data can be used for predictive maintenance. Sensors on industrial machines, for instance, can detect signs of wear and tear, allowing maintenance teams to schedule repairs before breakdowns occur.

Enhanced Efficiency: IoT and sensors enable process optimization. In a retail environment, IoT-enabled inventory management systems can track stock levels in real-time, reducing waste and ensuring products are always available.

Energy Efficiency: Sensors can monitor energy consumption and usage patterns in commercial buildings. IoT systems can adjust lighting, heating, and cooling automatically to optimize energy efficiency.

Security and Safety: Sensors, such as surveillance cameras and motion detectors, enhance security in commercial spaces. IoT-based alarm systems can alert security personnel in case of unauthorized access.

Environmental Monitoring: In agriculture and food production, sensors can track soil conditions, humidity, and weather data. This information is valuable for optimizing crop yields and ensuring food safety.

Inventory Management: RFID and IoT sensors can track the movement of goods and assets throughout the supply chain, improving inventory accuracy and reducing losses.

Customer Insights: IoT sensors in retail and hospitality settings can capture data on customer behavior and preferences. This data can be used to personalize services and offerings.

Compliance and Reporting: IoT and sensor data can be used for compliance reporting in regulated industries, ensuring that commercial enterprises meet regulatory requirements.

IoT and sensors are tightly intertwined in commercial enterprises, providing valuable data for monitoring, optimizing operations, enhancing efficiency, ensuring safety, and enabling data-driven decision-making. This integration has the potential to revolutionize industries by providing unprecedented visibility and control over various aspects of business operations.

Edge Computing and Fog Computing in IoT

Edge computing and fog computing are two paradigms that address the challenges of processing and managing data in the Internet of Things (IoT) by bringing computation closer to the data source. Here, we'll explore these concepts and their significance in IoT.

Edge Computing:

Definition: Edge computing refers to the practice of processing data closer to the data source, typically on or near the IoT devices themselves, rather than sending all data to a centralized cloud server for processing.

Key Features and Benefits:

Low Latency: Edge computing reduces data transfer times, enabling real-time or near-real-time processing, crucial for applications like autonomous vehicles and industrial automation.

Bandwidth Efficiency: By processing data at the edge, only relevant information is sent to the cloud, reducing the burden on network bandwidth and associated costs.

Privacy and Security: Sensitive data can be processed locally, enhancing privacy and security, as it doesn't leave the device.

Offline Functionality: Edge devices can continue to operate even when disconnected from the cloud, ensuring system resilience.

Scalability: Edge nodes can be easily added or removed to scale the IoT system as needed.

Use Cases:

Smart Cities: Edge computing can be used for real-time traffic management, street lighting control, and waste management.

Healthcare: Medical devices can process patient data locally, ensuring timely responses and patient privacy.

Manufacturing: Industrial robots and machines benefit from low-latency control and predictive maintenance through edge computing.

Fog Computing:

Definition: Fog computing extends the concept of edge computing by introducing intermediary computing nodes (fog nodes) between edge devices and the centralized cloud. These fog nodes perform data processing and management tasks.

Key Features and Benefits:

Hierarchical Architecture: Fog nodes create a hierarchical architecture, distributing computing resources in a scalable and organized manner.

Aggregation and Filtering: Fog nodes can aggregate and filter data from multiple edge devices, reducing the volume of data sent to the cloud.

Location Awareness: Fog nodes can make decisions based on location-specific information, enabling location-aware applications.

Resource Optimization: Fog nodes can optimize resource usage, allocating processing tasks efficiently based on the workload.

Use Cases:

Smart Grids: Fog computing helps manage energy distribution in real-time by processing data from smart meters and grid devices.

Retail: Inventory management, customer analytics, and personalized advertising benefit from fog computing in retail settings.

Telecommunications: Fog nodes in cellular networks can optimize traffic and ensure low-latency services.

In summary, edge computing and fog computing are essential strategies for optimizing IoT data processing, reducing latency, enhancing security, and ensuring efficient use of network resources. The choice between them depends on the specific requirements and architecture of the IoT application.

IP addressing in IoT

IP (Internet Protocol) addressing is a fundamental aspect of IoT (Internet of Things) because it enables devices to communicate over the internet or within a network. Here's a note on IP addressing in IoT:

Importance of IP Addressing in IoT: IP addressing in IoT is crucial for several reasons:

Identification and Location: IP addresses uniquely identify IoT devices on the internet or within a network. They allow devices to be located and communicate with each other, enabling seamless data exchange.

Interoperability: Standard IP addressing ensures interoperability between devices from different manufacturers and across various IoT platforms. Devices can communicate regardless of their origins.

Scalability: IoT networks can consist of thousands or even millions of devices. IP addressing provides a scalable structure to manage these devices efficiently.

Routing and Data Forwarding: IP addresses are used by routers and network infrastructure to route data packets to their intended destinations. This routing capability is essential for IoT data to reach the right device or service.

Security: IP addresses can be used in conjunction with security measures such as firewalls and access control lists to secure IoT networks and prevent unauthorized access.

Remote Management: IP addressing allows remote management of IoT devices, enabling updates, maintenance, and troubleshooting from anywhere with internet access.

Types of IP Addressing in IoT:

IPv4 (Internet Protocol version 4):

IPv4 is the most widely used IP addressing scheme and has been in use for decades.

It uses a 32-bit address format, allowing for approximately 4.3 billion unique addresses.

However, the rapid growth of IoT has led to IP address exhaustion issues with IPv4.

IPv6 (Internet Protocol version 6):

IPv6 was developed to address the limitations of IPv4 and accommodate the growing number of IoT devices.

It uses a 128-bit address format, providing an almost unlimited number of unique addresses (approximately 340 undecillion).

IPv6 adoption is gradually increasing to support the expanding IoT ecosystem.

Challenges and Considerations:

Address Management: Managing a large number of IP addresses efficiently can be challenging. IoT solutions often require robust IP address management strategies.

Security: IP addressing plays a crucial role in IoT security. Proper security measures, including authentication and encryption, are necessary to protect IoT devices from cyber threats.

Dynamic vs. Static IP: IoT devices may use dynamic (assigned by a DHCP server) or static (manually configured) IP addressing. The choice depends on factors like device mobility and network architecture.

Address Resolution: IoT devices need mechanisms for resolving IP addresses to physical addresses (e.g., MAC addresses) within local networks. Protocols like ARP (Address Resolution Protocol) or ND (Neighbour Discovery) serve this purpose.

IPv4 to IPv6 Transition: As IPv4 addresses become scarce, transitioning to IPv6 is essential for IoT scalability. Transition strategies and compatibility mechanisms need to be implemented.

In conclusion, IP addressing is a foundational element of IoT, enabling devices to communicate, be identified, and operate efficiently within the IoT ecosystem. IPv6 adoption is a significant step to address the scalability challenges posed by the ever-expanding IoT landscape, ensuring that IoT can continue to grow and evolve seamlessly.

Software Defined Network (SDN) for IoT

Software Defined Networking (SDN) is a revolutionary approach to network management and control that centralizes network intelligence and programmability. In traditional network architectures, network devices such as routers and switches have embedded control logic that determines how data packets are forwarded. SDN decouples the control plane (decision-making) from the data plane (packet forwarding) and introduces a centralized controller that orchestrates and manages the entire network.

Key components and concepts of SDN include:

SDN Controller: The central element of SDN, the controller, acts as the brain of the network. It communicates with network devices and makes decisions about how data packets should be forwarded based on policies and network conditions. Open-source controllers like Open Daylight and commercial solutions like Cisco's Application Centric Infrastructure (ACI) are examples.

Southbound APIs: These interfaces allow the SDN controller to communicate with network devices in the data plane. Protocols like OpenFlow are commonly used for this purpose, enabling the controller to instruct devices on how to handle packets.

Northbound APIs: These interfaces enable communication between the SDN controller and applications or network services. They allow applications to request specific network services and policies from the controller.

Network Virtualization: SDN allows for network virtualization, creating multiple virtual networks or segments on the same physical infrastructure. This feature is essential for multi-tenancy and creating isolated environments.

Dynamic Network Management: SDN enables dynamic and automated network management. Network policies can be adjusted in real-time to meet application requirements, improve security, or optimize traffic flow.

SDN for IoT:

SDN can significantly benefit IoT (Internet of Things) deployments by providing flexibility, scalability, and improved management capabilities. Here's how SDN can be leveraged for IoT:

Traffic Segmentation: IoT devices often belong to different categories with varying network requirements. SDN allows for the creation of separate virtual networks, ensuring that critical IoT traffic is prioritized and isolated from non-critical traffic.

Network Optimization: SDN can dynamically adjust network routes and resources to optimize the flow of data from IoT devices. This is especially useful in scenarios where IoT devices are mobile or where traffic patterns change frequently.

Security: SDN enhances IoT security by segmenting IoT devices into secure zones, enforcing access control policies, and monitoring network traffic for anomalies. It can isolate compromised devices and quarantine them from the network.

Scale and Manageability: As IoT deployments grow, managing a large number of devices can become challenging. SDN provides centralized control and automation, making it easier to manage and scale IoT networks.

Quality of Service (QoS): IoT applications often have strict latency and reliability requirements. SDN can prioritize and ensure the QoS for mission-critical IoT traffic, improving overall system performance.

Real-time Analytics: SDN can provide real-time visibility into IoT network traffic and device behaviour, enabling organizations to make data-driven decisions and respond to events quickly.

Energy Efficiency: In some IoT applications, energy efficiency is crucial. SDN can help optimize network resources and reduce energy consumption by intelligently turning off unused devices or adjusting network configurations.

In summary, SDN offers a flexible and intelligent approach to managing IoT networks, allowing organizations to adapt to changing IoT requirements, enhance security, and efficiently utilize network resources. It plays a pivotal role in supporting the diverse and dynamic nature of IoT deployments.

Gateway Prefix Allotment

Gateway Prefix Allotment refers to the process of allocating and managing network prefixes to gateways in an Internet of Things (IoT) or networking context. Network prefixes are blocks of IP addresses that are assigned to subnetworks within a larger network. This allotment is essential for the proper functioning and organization of IoT networks. Here are key points related to gateway prefix allotment:

IP Addressing: IoT devices, including gateways, require unique IP addresses to communicate over the internet or a private network. IP addresses are typically grouped into subnetworks, and each subnetwork is identified by a network prefix.

Subnetting: Subnetting involves dividing a large IP address space into smaller, manageable subnetworks. Each subnet is assigned its own network prefix. This practice helps in efficient IP address management and routing.

Gateway Role: Gateways in IoT networks serve as intermediaries between IoT devices and the broader network, such as the internet or a cloud platform. They are responsible for routing data between IoT devices and external networks.

Prefix Allocation: Network administrators or IoT system architects allocate specific network prefixes to gateways based on various factors. These factors may include the number of devices to be connected, network topology, and security considerations.

Scalability: Proper gateway prefix allotment ensures scalability within IoT networks. As more devices are added, the allocation of unique prefixes to gateways accommodates the growth without IP address conflicts.

Security and Isolation: Assigning separate network prefixes to gateways enhances network security and isolation. It prevents unauthorized access and data breaches by segmenting IoT traffic logically.

Routing Efficiency: Organized gateway prefix allotment simplifies routing within IoT networks. Routing tables are more manageable when gateways are associated with specific prefixes.

Dynamic Address Assignment: In some cases, dynamic address assignment protocols like DHCP (Dynamic Host Configuration Protocol) may be used to automatically assign network prefixes to gateways and devices as they join the network.

IPv4 and IPv6:IPv6, with its vast address space, is increasingly used in IoT to accommodate the growing number of connected devices. Gateway prefix allotment applies to both IPv4 and IPv6 networks.

Centralized Management: Centralized management tools and network management platforms often facilitate gateway prefix allotment and IP address assignment, ensuring efficient resource utilization.

In summary, gateway prefix allotment is a critical aspect of network management within IoT deployments. It involves the allocation of unique network prefixes to gateways, ensuring proper addressing, routing, scalability, security, and efficient traffic management within IoT networks. This practice contributes to the successful operation of IoT ecosystems and the seamless communication of devices with external networks.

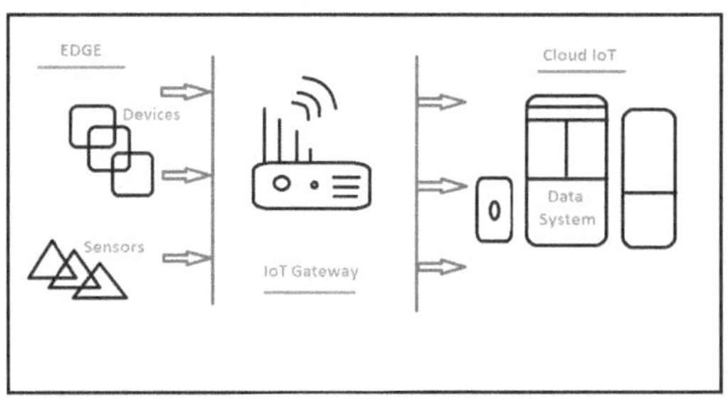

Mobility introduces several challenges and considerations related to how devices are assigned and manage their addresses within networks. Here are the key impacts:

Dynamic IP Address Assignment: Mobile devices often move between different networks or access points, such as switching from Wi-Fi to cellular data or moving between geographic locations. Dynamic IP address assignment protocols like DHCP (Dynamic Host Configuration Protocol) are commonly used to assign and manage IP addresses for mobile devices. This allows devices to obtain an IP address dynamically when they connect to a new network.

Address Pool Management: Mobility necessitates the efficient management of IP address pools. Network administrators need to ensure an adequate pool of available addresses to accommodate the varying number of devices that may connect or disconnect from the network at any given time.

IP Address Preservation: In some cases, preserving a consistent IP address for a mobile device can be essential. For example, in IoT applications, a mobile sensor may need to maintain the same address to ensure data continuity. Techniques like DHCP reservations or Mobile IP (MIP) can be employed for address preservation.

Roaming and Handovers: In cellular networks and mobile communication systems, devices frequently roam between cell towers or base stations. This requires seamless handovers while maintaining connectivity and IP address continuity. Mobile IP and protocols like SIP (Session Initiation Protocol) support such mobility scenarios.

IPv4 Address Exhaustion: The mobility of a large number of devices exacerbates the issue of IPv4 address exhaustion. The adoption of IPv6, with its vast address space, addresses this concern by providing unique and abundant addresses for all connected devices, including mobile ones.

Network Address Translation (NAT): NAT is often used to conserve IPv4 addresses by allowing multiple devices to share a single public IP address. However, NAT can complicate mobile device addressing because it hides the internal IP addresses of devices. Solutions like Carrier-Grade NAT (CGNAT) may be necessary in carrier networks to handle the large number of mobile devices.

Security Considerations: The mobility of devices introduces security challenges. Devices may connect to untrusted networks, increasing the risk of security breaches. Network security measures such as firewalls, VPNs (Virtual Private Networks), and secure authentication become crucial in addressing security concerns related to mobility.

Geolocation-Based Services: Mobility enables location-aware applications and services. Mobile devices can dynamically acquire location-specific information and services based on their current geographic position. Geolocation services rely on addressing information to deliver relevant content.

Scalability: As the number of mobile devices continues to grow, addressing and routing scalability become paramount. Network infrastructure must efficiently manage and route traffic for large numbers of mobile devices.

Quality of Service (QoS): Mobility affects QoS requirements, especially for real-time applications like voice and video. Network policies for addressing and routing may prioritize traffic to ensure low-latency and high-quality connections.

In conclusion, the mobility of devices, whether in IoT or traditional mobile networks, has a profound impact on addressing and network management. Dynamic IP address assignment, preservation, security, and scalability considerations become crucial in addressing the challenges and opportunities presented by mobile devices as they move within and between networks. IPv6 adoption and advanced network technologies are helping address many of these challenges and support the seamless mobility of devices.

Multihoming

Multihoming in IoT (Internet of Things) refers to the practice of connecting IoT devices to multiple networks or service providers simultaneously. While multihoming is more commonly associated with traditional networks and data centers, it has specific implications and applications within the IoT context:

Reliability and Redundancy: Multihoming in IoT enhances device reliability and redundancy. IoT devices often operate in critical environments where uninterrupted connectivity is essential. By connecting to multiple networks or access points, devices can automatically switch to an alternative network if one experiences connectivity issues or downtime. This ensures continuous data transmission and reduces the risk of service disruptions.

Load Balancing: In scenarios where IoT devices generate substantial data traffic, multihoming can be used to distribute the load across multiple networks. This load balancing optimizes network performance, prevents congestion, and ensures efficient data transfer.

Geographic Coverage: Multihoming can be particularly valuable in IoT applications that require global or wide-area coverage. Devices can connect to multiple cellular networks or satellite providers, ensuring connectivity in remote or geographically diverse locations.

Network Resilience: IoT devices deployed in harsh or challenging environments may experience network outages due to environmental factors. Multihoming allows devices to maintain connectivity by switching to alternative networks with better signal strength or stability.

Security and Isolation: Security is a crucial consideration in IoT deployments. Multihoming can enhance security by isolating different types of traffic or data streams onto separate networks. Critical data can be routed through one network, while less sensitive data goes through another, improving network segmentation and security.

Dynamic Network Selection: IoT devices equipped with multihoming capabilities can dynamically select the best available network based on factors such as signal strength, cost, or quality of service (QoS). This ensures that devices are always connected through the most suitable network at any given time.

Global Reachability: IoT devices often need to remain reachable from various locations around the world. Multihoming can help ensure global reachability by connecting to multiple networks, making it easier for devices to maintain connectivity even in regions with limited network infrastructure.

IP Address Management: Multihoming requires careful IP address management to avoid conflicts and ensure efficient utilization of IP address resources. Each network interface of a multihomed device typically has its own IP address.

Network Protocol Support: IoT devices must support protocols and mechanisms that facilitate multihoming, such as Mobile IP (MIP) or protocols for seamless handovers between networks.
Complexity and Management: Managing multihomed IoT devices can introduce complexity in terms of configuration, monitoring, and troubleshooting. Network administrators or IoT device managers must ensure that multihomed devices are correctly configured and that network performance is monitored effectively.
Multihoming in IoT is particularly relevant in scenarios where device reliability, continuous data transmission, and network resilience are critical requirements. By leveraging multihoming capabilities, IoT deployments can maintain connectivity even in challenging environments and provide uninterrupted services to end-users.

Exercise

Exercise 1 – MCQ

1. Which wireless communication protocol is suitable for long range IoT applications and provides non-robust services, generally?
a) Wi-Fi
b) Bluetooth
c) Zigbee
d) LoRaWAN
2. What type of IoT sensor is commonly used for detecting the presence or absence of nearby objects and is found in applications like automated doors?
a) Temperature Sensor
b) Proximity Sensor
c) Humidity Sensor
d) Pressure Sensor

Exercise 2 – True/ False

1. LoRaWAN is a short-range wireless communication protocol used in IoT.
2. IoT sensors are devices that primarily generate data and do not collect information from the environment.

Exercise 3 – Fill in the blanks

1. IoT devices communicate with each other using different ____________ protocols to enable data exchange.
2. IoT relies on sensors to detect and measure physical properties or environmental conditions, converting these observations into ______ data.

Exercise 4 – Match case

Match the following terms with their descriptions:
1. Sensor
2. Cloud Platform
3. Connectivity Protocol
4. Actuator
Descriptions:
a) Converts physical data into digital information.
b) Enables data transmission between devices and the cloud.
c) Centralized system for data storage and processing.
d) Performs actions based on data and commands.

Exercise 5 – One word answer

1. What is the primary purpose of IoT device "authentication"?
2. What is the process of converting data into a secret code to protect it from unauthorized access?
Exercise 6 – Small answer
1. Name some connectivity protocols of IoT.
2. What are sensors in IoT?

Exercise 7 – Long answer

1. Explain the security considerations of IoT.
2. Explain the importance of secure boot processes in IoT devices and how they contribute to overall security.

Answer:
Exercise 1.
1. d) LoRaWAN

2. b)Proximity sensor
Exercise 2.
1. False
2. False
Exercise 3.
1. connectivity
2. digital
Exercise 4.
1. Sensor – a)
2. Connectivity Protocol – b)
3. Cloud Platform – c)
4. Actuator – d)
Exercise 5.
1.Verification
2. Encryption

Previous Year Question

1. Write a short note on RFID sensors (Anna University MTech. 2018)
2. Explain the Zigbee architecture with suitable diagram (SPPU B.Tech. 2017)
3. Write a detail note on NFC and its use in IoT applications. (SPPU B.Tech. 2018)
4. What are the challenges and issues in RFID system. (SPPU B.Tech. 2017)
5. Discuss various components of RFID system. (SPPU B.Tech. 2017)
6. What is the connection between IoT and sensors in the commercial enterprise? (SPPU B.Tech.2022)
7. What are communication technologies? (Uttar Pradesh university B.Tech. 2021-22)
8. What is Zigbee? (Uttar Pradesh university B.Tech. 2018-19)
9. Compare sensors and actuators in IoT (SPPU B.Tech. 2017)
10. Write short notes on the following: Actuator and it's any three types, Zigbee, NFC and RFID connectivity used in IoT application. (IGNOU MCA 2022)
11. Define a sensor with reference to an IoT device. Explain various characteristics of sensors. Also, mention and explain any four classifications of sensors. (IGNOU MCA 2022)
12. Write a detail note on NFC and its use in IoT applications. (Mumbai University B.Tech.2017)
13. Write a short note on RFID sensors. (Mumbai University B.Tech._2017)
14. What are IoT testing tools? (RTU B.Tech. 2022)
15. Explain the types of testing in IoT.(RTU B.Tech. 2022)
16. What is the connection between IoT and sensors in the commercial enterprise? (RTU B.Tech. 2022)
17. What are IoT enabling technologies? (Anna University MTech. 2018)
18. What constitutes IoT platforms? (Anna University MTech. 2018)

ONLINE RESOURCES

Link: https://forms.gle/qiKicDxrQr6QiudWA

QR Code

Link: https://www.youtube.com/playlist?list=PLzlh_31VWEFpYhMoHLS9_703YYXqlgF9A

QR Code

Chapter 3: IoT Applications

Development of IoT Application

The development of IoT (Internet of Things) applications refers to the process of creating software and hardware solutions that enable devices, sensors, and objects to connect to the internet, collect and exchange data, and interact with each other or with centralized systems. IoT applications have a wide range of use cases across various industries and domains, including smart homes, healthcare, agriculture, industrial automation, transportation, and more. Here is an overview of the key aspects involved in the development of IoT applications:

Use Case Definition: Start by identifying a specific problem or need that can be addressed through IoT technology. Define the objectives, requirements, and expected outcomes of the IoT project.

Hardware Selection: Choose the appropriate hardware components for your IoT solution. This may include sensors, actuators, microcontrollers, communication modules (Wi-Fi, Bluetooth, cellular, etc.), and power sources. The selection depends on the application and environmental conditions.

Communication Protocols: Determine the communication protocols that IoT devices will use to exchange data with each other or with cloud-based systems. Common IoT protocols include MQTT, CoAP, HTTP, and WebSocket.

Firmware and Software Development: Develop the firmware and software that run on IoT devices. This includes programming microcontrollers, handling sensor data, managing device-to-cloud communication, and implementing data processing and logic.

Security Implementation: IoT applications must prioritize security. Implement encryption, authentication, access control, and other security measures to protect data and devices from unauthorized access and cyberattacks.

Cloud Platform Selection: Choose a cloud platform or IoT platform to manage and process data from your devices. Cloud platforms such as AWS IoT, Azure IoT, and Google Cloud IoT offer services for device management, data storage, analytics, and scalability.

Data Collection and Processing: Design data pipelines for collecting, storing, and processing data from IoT devices. This may involve real-time data processing, data analytics, and the extraction of valuable insights.

User Interfaces (UI): Create user interfaces, such as web applications or mobile apps, to allow end-users to interact with and control IoT devices. These interfaces provide real-time data visualization and user-friendly controls.

Integration with Third-Party Services: Integrate your IoT application with third-party services, APIs, or external data sources to enhance functionality. This can include weather data, mapping services, or social media integration.

Testing and Quality Assurance: Conduct thorough testing, including unit testing, integration testing, and performance testing, to identify and address issues related to reliability, scalability, and security.

Deployment: Deploy IoT devices in the field or target environment, ensuring proper configuration and connectivity to the cloud platform.

Monitoring and Maintenance: Implement continuous monitoring of IoT devices and the cloud infrastructure. Set up alerts for anomalies and perform regular maintenance tasks to ensure system reliability.

Scalability: Plan for scalability as your IoT network grows. Ensure that your infrastructure can handle an increasing number of devices and the associated data volume.

Data Privacy and Compliance: Comply with data privacy regulations (e.g., GDPR, HIPAA) and ensure that data handling practices are in line with legal requirements.

Feedback and Iteration: Collect feedback from users and monitor the performance of your IoT application. Use this feedback to make improvements and iterate on your IoT solution.

The development of IoT applications is a multidisciplinary field that combines expertise in hardware design, software development, networking, security, and data analytics. Successful IoT applications require careful planning, attention to user needs, and a focus on reliability and security.

Implementation of Device Integration

Here are the steps involved in implementing device integration for an IoT application with brief descriptions:

Device Identification: Identify and discover IoT devices to be integrated into the application. This step involves recognizing the devices that will be part of the IoT ecosystem.

Communication Protocols: Determine the communication protocols supported by IoT devices. This is crucial for establishing how the application will interact with the devices, whether through MQTT, HTTP, or other protocols.

Authentication and Security: Implement robust security measures to ensure that only authorized devices can connect to the application. Encryption and secure communication protocols should protect data in transit.

Data Ingestion and Processing: Create pipelines to ingest and process data from IoT devices. This involves collecting and transforming data into a usable format within the application.

Device Management: Develop functionalities for provisioning, configuring, and managing IoT devices. Remote management capabilities for updates and diagnostics are important.

Scalability and Load Balancing: Consider the application's scalability as the number of connected devices grows. Implement load balancing to evenly distribute data traffic across multiple servers or instances.

Error Handling and Logging: Set up mechanisms to handle errors related to connectivity, data transmission, and device disconnections. Robust logging ensures effective troubleshooting.

Real-time and Batch Processing: Depending on requirements, support real-time data processing for immediate actions and batch processing for historical data analysis.

API Design: Design a clear and consistent API that allows other parts of the application to interact with integrated IoT devices. Documentation is key for developers and users.

Testing and Quality Assurance: Thoroughly test device integration features, including communication, security, and data processing, and assess the system's performance under stress.

Monitoring and Analytics: Implement monitoring tools to track device health and performance in real-time. Analytics can provide valuable insights from IoT data.

Compliance and Regulations: Ensure that the IoT application complies with industry standards and regulations, especially those related to data privacy and security.

User Interface (UI): If the application includes a user interface, design and develop it to provide users access to device data and control features.

Documentation and Support: Create comprehensive documentation for device integration, including setup guides and troubleshooting instructions. Offer customer support channels for user assistance.

Effective device integration is essential for enabling IoT applications to function seamlessly and deliver value to users while ensuring security, scalability, and compliance with industry standards.

Data Acquisition and Integration

The development of an IoT application involves several stages, and Data Acquisition and Integration is a critical component. This process focuses on collecting data from various IoT devices, sensors, and sources and integrating it into a unified and structured format for analysis and application. Here's an overview of this stage:

Device Connectivity: Identify and connect IoT devices and sensors to the application's network or cloud infrastructure. Ensure compatibility with communication protocols like MQTT, CoAP, HTTP, or proprietary protocols used by the devices.

Data Collection: Continuously collect data from IoT devices and sensors. This may include environmental data (temperature, humidity), sensor readings, GPS coordinates, or any other relevant data generated by the devices.Implement mechanisms to handle real-time data streams from sensors.

Data Transformation: Raw data from different sources often varies in format and structure. Implement data transformation processes to standardize and normalize the data.Convert data into a consistent format that the application can work with.

Data Cleaning and Validation: Raw data may contain errors, missing values, or outliers. Apply data cleaning procedures to identify and rectify or discard problematic data points.Validate data for accuracy and integrity, ensuring it meets predefined quality standards.

Data Aggregation: Aggregate data from multiple IoT devices and sources into a single dataset. This consolidation allows for a comprehensive view of the IoT ecosystem.Summarize and group data as needed for analysis and application.

Data Storage: Choose appropriate data storage solutions, such as databases, data lakes, or cloud storage, to store the integrated data.Ensure that the selected storage system can handle the volume and velocity of IoT data.

Real-time and Batch Processing: Support real-time data processing for immediate actions and insights based on the latest data.Implement batch processing for historical data analysis, reporting, and trend identification.

Data Security and Privacy: Implement security measures to protect the collected data, including encryption, access controls, and authentication.Comply with data privacy regulations and ensure that sensitive information is handled appropriately.

Data Quality Assurance: Continuously monitor data quality and implement quality assurance processes to address anomalies and discrepancies.Employ automated checks and alerts for data anomalies.

Scalability and Performance: Design the data acquisition and integration processes to be scalable to accommodate a growing number of IoT devices and increasing data volumes.Optimize performance to ensure real-time responsiveness.

Data Governance and Metadata: Establish data governance practices to manage data ownership, access, and compliance.Maintain metadata and documentation for integrated data sources for transparency and accountability.

Analytics and Applications: Utilize the integrated data for various purposes, including analytics, machine learning, reporting, and visualization.Develop IoT applications that leverage the integrated data to provide insights and value to end-users.

Monitoring and Maintenance: Implement monitoring and alerting systems to track the health and performance of data acquisition and integration processes.Regularly maintain and update the processes to adapt to changing IoT device configurations and requirements.

Data acquisition and integration are foundational to the success of an IoT application. They enable the application to harness the full potential of IoT data, facilitating real-time decision-making, insights, and actionable outcomes for businesses and users.

Device Data Storage

In the development of an IoT application, Device Data Storage plays a crucial role in securely and efficiently managing the data generated by IoT devices. Here's an overview of this stage:

Data Storage Selection: Choose the appropriate data storage solutions based on the application's requirements. Options include databases, data lakes, cloud storage, and edge storage.

Database Design: If using a relational database, design the database schema to accommodate the types of data generated by IoT devices. Consider factors like data types, relationships, and indexing.

NoSQL Databases: For unstructured or semi-structured data, consider using NoSQL databases, which are well-suited for handling the variability and scale of IoT data.

Data Partitioning: Implement data partitioning strategies to distribute data across multiple storage nodes or shards. This helps improve data retrieval and scalability.

Data Compression and Encoding: Implement data compression and encoding techniques to optimize storage efficiency, especially when dealing with large volumes of IoT data.

Time-Series Databases: Consider using time-series databases for IoT applications, as they are designed to efficiently store and query time-stamped data.

Edge Storage: In scenarios with limited network connectivity or latency constraints, implement edge storage solutions on IoT devices to temporarily store data before transmitting it to a central storage location.

Data Retention Policies: Define data retention policies to determine how long data should be stored. Some data may be kept for real-time analytics, while older data may be archived or purged.

Security Measures: Implement robust security measures to protect stored IoT data. This includes encryption at rest, access controls, and data masking for sensitive information.

Data Backups: Regularly backup IoT data to prevent data loss due to hardware failures or other unforeseen events. Implement automated backup routines.

Data Replication: Set up data replication for redundancy and disaster recovery purposes. Multiple copies of data can be stored across different geographical regions or data centres.

Data Indexing: Create appropriate data indexes to facilitate fast and efficient data retrieval. Indexes can significantly improvequery performance.

Scalability: Ensure that the chosen data storage solution can scale horizontally or vertically to accommodate the growing volume of IoT data as the number of devices increases.

Integration with Data Processing: Integrate data storage with data processing components, such as analytics engines or machine learning models, to enable real-time data analysis and insights.

Compliance and Data Governance: Comply with data governance regulations and standards relevant to your industry and region. Document data storage practices for transparency and compliance.

Monitoring and Maintenance: Implement monitoring and alerting systems to track the health and performance of data storage infrastructure.Regularly maintain and optimize the storage system to ensure efficient data retrieval and storage capacity.

Device Data Storage is a critical aspect of IoT application development, as it directly impacts the application's ability to store, retrieve, and analyse data generated by IoT devices. Careful consideration of storage solutions, security, scalability, and data management practices is essential for the success of IoT applications.

Unstructured Data Storage on Cloud/Local Server

Here are the steps involved in the Development of IoT Application - Unstructured Data Storage on Cloud/Local Server.

Data Type Selection: Decide whether unstructured data, such as images, videos, audio, or text, needs to be stored. Unstructured data lacks a fixed schema and doesn't fit neatly into traditional databases.

Cloud vs. Local Server: Choose between storing unstructured data in the cloud (e.g., AWS S3, Azure Blob Storage) or on a local server, based on factors like scalability, cost, and accessibility.

Data Storage Infrastructure: Set up the necessary infrastructure for data storage, whether it's cloud-based storage buckets or dedicated servers with sufficient storage capacity.
Data Ingestion: Develop mechanisms for ingesting unstructured data into the chosen storage infrastructure. This may involve data upload APIs, direct data streaming, or batch uploads.
Data Organization: Implement a structured organization system for unstructured data. Use appropriate naming conventions and folders to categorize and manage data efficiently.
Metadata Management: Store metadata alongside unstructured data to provide context and enable easy searching and retrieval. Metadata can include timestamps, descriptions, and tags.
Data Security: Implement security measures to protect unstructured data, including access controls, encryption, and authentication mechanisms.
Backup and Redundancy: Establish backup and redundancy strategies to ensure data availability and prevent data loss due to hardware failures or other issues.
Scalability: Ensure that the chosen data storage solution can scale to accommodate the growing volume of unstructured data generated by IoT devices.
Data Retention Policies: Define policies for how long unstructured data should be retained. Different types of data may have varying retention requirements.
Integration with IoT Devices: Integrate data storage with IoT devices and sensors to facilitate seamless data uploads and storage.
Access Control and Permissions: Set granular access control and permissions to restrict or grant access to specific users or applications based on their roles and responsibilities.
Data Lifecycle Management: Implement data lifecycle management practices to efficiently manage data from creation to archiving or deletion.
Compliance and Regulations: Ensure compliance with data privacy and regulatory requirements, especially when dealing with sensitive or personally identifiable information.
Monitoring and Analytics: Implement monitoring and analytics tools to track data storage performance, usage, and trends. This data can inform optimization efforts.
Maintenance and Optimization: Regularly maintain and optimize the storage infrastructure to maximize efficiency, reduce costs, and improve data access speeds.
Disaster Recovery Planning: Develop disaster recovery plans and backup procedures to minimize data loss in case of unforeseen events.
Unstructured data storage for IoT applications is crucial for managing the diverse and often voluminous data generated by IoT devices. Proper organization, security, and scalability are key considerations for successful implementation.

Authentication, Authorization of Devices

In the development of an IoT application, Authentication and Authorization of Devices is a fundamental aspect to ensure the security and access control of IoT devices. Here are the key steps involved:
Device Identification: Assign a unique identifier to each IoT device, such as a device ID or certificate. This helps distinguish and authenticate devices.
Authentication: Implement strong authentication mechanisms to verify the identity of IoT devices when they attempt to connect to the application. Common methods include device certificates, API keys, or tokens.
Authorization Rules: Define authorization rules that specify what actions or data each authenticated device is allowed to access or perform. Authorization rules are typically based on device roles or permissions.
Role-Based Access Control (RBAC): Implement RBAC to group devices into roles (e.g., admin, user, guest), each with its own set of permissions. Devices are then authorized based on their assigned roles.
Access Policies: Create access policies that detail the specific resources, data, or functionalities that each device is authorized to access. Access policies are often based on predefined templates.
Access Tokens: Issue access tokens to authenticated devices, which contain information about the device's permissions. Tokens are presented with each request to access protected resources.
Token Validation: Validate access tokens upon each device request to ensure they haven't expired, haven't been tampered with, and are associated with the correct device.
Secure Communication: Enforce secure communication between devices and the application using encryption (e.g., TLS/SSL) to protect data in transit.
Device Registration: Implement a device registration process where devices are onboarded into the application. During registration, authentication credentials and authorization settings are established.
Multi-Factor Authentication (MFA): Enhance security by implementing MFA for device authentication. Require devices to provide multiple forms of verification, such as a certificate and a token.

Revocation and De-provisioning: Develop processes for revoking access or de-provisioning devices that are no longer authorized or in use. This prevents unauthorized access.
Auditing and Logging: Implement auditing and logging mechanisms to record device authentication and authorization events. These logs are critical for security monitoring and compliance.
Regulatory Compliance: Ensure that the authentication and authorization processes comply with relevant regulations and standards, especially if the IoT application handles sensitive or personal data.
Security Testing: Regularly conduct security testing, including penetration testing and vulnerability assessments, to identify and address potential security weaknesses in the authentication and authorization system.
Incident Response Plan: Develop an incident response plan to address security breaches or unauthorized access promptly. Define steps to mitigate risks and restore security.
Authentication and authorization of IoT devices are essential to protect the application and the data it handles. These measures ensure that only trusted and authorized devices can interact with the application's resources, reducing the risk of security breaches and unauthorized access.

Smart Home Automation

Definition: Smart home automation refers to the use of technology to control and manage various household devices and systems remotely or automatically for increased convenience, energy efficiency, and security.
Connected Devices: Smart homes incorporate a variety of connected devices, including thermostats, lights, door locks, cameras, speakers, and appliances.
Voice Control: Many smart home systems offer voice control through virtual assistants like Amazon Alexa, Google Assistant, or Apple HomeKit.
Remote Access: Homeowners can control and monitor their smart devices from anywhere using smartphone apps or web interfaces.
Energy Efficiency: Smart thermostats and lighting systems can optimize energy usage, reducing utility bills and environmental impact.
Security: Smart security cameras, doorbells, and motion sensors enhance home security by providing real-time alerts and remote monitoring.
Convenience: Automation routines can be set up to perform tasks automatically, such as adjusting lighting, temperature, and music based on preset preferences.
Integration: Smart home devices from different manufacturers can often be integrated into a single ecosystem, allowing for centralized control.
Customization: Homeowners can tailor their smart home systems to their specific needs, adding or removing devices as desired.
Health and Wellness: Smart home technology can also support health and wellness, with devices like fitness trackers and health monitors.
Entertainment: Smart TVs and audio systems can stream content from various sources and be controlled through voice commands.
Privacy Considerations: The collection of data by smart devices raises privacy concerns, and users should be aware of data usage and security settings.
Scalability: Smart home systems can be expanded over time, allowing homeowners to start with a few devices and gradually add more.
Costs: While smart home technology offers numerous benefits, there are upfront costs associated with purchasing and installing devices.
Compatibility: It's important to ensure that devices are compatible with each other and with the chosen smart home ecosystem.
Maintenance: Regular updates and maintenance may be required to keep smart devices functioning optimally and secure from vulnerabilities.
Future Trends: Smart home technology continues to evolve, with advancements in AI, IoT, and 5G expected to bring new capabilities and applications.
Smart home automation enhances convenience, security, and energy efficiency while providing homeowners with greater control and customization over their living spaces. As technology continues to advance, the possibilities for smart homes are expected to expand further.

Process Specification for Home Automation System

A process specification for a home automation system outlines the detailed steps and procedures that govern the operation and functionality of the system. It serves as a comprehensive document that defines how the home automation system should behave, respond to user inputs, and interact with various devices and sensors within a home. Below, I'll provide an overview of the key components that should be included in a process specification for a home automation system:

System Overview:

Start with an overview of the entire home automation system, including its purpose, objectives, and the main components involved.

Describe the scope of the system, including the types of devices to be controlled (lights, thermostats, security systems, etc.).

Provide an architectural diagram that illustrates the system's structure and how different components interact.

Functional Requirements:

Enumerate the different modes of operation (e.g., normal mode, sleep mode, away mode) and describe the behaviour of the system in each mode.

Specify how the system will respond to user inputs, both physical (e.g., button presses) and digital (e.g., smartphone app commands).

User Interfaces:

Describe the user interfaces through which homeowners or authorized users can interact with the system, such as mobile apps, web interfaces, physical control panels, or voice commands.

Explain how users can set preferences, schedules, and automation rules.

Device Integration:

Specify how the home automation system will integrate with various devices and sensors. This includes listing compatible devices (e.g., smart thermostats, smart locks) and communication protocols (e.g., Zigbee, Z-Wave, Wi-Fi) supported by the system.

Detail how the system will discover, pair, and manage connected devices.

Automation Rules:

Define the automation rules and scenarios that the system can execute. For example, "If motion is detected in the living room during nighttime, turn on the lights."

Explain how users can create, modify, and delete automation rules.

Security and Access Control:

Outline the security measures in place to protect the system from unauthorized access and cyber threats.

Describe the authentication and authorization mechanisms for users, including user roles and permissions.

Notifications and Alerts:

Specify the types of notifications and alerts that the system can generate, such as security breach alerts, device malfunction notifications, or energy usage reports.

Explain how users can customize notification preferences.

Energy Efficiency:

If applicable, describe the system's energy-saving features and how it optimizes energy usage within the home.

Detail any energy monitoring and reporting capabilities.

Error Handling and Recovery:

Outline how the system handles errors, exceptions, and unexpected situations.

Provide procedures for system recovery and troubleshooting.

Testing and Quality Assurance:

Describe the testing procedures and quality assurance processes that will be used to ensure the reliability and functionality of the home automation system.

Specify performance benchmarks and criteria for acceptance testing.

Maintenance and Updates:

Explain how the system will receive software updates, bug fixes, and security patches.

Provide recommendations for regular system maintenance and backups.

Documentation and Training:

Specify the documentation that will be provided to end-users, including user manuals and guides.

Outline any training or support services that will be available to users.

Creating a comprehensive process specification for a home automation system is essential for ensuring that the system functions as intended, meets user needs, and provides a reliable and secure smart home environment. It serves as a crucial reference document for system designers, developers, and end-users alike.

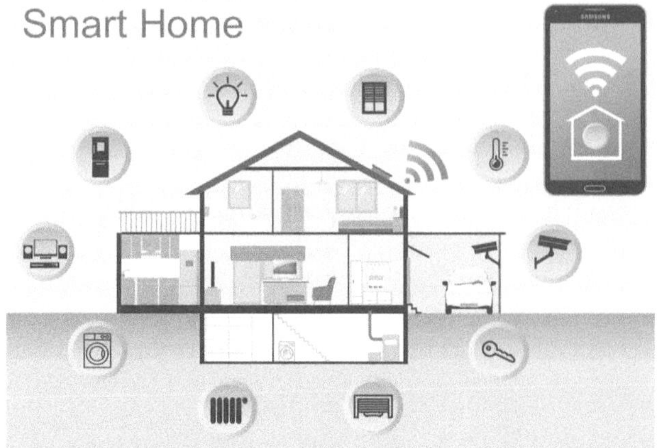

Certainly, here are some key points about the Industrial Internet of Things (IIoT) and its applications:
Definition: IIoT, or Industrial Internet of Things, is the application of IoT technology in industrial settings to improve efficiency, productivity, and safety.
Sensors and Devices: IIoT relies on sensors and connected devices to collect data from industrial equipment, processes, and environments.
Data Analytics: Collected data is analysed using advanced analytics and machine learning to gain insights, optimize operations, and make data-driven decisions.
Predictive Maintenance: IIoT enables predictive maintenance by monitoring equipment in real-time and predicting when maintenance is needed to prevent breakdowns.
Energy Management: Industries use IIoT to monitor energy consumption and optimize energy usage, reducing costs and environmental impact.
Supply Chain Optimization: IIoT helps track and optimize the supply chain, improving inventory management, logistics, and production scheduling.
Quality Control: Sensors and cameras ensure product quality by monitoring production processes and identifying defects early.
Remote Monitoring: IIoT allows for remote monitoring and control of industrial processes and equipment, reducing the need for physical presence.
Safety and Compliance: IIoT enhances workplace safety by monitoring hazardous conditions and ensuring compliance with safety regulations.
Asset Tracking: Industries use IIoT to track the location and condition of assets like vehicles, machinery, and tools.
Smart Manufacturing: IIoT facilitates the transition to smart factories with interconnected machines, automated processes, and real-time data analysis.
Environmental Monitoring: IIoT monitors environmental factors like air quality, emissions, and water quality, promoting sustainability and compliance.
Healthcare: IIoT is used in healthcare for remote patient monitoring, medical device management, and drug supply chain tracking.
Oil and Gas: In the oil and gas industry, IIoT monitors pipelines, equipment, and safety systems to improve operational efficiency and safety.
Agriculture: IIoT applications in agriculture include precision farming, crop monitoring, and livestock management.
Retail: IIoT improves inventory management and customer experiences through smart shelves, supply chain tracking, and personalized marketing.
Transportation: IIoT enhances transportation systems with real-time tracking, route optimization, and predictive maintenance for vehicles.
Waste Management: IIoT aids in optimizing waste collection and recycling processes, reducing costs and environmental impact.
Cybersecurity: Securing IIoT systems against cyber threats is crucial to protect critical infrastructure and sensitive data.

Scalability: IIoT solutions can scale to accommodate the unique needs and challenges of various industries and organizations.

IIoT is transforming industries by enabling data-driven decision-making, improving efficiency, and enhancing safety. Its applications continue to expand as technology evolves, making it a fundamental component of modern industrial operations.

Process specification for an Industrial IoT (IIoT)

It involves defining the step-by-step procedures and guidelines for deploying, managing, and maintaining IIoT systems within an industrial environment. Below is an outline of the key components of a process specification for an IIoT application:

Objective and Scope:

Clearly define the purpose and scope of the IIoT application, including its intended industrial processes and goals.

System Architecture:

Describe the overall architecture of the IIoT system, including edge devices, gateways, cloud services, and data flows.

Device Selection and Deployment:

Specify the criteria for selecting IoT devices and sensors suitable for the industrial environment.

Define procedures for deploying and provisioning IoT devices, including hardware installation and software configuration.

Data Collection and Sensors:

Detail the types of data to be collected, such as sensor readings, machine data, and environmental parameters.

Specify the sensors and data sources used and their locations within the industrial facility.

Connectivity:

Define the communication protocols and technologies for device-to-device and device-to-cloud communication.

Specify network infrastructure requirements, including Wi-Fi, Ethernet, cellular, or other connectivity options

Data Processing and Edge Computing:

Describe how data is processed at the edge, including data preprocessing, filtering, and analysis.

Explain the use of edge computing devices for real-time analytics and decision-making

Cloud Services:

Specify the cloud platforms and services used for data storage, processing, and analytics.

Detail data ingestion processes, data retention policies, and cloud security measures.

Data Visualization and Dashboards:

Define the user interfaces and dashboards used to monitor and visualize data.

Explain how stakeholders' access and interact with real-time data and insights.

Data Security and Privacy:

Describe security measures, such as encryption, access controls, and authentication mechanisms.

Address data privacy concerns, compliance with industry standards, and data ownership issues

Maintenance and Monitoring:

Provide guidelines for routine maintenance, including firmware updates and hardware maintenance.

Explain how monitoring and alerting systems are set up to detect and respond to anomalies or failures.

Scalability and Expansion:

Discuss strategies for scaling the IIoT system to accommodate additional devices and data volume.

Outline the process for integrating new sensors or devices into the existing infrastructure.

Disaster Recovery and Redundancy:

Define backup and disaster recovery plans to ensure business continuity in case of system failures.

Address redundancy and failover mechanisms for critical components.

Compliance and Reporting:

Specify any regulatory or compliance requirements applicable to the IIoT application.

Outline reporting mechanisms and procedures for compliance audits.

Training and Documentation:

Detail training programs for personnel involved in IIoT operations.

Provide comprehensive documentation for system configuration, troubleshooting, and maintenance.

Testing and Validation:

Describe testing procedures, including unit testing, integration testing, and validation of system performance against predefined benchmarks.

Stakeholder Communication:
Define communication channels and protocols for sharing IIoT insights and reports with relevant stakeholders.
Change Management:
Establish a change management process for introducing updates, modifications, or enhancements to the IIoT system.
Performance Metrics:
Specify key performance indicators (KPIs) and metrics to evaluate the effectiveness and efficiency of the IIoT application.

A well-defined process specification ensures that the deployment and operation of the Industrial IoT application align with the organization's objectives, industry standards, and best practices, ultimately leading to improved industrial processes and outcomes.

Healthcare and IoT

Here are some key points about the application of IoT in healthcare:

Remote Patient Monitoring: IoT devices like wearables and medical sensors allow for continuous remote monitoring of patients' vital signs and health metrics.

Telemedicine: IoT enables virtual healthcare consultations and remote diagnosis, improving access to medical services, especially in remote areas.

Medication Adherence: Smart pill dispensers and medication tracking systems help patients adhere to their prescribed medication schedules.

Health Tracking: IoT wearables, such as fitness trackers, collect data on physical activity, sleep, and overall wellness, helping individuals monitor their health.

Chronic Disease Management: IoT assists in managing chronic diseases like diabetes and hypertension by providing real-time data to healthcare providers.

Emergency Response: Wearable panic buttons and fall detection devices can automatically alert caregivers or emergency services in case of accidents.

Hospital Asset Tracking: IoT is used to track the location and status of medical equipment and assets in hospitals, improving resource management.

Infection Control: IoT solutions help monitor and control the spread of infections in healthcare settings by tracking hand hygiene compliance and air quality.

Supply Chain Management: IoT optimizes the supply chain for pharmaceuticals and medical supplies, ensuring timely delivery and reducing wastage.

Clinical Trials: IoT sensors and devices aid in remote data collection and monitoring during clinical trials, accelerating research and development.

Data Security: Ensuring the security and privacy of patient data is critical in healthcare IoT deployments.

Predictive Analytics: IoT data can be used to predict disease outbreaks, hospital bed occupancy, and equipmentmaintenance needs.

AI and Machine Learning: IoTdata, when combined with AI and machine learning, can provide valuable insights into patient care and treatment effectiveness.

Elderly Care: IoT solutions assist in elderly care by monitoring daily activities, detecting falls, and providing caregivers with insights into their well-being.

Cost Reduction: IoT can reduce healthcare costs by optimizing resource allocation, preventing readmissions, and improving overall operational efficiency.

Regulatory Compliance: Healthcare IoT must adhere to strict regulatory standards like HIPAA to protect patient data and ensure compliance.

Integration: Integrating IoT data with electronic health records (EHRs) and other healthcare systems enhances patient care and streamlines workflows.

Scalability: Healthcare IoT solutions should be scalable to accommodate the growing demand for connected devices and data.

IoT is revolutionizing healthcare by providing real-time data, improving patient outcomes, enhancing efficiency, and transforming the way medical services are delivered and managed.

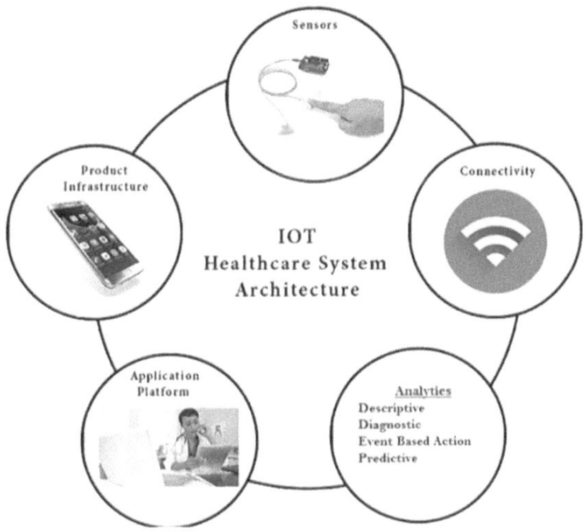

Process specification for healthcare and IoT

Process specification for healthcare and IoT (Internet of Things) involves defining the procedures and guidelines for implementing IoT-based solutions in healthcare settings. Below is an outline of key components of a process specification for IoT in healthcare:

Objective and Scope:

Clearly define the objectives and scope of the IoT implementation in healthcare, including the specific use cases and goals.

Regulatory Compliance:

Ensure compliance with healthcare regulations and standards, such as HIPAA (Health Insurance Portability and Accountability Act) for data privacy and security.

Data Collection and Sensors:

Specify the types of medical data to be collected, such as patient vitals, diagnostic information, or medication adherence.

Define the sensors and IoT devices to be used, including wearable devices, medical sensors, and monitoring equipment.

Connectivity and Network Infrastructure:

Detail the communication protocols and technologies for connecting IoT devices, ensuring secure and reliable data transmission.

Specify network infrastructure requirements, including Wi-Fi, cellular, or dedicated IoT networks.

Data Storage and Management:

Describe data storage solutions, including secure cloud platforms or on-premises servers.

Outline data retention policies, access controls, and encryption measures to protect patient data.

Device Integration and Compatibility:

Specify how IoT devices will be integrated with existing healthcare systems, such as electronic health records (EHRs) or hospital information systems (HIS).

Ensure compatibility with other medical equipment and devices.

Security and Privacy:

Define security measures, including authentication, encryption, and access controls, to safeguard patient data.

Address data privacy considerations and consent mechanisms for patients.

Device Deployment and Maintenance:

Provide guidelines for deploying IoT devices in healthcare facilities, including hardware installation and software configuration.

Detail maintenance procedures, including firmware updates, battery replacement, and troubleshooting.

Data Analytics and Insights:

Explain how collected data will be analysed using analytics tools and machine learning algorithms to extract valuable insights.

Define key performance indicators (KPIs) and metrics for monitoring patient health and system performance.

Alarm and Alerting Systems:

Specify alarm thresholds and notification mechanisms for healthcare professionals in case of critical patient conditions.

Ensure timely responses to alerts and emergencies.

Training and Education:

Develop training programs for healthcare staff and providers on using IoT devices and interpreting IoT-generated data.

Create user manuals and educational materials.

Patient Engagement:

Outline strategies for engaging patients in their care using IoT data and devices, including patient portals and mobile apps.

Promote patient education and empowerment.

Integration with Telemedicine:

Describe how IoT data can be integrated with telemedicine platforms to support remote patient monitoring and virtual consultations.

Data Backup and Disaster Recovery:

Establish data backup and disaster recovery plans to ensure data availability and system resilience in case of failures.

Compliance Audits and Reporting:

Define procedures for conducting compliance audits and generating reports for regulatory authorities or internal stakeholders.

Evaluation and Continuous Improvement:

Implement mechanisms for evaluating the effectiveness of the IoT solution in healthcare and make continuous improvements based on feedback and outcomes.

Scalability and Future Expansion:

Ensure that the IoT solution can scale to accommodate additional devices, healthcare facilities, or new use cases in the future.

A well-documented process specification for IoT in healthcare is essential to ensure the successful deployment, operation, and maintenance of IoT solutions while maintaining patient privacy and data security.

Agriculture and IoT

Certainly, here are some key points about the application of IoT in agriculture:

Precision Farming: IoT sensors and drones enable precision agriculture, allowing farmers to monitor and manage crop conditions with high accuracy.

Soil Health Monitoring: IoT devices measure soil moisture, nutrient levels, and temperature, helping farmers optimize irrigation and fertilization.

Crop Monitoring: IoT sensors and cameras track crop growth, detect diseases, and identify pest infestations in real-time.

Livestock Management: IoT tags and sensors track the health and location of livestock, improving herd management and preventing diseases.

Weather Forecasting: IoT weather stations provide localized weather data, aiding in crop planning and risk management.

Automated Irrigation: IoT-controlled irrigation systems adjust water usage based on soil moisture levels and weather forecasts, conserving water resources.

Smart Greenhouses: IoT in greenhouses regulates temperature, humidity, and lighting to optimize plant growth.

Crop Yield Prediction: Data from IoT devices and analytics tools help predict crop yields, aiding in production planning and market forecasting.

Supply Chain Tracking: IoT ensures the freshness and quality of produce by tracking it from farm to table through temperature and humidity sensors.

Drones and Robots: Autonomous drones and robots perform tasks like planting, spraying, and harvesting, reducing labour costs and increasing efficiency.

Farm Management Software: IoT data is integrated into farm management software, allowing farmers to make data-driven decisions and optimize operations.

Water Management: IoT helps manage water resources efficiently by monitoring water quality, levels, and distribution in irrigation systems.

Pest Control: Smart traps and sensors detect pest activity and enable targeted pest control measures.

Market Access: IoT connects farmers directly to markets, eliminating intermediaries and improving access to consumers.
Environmental Sustainability: IoT promotes sustainable farming practices by optimizing resource use and reducing waste.
Remote Monitoring: Farmers can remotely monitor and control IoT-enabled farm equipment and systems, enhancing productivity.
Data Analytics: Big data analytics and machine learning are used to derive valuable insights from IoT-generated data for better decision-making.
Education and Training: IoT technology provides farmers with access to online resources and training materials for improving agricultural practices.
Cost Reduction: By optimizing resource use and reducing waste, IoT helps lower operational costs for farmers.
Scalability: IoT solutions can be scaled up or down to suit the needs of both small-scale and large-scale farming operations.
IoT is transforming agriculture by making it more efficient, sustainable, and data-driven, ultimately improving crop yields and food security while conserving resources.

Process specification

Process specification for agriculture and IoT (Internet of Things) involves defining the procedures and guidelines for implementing IoT-based solutions in agricultural settings. Here is an outline of key components of a process specification for IoT in agriculture:

Objective and Scope:

Clearly define the objectives and scope of the IoT implementation in agriculture, including the specific use cases and goals.

Data Collection and Sensors:

Specify the types of agricultural data to be collected, such as soil moisture, temperature, crop health, and weather conditions.

Define the sensors and IoT devices to be used, including soil sensors, weather stations, drones, and cameras.

Connectivity and Network Infrastructure:

Detail the communication protocols and technologies for connecting IoT devices, ensuring secure and reliable data transmission.

Specify network infrastructure requirements, including Wi-Fi, cellular, or low-power wide-area networks (LPWANs).

Data Storage and Management:

Describe data storage solutions, including secure cloud platforms or on-premises servers.

Outline data retention policies, access controls, and encryption measures to protect agricultural data.

Device Integration and Compatibility:

Specify how IoT devices will be integrated with existing agricultural systems, such as farm management software, irrigation systems, or machinery.

Ensure compatibility with other agricultural equipment and technologies.

Security and Privacy:

Define security measures, including authentication, encryption, and access controls, to safeguard agricultural data.

Address data privacy considerations and consent mechanisms for stakeholders.

Data Analytics and Insights:

Explain how collected data will be analysed using analytics tools and machine learning algorithms to extract valuable insights.

Define key performance indicators (KPIs) for monitoring crop health, soil conditions, and resource usage.

Automated Control Systems:

Detail the automation processes enabled by IoT, such as automated irrigation, pest control, and crop monitoring.

Specify trigger conditions and thresholds for automated actions

Remote Monitoring and Control:

Describe how farmers and agricultural experts can remotely monitor and control IoT-enabled devices and systems.

Ensure ease of access through mobile apps or web interfaces.

Training and Education:

Develop training programs and resources for farmers and farmworkers on using IoT devices and interpreting agricultural data.

Provide user manuals and educational materials.

Maintenance and Support:

Outline procedures for routine maintenance of IoT devices, including battery replacement, firmware updates, and troubleshooting.

Define support channels for addressing technical issues or queries.

Data Backup and Disaster Recovery:

Establish data backup and disaster recovery plans to ensure data availability and system resilience in case of failures or natural disasters.

Compliance Audits and Reporting:

Define procedures for conducting compliance audits and generating reports for regulatory authorities or funding agencies.

Evaluation and Continuous Improvement:

Implement mechanisms for evaluating the effectiveness of the IoT solution in agriculture and make continuous improvements based on feedback and outcomes.

Scalability and Future Expansion:

Ensure that the IoT solution can scale to accommodate additional devices, crop types, or new use cases as agriculture evolves.

A well-documented process specification for IoT in agriculture is essential to ensure the successful deployment, operation, and maintenance of IoT solutions while promoting sustainable and data-driven agricultural practices.

Transportation and Smart Cities

Certainly, here are some key points about the application of IoT in transportation and smart cities:

Transportation:

Traffic Management: IoT sensors and cameras monitor traffic conditions, allowing for real-time traffic management and congestion reduction.

Smart Parking: IoT-enabled parking systems guide drivers to available parking spots, reducing search time and traffic congestion.

Public Transportation: IoT provides real-time information on bus and train schedules, helping commuters plan their journeys more efficiently.

Fleet Management: IoT solutions track and optimize the routes and maintenance of vehicles in commercial fleets, reducing costs and improving efficiency.

Road Safety: IoT-connected vehicles and infrastructure exchange data to enhance road safety through features like collision avoidance and traffic sign recognition.

Environmental Impact: IoT helps reduce the carbon footprint of transportation by optimizing routes, promoting carpooling, and monitoring vehicle emissions.

Transportation as a Service (TaaS): IoT platforms enable mobility-as-a-service models, allowing users to access various transportation modes seamlessly.

Logistics and Supply Chain: IoT tracks the movement of goods, providing real-time visibility into the supply chain and ensuring timely deliveries.

Smart Cities:

Urban Planning: IoT data aids urban planners in making informed decisions regarding infrastructure development, housing, and public services.

Waste Management: Smart waste bins equipped with IoT sensors optimize waste collection routes and schedules, reducing costs and improving efficiency.

Energy Efficiency: IoT manages energy usage in buildings, streetlights, and public spaces, contributing to energy conservation and cost savings.

Air Quality Monitoring: IoT sensors measure air quality and pollutants, enabling cities to take actions to improve air quality and public health.

Water Management: IoT helps monitor water distribution, leak detection, and wastewater treatment, ensuring efficient use of water resources.

Emergency Services: IoT facilitates rapid response to emergencies by providing real-time information to first responders and city officials.
Digital Signage and Wayfinding: Smart city displays provide real-time information on transportation, events, and services, improving the urban experience.
Citizen Engagement: IoT platforms allow citizens to participate in governance through real-time feedback, reporting issues, and accessing public services.
Security and Surveillance: Smart city surveillance systems enhance security through IoT-connected cameras and sensors.
Healthcare: IoT supports healthcare services with remote patient monitoring, telemedicine, and health data analytics.
Education: Smart classrooms and digital education tools enhance learning experiences in schools and universities.
Data-driven Governance: Smart cities leverage data analytics and IoT insights to improve decision-making and service delivery.
IoT in transportation and smart cities enhances urban mobility, sustainability, and quality of life, contributing to more efficient and connected urban environments.

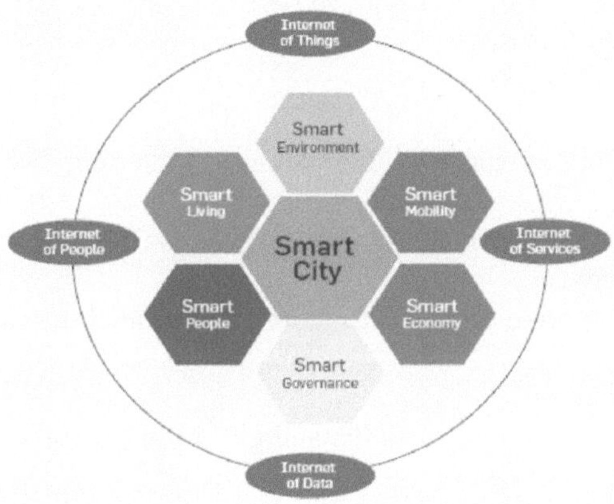

Process specification for implementing IoT in transportation and smart cities

Process specification for implementing IoT in transportation and smart cities involves defining the procedures and guidelines for deploying IoT-based solutions in urban environments. Here is an outline of key components of a process specification for IoT in transportation and smart cities

Objective and Scope:

Clearly define the objectives and scope of the IoT implementation in transportation and smart cities, including specific use cases and goals.

Regulatory Compliance:

Ensure compliance with relevant regulations and standards, such as data privacy laws and transportation safety regulations.

Data Collection and Sensors:

Specify the types of data to be collected, such as traffic data, environmental data, or public transportation information.
Define the sensors and IoT devices to be used, including cameras, traffic sensors, and environmental sensors.

Connectivity and Network Infrastructure:

Detail the communication protocols and technologies for connecting IoT devices, ensuring secure and reliable data transmission.
Specify network infrastructure requirements, including Wi-Fi, 4G/5G, or dedicated IoT networks.

Data Storage and Management:

Describe data storage solutions, including secure cloud platforms or on-premises servers.
Outline data retention policies, access controls, and encryption measures to protect sensitive data.

Device Integration and Compatibility:
Specify how IoT devices will be integrated with existing transportation and city systems, such as traffic management systems or public transportation networks.
Ensure compatibility with other urban infrastructure and technologies.
Security and Privacy:
Define security measures, including authentication, encryption, and access controls, to safeguard data and infrastructure.
Address data privacy considerations and consent mechanisms for citizens' data.
Data Analytics and Insights:
Explain how collected data will be analysed using analytics tools and machine learning algorithms to derive valuable insights.
Define key performance indicators (KPIs) for monitoring transportation efficiency, urban planning, and environmental sustainability.
Automated Systems and Services:
Detail the automation processes enabled by IoT, such as traffic signal optimization, public transportation scheduling, and waste management.
Specify trigger conditions and thresholds for automated actions.
Citizen Engagement and Services:
Describe how citizens can access and interact with IoT-driven services, such as real-time transportation updates or urban event information.
Ensure user-friendly interfaces and accessibility.
Maintenance and Support:
Outline procedures for routine maintenance of IoT devices, including firmware updates, sensor calibration, and equipment replacement.
Define support channels for addressing technical issues or queries from citizens and city personnel.
Data Backup and Disaster Recovery:
Establish data backup and disaster recovery plans to ensure data availability and system resilience in case of failures, cyberattacks, or natural disasters.
Compliance Audits and Reporting:
Define procedures for conducting compliance audits and generating reports for regulatory authorities, city officials, and stakeholders.
Evaluation and Continuous Improvement:
Implement mechanisms for evaluating the effectiveness of the IoT solution in transportation and smart cities.
Make continuous improvements based on feedback and outcomes to enhance urban mobility and sustainability.
Scalability and Future Expansion:
Ensure that the IoT solution can scale to accommodate additional devices, urban areas, or new use cases as transportation and smart city needs evolve.
A well-documented process specification for IoT in transportation and smart cities is crucial to ensure the successful deployment, operation, and maintenance of IoT solutions while enhancing urban mobility, sustainability, and the quality of life for citizens.

Smart Energy

Smart energy is a transformative application of the Internet of Things (IoT) that is revolutionizing the way we produce, distribute, and consume energy. It leverages IoT technologies to create efficient, sustainable, and intelligent energy systems. Here's a brief overview of smart energy and its key applications:

Smart Grids: IoT sensors, smart meters, and communication networks are integrated into power grids to create smart grids. These grids enable real-time monitoring, control, and optimization of electricity distribution. Smart grids enhance grid reliability, reduce losses, and enable two-way communication between utilities and consumers. They also support renewable energy integration and demand response programs.

Smart Metering: Smart meters are IoT-enabled devices installed at homes and businesses to monitor and report energy consumption in real-time. They provide consumers with insights into their energy usage, promote energy conservation, and enable accurate billing based on actual consumption.

Energy Management: IoT-based energy management systems help businesses and homeowners optimize energy usage. Sensors and smart devices collect data on temperature, lighting, and appliance usage, allowing for intelligent control and automation. This results in energy savings, reduced costs, and improved sustainability.

Renewable Energy Integration: IoT plays a vital role in integrating renewable energy sources like solar panels and wind turbines into the grid. IoT sensors monitor weather conditions, energy production, and grid demand, enabling efficient utilization of renewable resources and grid stability.

Demand Response: IoT-driven demand response programs encourage consumers to adjust their energy usage during peak periods. This helps utilities balance supply and demand, reduce grid stress, and avoid blackouts. Smart thermostats and appliances can automatically participate in demand response events.

Energy Efficiency in Buildings: Smart building solutions use IoT sensors to optimize lighting, heating, ventilation, and air conditioning (HVAC) systems. These systems adjust in real-time based on occupancy and environmental conditions, resulting in energy savings without sacrificing comfort.

Electric Vehicle (EV) Charging: IoT-enabled EV charging stations offer real-time data on charging status, availability, and energy cost. This information helps EV owners find convenient charging points and utilities manage the increased demand for electricity.

Grid Analytics: IoT-driven analytics provide utilities with valuable insights into grid performance, asset maintenance, and predictive maintenance. This enables proactive grid management, reducing downtime and improving overall grid reliability.

Energy Storage: IoT technology is utilized in energy storage systems to monitor and manage battery performance. This ensures efficient energy storage and release, supporting grid stability and renewable energy integration.

Environmental Sustainability: Smart energy solutions contribute to reducing greenhouse gas emissions by promoting energy efficiency, renewable energy adoption, and better resource management.

Smart energy, powered by IoT, offers numerous benefits, including cost savings, environmental sustainability, grid resilience, and improved energy management. As technology continues to advance, smart energy applications will play an increasingly vital role in shaping a more sustainable and efficient energy future.

Smart Irrigation System

A smart irrigation system is a technologically advanced approach to managing and optimizing the watering of plants, crops, and landscapes. It leverages various sensors, weather data, automation, and connectivity to deliver precise and efficient irrigation while conserving water resources. Here's an overview of a smart irrigation system:

Sensors and Data Collection:

Soil Moisture Sensors: These sensors measure the moisture level in the soil, providing real-time data on whether the plants need watering.

Weather Stations: Smart irrigation systems often integrate with weather stations or access weather data online to adjust watering schedules based on current weather conditions, including temperature, humidity, and rainfall predictions.

Central Controller:

A central controller, often cloud-based, receives data from sensors and weather sources.

It processes this information to make decisions regarding irrigation schedules and watering durations.

Precision Irrigation:

The system delivers water directly to the root zone of plants, minimizing wastage and ensuring that the right amount of water is provided.

Drip irrigation, soaker hoses, or precision spray nozzles are commonly used for this purpose.

Automation and Remote Control:

Smart irrigation systems automate watering schedules, reducing the need for manual adjustments.

Users can access and control the system remotely via smartphone apps or web interfaces, allowing for real-time adjustments and monitoring.

Water Conservation:

By responding to real-time conditions and only irrigating, when necessary, smart irrigation systems significantly reduce water wastage compared to traditional irrigation methods.

They contribute to water conservation efforts and help lower water bills.

Customizable Scheduling:

Users can customize watering schedules based on plant types, soil types, and local climate conditions.

Some systems even consider factors like plant age and specific watering needs.

Alerts and Notifications:

Smart irrigation systems can send alerts and notifications to users in case of system malfunctions or when unusual conditions are detected, such as a sudden drop in soil moisture.

Integration with Other Systems:

They can integrate with other smart home or agriculture systems, such as home automation platforms or farm management software, to create a holistic solution.

Energy Efficiency:

Some systems use solar power or energy-efficient components to reduce their environmental impact.

Benefits:

Increased Efficiency: Smart irrigation reduces overwatering and underwatering, promoting healthier plants and improved crop yields.

Water Savings: The precise control of water usage leads to significant water savings.

Time Savings: Users spend less time manually adjusting irrigation schedules.

Environmental Benefits: Conservation of water resources and reduced runoff contribute to environmental sustainability.

Cost Savings: Lower water bills and potentially reduced energy costs make smart irrigation systems cost-effective in the long run.

Applications:

Smart irrigation systems find applications in agriculture, landscaping, urban gardening, golf course management, and residential gardens.

Process specification for smart irrigation IoT system

Creating a process specification for a smart irrigation IoT system involves outlining the steps and requirements necessary to design, develop, deploy, and maintain such a system. Here's a general process specification for a smart irrigation IoT system:

Project Initiation:

Objective Definition: Clearly define the objectives and goals of the smart irrigation system, including water conservation, plant health, or crop yield optimization.

Stakeholder Identification: Identify all stakeholders, including end-users, farmers, technicians, and decision-makers.

System Requirements:

Functional Requirements: Specify the core functions of the system, such as soil moisture sensing, weather data integration, and irrigation control.

Non-Functional Requirements: Define performance, security, scalability, and reliability requirements.

User Interface Requirements: Outline user interface design requirements for web and mobile applications.

System Design:

Architecture Design: Create an architectural overview, detailing components like sensors, actuators, controllers, and cloud services.

Database Design: Define the data schema and database structure for storing sensor data, user profiles, and device configurations.

Communication Protocols: Specify the communication protocols between IoT devices, gateway, and cloud services.

Hardware and Sensor Selection:

Select Sensors: Choose appropriate sensors for soil moisture, temperature, humidity, and weather data.

Microcontroller Selection: Choose microcontrollers or IoT platforms capable of interfacing with sensors and communicating with the cloud.

IoT Device Development:

Sensor Integration: Develop firmware to read data from sensors and transmit it to the cloud.

Actuator Control: Implement control logic to operate irrigation valves based on sensor data and user-defined schedules.

Gateway Development: If necessary, develop a gateway to aggregate data from multiple devices and relay it to the cloud

Cloud Services and Backend Development:

Cloud Infrastructure: Set up cloud servers, databases, and necessary services (e.g., AWS, Azure, Google Cloud).

API Development: Create APIs for data ingestion, device management, and user interactions.

Data Processing: Implement data processing and analytics to generate insights and control irrigation.

User Interface Development:

Web and Mobile Apps: Develop user-friendly web and mobile applications for device configuration, monitoring, and control.

Dashboard Design: Create dashboards to visualize sensor data, weather forecasts, and irrigation schedules.
Security Measures:
Data Encryption: Implement data encryption for communication and storage.
Access Control: Develop authentication and authorization mechanisms for user and device **access.**
Security Audits: Conduct security audits and penetration testing to identify vulnerabilities.
Testing and Quality Assurance:
Unit Testing: Test individual components and functions.
Integration Testing: Verify interactions between components.
User Acceptance Testing: Involve stakeholders in testing to ensure the system meets requirements.
Deployment:
Deploy IoT devices in the field, ensuring they are properly calibrated and connected.
Set up cloud infrastructure and deploy web/mobile applications.
User Training:
Train end-users, technicians, and maintenance personnel on system operation and maintenance.
Maintenance and Support:
Establish a maintenance schedule for sensor calibration, battery replacement, and software updates.
Provide ongoing support for users and troubleshoot issues.
Data Analytics and Continuous Improvement:
Implement data analytics to gain insights into system performance and plant health.
Continuously improve the system based on data-driven feedback.
Compliance and Regulation:
Ensure compliance with local regulations related to water usage and environmental impact.
Documentation:
Maintain comprehensive documentation for the system, including user manuals, technical specifications, and troubleshooting guides.
Scalability and Expansion:
Plan for system scalability to accommodate future growth and additional sensors or devices.
Evaluation:
Regularly evaluate system performance against defined objectives and user feedback.
Creating a process specification helps ensure that the smart irrigation IoT system is developed efficiently, meets user needs, and operates effectively over the long term. It also provides a structured approach to system design and deployment.

Domain model of Smart irrigation IoT system

A domain model for a smart irrigation IoT system represents the key concepts, entities, and their relationships within the system's domain. Here's a simplified domain model for a smart irrigation IoT system:
User:
Represents individuals or organizations using the smart irrigation system.
Attributes may include user ID, name, contact information, and login credentials.
Can have multiple roles, such as admin, farmer, or technician.
Device:
Represents IoT devices used for irrigation control and data collection.
Attributes include device ID, device type, location, and status (active/inactive).
Belongs to a specific user.
Sensor:
Subtype of the device that collects environmental data.
Attributes include sensor type (e.g., soil moisture, temperature), accuracy, and calibration status.
Belongs to a specific device.
Actuator:
Subtype of the device responsible for controlling irrigation equipment.
Attributes include actuator type (e.g., valve, pump), status, and activation settings.
Belongs to a specific device.
Gateway:
Represents a communication gateway that collects data from multiple devices and sends it to the cloud.
Attributes may include gateway ID, connectivity status, and data transmission rate.

Cloud Service:
Represents the cloud-based infrastructure used for data storage, processing, and application logic.
Includes databases, APIs, and data processing services.
Data:
Represents collected sensor data, including soil moisture readings, temperature, humidity, and weather forecasts.
Attributes include timestamp, sensor ID, and measured values
Irrigation Schedule:
Represents user-defined schedules for when and how much to irrigate.
Includes start times, duration, and frequency settings.
User Interface:
Represents the web and mobile applications used by users to interact with the system.
Includes dashboards, settings, and reporting modules.
Authentication & Authorization:
Represents security mechanisms for user authentication and device authorization.
Ensures that users can access only their devices and data.
Alerts & Notifications:
Represents a subsystem that generates alerts and notifications based on sensor data, system health, and user-defined thresholds.
Analytics Engine:
Subsystem responsible for processing sensor data and generating insights, including recommendations for irrigation adjustments.
Maintenance Schedule:
Represents planned maintenance tasks for sensor calibration, battery replacement, and device servicing
Environmental Data Source:
Represents external sources of environmental data, such as weather forecasts and historical climate data
Regulatory Compliance:
Includes rules and regulations related to water usage and environmental conservation.
System Logs:
Records system events, user interactions, and device activities for auditing and troubleshooting.
Localization & Customization:
Represents features for customizing the system's language, units of measurement, and user interface branding.
This domain model provides a high-level view of the entities and relationships within a smart irrigation IoT system. Depending on the specific requirements and complexity of the system, additional entities and attributes may be included in the model.

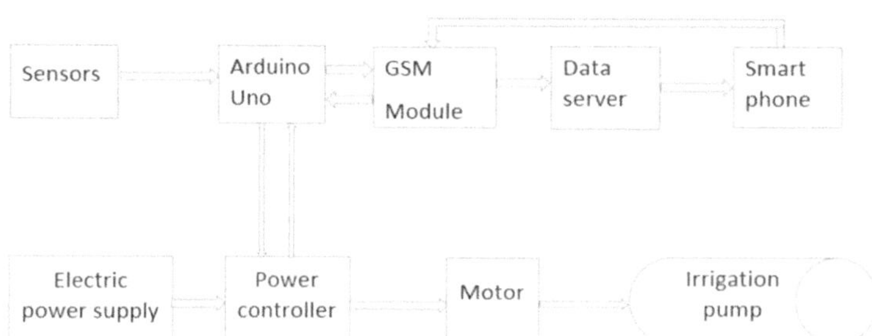

Information model of Smart irrigation IoT system
An information model for a smart irrigation IoT system defines the structure and organization of data and information within the system. It outlines the entities, attributes, and relationships that are essential for the system's operation and functionality. Here's an information model for a smart irrigation IoT system:
Entities:
User:
Attributes: User ID (Primary Key), Username, Password (hashed), First Name, Last Name, Email, Phone Number, Role (e.g., Admin, Farmer, Technician).
Device:

Attributes: Device ID (Primary Key), Device Name, Device Type, Location (Latitude and Longitude), Activation Status, User ID (Foreign Key).

Sensor:

Attributes: Sensor ID (Primary Key), Sensor Type, Accuracy, Calibration Status, Device ID (Foreign Key).

Actuator:

Attributes: Actuator ID (Primary Key), Actuator Type, Activation Status, Device ID (Foreign Key).

Gateway:

Attributes: Gateway ID (Primary Key), Gateway Name, Connectivity Status.

Cloud Service:

Attributes: Service ID (Primary Key), Service Name, Description, Hosting Provider (e.g., AWS, Azure), API Endpoints.

Data:

Attributes: Data ID (Primary Key), Timestamp, Sensor ID (Foreign Key), Value (e.g., soil moisture reading, temperature), Weather Forecast (if applicable).

Irrigation Schedule:

Attributes: Schedule ID (Primary Key), User ID (Foreign Key), Start Time, Duration, Frequency, Device ID (Foreign Key).

User Interface:

Attributes: Interface ID (Primary Key), Interface Type (e.g., Web, Mobile), User ID (Foreign Key).

Authentication & Authorization:

Attributes: Authentication Token, Authorization Roles and Permissions.

Alerts & Notifications:

Attributes: Notification ID (Primary Key), Timestamp, User ID (Foreign Key), Message, Alert Type.

Analytics Engine:

Attributes: Engine ID (Primary Key), Engine Name, Algorithms Used, Data Sources (e.g., Sensor Data).

Maintenance Schedule:

Attributes: Maintenance ID (Primary Key), Task Description, Schedule Date, Device ID (Foreign Key).

Environmental Data Source:

Attributes: Source ID (Primary Key), Source Name, Data Type (e.g., Weather Forecast, Historical Climate Data), Data Provider.

Regulatory Compliance:

Attributes: Regulation ID (Primary Key), Regulation Name, Description, Compliance Status.

System Logs:

Attributes: Log ID (Primary Key), Timestamp, Event Type, User ID (if applicable), Device ID (if applicable), Log Details.

Localization & Customization:

Attributes: Localization Settings (e.g., Language), Customization Settings (e.g., Branding).

Relationships:

Users can have multiple devices, and each device belongs to one user (One-to-Many Relationship: User - Device).

Devices can have multiple sensors and actuators, and each sensor/actuator belongs to one device (One-to-Many Relationship:Device - Sensor/Actuator).

Sensor data is collected at specific timestamps and belongs to a sensor (One-to-Many Relationship: Sensor - Data).

Users can define multiple irrigation schedules, and each schedule belongs to one user (One-to-Many Relationship: User - Irrigation Schedule).

Users can receive multiple alerts and notifications, and each notification belongs to one user (One-to-Many Relationship: User - Alerts & Notifications).

Maintenance tasks can be associated with specific devices, and each task belongs to one device (One-to-Many Relationship: Device - Maintenance Schedule).

This information model provides a structured representation of the key data entities and their relationships within a smart irrigation IoT system. It serves as a foundation for database design, API development, and data management in the system. Depending on the system's complexity and requirements, additional entities and attributes may be added to capture specific details and functionalities.

Controller service of Smart irrigation IoT system

In a smart irrigation IoT system, a controller service plays a critical role in managing and controlling the irrigation process based on various inputs, including sensor data, weather forecasts, user-defined schedules, and specific algorithms. Here's an overview of a controller service in such a system:

Data Aggregation and Processing:

The controller service aggregates data from various sources, such as soil moisture sensors, weather forecasts, and user-defined irrigation schedules.

It processes this data to make informed decisions about when, where, and how much to irrigate.

Decision-Making Logic:

Using predefined algorithms or machine learning models, the controller service determines the irrigation needs for different areas or zones within the irrigation system.

It considers factors like soil moisture levels, plant types, weather conditions, and historical data to make decisions.

Irrigation Control:

The controller service sends commands to actuators (e.g., irrigation valves, pumps) to control the flow of water to specific zones or areas.

It ensures that the irrigation process is precise, efficient, and tailored to the specific requirements of each plant or crop.

Real-Time Monitoring:

It continuously monitors sensor data and system conditions in real-time to make dynamic adjustments to irrigation schedules.

For example, if unexpected rain is detected, it may delay or cancel scheduled irrigation to prevent overwatering.

User Interaction:

The controller service interfaces with user applications, allowing users to set irrigation schedules, configure system parameters, and receive notifications or alerts.

Users can interact with the service through web or mobile applications.

Optimization:

The controller service aims to optimize water usage, energy consumption, and plant health.

It may adjust irrigation schedules based on changing conditions to minimize water wastage and reduce operating costs.

Reporting and Analytics:

It provides users with reports and analytics on irrigation activities, water consumption, plant health, and system performance.

Users can use these insights to make informed decisions and adjustments.

Alerts and Notifications:

The service generates alerts and notifications for users in case of system malfunctions, low battery levels, or unusual sensor readings.

This ensures timely maintenance and issue resolution.

Scalability:

The controller service is designed to handle a growing number of IoT devices and zones as the irrigation system expands.

It can scale horizontally to accommodate additional sensors and actuators.

Integration:

It can integrate with external data sources, such as weather services or soil databases, to enhance decision-making accuracy.

It may also integrate with other smart home or farm management systems for a holistic solution.

A well-designed controller service is essential for the efficient and effective operation of a smart irrigation IoT system, ensuring that plants receive the right amount of water while conserving resources and minimizing environmental impact.

Smart Services

Smart Services: Smart services in the IoT context are innovative and value-added offerings enabled by IoT technologies. These services leverage data from IoT devices to deliver enhanced and intelligent experiences to users or organizations. Examples of smart services include smart home automation, predictive healthcare monitoring, intelligent transportation systems, and more.

Key Characteristics: Smart services often incorporate data analytics, real-time decision-making, automation, and connectivity. They aim to provide convenience, efficiency, and improved quality of life or business operations. Smart services can also adapt and evolve based on user preferences and changing conditions.

Some more applications of IoT are:

Smart Lighting
Smart Appliances
Intrusion Detection
Smoke/Gas Detectors Cities
Smart Parking
Smart Roads
Surveillance
Emergency Response Environment
Weather Monitoring
Air Pollution Monitoring
Noise Pollution Monitoring
Forest Fire Detection
River Floods Detection Energy
Smart Grids
Renewable Energy Systems
Prognostics Retail
Inventory Management
Smart Payments
Smart Vending Machines Agriculture
Green House Control Industry
Machine Diagnosis & Prognosis
Indoor Air Quality Monitoring

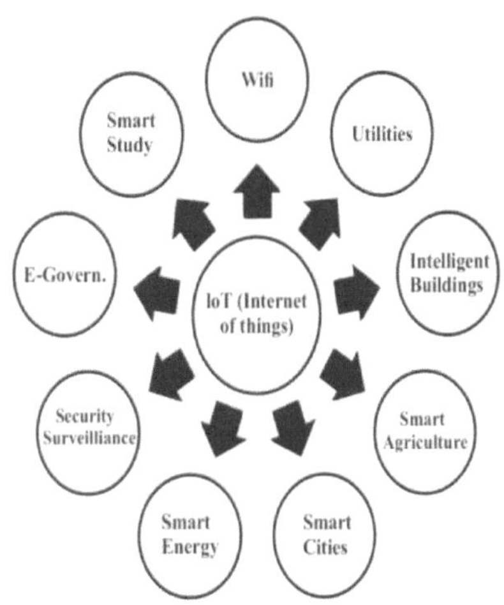

Secured communication for smart IoT

Secured communication for smart IoT (Internet of Things) devices is a critical aspect of ensuring the safety and integrity of IoT deployments. IoT devices are often utilized in diverse and uncontrolled environments, making them vulnerable to various security risks. Here is an explanation of how secured communication is achieved for smart IoT objects.

Authentication:

IoT devices must undergo authentication processes to establish their legitimacy before initiating communication. Various authentication methods are employed, including digital certificates, username-password combinations, or token-based systems. Mutual authentication ensures that both the device and the network or service can confirm each other's identities.

Encryption:

To prevent eavesdropping and data theft, it is essential to encrypt data transmitted between IoT devices and backend systems. The use of protocols like TLS/SSL (Transport Layer Security/Secure Sockets Layer) is common for securing data in transit. Implementing end-to-end encryption ensures data remains confidential throughout the communication process.

Access Control:

Strict access control policies are implemented to define who can access IoT devices and the data they generate. Role-based access control (RBAC) and access tokens are often used to manage permissions effectively. Regularly auditing and updating access control policies help minimize security risks.

Firewalls and Intrusion Detection/Prevention Systems (IDS/IPS):

To monitor network traffic for potential threats, firewalls and IDS/IPS systems are deployed. Firewalls filter incoming and outgoing traffic based on predefined rules, while IDS/IPS systems detect and respond to potential threats, blocking or alerting on malicious activities.

Security Updates and Patch Management:

Regularly updating and patching IoT devices' firmware and software is crucial to address known vulnerabilities. Establishing an efficient patch management system ensures timely updates without compromising device functionality.

Secure Boot and Hardware-Based Security:

IoT devices should have a secure boot process that verifies the integrity of firmware and software during startup. Hardware-based security features, such as Trusted Platform Modules (TPMs) or Hardware Security Modules (HSMs), can be utilized to protect cryptographic keys and sensitive data.

Network Segmentation:

Segmenting IoT devices onto separate networks or VLANs (Virtual Local Area Networks) isolates them from critical infrastructure and sensitive data, reducing the potential attack surface and containing breaches in case of device compromise.

Security Standards and Protocols:

Adhering to industry-specific security standards and protocols, such as Zigbee, Z-Wave, MQTT, CoAP, or OPC UA, ensures that IoT deployments incorporate security features tailored to their specific requirements.

Data Integrity:

Implementing mechanisms to verify the integrity of data transmitted and received by IoT devices is crucial. Techniques like hash functions and digital signatures ensure that data remains unaltered during transit.

Incident Response Plan:

Developing and regularly testing an incident response plan is essential for addressing security breaches or anomalies promptly. The plan should outline procedures for containment, investigation, and recovery.

Secured communication for smart IoT devices requires a comprehensive approach, considering not only the devices but also the network infrastructure and backend services. Regular security audits and updates are essential to proactively address emerging threats and vulnerabilities in the ever-evolving IoT landscape.

Challenges in IoT Application Development

Developing IoT (Internet of Things) applications offers numerous opportunities but also comes with its fair share of challenges. Here are some of the key challenges that developers and organizations face when creating IoT applications:

Interoperability: IoT involves a multitude of devices from different manufacturers, running various operating systems and communication protocols. Ensuring seamless interoperability and data exchange among these devices can be challenging.

Scalability: IoT systems can scale from a few devices to thousands or even millions. Designing applications that can handle this level of scalability in terms of data management, processing, and communication can be complex.

Security: IoT devices are often vulnerable to cybersecurity threats. Developers must implement robust security measures to protect data, devices, and the network. This includes device authentication, encryption, and secure firmware updates.

Privacy: IoT applications collect and process vast amounts of personal data. Ensuring that data is handled in compliance with privacy regulations and user consent is a significant challenge.

Data Management: IoT generates enormous amounts of data. Efficiently storing, managing, and processing this data is a challenge, particularly when considering real-time analytics and historical data storage.

Latency: Some IoT applications require low-latency communication, such as autonomous vehicles or industrial automation. Ensuring real-time response and minimal delay can be demanding.

Power Efficiency: Many IoT devices are battery-powered or have limited power sources. Optimizing power consumption while maintaining functionality is essential for prolonged device lifespan.
Connectivity: IoT devices may operate in diverse environments, including areas with poor connectivity. Ensuring reliable communication and handling intermittent connectivity can be challenging.
Firmware Updates: Managing and distributing firmware updates to IoT devices, especially those deployed in remote or inaccessible locations, requires careful planning and security considerations.
Standards and Protocols: The IoT ecosystem lacks universal standards, resulting in fragmentation. Developers may need to navigate a variety of protocols and technologies, making interoperability a challenge.
Cost Constraints: IoT devices often have cost constraints. Balancing functionality and performance with cost-effectiveness is a constant challenge.
Regulatory Compliance: IoT applications must adhere to local and international regulations and standards, which can vary significantly from one region to another.
Data Quality: IoT data may be noisy or inaccurate due to various environmental factors or device limitations. Ensuring data quality and reliability is essential for decision-making.
Ethical Considerations: As IoT applications become more prevalent, ethical concerns, such as the impact on employment, surveillance, and environmental sustainability, must be addressed.
Legacy Systems Integration: Many IoT deployments involve integrating with existing legacy systems, which can be complex and require careful planning to ensure compatibility and data exchange.
Addressing these challenges requires a multidisciplinary approach, involving expertise in hardware design, software development, security, data analytics, and domain-specific knowledge. It also demands a proactive approach to staying updated with emerging technologies and best practices in the ever-evolving field of IoT.

Monitor Air-Pollution

In the context of IoT (Internet of Things), monitoring air pollution involves the use of IoT devices and sensors to collect, transmit, and analyse data related to air quality. IoT technologies enhance traditional air pollution monitoring by providing real-time data, remote accessibility, and scalability. Here's how air pollution monitoring can be done using IoT:
Sensor Selection: Choose IoT-compatible air quality sensors that can measure specific pollutants, such as particulate matter (PM2.5 and PM10), gases (NO2, SO2, CO, O3), temperature, humidity, and more. These sensors should be capable of providing digital data output.
IoT Devices: Deploy IoT devices that incorporate the selected sensors. These devices are equipped with microcontrollers, communication modules (e.g., Wi-Fi, cellular, LoRa), and power sources (e.g., batteries or solar panels).
Sensor Placement: Place IoT devices with sensors at strategic locations within the area of interest. Ensure they are properly calibrated and protected from environmental factors that may affect sensor accuracy.
Data Collection: IoT devices continuously collect air quality data from the sensors. This data includes pollutant concentrations, temperature, humidity, and other relevant environmental parameters.
Data Transmission: IoT devices transmit the collected data to a central IoT platform or cloud-based server using wireless communication protocols. This allows for real-time data transfer and remote monitoring.
Data Storage and Processing: The IoT platform or cloud server stores the received data and processes it in real-time. Data processing may involve aggregating, analyzing, and visualizing the information.
Real-Time Monitoring: Stakeholders, including environmental agencies, local authorities, and the public, can access real-time air quality data through web interfaces or mobile applications. This provides up-to-date information on air quality conditions.
Alerts and Notifications: Implement alert systems that automatically notify relevant parties when air quality deteriorates or crosses predefined thresholds. These notifications can be sent via email, SMS, or app notifications.
Historical Data and Analytics: IoT platforms enable the storage of historical air quality data, allowing for trend analysis, identification of pollution sources, and long-term assessment of air quality.
Integration with Geographic Information Systems (GIS): Integrate IoT air quality data with GIS systems to visualize pollution patterns on maps. This aids in spatial analysis and decision-making.
Remote Management: IoT devices can be remotely managed and updated, ensuring that they operate efficiently and stay calibrated over time.
Scalability: As needed, additional IoT devices and sensors can be deployed to expand monitoring coverage to more locations or to monitor additional pollutants.

IoT-based air pollution monitoring enhances environmental monitoring capabilities by providing real-time, comprehensive, and accessible data. It enables timely responses to pollution events, supports policy decisions, and empowers citizens with information to protect their health and the environment.

Frameworks For IoT Applications

Developing IoT applications can be a complex task, but using frameworks can significantly simplify the process and accelerate development. IoT frameworks provide a set of pre-built tools, libraries, and components that streamline common tasks and challenges associated with IoT application development. Here are some popular IoT frameworks and platforms that can be used to develop IoT applications:

IoT Platforms:

IoT platforms are comprehensive solutions that provide end-to-end capabilities for developing, deploying, and managing IoT applications. They often include device management, data storage, analytics, and integration with cloud services. Examples include:

AWS IoT: Amazon Web Services offers a robust IoT platform with a wide range of services for device management, data processing, and integration with other AWS services.

Azure IoT: Microsoft's Azure IoT platform provides tools for device management, data analytics, and integration with Azure services.

Google Cloud IoT: Google Cloud offers a suite of services for IoT device management, data processing, and machine learning.

Arduino IoT Cloud: Arduino provides a platform for building IoT applications with Arduino boards. It includes cloud-based tools for device management, data visualization, and remote control of Arduino devices.

Particle: Particle is an IoT platform that offers hardware, connectivity, and cloud services. It is suitable for both prototyping and production-grade IoT applications.

Platform IO: Platform IO is an open-source IoT development platform that supports multiple hardware platforms and integrates with various development environments. It simplifies the development and management of IoT firmware.

Node-RED: Node-RED is a flow-based development tool for visual programming of IoT applications. It provides a graphical interface for wiring together devices, APIs, and online services.

Open HAB: Open HAB is an open-source home automation framework that allows you to build smart home IoT applications. It supports a wide range of devices and protocols and provides rule engines for automation.

Home Assistant: Home Assistant is another open-source home automation platform with a strong community following. It offers integrations with various IoT devices and services.

Thing Speak: Thing Speak is an IoT analytics platform from MathWorks (makers of MATLAB) that allows you to collect, analyse, and visualize IoT data. It's suitable for research and prototyping IoT applications.

Tessel: Tessel is an open-source IoT platform that provides a JavaScript runtime for IoT devices. It simplifies IoT development for JavaScript developers.

Mongoose OS: Mongoose OS is an open-source IoT firmware development framework that supports various microcontrollers and platforms. It's designed to simplify IoT device management and connectivity.

RIOT OS: RIOT is an open-source real-time operating system for the Internet of Things. It's suitable for resource-constrained IoT devices and offers a robust development environment.

Free RTOS: Free RTOS is another open-source real-time operating system designed for IoT and embedded systems. It provides a lightweight and efficient platform for building IoT applications.

When choosing an IoT framework or platform, consider factors such as your specific use case, the hardware you plan to use, scalability requirements, and the level of customization and control you need. Each framework has its strengths and may be better suited to different types of IoT applications.

Exercise

Exercise 1 – MCQ

1. Which of the following is an example of an IoT application in the healthcare sector?
a) Smart thermostat
b) Connected car
c) Remote patient monitoring
d) Smart refrigerator

2. In which of the following scenarios is an IoT application commonly used for energy conservation?
a) Smart traffic management
b) Online shopping

c) Home security
d) Smart grid for electricity distribution

Exercise 2 – True/False

1. IoT applications are primarily focused on consumer products and have limited relevance in industrial and healthcare sectors.
2. IoT applications are limited to the healthcare sector and cannot be applied to other industries.

Exercise 3 – Fill in the blanks

1. IoT applications in healthcare improve _______ by enabling remote patient monitoring and personalized treatment.
2. In smart cities, IoT enhances _______ through optimized traffic management and resource utilization.

Exercise 4 – One word answer

1. What does "mHealth" refer to in IoT applications?
2. Which technology is at the core of many IoT applications involving tracking and identification?

Exercise 5 – Small answer

1. What is a common application of IoT in the agriculture sector?
2. Which industry often uses IoT for predictive maintenance of machinery and equipment?

Exercise 6 – Long answer

1. Explain how IoT can be applied in the transportation sector for traffic management and optimization.
2.Describe the potential benefits and challenges of implementing IoT in the healthcare sector for remote patient monitoring.

Answer:

Exercise 1.
1. c) Remote patient monitoring
2. a) Smart grid for electricity distribution

Exercise 2.
1. False
2. False

Exercise 3.
1. patient care
2. urban living

Exercise 4.
1.Mobile Health
2. RFID (Radio-Frequency Identification)

Previous Year Questions

1. Write Short note on (any 2)
a) Energy Management and smart homes
b) Internet of things for ambient assisted living
c) Intelligent Transport (SPPU B.Tech. 2019)
2. Explain challenges in developing IoT applications. (SPPU B.Tech. 2017)
3. Write a detail note on -i. Smart Energy ii. Application Smart homes and IoT. (SPPU B.Tech. 2017)
4. Explain secured communication for smart IoT object. (RTU B.Tech. 2017)
5. List and explain in short IoT applications. (RTU B.Tech. 2018)
6. Write a short note to give abstract view of Internet of Things
7. Write in detail Application of Internet of Things. (SPPU B.Tech. 2017)
8. Explain in detail application of Internet of Things in city automation and home automation. (SPPU B.Tech. 2017)
9. Write applications of Internet of Things for e health body area network. (SPPU B.Tech. 2017)
10. Explain in detail application of Internet of Things in city automation and home automation. (SPPU 2017)
11. Explain the application of lot in home automation systems. (Uttar Pradesh university B.Tech. 2018-19)
12. Explain process specification for home automation system. (Mumbai University B.Tech. 2017)
13. Design smart irrigation system based on followings:
(1) Define process specification for smart irrigation IoT system
(2)Domain model of Smart irrigation IoT system. (Mumbai University B.Tech. 2017)
15. Explain in detail Arduino and sensors and interfacing for it. (Mumbai University B.Tech. 2017)

16.Write a detail note on secured communication in IoT applications for data transfer and its importance. (Mumbai University B.Tech. 2017)
17. List and explain in short IoT applications. (Mumbai University B.Tech. 2017)
18. Information model of Smart irrigation IoT system. (Mumbai University B.Tech. 2017)
19. Controller service of Smart irrigation IoT system (SPPU B.Tech. 2019)
20. Mention six applications of IOT (Chaudhary Charan Singh University B. Tech 2017)
21. Write about the application layer of IOT. (Chaudhary Charan Singh University B. Tech 2017)
22. What are the three major blocks of any IOT application? (Chaudhary Charan Singh University B. Tech 2017)
23. How to monitor Air-Pollution?(RTU B.Tech. 2017)

ONLINE RESOURCES

Link: https://forms.gle/YkxujR1NNBfW7XXq7

QR Code

Link: https://www.youtube.com/playlist?list=PLzlh_31VWEFqPWJ6IvPUrFlqwH16FqrwT

QR Code

Chapter 4: IoT Design Methodology

Designing IoT systems

Designing IoT systems can indeed be a complex undertaking due to the intricate interactions among various components. IoT designers often find themselves considering specific products or services during the design process. However, adopting a generic design methodology, which remains agnostic to particular products, services, or programming languages, can offer several advantages. These include reduced design time, streamlined testing and maintenance, decreased complexity, and improved interoperability. Below is a breakdown of the key stages in this generic IoT design methodology:

Purpose and Requirements Specification:

In this initial phase, the primary goal is to define the purpose and objectives of the IoT system.

Specify the functional and non-functional requirements, taking into account factors such as scalability, security, and data processing speed.

Process Specification:

Identify and document the various processes and workflows that the IoT system will involve.

This step helps in understanding how data will flow and how components will interact.

Domain Model Specification:

Develop a domain model that represents the entities, their attributes, and relationships within the IoT ecosystem.

This model helps in clarifying the structure of the system and its various components.

Information Model Specification:

Create an information model that defines how data is structured and organized within the IoT system.

Specify data formats, data sources, and data storage requirements.

Service Specifications:

Define the services that the IoT system will offer to users or other components.

Specify the interfaces and protocols for accessing these services.

Functional View Specification:

Detail the functional aspects of the system, including how data is processed and transformed.

Describe the logic and algorithms that drive the system's functionality.

Operational View Specification:

Outline how the IoT system will operate in different scenarios, including startup, shutdown, and error-handling.

Define performance metrics and monitoring requirements.

Device and Component Integration:

Determine how various devices and components will be integrated into the system.

Specify communication protocols and data exchange formats.

Application Development:

Develop the software applications and services needed to implement the IoT system.

Follow best practices for coding, testing, and documentation.

Purpose of IoT System Design Methodology

The purpose of an IoT system design methodology is to provide a structured approach to conceptualizing, planning, and implementing IoT solutions. It aims to ensure that IoT systems meet their intended goals effectively and efficiently. This methodology guides developers and stakeholders through various stages of the IoT system's lifecycle, from conceptualization to deployment and maintenance.

In the context of a smart IoT-based home automation system, the purpose of the design methodology is to:

Define Objectives: Clearly articulate the goals and objectives of the home automation system. For example, in a smart home, the objective might be to enhance convenience, security, energy efficiency, and comfort.

Specify Requirements: Identify and document the functional and non-functional requirements of the system. This includes determining what devices will be controlled, how they will communicate, what user interfaces are needed, and the performance criteria (e.g., response time, scalability, security).

Design Architecture: Develop a high-level architectural design that outlines how devices will be interconnected, how data will flow, and how various components (sensors, actuators, controllers, user interfaces) will interact.

Select Technologies: Choose appropriate IoT protocols, communication technologies (e.g., Wi-Fi, Zigbee, Bluetooth), and hardware components (sensors, actuators) that align with the system's requirements.

Ensure Security: Integrate security measures to protect the home automation system from unauthorized access and data breaches. This includes authentication, encryption, and secure device management.

Optimize Performance: Consider strategies for optimizing system performance and responsiveness, such as load balancing, data caching, and real-time data processing.

Scalability and Upgradability: Plan for the ability to scale the system as more devices are added or upgrade components over time.

User Experience: Design user-friendly interfaces (e.g., mobile apps, web dashboards) that allow homeowners to control and monitor the automation system easily.

Energy Efficiency: Implement strategies to optimize energy usage, such as scheduling and power management for connected devices.

Compliance: Ensure that the IoT home automation system complies with relevant regulations and standards, including data privacy and electrical safety.

Requirements Specification in IoT System Design:

The requirements specification phase in IoT system design is crucial for understanding and documenting what the system must achieve. For a smart IoT-based home automation system, this phase involves the following steps:

Gather Requirements: Engage with stakeholders, including homeowners, to gather requirements. Identify the specific devices to be controlled (e.g., lights, thermostat, locks), the desired automation scenarios (e.g., motion-activated lighting, remote temperature control), and user preferences.

Prioritize Requirements: Rank requirements based on importance and feasibility. Prioritization ensures that essential features are addressed first and aligns with the system's objectives.

Functional Requirements: Detail the specific functions the system must perform, such as turning on lights when motion is detected, adjusting the thermostat based on user preferences, or sending security alerts.

Non-Functional Requirements: Document non-functional requirements related to performance, security, scalability, and usability. For instance, specify response time expectations, encryption requirements, and the number of supported devices.

Use Cases and User Stories: Create use cases or user stories to describe system interactions from the user's perspective. For example, describe how a user can set up automation rules through a mobile app.

System Constraints: Identify any constraints that may impact system design, such as budget limitations, hardware availability, or compatibility with existing infrastructure.

Validation and Review: Review the requirements with stakeholders to ensure they accurately reflect their needs and expectations. This step helps avoid misunderstandings and scope changes later in the project.

Documentation: Document the requirements specification in a clear and organized manner, making it accessible to all project stakeholders.

The requirements specification phase serves as the foundation for subsequent design and development activities. It guides the creation of system architectures, the selection of components, and the development of software and user interfaces to meet the identified needs and goals of the smart IoT-based home automation system.

Process Specification in IoT Design Methodology

Process specification in IoT (Internet of Things) design methodology outlines the step-by-step approach and activities involved in conceptualizing, developing, and implementing an IoT solution. It provides a structured framework to ensure that the IoT project progresses smoothly from inception to deployment. Here is a detailed explanation of the process specification in IoT design methodology:

Define Objectives and Scope: Begin by clearly defining the objectives of the IoT project. What problem does it aim to solve, and what are the desired outcomes? Determine the project's scope, including the range of devices, applications, and functionalities to be included.

Gather Requirements: Collaborate with stakeholders, including end-users, business owners, and technical experts, to gather and document both functional and non-functional requirements. These requirements serve as the foundation for the design and development phases.

System Architecture Design: Develop a high-level system architecture that outlines the structure of the IoT solution. Define the components, their interactions, and data flows within the system. Decide on the deployment model (edge, cloud, hybrid) and communication protocols.

Technology Selection: Choose the appropriate hardware components (sensors, actuators, gateways), software platforms, communication technologies (e.g., Wi-Fi, Bluetooth, LoRa), and IoT development tools based on the project's requirements.

Security Integration: Integrate robust security measures into the design, encompassing device authentication, data encryption, access control, and secure firmware updates. Ensure that security is a fundamental aspect of the architecture.

Data Management and Analytics: Define how data will be collected, processed, stored, and analysed. Determine the data storage solutions, databases, and analytics tools that will be used to derive actionable insights from IoT-generated data.

Device Management: Establish device management protocols to monitor and control IoT devices remotely. This includes tasks like device provisioning, firmware updates, and error handling.
User Interface Design: Create user-friendly interfaces (e.g., web dashboards, mobile apps) for end-users to interact with and control IoT devices. Ensure that the interface aligns with user expectations and project goals
Prototyping and Testing: Develop prototypes or proof-of-concept implementations to validate the design and functionality of the IoT system. Conduct thorough testing to identify and address any issues or performance bottlenecks.
Scalability and Upgradability: Plan for scalability to accommodate future growth and increased device deployments. Ensure that the system can be easily upgraded to support new features or technologies.
Compliance and Regulations: Assess and address regulatory requirements and standards relevant to the IoT project, such as data privacy, safety, and industry-specific regulations.
Documentation: Maintain detailed documentation throughout the design process. Document system architecture, component specifications, protocols, and any custom code or configurations.
Deployment and Monitoring: Deploy the IoT solution in the intended environment, whether it's a smart home, industrial setting, or urban infrastructure. Continuously monitor system performance, security, and data quality post-deployment.
Maintenance and Updates: Establish procedures for ongoing maintenance, including device maintenance, software updates, and security patch management. Ensure that the IoT solution remains reliable and secure over time.
Feedback and Improvement: Collect feedback from end-users and stakeholders to identify areas for improvement. Iterate on the design and functionality based on real-world usage and evolving requirements.
Process specification in IoT design methodology ensures that the development process is systematic, efficient, and aligned with project goals. It helps in managing complexities, mitigating risks, and delivering IoT solutions that meet user expectations and business objectives.

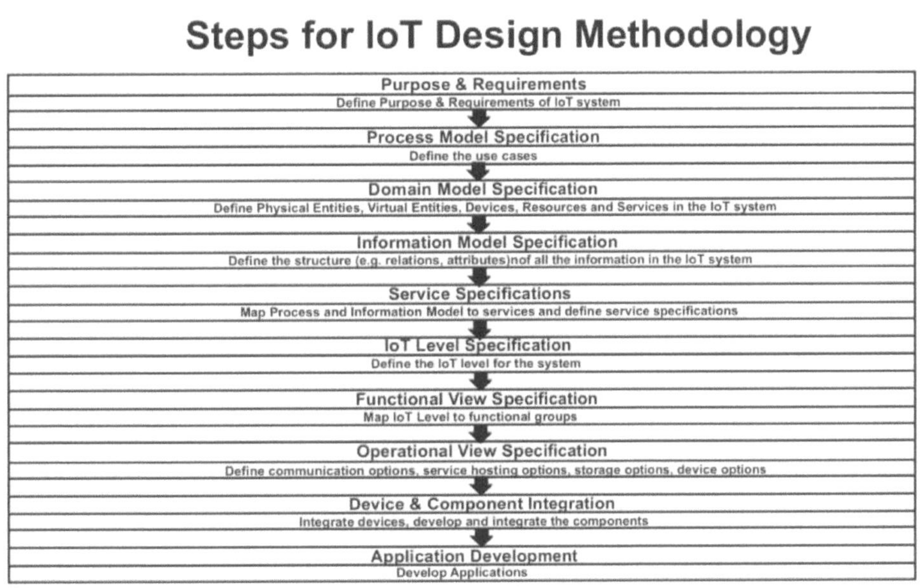

Domain Model Specification

A domain model specification is a conceptual framework that defines the key elements, concepts, relationships, and rules within a specific domain or subject area. It serves as a visual representation or abstraction of the real-world entities and their interactions, helping stakeholders better understand and communicate the structure and behavior of a system or domain. Key components of a domain model specification typically include:

Entities: These are the main objects or concepts within the domain. Entities represent nouns, such as customers, products, or orders, and capture the essential characteristics and attributes associated with them.
Attributes: Attributes describe the properties or characteristics of entities. For example, a "customer" entity may have attributes like "name," "email," and "address."
Relationships: Relationships define how entities are connected or associated with one another. Relationships can be one-to-one, one-to-many, or many-to-many and represent connections between entities.
Constraints: Constraints specify rules, conditions, or limitations within the domain. These constraints ensure data integrity and guide the behaviour of the system. Examples include uniqueness constraints or validation rules.
The Domain Model Specification is an essential component of software engineering and system design. Its primary purpose is to facilitate a deep understanding of the problem domain, define the requirements and constraints of the system, guide the design and development process, and ensure alignment between the software solution and the real-world domain it serves. A well-crafted Domain Model contributes to more effective communication, problem-solving, and system development.

Need and purpose of Domain Model Specification:

The Domain Model Specification is a critical aspect of software engineering and system design, especially when developing complex systems. Its primary purpose is to define and represent the fundamental concepts, entities, relationships, and rules within a specific domain or problem space. Here are the key needs and purposes of Domain Model Specification:
Domain Understanding: The primary need for a Domain Model Specification is to gain a deep understanding of the problem domain. It helps stakeholders, including developers, designers, and business analysts, become familiar with the domain's concepts and intricacies.
Conceptual Clarity: It provides a clear and precise representation of the domain's essential elements, such as entities, attributes, and relationships. This clarity aids in avoiding misunderstandings and ambiguities during the development process.
Common Vocabulary: A Domain Model creates a common vocabulary that all stakeholders can use to discuss and describe the domain. This shared terminology enhancescommunication and collaboration among team members.
Requirements Elicitation: By exploring and defining the domain thoroughly, it becomes easier to identify and document requirements for the software or system. This ensures that the resulting solution aligns with the needs of the domain.
Design Guidance: Domain models can serve as the foundation for system design. They help in identifying the structural and behavioural aspects of the system by mapping domain concepts to software components.
Complexity Management: In complex systems, a Domain Model helps manage the complexity by breaking it down into manageable and understandable parts. It aids in dividing the system into subsystems or modules that can be developed and tested independently.
Abstraction: Domain models provide an abstraction of the domain, focusing on the most relevant aspects while omitting unnecessary details. This abstraction aids in simplifying the problem-solving process.
Consistency and Integrity: A well-defined Domain Model can enforce consistency and data integrity rules within the system. It specifies the valid relationships and constraints between domain entities.
Visualization and Communication: Domain models, often represented graphically using tools like UML (Unified Modelling Language), provide visual representations of the domain structure. These visual models make it easier for stakeholders to comprehend complex domain structures.
Testing and Validation: Domain models can serve as the basis for test planning and validation activities. Test cases can be derived directly from the model, ensuring comprehensive coverage of domain-related scenarios.
Documentation and Knowledge Transfer: Domain models serve as valuable documentation for the domain itself, which can be useful for training new team members, onboarding stakeholders, and maintaining the system in the long term.
Agility and Adaptability: A well-structured Domain Model can make a system more adaptable to changes within the domain. It allows for easier incorporation of new concepts or modifications to existing ones.
Domain model specifications are valuable tools in software engineering and system design. They help in modeling complex systems, understanding business requirements, and facilitating effective communication among project stakeholders, including developers, designers, and domain experts. Domain models can be used as a basis for designing databases, creating class diagrams in object-oriented programming, or structuring data for various software applications.

Information Model Specification

An information model specification is a comprehensive framework that delineates how data and information are structured, organized, and interconnected within a particular system, application, or domain. It serves as a blueprint for defining the types of data entities, their attributes, relationships, and the rules governing data manipulation and interactions.

Key components of an information model specification typically encompass:

Entities: These represent fundamental data objects or concepts within the domain. Entities encapsulate data with specific attributes, characterizing the properties and characteristics of each entity. For instance, in a healthcare information model, entities could include "patients," "medical procedures," and "diagnoses."

Attributes: Attributes are the descriptive properties or fields associated with each entity. They define the data elements that need to be captured and processed. For instance, a "patient" entity might have attributes such as "name," "date of birth," and "medical history."

Relationships: Relationships establish how entities are related or connected to one another. They describe the associations and dependencies between data entities. Relationships can be one-to-one, one-to-many, or many-to-many, and they play a crucial role in modelling data flows and dependencies.

Constraints: Constraints specify rules, conditions, or limitations on the data. These constraints can include data validation rules, uniqueness requirements, or referential integrity constraints, ensuring data quality and consistency.

Semantic Meaning: Information models often include definitions and descriptions that provide a shared understanding of the data elements and their semantics. This helps ensure that all stakeholders interpret data consistently.

Information models are pivotal in various fields, including software engineering, database design, and system architecture. They serve as a guide for designing databases, creating data-driven applications, and facilitating effective data management and integration. Information model specifications enable stakeholders to collaborate efficiently, ensuring that data is accurately represented, processed, and utilized within a given system or domain.

Need and purpose of Information Model Specification

The Information Model Specification is a critical component in the design and development of complex systems, particularly in the context of IoT (Internet of Things) and other interconnected technologies. It serves several important needs and purposes:

Common Understanding: Information Model Specification provides a standardized and structured way to define the various data, entities, and relationships within a system. It ensures that all stakeholders, including developers, engineers, and users, have a common understanding of the system's data and its organization.

Interoperability: In interconnected systems like IoT, devices and services from different vendors need to work together seamlessly. An Information Model Specification helps achieve interoperability by defining standardized data formats and communication protocols. This ensures that data can be exchanged and interpreted consistently across different devices and platforms.

Data Integration: In many systems, data is generated and consumed by multiple components. An Information Model Specification enables data integration by defining how data should be structured, shared, and transformed between different parts of the system. This is crucial for real-time decision-making and analytics.

Scalability: As systems grow and evolve, it's essential to have a clear information model in place. This allows for the easy addition of new components, devices, or services without disrupting the existing system. Scalability is especially critical in IoT systems that may expand rapidly.

Security: Information Model Specification plays a role in ensuring data security. It defines how data is accessed, protected, and shared within the system. By specifying security requirements and access controls within the model, potential vulnerabilities can be identified and addressed proactively.

Efficient Development: Developers rely on Information Model Specifications as blueprints for building software and hardware components. Having a well-defined information model reduces ambiguity and accelerates the development process. Developers can work based on a common set of data structures and interfaces.

Data Quality: A clear information model helps maintain data quality and consistency. It enforces rules and constraints on how data is collected, stored, and processed, reducing the likelihood of errors and data inconsistencies.

Maintenance and Evolution: Systems evolve over time, and the Information Model Specification provides a reference point for making changes and updates. It helps ensure that modifications are made with a clear understanding of how they impact data and system behaviour.

Communication: Information Model Specifications are valuable tools for communicating system requirements and capabilities to stakeholders, including clients, partners, and regulatory authorities. They serve as documentation that can be easily understood and reviewed.

Compliance and Standardization: In regulated industries or sectors with industry standards, Information Model Specifications help ensure compliance with requirements and standards. They provide a basis for demonstrating that a system adheres to predefined rules and regulations.

In summary, Information Model Specification is a foundational element in system design and development, offering a structured and standardized approach to defining and managing data within complex systems. It addresses the need for clarity, interoperability, security, efficiency, and adaptability in modern interconnected technologies like IoT.

Service Specifications

Service specifications outline the detailed characteristics, functionalities, and requirements of a particular service or set of services offered within a system, organization, or industry. These specifications are critical in ensuring that services meet predefined standards, performance criteria, and user expectations. Service specifications typically include:

Service Description: A clear and concise description of the service, including its purpose, scope, and intended audience.

Functional Requirements: Detailed specifications of the service's features and capabilities. This section outlines what the service is expected to do and how it will perform its functions.

Performance Metrics: Quantifiable criteria that define the expected performance of the service, such as response times, throughput, availability, and reliability.

Interfaces and APIs: Specifications of how the service interfaces with other services, systems, or external entities. This may include API documentation, data formats, and communication protocols.

Security Requirements: Guidelines and measures to ensure the security and privacy of data and transactions handled by the service. This may involve authentication, encryption, access control, and compliance with security standards.

Scalability and Resource Requirements: Information on how the service can scale to accommodate increased demand, including hardware and software resource requirements.

Service-Level Agreements (SLAs): Agreed-upon commitments regarding service performance, availability, and support, often formalized in SLA contracts.

Dependencies: Identification of dependencies on other services, components, or third-party resources that the service relies on.

Error Handling and Recovery: Guidelines for handling errors, exceptions, and failures gracefully, including strategies for fault tolerance and recovery.

Testing and Quality Assurance: Procedures and criteria for testing the service to ensure it meets specifications, including test cases, scenarios, and validation criteria.

Regulatory Compliance: Compliance requirements and regulations that the service must adhere to, especially in regulated industries like healthcare or finance.

Documentation and Support: Documentation resources, user manuals, training materials, and support channels to assist users in understanding and utilizing the service effectively.

Within the Service Specification step, there are three important service types: Mode Service, State Service, and Controller Service.

Mode Service:

Definition: A Mode Service is responsible for defining the operational modes or states that an IoT device or system can assume. Each mode represents a specific configuration or behaviour.

Purpose: Mode Services are used to control the operation of IoT devices based on different scenarios or user-defined preferences. They allow devices to adapt to changing conditions or requirements.

Example: In a smart thermostat, a Mode Service might define modes like "Heating," "Cooling," "Eco," and "Off," each with its own temperature settings and behaviour.

State Service:

Definition: A State Service monitors and reports the current state or condition of an IoT device or system. It provides information about the device's status or the environment it's monitoring.

Purpose: State Services are essential for real-time monitoring and decision-making. They enable other components of the IoT system to react to changes in device or environmental states.

Example: A State Service in a smart lighting system report whether a light is "On" or "Off" and the current brightness level.

Controller Service:

Definition: A Controller Service is responsible for managing the control and coordination of actions within the IoT system. It often receives input from Mode and State Services to make decisions.

Purpose: Controller Services play a pivotal role in orchestrating the behaviour of IoT devices and ensuring that they respond appropriately to various conditions or commands.

Example: In a home automation system, a Controller Service might receive input from a Mode Service to switch to "Security Mode" and then activate State Services to lock doors, arm security cameras, and set up motion detectors.

Service specifications are crucial in various domains, including software development, telecommunications, healthcare, and manufacturing. They serve as a reference for service providers, developers, quality assurance teams, and users, ensuring that services are designed, implemented, and maintained to meet predefined standards and expectations.

Need and Purpose of Service Specifications

Service Specifications play a crucial role in the design and development of systems, particularly in the context of software development and service-oriented architectures. They serve several important needs and purposes:

Clear Definition of Services: Service Specifications provide a clear and unambiguous definition of the services that a system or application will offer. This is essential for ensuring that all stakeholders have a common understanding of what the services do and how they can be used.

Functional Requirements: Service Specifications outline the functional requirements of each service, including what inputs they accept, what processing they perform, and what outputs or results they provide. This information is vital for developers who need to implement the services.

Service Dependencies: In complex systems, services often depend on one another. Service Specifications document these dependencies, helping developers understand how different services interact and ensuring that these interactions are well-defined and structured.

Data Formats and Protocols: Service Specifications define the data formats and communication protocols that services use to exchange information. This is essential for ensuring that services can communicate effectively with each other.

Service Behaviour: Service Specifications describe the expected behaviour of each service, including error handling, response times, and other quality-of-service attributes. This helps set expectations for performance and reliability.

Scalability and Performance: Service Specifications may include information about how services can be scaled to handle increased load or demand. This is critical for systems that need to accommodate changing workloads.

Service Contracts: They establish contracts between service providers and consumers. These contracts specify what a service will provide and what is expected from service consumers, promoting a clear understanding of responsibilities.

Security Requirements: Service Specifications may outline security requirements, including authentication, authorization, encryption, and data protection measures. This helps ensure that services are developed with security in mind.

Interoperability: Service Specifications can define standards and protocols for interoperability with other systems or external services. This is crucial in systems that need to work with third-party services or integrate with existing infrastructure.

Documentation: They serve as comprehensive documentation for each service, making it easier for developers, testers, and other stakeholders to understand and work with the services.

Testing and Validation: Service Specifications are used as the basis for creating test cases and validation procedures. This ensures that services meet their functional and non-functional requirements.

Change Management: As systems evolve, Service Specifications provide a reference point for making changes and updates to services. They help ensure that modifications are made with a clear understanding of their impact on the system.

Contract Negotiation: Service Specifications can be used in contract negotiations with external service providers or clients. They specify the terms and conditions under which services will be delivered or consumed.

In summary, Service Specifications are essential for defining, documenting, and managing services within a system or architecture. They promote clarity, consistency, and alignment with stakeholder expectations, ultimately contributing to the successful design, development, and operation of systems and services.

Functional View Specification

A functional view specification is a detailed document that focuses on describing the functional aspects and capabilities of a system, software application, or component. It provides a comprehensive understanding of how the system's functions operate and interact to achieve specific objectives. This specification typically includes the following components:

Functional Requirements: A list of specific functions or features that the system is expected to perform. Each requirement is described in detail, specifying its purpose, inputs, expected behaviour, and outputs.

Use Cases: Detailed descriptions of various scenarios or interactions between users and the system. Use cases illustrate how users interact with the system to achieve specific goals and capture the flow of activities.

Functional Flow Diagrams: Visual representations, such as flowcharts or sequence diagrams, that depict the flow of data, processes, and interactions among different functions within the system.

System Interfaces: Descriptions of the interfaces, both internal and external, that the system interacts with. This includes APIs, databases, hardware components, and third-party services.
Data Requirements: Specifications of the data sources, formats, and structures that the system uses or produces during its operations. It outlines how data is collected, processed, stored, and communicated.
User Interfaces: Details about the graphical user interfaces (GUIs) or command-line interfaces (CLIs) that users interact with. This includes screen layouts, menu structures, and user input/output interactions.
Functional Constraints: Any limitations or restrictions that affect the system's functions, such as performance constraints, compatibility requirements, and regulatory compliance.
Business Rules: Specific rules or policies that govern how certain functions should behave. These rules often reflect the organization's business processes and practices.
Functional Testing Criteria: Criteria and test cases that will be used to verify and validate that the system's functions perform as specified. This includes acceptance criteria for each requirement.
Dependencies: Identification of dependencies between different functions or components within the system. This helps in understanding how changes to one function may impact others.
Non-Functional Requirements: Consideration of non-functional aspects that may influence the functional behaviour, such as security, performance, scalability, and usability requirements.
The functional view specification serves as a critical reference for developers, testers, and stakeholders involved in the system's design, development, and quality assurance. It ensures that the system's functions align with user needs and business objectives while providing a clear roadmap for implementation and testing.

Operational View Specification:

An operational view specification provides an in-depth overview of how a system or software application functions in a real-world operational context. It encompasses:
Deployment Architecture: Describes the system's physical and logical deployment across hardware infrastructure.
System Components: Lists and describes software and hardware components.
Configuration Management: Details version control and release management.
Monitoring: Explains system health and performance monitoring.
Fault Tolerance: Describes measures for system reliability and redundancy.
Scalability: Discusses system capacity scaling strategies.
Security Measures: Addresses access control, authentication, and encryption.
Backup and Recovery: Outlines data backup and disaster recovery plans.
Support and Maintenance: Covers helpdesk procedures and software updates.
Compliance: Addresses regulatory and compliance requirements.
Operational Testing: Specifies testing procedures and criteria.
This specification guides IT administrators and support teams in effectively deploying, maintaining, and monitoring the system in a real-world environment.

Device and Component Integration in IoT Design:

Device and component integration is a crucial phase in IoT design that focuses on connecting and coordinating various IoT devices, sensors, and software components to create a functional system. Here's a streamlined overview:
Device Selection: Choose suitable devices based on project requirements.
Communication Protocols: Define communication protocols (e.g., MQTT, Wi-Fi) for device data exchange.
Interoperability: Ensure devices can work together, using standardized protocols.
Gateway Integration: Incorporate gateways if needed to preprocess data and enhance connectivity.
Network Setup: Configure the network infrastructure for device communication.
Data Handling: Design data ingestion processes, validation rules, and data transformations.
Cloud or Server Integration: Connect devices to cloud platforms or central servers securely.
Data Processing: Implement real-time data processing and analytics pipelines.
Security: Secure data and device communication through authentication and encryption.
Configuration Management: Enable remote device configuration and updates.
Testing: Thoroughly test device functionality, data accuracy, and error handling.
Scalability: Plan for system scalability to accommodate more devices and data.
Monitoring: Implement monitoring tools for system health and performance.
Documentation: Maintain comprehensive documentation for troubleshooting and future reference.
Efficient device and component integration ensure that the IoT system operates smoothly, providing valuable data and insights while meeting project goals.

Application Development in IoT Design:

In IoT design, application development is a crucial phase where software components and interfaces are created to harness data from IoT devices. Key points in this phase include:

Use Cases: Analyse use cases to define how users and devices will interact within the IoT ecosystem.

Software Architecture: Design the software structure, specifying the roles of devices, servers, and user interfaces.

User Interfaces (UI): Create user-friendly interfaces for web, mobile, or IoT dashboards.

Data Handling: Develop data collection and processing mechanisms for IoT-generated data.

Device Communication: Establish secure communication protocols for device-to-application data exchange.

Data Analytics: Integrate analytics tools to extract insights from IoT data.

Security: Implement strong security measures for data protection and device communication.

Performance Optimization: Ensure the application scales and performs well with increased data and users.

Testing: Thoroughly test the application for functionality, integration, and performance.

Deployment: Deploy the application in production, either on-premises or in the cloud.

Documentation: Maintain documentation for user guidance, APIs, and system architecture.

User Support: Provide training and support resources for users.

Continuous Improvement: Continuously monitor performance, gather feedback, and iterate for enhancements.

Application development is the linchpin of IoT design, enabling data-driven value delivery and user interaction.

Steps involves in the IoT system design methodology

IoT (Internet of Things) system design is a structured process that involves several steps to create a functional and effective IoT solution. These steps ensure that the IoT system aligns with the desired objectives, meets the needs of stakeholders, and functions reliably. Here are the key steps involved in the IoT system design methodology:

Define Objectives and Requirements:

Identify Stakeholders: Determine who the key stakeholders are, including users, clients, and decision-makers. Understand their needs and expectations.

Set Clear Objectives: Define the specific goals and objectives of the IoT system. Understand what you aim to achieve, whether it's improved efficiency, cost reduction, enhanced user experiences, or other outcomes.

Gather Requirements: Collect and document functional and non-functional requirements, such as data types, communication protocols, scalability, security, and compliance standards.

Conceptual Design:

System Architecture: Develop a high-level architecture for the IoT system. Decide on the overall structure, including components like sensors, actuators, communication protocols, data storage, analytics, and user interfaces.

Data Flow: Create a data flow diagram to illustrate how data will move within the system, from sensors to processing units and user interfaces.

Component Selection and Integration:

Select Hardware: Choose the appropriate IoT devices, sensors, actuators, and edge computing components based on your requirements.

Choose Software Stack: Select the software components, platforms, and frameworks needed for data processing, analytics, and application development.

Integration Planning: Define how different hardware and software components will integrate and communicate within the system.

Network Design:

Connectivity: Determine the communication protocols and network technologies (e.g., Wi-Fi, Bluetooth, cellular, LPWAN) required for IoT device connectivity.

Network Topology: Design the network topology to ensure reliable data transmission, low latency, and scalability.

Data Management and Analytics:

Data Storage: Decide where and how IoT data will be stored, whether it's in the cloud, on-premises, or at the edge. Consider data security and privacy.

Data Processing: Plan data processing pipelines, including real-time and batch processing, to extract insights and actionable information from IoT data.

Analytics and Machine Learning: Determine if and how machine learning and analytics will be applied to the data for decision-making and automation.

Security and Privacy:

Security Measures: Implement security measures such as encryption, authentication, access control, and intrusion detection to protect IoT devices and data.

Privacy Compliance: Ensure compliance with relevant privacy regulations and standards, such as GDPR or HIPAA, and implement mechanisms for user consent and data anonymization.

User Interface and Experience:

Design UI/UX: Create user interfaces (e.g., web applications, mobile apps) that allow users to interact with and control IoT devices. Focus on user experience to make interfaces intuitive and user-friendly.

Testing and Validation:

Test Plan: Develop a comprehensive testing plan that covers functional, performance, security, and usability testing.

Prototyping: Build prototypes or proof-of-concept systems to validate the design and gather feedback from stakeholders.

Deployment:

Pilot Deployment: Launch a pilot deployment of the IoT system in a controlled environment to identify and address any issues before full-scale deployment.

Scaling: Scale up the deployment based on the success of the pilot phase.

Monitoring and Maintenance:

Real-Time Monitoring: Implement continuous monitoring of the IoT system to detect and respond to issues promptly.

Routine Maintenance: Establish regular maintenance procedures for updates, patches, and hardware maintenance.

Feedback and Iteration:

Gather feedback from users and stakeholders to identify areas for improvement and iterate on the IoT system's design and functionality accordingly.

Documentation and Knowledge Transfer:

Create comprehensive documentation, including design documents, user manuals, and operational guidelines, to facilitate knowledge transfer and support.

Business Value Measurement:

Evaluate the return on investment (ROI) and assess the system's impact on business objectives to ensure it aligns with organizational goals.

IoT system design is an iterative process, and adjustments may be necessary as the system evolves and new requirements arise. Collaboration among multidisciplinary teams, including hardware and software engineers, data scientists, security experts, and domain specialists, is essential for a successful IoT system design and implementation.

IoT Communication Models

IoT (Internet of Things) communication models refer to the ways in which devices and components within an IoT ecosystem exchange data and interact with each other. These communication models play a pivotal role in enabling the flow of information, control, and decision-making processes within IoT systems. In the world of IoT, several communication models are commonly used, each tailored to specific requirements and use cases.

Request & Response Model:

In the Request & Response model, communication occurs between a client (requester) and a server (responder).

The client sends a request to the server, specifying the desired action or information.

The server processes the request and sends a response back to the client.

This model is commonly used in IoT applications where real-time interaction between devices and a centralized server is required. For example, a smart thermostat requesting weather updates from an online service.

Publisher-Subscriber Model:

The Publisher-Subscriber (Pub-Sub) model is an asynchronous communication model.

In this model, there are publishers that send messages (topics) and subscribers that express interest in specific topics.

Publishers publish messages to specific topics, and subscribers receive messages from topics they are subscribed to.

Pub-Sub is well-suited for scenarios where many devices need to receive updates or notifications based on specific events. For instance, in a smart city, sensors can publish data, and various applications can subscribe to relevant sensor data.

Push-Pull Model:

The Push-Pull model is a variant of the Pub-Sub model, often used in scenarios where devices need to control data flow actively.

In this model, subscribers can request data (pull) from specific topics, and publishers can actively send data updates (push) to subscribers.

It offers a balance between proactive data dissemination (push) and on-demand data retrieval (pull).

For instance, in an industrial automation system, sensors can push real-time data updates, but control systems can also pull historical data for analysis as needed.

Exclusive Pair:

The Exclusive Pair model involves a one-to-one relationship between two devices or entities.
It represents a direct and exclusive communication link between two entities, ensuring that data is exchanged only between these paired devices.
This model is valuable for secure and private communication between specific IoT devices. For instance, pairing a smartphone with a Bluetooth-enabled door lock for remote access control.
These communication models offer flexibility and versatility in IoT applications, allowing designers and developers to choose the most appropriate model based on the specific requirements of their projects. Whether it's real-time interactions, data distribution, or exclusive one-to-one connections, these models enable effective communication within the IoT ecosystem.

The process model specification step involves in IOT

In the context of IoT system design methodology, the process model specification step involves defining and describing the various processes, workflows, and interactions that occur within the IoT system. This step is essential for understanding how different components of the system will work together to achieve the desired functionality. Let's consider a smart IoT-based home automation system as an example to explain the process model specification step:
Process Model Specification for a Smart IoT-based Home Automation System

Identify System Components: Begin by identifying and listing all the components and devices that will be part of the smart home automation system. This may include sensors (e.g., motion detectors, temperature sensors), actuators (e.g., smart locks, lights, thermostats), a central controller or hub, and user interfaces (e.g., smartphone apps, web interfaces).

Define Use Cases: Identify the primary use cases or scenarios that the system will support. For example, use cases could include "Home Security," "Energy Management," "Lighting Control," and "Climate Control." Each use case represents a specific functionality or task that the system will enable.

Map Interactions: Determine how these system components interact with each other and with external entities, such as users or cloud-based services. For example, when motion is detected by a sensor, it triggers an interaction with the lighting system to turn on the lights.

Sequence Diagrams: Create sequence diagrams for each use case to illustrate the sequence of interactions and messages exchanged between system components. For instance, a sequence diagram for the "Home Security" use case might show how a motion sensor triggers an alert on the user's smartphone via the central controller.

State Diagrams: Use state diagrams to model the various states that system components can be in and the transitions between these states. For example, a state diagram for a smart thermostat might show states like "Heating," "Cooling," and "Idle" and transitions between these states based on temperature readings.

Define Data Flows: Specify the flow of data within the system. Identify what data is generated by sensors, how it is processed by the central controller, and how it is acted upon by actuators. This step is crucial for understanding how sensor data is utilized to make decisions.

Error Handling: Describe how the system handles errors and exceptions. For example, if a sensor malfunctions or loses connectivity, what actions should be taken? Define error messages and recovery procedures.

User Interfaces: If the system has user interfaces (e.g., mobile apps or web interfaces), define the user interaction workflows. How do users interact with the system to set preferences, monitor device status, or receive alerts?

Security Considerations: Integrate security measures into the process model, such as authentication, authorization, and encryption. Specify how sensitive data is protected and how access control is enforced.

Scalability and Performance: Consider scalability and performance requirements. How does the system handle a growing number of devices or users? Are there performance benchmarks or thresholds that need to be met?

Testing and Validation: Outline the testing and validation procedures for the IoT system. Define test cases, scenarios, and performance benchmarks to ensure that the system functions as intended.

Documentation: Document the entire process model specification, including diagrams, descriptions, and any relevant standards or protocols used.

The process model specification step is a crucial part of IoT system design as it provides a clear blueprint of how the IoT ecosystem will operate, how data flows, and how different components interact. This documentation serves as a reference for development, testing, and maintenance phases of the smart IoT-based home automation system.

IoT Communication API's

IoT (Internet of Things) communication APIs come in various types, each designed to address specific communication requirements within the IoT ecosystem. Here are some common types of IoT communication APIs along with explanations for each:

RESTful APIs (Representational State Transfer):

RESTful APIs are based on a set of architectural principles that use HTTP methods (GET, POST, PUT, DELETE) for communication. They are resource-oriented, where resources (e.g., devices, data points) are represented as URLs. Clients interact with these resources using HTTP requests.

Use Cases: RESTful APIs are well-suited for IoT applications involving data retrieval, configuration, and management. They are often used when real-time communication is not critical.

WebSocket APIs:

WebSocket APIs provide full-duplex, bidirectional communication channels over a single, long-lived connection. They are ideal for real-time and low-latency IoT scenarios, allowing devices to send and receive data and commands without the overhead of repeated connections.

Use Cases: WebSocket APIs are commonly used in IoT applications that require instant data updates, real-time control, and push-based communication. Examples include remote monitoring, gaming, and collaboration among IoT devices.

MQTT (Message Queuing Telemetry Transport):

MQTT is a lightweight, publish-subscribe messaging protocol designed for constrained devices and low-bandwidth, high-latency, or unreliable networks. It uses a broker to manage message distribution to subscribers.

Use Cases: MQTT is widely used in IoT for scenarios like sensor data collection, home automation, and industrial applications, where low power consumption and efficient communication are essential.

AMQP (Advanced Message Queuing Protocol):

AMQP is a messaging protocol that supports both message queuing and publish-subscribe models. It provides features like message persistence, reliability, and message routing.

Use Cases: AMQP is used in IoT scenarios where message reliability and queuing are critical, such as logistics, supply chain management, and asset tracking.

CoAP (Constrained Application Protocol):

CoAP is a lightweight, UDP-based protocol designed for constrained IoT devices. It offers a RESTful architecture and supports request-response and publish-subscribe communication patterns.

Use Cases: CoAP is suitable for IoT applications with resource-constrained devices, such as smart agriculture, wearable devices, and industrial IoT.

HTTP/HTTPS APIs:

HTTP and HTTPS APIs are widely used for IoT communication due to their compatibility with existing web infrastructure. They are suitable for various IoT applications, including data exchange, device management, and integration with web services.

Use Cases: HTTP/HTTPS APIs are versatile and can be used in a wide range of IoT applications, from smart home devices to industrial automation.

Graph QL APIs:

Graph QL is a query language for APIs that allows clients to request precisely the data they need. It offers flexibility in data retrieval, reducing over-fetching and under-fetching of data.

Use Cases: Graph QL is useful in IoT applications where devices generate complex data structures, and clients require customized data queries, such as mobile apps interacting with IoT.

WebSocket-based communication APIs

WebSocket-based communication APIs are a set of protocols and technologies that enable real-time, bidirectional communication between clients (typically web browsers) and servers over a single, long-lived connection. Unlike traditional HTTP-based communication, where the client initiates a request and the server responds, WebSocket allows data to be sent and received by both parties at any time, facilitating interactive and dynamic web applications. Here's an explanation of WebSocket-based communication APIs:

WebSocket Protocol: WebSocket is a protocol standardized by the IETF (Internet Engineering Task Force) through RFC 6455. It is designed to provide a full-duplex, low-latency communication channel over a single TCP connection.

Initial Handshake: The communication begins with an initial HTTP handshake between the client and server. The client sends a standard HTTP request to the server.If the server supports WebSocket, it responds with an HTTP 101 status code (Switching Protocols), indicating the switch to the WebSocket protocol.

Establishing a Persistent Connection: Once the handshake is successful, a WebSocket connection is established and remains open as long as both the client and server desire. This persistence eliminates the need for repeated connections, reducing overhead.

Bi-directional Communication: WebSocket enables both the client and server to send data to each other without waiting for a request-response cycle.Data is transmitted in the form of messages, which can be text or binary data. These messages can be sent back and forth between the client and server as needed.

Low Latency and Efficiency: WebSocket is designed for low-latency communication, making it ideal for applications requiring real-time updates, such as chat applications, online gaming, and financial trading platforms.It reduces latency compared to traditional HTTP polling or long polling, where clients repeatedly request updates from the server.

Event-Driven Model: WebSocket-based communication APIs use an event-driven model, where clients and servers can register callback functions or event handlers to process incoming messages or events.This model allows developers to create responsive and interactive web applications.

Security:WebSocket connections are secured through the same mechanisms as HTTPS connections, using TLS/SSL encryption **to protect data in transit.**

Cross-Origin Communication: WebSocket-based communication APIs adhere to the same-origin policy by default, but they can also support cross-origin communication through the use of appropriate headers and security mechanisms.

Closing the Connection: Either the client or server can initiate the closing of a WebSocket connection by sending a close message. Upon receiving the close message, both parties gracefully close the connection.

WebSocket-based communication APIs have become a fundamental technology for building modern web applications that require real-time interactions and live updates. They provide a more efficient and responsive alternative to traditional HTTP-based communication for a wide range of use cases.

The communication functional block in an IoT

The communication functional block in an IoT (Internet of Things) system plays a crucial role in facilitating data exchange between IoT devices, sensors, and the central control or cloud platform. It is responsible for ensuring that data generated by sensors and devices can be transmitted, received, and processed effectively. In a complete IoT system, various components work together to enable seamless communication, data processing, and decision-making. Here's an explanation of the communication functional block and other key components, illustrated with a simple diagram:

Communication Functional Block:

Function: The communication functional block enables devices and sensors in the IoT ecosystem to transmit data to a central control or cloud platform and receive commands or updates from the platform. It handles data exchange using various communication protocols, ensures data security and reliability, and manages device connectivity.

IoT Devices and Sensors:

Function: These are the physical components that collect data from the physical environment. They include sensors (e.g., temperature sensors, motion detectors, GPS modules), actuators (e.g., motors, valves), and edge devices. IoT devices generate data and send it to the communication functional block.

Network Layer:

Function: The network layer is responsible for routing and transporting data between IoT devices and the central control or cloud platform. It ensures data is transmitted securely and efficiently. Components in this layer include routers, gateways, and communication protocols (e.g., MQTT, CoAP, HTTP).

Central Control or Cloud Platform:

Function: This central component of the IoT system receives data from devices, processes it, stores it, and enables decision-making and control. It hosts IoT applications and services, performs analytics, and provides user interfaces for monitoring and managing IoT data and devices.

Data Processing and Analytics:

Function: This component within the central control or cloud platform processes and analyses the data received from IoT devices. It may involve real-time analytics, data storage in databases, machine learning algorithms for insights generation, and the presentation of results.

User Interface and Applications:

Function: The user interface and applications layer provide user-friendly interfaces, dashboards, and applications for end-users and administrators to interact with the IoT system. It allows users to view data, set preferences, and receive alerts or notifications.

Integration Points:

Function: These are interfaces and connectors that enable the IoT system to integrate with external systems, databases, and cloud services. Integration points facilitate data exchange and enhance the functionality of the IoT system.

Four Pillars of IoT

The concept of the "Four Pillars of IoT" highlights the foundational components that constitute the Internet of Things (IoT) ecosystem. These four pillars encompass crucial aspects of IoT technology and its deployment. The four pillars of IoT consist of:

Sensors and Actuators:

Sensors and actuators are at the core of IoT. Sensors are responsible for gathering data from the physical environment, measuring parameters like temperature, humidity, motion, or light. Actuators, on the other hand, take actions based on the data received from sensors. For example, a temperature sensor might collect data, and an actuator could adjust a heating or cooling system based on that data.

Importance: Sensors and actuators are fundamental for enabling IoT devices to interact with and monitor the physical world. They are the basis for data collection and control in IoT applications.

Connectivity:

Connectivity refers to the network infrastructure that facilitates communication between IoT devices, allowing them to communicate with each other and with central systems, typically over the internet. IoT devices can employ various communication technologies such as Wi-Fi, cellular networks, Bluetooth, Zigbee, LoRa, etc., to transmit data to and receive commands from other devices or cloud-based platforms.

Importance: Connectivity serves as the foundation for data exchange between IoT devices, edge devices, and cloud services, enabling remote monitoring, control, and data analysis.

Data Processing and Analytics:

Data processing and analytics encompass activities related to collecting, storing, analysing, and interpreting the extensive data generated by IoT devices. This pillar includes cloud computing, edge computing, and data analytics platforms that process the data and transform it into actionable insights or valuable information.

Importance: Data processing and analytics provide the intelligence behind IoT, allowing organizations to make informed decisions, optimize processes, identify anomalies, and derive valuable insights from the data generated by IoT devices.

User Interface and Applications:

The user interface and applications layer involve components of IoT that interact with end-users, whether individuals or other systems. This encompasses web and mobile applications, dashboards, and user-friendly interfaces that enable users to control IoT devices, monitor data, and make decisions based on the information generated by IoT devices.

Importance: User interfaces and applications bridge the gap between IoT technology and human users, making IoT accessible and user-friendly. They facilitate interactions and decision-making, enabling individuals and organizations to benefit from IoT solutions.

The four pillars of IoT work together to create a comprehensive IoT ecosystem. IoT devices collect data from sensors, transmit data through various connectivity options, process and analyse data at the edge or in the cloud, and present results from user interfaces and applications. This holistic approach to IoT design and implementation supports a variety of applications across industries, including smart cities, industrial automation, healthcare, agriculture, and more, enabling more efficient, convenient, and informed decision-making.

REST

REST (Representational State Transfer) is an architectural style for designing networked applications and services. It was introduced by Roy Fielding in his doctoral dissertation in 2000 and has since become a popular choice for building web services and APIs, including those used in the Internet of Things (IoT). RESTful principles play a significant role in IoT for several reasons:

Simplicity and Scalability: REST emphasizes simplicity in its design, making it easier to implement and scale. In IoT, where there can be a large number of devices with varying capabilities, simplicity is crucial for widespread adoption.

Statelessness: RESTful interactions are stateless, meaning each request from a client to a server must contain all the information needed to understand and process the request. This aligns well with the stateless nature of many IoT devices that may come online and offline frequently.

Resource-Oriented: REST models resources as entities that can be accessed and manipulated using standard HTTP methods like GET, POST, PUT, and DELETE. IoT devices can be represented as resources, and their data and functionality can be exposed through RESTful APIs.

HTTP as the Transport Protocol: REST often uses HTTP as the underlying communication protocol. Since many IoT devices have HTTP capabilities, it's a natural fit for IoT applications. IoT devices can make HTTP requests to send and receive data.

Uniform Interface: REST promotes a uniform and consistent interface for interacting with resources. This uniformity simplifies the development of IoT applications because clients and servers follow the same conventions.
Data Representation: RESTful APIs typically use standard data formats like JSON or XML to represent data. This simplifies data exchange between IoT devices and applications, ensuring interoperability.
Scalability and Caching: REST supports caching mechanisms, which can be beneficial for IoT applications. Caching allows responses to be stored and reused, reducing the load on IoT devices and servers.
HATEOAS (Hypermedia as the Engine of Application State): While not as commonly implemented in IoT as in web applications, HATEOAS can be used to provide discoverability and navigation features in IoT APIs. Devices and applications can follow links provided in responses to discover related resources and actions.

REST Model, Importance of REST and Common REST Methods:

The REST (Representational State Transfer) architectural style is a set of constraints and principles for designing networked applications and web services. It was introduced by Roy Fielding in his doctoral dissertation in 2000. REST is widely used in web development and is the foundation for many modern web APIs, including those used in IoT (Internet of Things). Let's explore the REST model, its importance, and the common REST methods:

REST Model:

The REST model is based on the following key principles and constraints:
Statelessness: Each client request to the server must contain all the information needed to understand and process the request. The server does not store any client state between requests. This simplifies server design and enhances scalability.
Client-Server Architecture: REST separates the client (user interface) and server (data storage and processing) components. This separation enables the client and server to evolve independently, improving scalability and flexibility.
Uniform Interface: REST defines a uniform and consistent way to interact with resources. This constraint is divided into several sub-constraints:
Identification of Resources: Resources are identified by unique URIs (Uniform Resource Identifiers).
Manipulation of Resources Through Representations: Clients interact with resources using representations, such as JSON or XML.
Self-Descriptive Messages: Messages between clients and servers must contain all the information needed to understand the message without relying on server state.
Hypermedia as the Engine of Application State (HATEOAS): Clients navigate the application's state by following links provided in the representations. HATEOAS makes the application more self-explanatory and allows for better decoupling between clients and servers.
Layered System: REST supports a layered system architecture, where each layer (e.g., load balancers, proxies, caches) has a specific role and does not need to know the details of other layers. This separation improves scalability and flexibility.
Cache ability: Responses from the server can be explicitly marked as cacheable or non-cacheable. Caching mechanisms can store and reuse responses to reduce server load and improve performance.

Importance of REST:

The REST architectural style is important for several reasons:
Simplicity: RESTful APIs are simple to understand and use, making them accessible to a wide range of developers and applications.
Scalability: REST's statelessness and layered system support scalability, enabling applications to handle growing numbers of users and requests.
Interoperability: REST is based on standard HTTP methods and data formats (e.g., JSON, XML), ensuring interoperability across diverse platforms and languages.
Flexibility: REST's separation of concerns allows clients and servers to evolve independently, promoting flexibility and adaptability in rapidly changing environments.
Performance: REST's lightweight design and caching mechanisms contribute to improved performance, especially when handling large-scale applications.

Common REST Methods:

REST defines a set of HTTP methods (also known as CRUD operations) to interact with resources. The common REST methods include:
GET: Retrieves data from a resource. It should not have side effects on the resource (read-only).
POST: Creates a new resource or submits data to be processed. It may result in the creation of a new resource.
PUT: Updates an existing resource or creates one if it doesn't exist. It replaces the entire resource with the new data.

DELETE: Removes a resource.

PATCH: Partially updates a resource with new data. It only modifies the specified fields of the resource.

HEAD: Retrieves metadata about a resource without fetching the resource itself. It's useful for checking resource availability.

OPTIONS: Retrieves information about the communication options available for a resource.

These methods provide a standardized way to perform operations on resources, making it easier to design and implement web services and APIs that follow the REST architectural style.

Architectural constraints of REST

REST's role in IoT is to provide a lightweight, scalable, and standardized way to design APIs and services that enable communication and interaction between IoT devices, applications, and cloud services. It simplifies the development process, promotes interoperability, and is well-suited for the diverse and dynamic nature of IoT ecosystems.

The architectural constraints of REST, which stands for Representational State Transfer, are key principles that guide the design of RESTful web services. These constraints were defined by Roy Fielding in his doctoral dissertation in 2000. RESTful systems adhere to these constraints to ensure a scalable, efficient, and maintainable architecture. The primary constraints of REST are:

Client-Server Architecture:

REST separates the client (user interface) and server (data storage and processing) components, allowing them to evolve independently. This separation simplifies scalability, improves flexibility, and enhances the overall system's reliability.

Statelessness:

Each client request to the server must contain all the information needed to understand and process the request. The server should not store any client state between requests. Statelessness simplifies server design, improves scalability, and supports better fault tolerance.

Cache ability:

Responses from the server can be explicitly marked as cacheable or non-cacheable. Caching mechanisms, such as in the client or intermediary proxies, can store and reuse responses to improve performance and reduce the load on the server.

Layered System:

REST supports a layered system architecture, where each layer (e.g., load balancers, gateways, caches) has a specific role and does not need to know the details of other layers. This separation allows for better scalability, flexibility, and ease of maintenance.

Uniform Interface:

The uniform interface constraint defines a consistent and standardized way to interact with resources. It is divided into several sub-constraints:

Identification of Resources: Resources are identified by URIs (Uniform Resource Identifiers).

Manipulation of Resources Through Representations: Clients interact with resources through representations, such as JSON or XML.

Self-Descriptive Messages: Messages sent between clients and servers should contain all the information needed to understand the message without relying on server state.

Hypermedia as the Engine of Application State (HATEOAS): Clients should navigate the application's state by following links provided in the representations. HATEOAS makes the application more self-explanatory and allows for better decoupling between clients and servers.

Code on Demand (Optional):

This constraint is optional, meaning that servers can provide executable code (e.g., JavaScript) to be executed by the client. This feature is rarely used in practice and is typically reserved for specific use cases like web applications.

Adhering to these architectural constraints helps ensure that RESTful systems are scalable, maintainable, and efficient, making them a popular choice for designing web services and APIs.

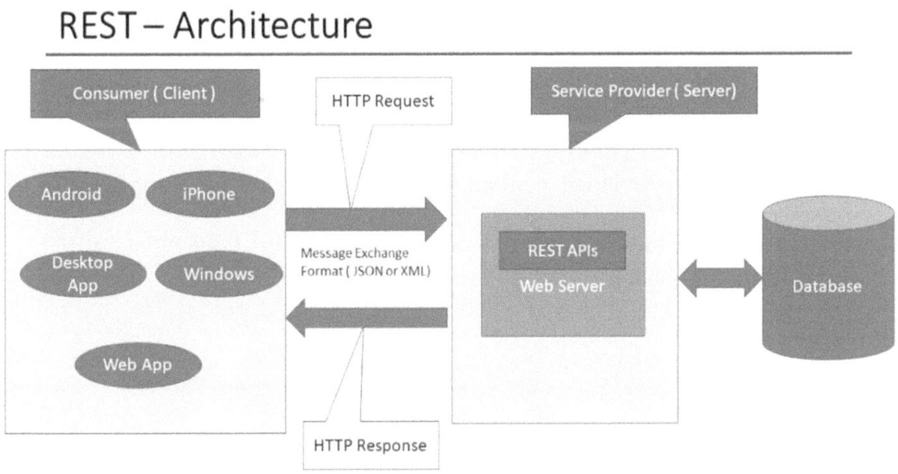

Exercise

Exercise 1 – MCQ

1. Which type of API is commonly used in IoT for real-time and low-latency communication, making it suitable for scenarios like remote control and monitoring of IoT devices?
a) REST-based API
b) WebSocket-based API
c) MQTT-based API
d) CoAP-based API
2. Which of the Four Pillars of IoT involves collecting, storing, analysing, and interpreting the vast amounts of data generated by IoT devices?
a) Sensors and Actuators
b) Connectivity
c) Data Processing and Analytics
d) User Interface and Applications

Exercise 2 – True/False

1. REST-based APIs are ideal for IoT applications that require real-time communication and low-latency data exchange.
2. WebSocket-based APIs establish a persistent connection between clients and servers, making them suitable for applications requiring instant data updates and push-based communication.

Exercise 3 – Fill in the blanks

1. WebSocket-based APIs are commonly used in IoT for _________ and _________ communication, making them suitable for real-time applications.
2. REST-based APIs typically use the __________ protocol for communication, while WebSocket-based APIs provide full-duplex, bidirectional communication channels over a single, long-lived __________.

Exercise 4 – Match case

Match the following terms with their descriptions:
1. WebSocket-based API
2. Data Processing and Analytics
3. REST-based API
4. Sensors and Actuators
Descriptions:
a) Provides full-duplex, bidirectional communication for real-time IoT applications.
b) Involves collecting, storing, analysing, and interpreting IoT data.
c) Uses HTTP for communication and is commonly used for IoT device management.
d) Fundamental components that collect data from the physical

Exercise 5 – One word answer

1. MQTT stands for?
2. CoAP stands for?

Exercise 6 – Small answer

1. What is the primary advantage of using WebSocket-based APIs in IoT communication?
2. Which one of the Four Pillars of IoT involves sensors and actuators?

Exercise 7 – Long answer

1. Explain the role of REST-based APIs in IoT communication, and provide an example of an IoT application where REST APIs are commonly used.
2. Describe the significance of Data Processing and Analytics as one of the Four Pillars of IoT. Provide examples of how data processing and analytics are applied in IoT scenarios.

Answer:

Exercise 1.
1. b) WebSocket-based API
2. c) Data Processing and Analytics

Exercise 2.
1. False
2. True

Exercise 3.
1. real-time and low-latency
2. HTTP (or HTTPS); connection

Exercise 4.
1. WebSocket-based API – a)
2. Data Processing and Analytics – b)
3. REST-based API – c)
4. Sensors and Actuators – d)

Exercise 5.
1. Message Queuing Telemetry Transport
2. Constrained Application Protocol

Previous Year Questions

1. With the help of appropriate diagram explain WebSocket-based communication APIs. (RTU B.Tech. 2017)
2. Draw and explain four pillars of IoT paradigms. (SPPU B.Tech. 2017)
3. Explain purpose and requirements specification step of IoT system design methodology, consider smart IoT-based home automation system as an example. (Mumbai University B.Tech. 2017)
4. Explain information model specification step of IoT system design methodology, consider smart IoT-based home automation system as an example. (SPPU B.Tech. 2018)
5. With the help of diagram list and briefly explain the steps involved in the IoT system design methodology. (SPPU B.Tech. 2018)
6. List various IoT communication models. (Uttar Pradesh university B.Tech. 2021-22)
7. Compare REST-based communication and WebSocket communication API. (SPPU B.Tech. 2019)
8. Explain about IoT Communication APIs in detail. (SPPU B.Tech. 2017)
9. Explain process model specification step of IoT system design methodology, consider smart IoT-based home automation system as an example. (SPPU B.Tech. 2017)
10. Explain the steps involved in the IoT system design methodology. (SPPU B.Tech. 2017)
11. Explain Functional view specification step of IoT system design methodology, consider smart IoT-based home automation system as an example. (SPPU B.Tech. 2018)
12. Explain with example MQTT Protocol. What is role of MQTT protocol in IoT (Uttar Pradesh university B.Tech. 2021-22)
13. What is the function of communication functional block in an IoT system? What are the other components of a complete IoT system? Explain with diagram. (SPPU B.Tech. 2017)
14. Explain in detail steps involved in Prototypedesign of IoT. (Mumbai University B.Tech. 2017)
15. Explain detail design guidelines for Internet of Things. (SPPU 2017)
16. Explain with example MQTT Protocol. What is role of MQTT protocol in IoT (Uttar Pradesh university B.Tech. 2018-19)

17.Explain service specification step of IoT system-design methodology. consider smart IoT based home automation stem as an example. (SPPU B.Tech. 2019)
18. Explain the Operational View Specification step of IoT system design. (SPPU B.Tech. 2019)
19.Explain service specification step of IoT system-design methodology. consider smart IoT based home automation stem as an example. (SPPU B.Tech. 2019)
20.Explain the Operational View Specification step of IoT system design. (SPPU B.Tech. 2019)
21.Justify the three-layer DCM classification is more about the lot value chain than its system architecture at runtime". (SPPU B.Tech. 2019)
22.With the help of diagram list and briefly explain the steps involved in the IoT system design methodology. (SPPU B.Tech. 2019)
23.Explain functional view specification step of IoT system design methodology, consider smart IoT-based home automation system (SPPU B.Tech. 2019)
24.Explain domain model specification step of IoT system design methodology, consider smart lo-based home automation system as an example. (Mumbai University 2017)
25. What is REST model? Why it is important? Explain the REST methods. (RTU B.Tech. 2022)
26. What are the architectural constraints of REST? (RTU B.Tech. 2017)
27. How sensors and actuators work? Explain with practical example. (SPPU B.Tech. 2019)
28. Explain IoT levels and deployment templates. Illustrate the significance of each level. (Anna University MTech 2018)
29. What do u mean by functional model of IoT? (Anna University MTech 2018)

ONLINE RESOURCES

Link : https://forms.gle/5ZGweBZ8d54iYzco8

QR Code :

Link : https://www.youtube.com/playlist?list=PLzlh_31VWEFr1CNkduYvwl1d42Oxq7Z_5

QR Code :

Chapter 5: IoT Protocols

Protocol Standardization for IoT

Standardization in IoT refers to the process of creating and implementing common technical standards, protocols, and guidelines. These standards act as a shared language that enables different IoT devices and systems to communicate and work together smoothly and securely. It is like establishing a universal set of rules that all IoT devices can understand and adhere to, ensuring compatibility and interoperability. Key aspects of IoT standardization include:

Interoperability: Standardization ensures that devices produced by different manufacturers can interact and share data effectively. For instance, a smart thermostat from one company can seamlessly operate with a smart speaker from another.

Security: IoT standards encompass security protocols and best practices to safeguard devices and data from cyber threats. This helps protect user privacy and prevent unauthorized access.

Data Exchange: Standardized data formats facilitate efficient and consistent data sharing between devices and systems, which is vital for IoT applications reliant on data collection and analysis.

Scalability: Standardization allows IoT solutions to expand effortlessly. As more devices and sensors are integrated into a network, they can do so seamlessly without causing compatibility issues.

Sustainability: Standardization defines energy-efficient protocols and practices, aiding in reducing power consumption, a crucial aspect for IoT devices operating on batteries or low-power sources.

Regulatory Compliance: IoT standards often align with legal and regulatory requirements, ensuring that IoT solutions meet industry and governmental standards for safety, privacy, and environmental considerations.

Global Adoption: International standards organizations, such as the ISO (International Organization for Standardization), collaborate with regional bodies to develop global IoT standards. This promotes consistency and facilitates IoT deployments worldwide.

IoT standardization simplifies the development, deployment, and management of IoT solutions. It enhances their reliability, security, and accessibility, benefiting a wide range of industries and applications, including smart homes, smart cities, industrial automation, and healthcare.

M2M and WSN Protocols

IoT protocols are like sets of rules that smart devices and machines use to talk to each other over the internet. Think of them as a common language that these devices understand, allowing them to share information and work together smoothly. These protocols help ensure that your smart thermostat, for example, can send temperature data to your smartphone, or your fitness tracker can share your workout stats with your computer. These rules make sure everything works well and securely in the world of the Internet of Things (IoT).

Machine-to-Machine (M2M) and Wireless Sensor Network (WSN) protocols are essential for enabling communication and data exchange in the fields of IoT (Internet of Things), industrial automation, and environmental monitoring. Let's explore these two types of protocols:

Certainly, here's an explanation of M2M (Machine-to-Machine) and WSN (Wireless Sensor Network) protocols:

Machine-to-Machine (M2M) Protocols:

M2M protocols are essential for enabling automated communication between machines, devices, and systems without the need for human intervention. They play a crucial role in a wide range of industries, including manufacturing, logistics, healthcare, and agriculture. Several key M2M protocols include:

MQTT (Message Queuing Telemetry Transport): MQTT is a lightweight and efficient publish-subscribe messaging protocol commonly used in IoT and M2M applications. It is well-suited for scenarios with low bandwidth, high latency, or unreliable network connections.

CoAP (Constrained Application Protocol): CoAP is specifically designed for resource-constrained IoT and M2M devices. It follows a RESTful architecture, making it easy to integrate with web services. CoAP finds application in areas like smart home automation and sensor networks.

XMPP (Extensible Messaging and Presence Protocol): Initially developed for instant messaging, XMPP has been adapted for M2M communication. It is known for its real-time capabilities and is used in applications such as home automation and energy management.

AMQP (Advanced Message Queuing Protocol): AMQP is a versatile messaging protocol that supports both message queuing and publish-subscribe models. It is widely employed in industrial and enterprise M2M applications, where message reliability and robust queuing are critical.

Wireless Sensor Network (WSN) Protocols:

Wireless Sensor Networks consist of sensor nodes that collect data from the physical environment and communicate wirelessly. These networks find applications in environmental monitoring, smart agriculture, healthcare, and more. Several notable WSN protocols include:

Zigbee:

Zigbee is a low-power, low-data-rate wireless communication protocol designed for WSNs. It is commonly utilized in applications such as home automation, smart lighting, and industrial control systems due to its reliability and energy efficiency.

LoRaWAN (Long Range Wide Area Network):

LoRaWAN is engineered for long-range communication and is well-suited for outdoor WSNs. It is frequently employed in applications like smart cities, agricultural monitoring, and asset tracking.

Bluetooth Low Energy (BLE):

BLE is a low-power wireless communication protocol commonly used in personal area networks and wearable devices. It is suitable for WSNs that require short-range communication.

6LoWPAN (IPv6 over Low-Power Wireless Personal Area Networks):

6LoWPAN serves as an adaptation layer enabling IPv6 communication over low-power wireless networks. It is instrumental in connecting WSNs to the internet, facilitating seamless data integration.

Wifi :

High Data Rates: Wi-Fi provides high data transmission rates, making it ideal for applications that require rapid data transfer, such as real-time monitoring, video surveillance, or large-scale data collection.

Compatibility: Wi-Fi modules can seamlessly integrate with existing Wi-Fi networks and infrastructure. This compatibility facilitates data exchange and management, especially in environments where Wi-Fi connectivity is prevalent.

GPS :

Location Tracking: GPS enables real-time tracking and precise geolocation of sensor nodes, assets, or vehicles within the WSN. This feature is invaluable for applications that require monitoring and tracking across wide areas.

Enhanced Contextual Data: GPS data enhances the contextual information collected by sensors, improving the accuracy and relevance of data analysis and decision-making.

GSM modules:

Wide Coverage: GSM networks offer extensive coverage, making them suitable for remote and wide-area applications where Wi-Fi access is limited. This capability ensures connectivity even in remote or rural regions.

Two-Way Communication: GSM modules support bidirectional communication, enabling not only data transmission from sensor nodes to remote servers but also remote control and command reception. This is valuable for applications requiring real-time response.

In conclusion, M2M and WSN protocols are vital components of IoT and M2M communication, enabling devices and sensors to connect, exchange data, and collaborate efficiently. Protocol selection hinges on factors such as the specific use case, network requirements, and power constraints, ensuring that communication is tailored to the unique demands of each application.

Ipv6

IPv6 (Internet Protocol version 6) is the latest version of the Internet Protocol, designed to replace IPv4 due to the exhaustion of IPv4 addresses. IPv6 introduces several improvements, including a larger address space and a simplified packet format. Below, I'll explain the IPv6 packet format in detail:

The IPv6 packet header consists of two main parts: the fixed header and the optional extension headers. Let's break down each part:

Fixed Header:

The fixed header in an IPv6 packet is 40 bytes in length and contains essential information for routing and delivering the packet. It includes the following fields:

Version (4 bits): Indicates the IP version. For IPv6, this field is set to '0110.'

Traffic Class (8 bits): Used for Quality of Service (QoS) and traffic classification. It allows routers to prioritize or classify packets based on the type of traffic.

Flow Label (20 bits): This field is reserved for future use and is intended to label packets belonging to the same flow **or** traffic stream.

Payload Length (16 bits): Specifies the length of the payload (data) in the packet, excluding the fixed header. This allows routers to determine the length of the packet.

Next Header (8 bits): Indicates the type of the next header in the packet. It points to the first extension header, if present, or the upper-layer protocol (e.g., TCP, UDP) if no extension headers are used.

Hop Limit (8 bits): Similar to IPv4's Time-to-Live (TTL) field, this value decrements by one at each hop in the network. If it reaches zero, the packet is discarded. The Hop Limit prevents packets from circulating endlessly.
Source Address (128 bits): This field contains the IPv6 address of the packet's source.
Destination Address (128 bits): This field contains the IPv6 address of the packet's intended destination.
Extension Headers (Optional):
IPv6 allows for optional extension headers, which can be included after the fixed header to provide additional functionality. Extension headers are used to support features like fragmentation, security, and routing. These headers may appear in a specific order, depending on the packet's requirements. Some common extension headers include:
Hop-by-Hop Options Header: Contains options that must be processed by all routers along the packet's path.
Routing Header: Used for source routing, where the sender specifies the route, the packet should follow.
Fragment Header: Used when a packet needs to be fragmented during transit, as IPv6 generally discourages fragmentation at routers.
Destination Options Header: Contains options that should be processed only by the packet's destination.
Authentication Header (AH): Provides data integrity, authentication, and anti-replay protection for the packet.
Encapsulating Security Payload (ESP) Header: Provides confidentiality, data integrity, and authentication services for the packet's payload.
Destination Options for Mobile IPv6 (Mobility Header): Supports mobile IPv6 features.
Each extension header has its specific format and purpose, and they can be used individually or in combination as needed by the packet's requirements

The Importance of LoWPAN over IPv6 in the IoT

In the rapidly evolving landscape of the Internet of Things (IoT), where billions of devices are interconnected to collect and exchange data, the choice of networking protocols becomes critical. One such protocol that plays a pivotal role in the IoT ecosystem is LoWPAN (Low-Power Wireless Personal Area Network) over IPv6 (Internet Protocol version 6). In this note, we will explore the significance of LoWPAN over IPv6 in the IoT context.
Scalability: IPv6 offers a vast address space, with 2^128 unique addresses, ensuring that every IoT device can have a unique IP address. This scalability is essential as the number of IoT devices continues to grow exponentially. LoWPAN over IPv6 allows IoT networks to accommodate this expansion seamlessly.
Low Power Consumption: IoT devices are often battery-powered and require energy-efficient communication protocols. LoWPAN, as the name suggests, is designed for low-power applications. When combined with IPv6, it allows devices to remain in low-power sleep modes while still being reachable when needed. This significantly extends the battery life of IoT devices.
Global Interoperability: IPv6 is a globally recognized standard, and its adoption ensures that IoT devices can communicate across different networks and regions without the need for complex translation mechanisms. This global interoperability simplifies IoT deployments on a larger scale.
Security: Security is a top concern in IoT, given the potential vulnerabilities of interconnected devices. IPv6 provides improved security features over its predecessor, IPv4. With LoWPAN over IPv6, IoT networks can take advantage of these security enhancements, making it more challenging for malicious actors to compromise IoT devices.
Quality of Service (QoS): Many IoT applications, such as industrial automation and healthcare monitoring, require low-latency and reliable communication. LoWPAN over IPv6 supports Quality of Service mechanisms, allowing for prioritization of traffic and ensuring that critical data is delivered with minimal delay.
Standardization and Support: LoWPAN over IPv6 is backed by industry standards and has gained wide support from IoT device manufacturers and network infrastructure providers. This ensures that IoT solutions built on this protocol stack are robust, reliable, and future-proof.
IPv6-Enabled IoT Ecosystem: As the world transitions from IPv4 to IPv6 due to the exhaustion of IPv4 addresses, IoT networks that use IPv6 are well-prepared for the future. By adopting LoWPAN over IPv6, organizations can align their IoT deployments with the broader technological trends and standards.
In conclusion, LoWPAN over IPv6 is a crucial networking protocol in the IoT context. It addresses the unique requirements of IoT, such as low power consumption, scalability, security, and global interoperability. By leveraging the advantages of IPv6, IoT ecosystems can ensure long-term sustainability and readiness for the evolving landscape of interconnected devices. As the IoT continues to reshape industries and daily life, the importance of protocols like LoWPAN over IPv6 cannot be overstated.

Three-layer architecture of a Wireless Sensor Node (WSN)

The three-layer architecture of a Wireless Sensor Node (WSN) consists of three main layers: the Sensing Layer, the Processing Layer, and the Communication Layer. Each layer has specific functions in collecting and transmitting data from the sensor node. Additionally, I'll list some common security attacks in WSN.

Three-Layer Architecture of Wireless Sensor Node:

Sensing Layer: This layer is responsible for capturing data from physical phenomena using various sensors (e.g., temperature, humidity, light, motion).

Functions:

Data collection from physical environment.

Analog-to-digital conversion (if sensors provide analog data).

Preprocessing and filtering of raw sensor data.

Event detection and data aggregation.

Processing Layer: The processing layer receives the pre-processed data from the sensing layer and performs computations or data analysis tasks.

Functions:

Data analysis, including statistical analysis or pattern recognition.

Computation of sensor node's operating parameters.

Execution of algorithms for event detection or localization.

Decision-making based on sensor data.

Communication Layer: The communication layer is responsible for transmitting the processed data or events to other sensor nodes or a central base station.

Functions:

Data routing and forwarding to the destination.

Establishing communication links with neighbouring nodes.

Data compression to reduce transmission overhead.

Handling communication protocols and addressing.

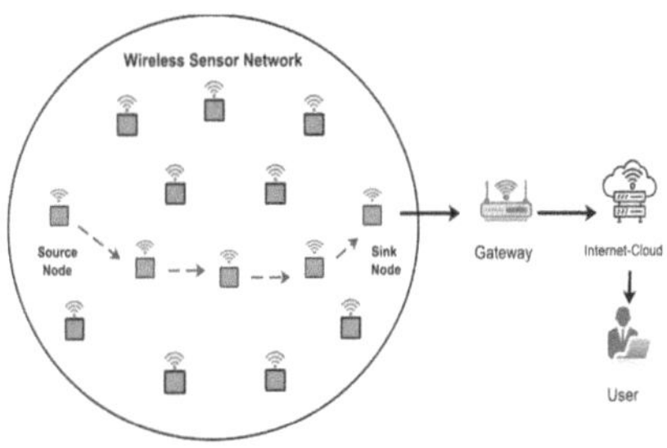

Common Security Attacks in Wireless Sensor Networks

Eavesdropping (Passive Attack): Attackers intercept and listen to communication between sensor nodes, potentially obtaining sensitive information.

Tampering (Active Attack): Attackers physically tamper with sensor nodes to disrupt their operation or modify data.

Replay Attack: Attackers capture and replay previously transmitted messages to deceive sensor nodes or the network.

Selective Forwarding (Black Hole Attack): Malicious nodes selectively drop or forward packets, causing network routing problems and data loss.

Sybil Attack: An attacker impersonates multiple fake nodes to disrupt communication or manipulate data.

Sinkhole Attack: Malicious nodesattract data packets toward themselves, diverting them away from their intended destination.

Wormhole Attack: Attackers create a tunnel between two distant points in the network, allowing them to forward packets through the tunnel, potentially bypassing security measures.

Denial of Service (DoS) Attack: Attackers flood the network with excessive traffic or malicious packets to overwhelm sensor nodes and disrupt normal operation.

Node Reprogramming or Code Injection: Attackers inject malicious code into sensor nodes to compromise their functionality or steal data.

Battery Drain Attack: Attackers force sensor nodes to consume excessive energy, depleting their battery life and rendering them non-operational.

Spoofing or Identity Impersonation: Attackers impersonate legitimate nodes or base stations, leading to unauthorized access or data manipulation.

Hello Flood Attack: Attackers flood the network with fake "hello" messages to disrupt routing and communication.

To secure WSNs, various security mechanisms, such as encryption, authentication, intrusion detection, and secure routing protocols, are employed to mitigate these attacks and protect the integrity, confidentiality, and availability of data in sensor networks.

RFID Protocol

RFID, which stands for Radio-Frequency Identification, is like a special communication system that helps objects talk to machines without any wires. It's a bit like a magic tag that can share information when it's near a special device.

Here's how it works: Objects, like products in a store or library books, have tiny RFID tags on them. These tags have a unique ID, like a name, that machines can read. When you bring an object close to an RFID reader (a special machine), it sends out a signal. The tag on the object receives this signal and sends back its unique ID. The reader then understands which object it is.

Think of it like a library where each book has a special label. When you walk out with a book, the library gate knows which book you took because of the label. RFID tags work in a similar way, helping machines identify and track objects quickly and accurately.

Usage: RFID is used in many places, like stores for tracking products, in transportation for managing goods, and even in passports for security. It's like a secret language between things and machines, making our world smarter and more efficient.

Here are some key concepts and terminology related to RFID applications:

RFID Tag: An RFID tag, also known as a transponder or label, is a small device that contains a unique identification code or data. Tags come in various forms, including passive, active, and semi-passive (battery-assisted) types.

RFID Reader: An RFID reader, also known as an interrogator, is a device that emits radio waves to communicate with RFID tags. Readers can read data from tags and, in some cases, write data to tags. They come in fixed, handheld, or mobile forms.

Antenna: The antenna is an integral part of both RFID tags and readers. It helps transmit and receive radio waves for communication. The size and design of the antenna impact the RFID system's performance.

Frequency Bands:RFID operates in various frequency bands, including Low Frequency (LF), High Frequency (HF), Ultra High Frequency (UHF), and Microwave. Each frequency band has its advantages and is suitable for different applications.

Passive RFID: Passive RFID tags do not have a built-in power source (battery) and rely on the energy transmitted by the RFID reader to operate. They are cost-effective and commonly used for tracking inventory, access control, and supply chain management.

Active RFID: Active RFID tags have their own power source (typically a battery) and can transmit data over longer distances compared to passive tags. They are often used for tracking high-value assets and monitoring the movement of objects over a wide area.

Semi-Passive (Battery-Assisted) RFID: Semi-passive RFID tags have a small battery that powers certain functions, such as the tag's sensor or memory. They strike a balance between the capabilities of passive and active tags.

Read Range: Read range refers to the distance at which an RFID reader can communicate with an RFID tag. The read range varies depending on factors like frequency, antenna design, and power output.

EPC (Electronic Product Code): EPC is a unique identifier used in RFID systems to distinguish individual items or products. It is often used in supply chain management for tracking goods throughout their journey.

RFID Middleware: RFID middleware is software that sits between RFID readers and enterprise systems. It helps manage RFID data, filter and aggregate information, and integrate it with existing business applications.

RFID Portal: An RFID portal is an entrance or gateway equipped with RFID readers and antennas. It is used for tracking and monitoring items as they pass through the portal, such as in retail stores or warehouses.

Inventory Management: RFID is commonly used for real-time inventory management in retail, warehouses, and manufacturing. It provides accurate and efficient tracking of items, reducing stockouts and overstock situations.

Access Control: RFID access control systems are used to grant or restrict access to secure areas. Employees or individuals can use RFID cards or badges to gain entry.

Asset Tracking:RFID is used for tracking and managing high-value assets in industries like healthcare, aviation, and construction. It ensures assets are accounted for, reduces loss, and streamlines maintenance.

Supply Chain Management: RFID plays a crucial role in supply chain visibility, enabling organizations to track shipments, monitor goods in transit, and improve logistics efficiency.

NFC (Near-Field Communication):NFC is a subset of RFID that operates in the HF band and is used for short-range communication, often between a smartphone and an NFC tag. It is used in contactless payments, ticketing, and smart device pairing.

These concepts and terminology provide a foundational understanding of how RFID technology is applied in various industries and applications for tracking, identification, and data exchange.

Technological issues in RFID IoT system design?

Designing an RFID (Radio-Frequency Identification) IoT system involves addressing various technological challenges to ensure its effectiveness, reliability, and security. Here are some key technological issues in RFID IoT system design:

Interference and Collision: In densely populated RFID environments, multiple RFID tags may transmit simultaneously, causing signal collisions and interference. Collision resolution techniques, anti-collision algorithms, and proper tag placement are essential to mitigate these issues.

Range and Readability: RFID tags have limited read ranges, which can be affected by factors like tag type, frequency, and interference. Designing the system to ensure consistent and reliable tag readability is a challenge, especially in dynamic environments.

Power Management: Many RFID tags are passive and rely on energy harvested from RFID readers' signals. Efficient power management techniques are needed to ensure tags remain operational for extended periods without battery replacements.

Security and Privacy: RFID systems are susceptible to security and privacy breaches. Unauthorized tag cloning, eavesdropping, and data manipulation are concerns. Implementing strong encryption, authentication, and access control mechanisms is vital to protect data and ensure privacy.

Data Integrity and Accuracy: Ensuring data accuracy and integrity during tag reading and data transmission is essential. Error correction codes, checksums, and data validation processes must be implemented to maintain data reliability.

Scalability: RFID IoT systems often need to scale to accommodate a growing number of tags and devices. Designing scalable architectures, databases, and communication protocols is necessary to handle large-scale deployments effectively.

Integration with IoT Platform: Integrating RFID data seamlessly with IoT platforms, analytics systems, and enterprise applications can be complex. Compatibility issues and data format conversions must be addressed for effective integration.

Real-Time Processing: Many IoT applications require real-time or near-real-time data processing. Designing the system to handle real-time data streams from RFID tags while maintaining low latency is a challenge.

Localization and Positioning: Determining the precise location of RFID-tagged assets can be challenging. Solutions like RFID-based triangulation or integrating RFID with other positioning technologies (e.g., GPS) may be necessary for accurate asset tracking.

Environmental Factors: RFID tags may be exposed to various environmental conditions, such as temperature extremes, moisture, and physical stress. Selecting durable tags and protective enclosures is critical for maintaining tag functionality.

Standards and Protocols: RFID operates under various standards and protocols, depending on the frequency band and application. Ensuring compatibility and compliance with industry standards is essential for interoperability and system performance.

Cost Management: Balancing the cost of RFID tags, readers, infrastructure, and software with the benefits gained from the IoT system is a significant challenge. Cost-effective RFID solutions must be designed to meet specific use cases.

Firmware and Software Updates: Managing firmware and software updates for RFID readers and tags across a large-scale deployment can be complex. Effective update mechanisms and version control are necessary to ensure system reliability.

Addressing these technological challenges requires a thorough understanding of RFID and IoT technologies, careful system design, and ongoing maintenance and optimization to keep the RFID IoT system efficient and secure.

IEEE 802.15.4 protocol

IEEE 802.15.4 is a standard that defines the physical (PHY) and media access control (MAC) layers for low-rate wireless personal area networks (LR-WPANs). This standard specifies the characteristics of the physical layer (e.g., frequency bands, modulation) and the data link layer (e.g., frame format, channel access mechanisms) for low-power, low-data-rate wireless communication. IEEE 802.15.4 is often associated with the development of wireless sensor networks (WSNs) and is a fundamental technology in the context of IoT (Internet of Things).

Here's how IEEE 802.15.4 is related to IoT:

Low-Power and Low-Data-Rate:IEEE 802.15.4 is designed to operate in environments where devices are power-constrained and transmit small amounts of data infrequently. This makes it well-suited for IoT devices that need to operate on battery power for extended periods.

Wireless Sensor Networks: Many IoT applications involve sensors and actuators distributed in an environment. IEEE 802.15.4 provides a foundation for creating wireless sensor networks by defining the communication protocols needed for these devices to communicate with each other and with a central controller or gateway.

Mesh Networking: IEEE 802.15.4 supports mesh networking, which is important for IoT deployments. In a mesh network, devices can relay data for each other, extending the network's coverage and improving reliability. This is particularly valuable in large-scale IoT deployments.

Multi-Channel Support: The standard allows devices to operate in different frequency bands, which helps in reducing interference and improving network robustness. This is essential for IoT applications where many devices might coexist in the same area.

Low Latency: While IEEE 802.15.4 is designed for low-power operation, it still provides relatively low-latency communication. This is important for applications where devices need to respond quickly to events, such as industrial automation and home automation.

Interoperability: IEEE 802.15.4 is an open standard, meaningthat devices from different manufacturers can be designed to adhere to the same communication protocols. This promotes interoperability in the IoT ecosystem, allowing devices from various vendors to work together seamlessly.

Security: The standard includes security features such as encryption and authentication, which are crucial for IoT devices that transmit sensitive data.

In summary, IEEE 802.15.4 is a key enabling technology for IoT because it provides a standardized, efficient, and low-power way for devices to communicate wirelessly. It addresses the specific requirements and constraints of IoT applications, making it a foundational protocol for building IoT networks and systems.

Topology model of IEEE 802.15.4 and PAN Coordinator.

IEEE 802.15.4 is a standard for low-rate wireless personal area networks (LR-WPANs), providing a framework for communication between low-power devices in a relatively small area. Within the IEEE 802.15.4 standard, different network topologies can be implemented to facilitate communication between devices. Two common topology models within IEEE 802.15.4 are the star topology and the peer-to-peer (P2P) topology. Additionally, the concept of a PAN (Personal Area Network) Coordinator plays a significant role in managing these topologies.

Star Topology: In a star topology model, devices communicate directly with a central PAN Coordinator, which serves as a hub. Each device in the network communicates exclusively with the PAN Coordinator, making it a simple and easy-to-manage arrangement. The PAN Coordinator controls the communication within the network, ensuring that devices take turns transmitting data to avoid collisions.

Advantages of the star topology:

Simplicity: Easy to set up and manage.

Centralized control: PAN Coordinator manages the network efficiently.

Low latency: Devices have a direct route to the PAN Coordinator.

Disadvantages:

Single point of failure: If the PAN Coordinator fails, the entire network may become inoperative.

Limited scalability: The number of devices that can be supported is limited by the PAN Coordinator's capacity.

Peer-to-Peer (P2P) Topology:

In a P2P topology, devices can communicate directly with one another without relying on a central hub like the PAN Coordinator. Each device in the network can act as both a sender and a receiver, allowing for more complex communication patterns. P2P networks are more robust in the sense that if one device fails, other devices can still communicate.

Advantages of the P2P topology:

Redundancy: Devices can communicate even if some devices fail.

Scalability: Can support a larger number of devices compared to the star topology.

Flexible communication patterns: Devices can communicate directly with each other in various ways.
Disadvantages:
More complex management: P2P networks may require more advanced protocols for device discovery and routing.
Potential for increased latency: Depending on the network size and routing complexity, latency may increase.
PAN Coordinator: The PAN Coordinator is a central device responsible for managing and coordinating activitieswithin an IEEE 802.15.4 network. Its primary roles include:
Network initialization: The PAN Coordinator initializes the network and assigns addresses to devices.
Beacon management: It broadcasts periodic beacons that allow devices to synchronize their communication.
Device association: The PAN Coordinator manages the association and disassociation of devices in the network.
Data routing: In P2P networks, the PAN Coordinator may assist in routing data between devices.
In a star topology, the PAN Coordinator is typically the central hub through which all communication flows. In a P2P topology, the PAN Coordinator still plays a crucial role in network management but may have a less centralized role compared to the star topology.
Overall, IEEE 802.15.4 provides flexibility in choosing the appropriate network topology model (star or P2P) based on the specific requirements of an application. The PAN Coordinator is a key element in managing and ensuring the efficient operation of these topologies within an LR-WPAN.

Layers of IoT Protocol

The term "IoT protocol" is quite broad, as there are numerous protocols used in the Internet of Things (IoT) ecosystem, each serving specific purposes and functions. These protocols can be organized into different layers, similar to the OSI (Open Systems Interconnection) model or the TCP/IP model. Here's a simplified representation of the layers commonly associated with IoT protocols:
Application Layer:
MQTT (Message Queuing Telemetry Transport)
CoAP (Constrained Application Protocol)
HTTP/HTTPS (Hypertext Transfer Protocol)
AMQP (Advanced Message Queuing Protocol)
WebSocket
OPC UA (Open Platform Communications Unified Architecture)
Transport Layer:
TCP (Transmission Control Protocol)
UDP (User Datagram Protocol)
DTLS (Datagram Transport Layer Security)
SCTP (Stream Control Transmission Protocol)
Network Layer:
IPv4 (Internet Protocol version 4)
IPv6 (Internet Protocol version 6)
6LoWPAN (IPv6 over Low-Power Wireless Personal Area Networks)
RPL (Routing Protocol for Low-Power and Lossy Networks)
Link Layer:
Wi-Fi (IEEE 802.11)
Bluetooth (Bluetooth Low Energy, BLE)
Zigbee (IEEE 802.15.4)
LoRa (Long Range)
Cellular (e.g., LTE-M, NB-IoT)
Ethernet
NFC (Near Field Communication)
Physical Layer:
Defines the hardware characteristics such as radio frequencies, modulation, and physical connectors used for communication.
It's important to note that IoT is a highly diverse and evolving field, and the choice of protocols depends on factors like device constraints, network requirements, and application needs. Different IoT ecosystems and use cases may employ various combinations of these protocols at different layers to meet their specific requirements.

Modbus Protocol

Modbus is a widely used communication protocol in industrial automation and control systems. It was developed in the late 1970s and has since become a standard for connecting and communicating between devices in various industries. Modbus is simple, robust, and easy to implement, making it a popular choice for industrial applications. Here are some key aspects of the Modbus protocol:

Communication Model: Modbus uses a client-server or master-slave communication model, where one device (the master or client) initiates requests, and one or more devices (the slaves or servers) respond to those requests.

Data Representation: Modbus uses a binary encoding scheme for data representation. It supports two data formats: RTU (RemoteTerminal Unit) and ASCII. RTU is the most commonly used format due to its efficiency and simplicity.

Data Types: Modbus supports various data types, including bits, integers (16-bit and 32-bit), floating-point numbers, and more. These data types are used to represent different types of data such as digital inputs, Analog values, and control commands.

Addressing: In Modbus, each device or register is assigned a unique address. Registers can be discrete (for binary values) or holding (for Analog or control values). Addresses typically range from 0 to 65,535.

Function Codes: Modbus defines a set of function codes that specify the type of action to be performed. For example, Function Code 3 is used to read multiple holding registers, while Function Code 16 is used to write multiple holding registers.

Supported Communication Types: Modbus can be implemented over various physical communication layers, including RS-232, RS-485, TCP/IP (Modbus TCP), and Ethernet (Modbus RTU over TCP). Modbus TCP is commonly used for Ethernet-based communication.

Request-Response: When a master device sends a request to a slave device, it includes the function code, data address, and additional information as needed. The slave device processes the request and responds with the requested data or an acknowledgment.

Error Handling: Modbus includes error-checking mechanisms to ensure data integrity. CRC (Cyclic Redundancy Check) is commonly used for error detection.

Use Cases: Modbus is extensively used in various industrial applications, including process control, manufacturing automation, building automation, and energy management systems.

Modbus Variants: Modbus has several variants, including Modbus RTU, Modbus ASCII, and Modbus TCP. Each variant is suited for different communication environments and requirements.

Limitations: While Modbus is widely adopted, it has some limitations, such as limited security features and lack of built-in support for more advanced data types. In critical applications, additional security measures may be required.

Modbus is known for its simplicity and reliability, which has contributed to its continued use in industrial automation and control systems. However, it's important to note that in modern industrial environments, where cybersecurity is a concern, additional security measures may need to be implemented to protect Modbus-based systems from unauthorized access and attacks.

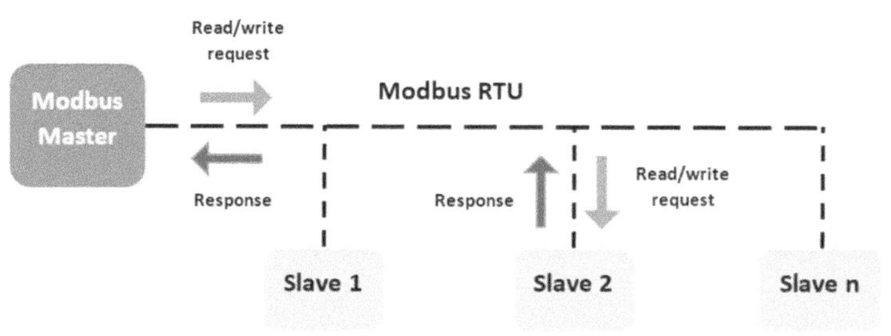

Issues in standardization

Standardization in the Internet of Things (IoT) is essential for ensuring interoperability, security, and scalability across IoT devices and systems. However, several challenges and issues are associated with IoT standardization:

Fragmentation of Standards: One of the most significant issues in IoT standardization is the proliferation of multiple, competing standards. Different industries, regions, and organizations may develop their own standards, leading to fragmentation. This makes it difficult to achieve universal compatibility and can hinder IoT adoption.

Lack of Global Consensus: Achieving global consensus on IoT standards is challenging due to diverse interests, regulations, and economic factors. Standards developed in one region or industry may not align with those in another, creating compatibility issues.

Rapid Technological Evolution: IoT technologies are rapidly evolving, and new innovations frequently emerge. This pace of change can make it difficult for standards bodies to keep up and may lead to outdated standards that do not address current IoT requirements.

Security Concerns: IoT devices are susceptible to security threats, including hacking and data breaches. Standardizing robust security measures is crucial, but achieving consensus on security standards can be complex due to varying security needs across industries.

Privacy and Data Protection: IoT devices collect and transmit vast amounts of data, raising concerns about user privacy and data protection. Ensuring that IoT standards address these concerns while allowing for innovation is challenging.

Resource Constraints: Many IoT devices operate with limited resources, including processing power, memory, and energy. Standardization efforts need to consider resource-constrained devices to ensure that standards are practical for implementation.

Interoperability Challenges: Ensuring interoperability among diverse IoT devices and platforms is a primary goal of standardization. However, achieving seamless interoperability across different devices, communication protocols, and ecosystems is a complex task.

Regulatory Compliance: IoT standards must align with regional and industry-specific regulations and compliance requirements. This adds complexity and can lead to variations in standards based on geographic location.

Cross-Domain Integration: IoT often spans multiple domains and industries, such as healthcare, transportation, and agriculture. Integrating standards across these domains to create comprehensive IoT solutions can be challenging.

Patent and Licensing Issues: IoT standards may incorporate patented technologies, leading to potential licensing disputes and royalty fees. Resolving intellectual property issues is essential for widespread adoption.

Legacy System Compatibility: Many IoT implementations involve the integration of IoT technologies with existing legacy systems. Ensuring that standards accommodate legacy systems can be complex and costly.

Standards Development Process: The process of developing IoT standards can be slow and bureaucratic, causing delays in the adoption of new technologies. Agile approaches are needed to keep pace with IoT advancements.

To address these issues, industry stakeholders, standards organizations, and governments must collaborate to develop and harmonize IoT standards. Additionally, ongoing efforts to update and refine standards as IoT technology evolves are essential for ensuring the long-term success of IoT implementations.

CoAP

CoAP, or Constrained Application Protocol, is a lightweight and efficient protocol designed for constrained devices and low-power, low-bandwidth networks, such as IoT (Internet of Things) devices. CoAP is designed to provide a simple and efficient way for devices to communicate over the Internet. CoAP messaging format is structured to be resource-oriented, similar to HTTP, but it is more suitable for constrained environments. Here's an explanation of the CoAP messaging format:

CoAP Header: The CoAP message begins with a fixed-size header, which is 4 bytes in length:

Version (2 bits): Indicates the CoAP version, which is typically set to 1 for CoAP version 1.

Type (2 bits): Specifies the message type, which can be one of the following:

`0`: Confirmable (CON)

`1`: Non-confirmable (NON)

`2`: Acknowledgment (ACK)

3`: Reset (RST)

Token Length (4 bits): Indicates the length of the variable-length Token field that follows the header. The Token is used to correlate requests and responses.

Code (8 bits): Specifies the CoAP method or response code. For requests, this field indicates the method (GET, POST, PUT, DELETE, etc.). For responses, it indicates the result of the request (e.g., 2.01 for Created).

Message ID (16 bits): A unique identifier for the message. Used to match requests and responses.

Token:

The Token field is of variable length (0-8 bytes) and is used to correlate requests and responses. It is typically used for confirmable (CON) messages and can be omitted in non-confirmable (NON) messages.

Options:

CoAP messages can include a list of options that provide additional information about the request or response. Options are variable in length and can include information such as URI paths, content type, observe, and more. Each option is encoded using a variable-length format, with a delta and length field to specify the option type and length. Some common CoAP options include:

URI Path: Specifies the path of the resource being accessed.

Content Type: Indicates the format of the message payload.

Max-Age: Specifies the maximum time in seconds for which the response is considered fresh.

Observe: Used for observing resources and receiving notifications when they change.

Payload:

The payload is optional and carries the application data. It can be empty or contain the data associated with the request or response. The length of the payload is determined by the message's Content-Length option.

Here's a simplified visual representation of a CoAP message:

```
+----------------------------------------------+
| CoAP Header (4 bytes)                        |
+----------------------------------------------+
| Token (variable length)                      |
+----------------------------------------------+
| Options (variable length)                    |
+----------------------------------------------+
| Payload (optional, variable length)          |
+----------------------------------------------+
```

CoAP is designed to be efficient and flexible, making it suitable for resource-constrained devices and constrained network environments. It borrows many concepts from HTTP but simplifies them to meet the needs of IoT and similar applications.

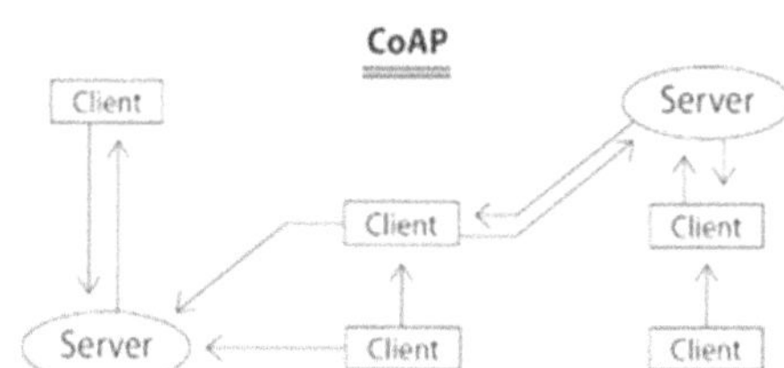

Piggyback and Separate responses in context with CoAP

In the context of CoAP (Constrained Application Protocol), piggybacking and separate responses are two different approaches for handling responses to client requests. These approaches are used to optimize communication between CoAP clients and servers, especially in scenarios where low overhead and efficiency are critical.

Piggybacked Responses:

Definition: Piggybacked responses involve the server including its response within an acknowledgment message (ACK) to the client. In other words, the server sends both the acknowledgment for the client's request and the response to that request in a single message.

Advantages:

Reduced Latency: Piggybacking reduces the round-trip time (RTT) for communication because the client doesn't need to wait for a separate response message.

Efficient Use of Resources: It minimizes the use of network resources and reduces the overall message count in the network.

Use Case Example:

Imagine a CoAP client sending a request to turn on a smart light bulb. The server receives the request, processes it, and immediately responds with an ACK that acknowledges the receipt of the request and includes the response status (e.g., "Success" or "Failure") in the ACK message. The client can quickly confirm the request's status without waiting for a separate response.

Separate Responses:

Definition: Separate responses, as the name suggests, involve the server acknowledging the receipt of the client's request with an empty acknowledgment message (ACK) and then sending the actual response in a separate CoAP message.

Advantages:

Flexibility: Separate responses allow the server to take more time to process the request and send a response when ready. This can be useful for handling complex requests or when responses are not readily available.

Non-blocking: Clients can continue to send other requests or perform other tasks while waiting for the separate response.

Use Case Example:

Consider a CoAP client requesting data from a remote weather sensor. The server may need some time to collect and process the data. In this case, the server sends an ACK to acknowledge the request's receipt and inform the client that it is processing the request. Once the data is ready, the server sends a separate response containing the weather data to the client.

Choosing Between Piggybacked and Separate Responses:

The choice between piggybacked and separate responses depends on the specific requirements of the CoAP application. Piggybacked responses are ideal for scenarios where low latency and efficient use of resources are critical, while separate responses offer flexibility when processing time varies or when clients need to remain non-blocking.

CoAP's design allows for both approaches, enabling developers to optimize communication based on the unique characteristics and needs of their IoT applications

Application Protocols for IoT- The Transport Layer

Application protocols at the transport layer play a crucial role in facilitating communication and data exchange between IoT devices and the network. These protocols define how data is transmitted, acknowledged, and managed in IoT systems. Here are some commonly used transport layer protocols for IoT:

TCP (Transmission Control Protocol):

Purpose: TCP is a connection-oriented transport protocol that provides reliable, error-checked, and ordered data transmission. It's widely used in IoT applications where data integrity and guaranteed delivery are critical.

Features: TCP establishes a connection between sender and receiver, handles congestion control, and ensures that data packets are delivered in the correct order. It's suitable for applications like remote monitoring, command and control, and firmware updates.

UDP (User Datagram Protocol):

Purpose: UDP is a connectionless transport protocol that offers lightweight, low-overhead communication. It's commonly used in IoT applications where real-time data transmission and low latency are more important than guaranteed delivery.

Features: UDP does not establish a connection and does not guarantee data delivery or packet order. It's suitable for applications like live video streaming, sensor data transmission, and voice over IP (VoIP) in IoT.

DTLS (Datagram Transport Layer Security):

Purpose: DTLS is a secure variant of UDP. It provides encryption and data integrity features, making it suitable for securing communications in IoT applications.

Features: DTLS adds security to UDP by enabling encryption and authentication. It's commonly used in IoT scenarios where data privacy and security are paramount, such as healthcare or industrial control systems.

MQTT-SN (MQTT for Sensor Networks):

Purpose: MQTT-SN is an adaptation of the MQTT protocol designed for constrained IoT devices and unreliable networks. It's suitable for low-power, low-bandwidth IoT applications.

Features: MQTT-SN retains the publish-subscribe messaging model of MQTT but is optimized for devices with limited resources. It's often used in applications like sensor data collection and monitoring.

HTTP/HTTPS:

Purpose: While not typically considered transport layer protocols, HTTP (Hypertext Transfer Protocol) and its secure version, HTTPS, are commonly used for IoT applications requiring web-based communication.

Features: HTTP/HTTPS enable RESTful interactions, making it easy to integrate IoT devices with web services and cloud platforms. They are used for device management, data retrieval, and web-based control interfaces in IoT.

WebSocket:

Purpose: WebSocket provide full-duplex, bidirectional communication over a single, long-lived connection. They are used for real-time, interactive IoT applications.

Features: WebSocket offer low-latency, real-time data exchange and are suitable for applications like remote control, monitoring, and live dashboards in IoT systems.

The choice of transport layer protocol in IoT depends on factors such as the nature of the IoT devices, communication requirements (e.g., reliability, latency, and security), and the specific use case. IoT systems often use a combination of these protocols to address various communication needs within the same network.

IoT Application Transport Methods

IoT application transport methods refer to the mechanisms and protocols used to facilitate data transfer and communication within Internet of Things (IoT) systems. These methods are essential for transmitting data generated by IoT devices to cloud platforms, servers, or other devices for processing, storage, and analysis. Here are some common IoT application transport methods:

HTTP/HTTPS (Hypertext Transfer Protocol/Secure Hypertext Transfer Protocol):

Purpose: HTTP and its secure variant, HTTPS, are widely used for IoT data transport, especially when interacting with web-based applications and services.

Features: HTTP/HTTPS enables communication using standard web protocols, making it easy to integrate IoT devices with web servers and cloud platforms. IoT devices can send data via HTTP POST requests, and HTTPS adds a layer of security through data encryption.

MQTT (Message Queuing Telemetry Transport):

Purpose: MQTT is a lightweight publish-subscribe messaging protocol designed for efficient and real-time data exchange in IoT applications.

Features: MQTT follows a publish-subscribe model, allowing IoT devices to publish data to specific topics, and other devices or services can subscribe to those topics to receive data updates. It's suitable for scenarios where low bandwidth and low power consumption are important.

CoAP (Constrained Application Protocol):

Purpose: CoAP is a protocol designed specifically for constrained IoT devices, enabling them to communicate efficiently in resource-constrained environments.

Features: CoAP is designed to work with constrained devices and low-power networks. It provides lightweight request-response interactions and is suitable for applications like smartcities and industrial IoT.

AMQP (Advanced Message Queuing Protocol):

Purpose: AMQP is a messaging protocol that provides message queuing capabilities for IoT applications with strict message delivery requirements.

Features: AMQP ensures reliable and ordered message delivery between sender and receiver. It's used in scenarios where message loss is not acceptable, such as in industrial control systems.

DDS (Data Distribution Service):

Purpose: DDS is a middleware standard designed for real-time and high-performance data distribution in IoT and industrial systems.

Features: DDS enables efficient data exchange between IoT devices, ensuring low-latency communication and scalability. It's commonly used in applications like autonomous vehicles and healthcare.

WebSocket:

Purpose: WebSocket provide full-duplex, bidirectional communication channels over a single connection, making them suitable for real-time IoT applications.

Features: WebSocket offer low-latency, persistent connections for interactive IoT use cases, such as remote control, monitoring, and live data streaming.

AMQP, Kafka, and Message Brokers:

Purpose: Message brokers like Apache Kafka and RabbitMQ, which support AMQP, provide centralized message queuing and routing capabilities for IoT applications.

Features: These message brokers help manage the distribution of data from IoT devices to various consumers, ensuring scalability and data integrity.

Custom Protocols:

Purpose: In some cases, IoT applications may require custom transport protocols tailored to specific requirements.

Features: Custom protocols are designed to meet the unique needs of IoT systems, taking into account factors like device capabilities, network conditions, and security requirements.

The choice of IoT application transport method depends on factors such as the nature of the IoT devices, communication requirements (e.g., real-time, reliability, and security), and the specific use case or industry. Many IoT systems use a combination of these transport methods to address various communication needs within the same network.

Application Layer Protocol Not Present

If an application layer protocol is not present or needed in an IoT system, it typically implies that direct communication between IoT devices and the destination (e.g., a cloud platform, server, or other devices) is established without the use of a specific application layer protocol. Instead, the communication might be based on more fundamental transport layer protocols like TCP or UDP, or it could be a proprietary communication method designed specifically for the IoT application. Here are a few scenarios where an application layer protocol might not be present or explicitly used:

Direct Communication over TCP or UDP: In some IoT applications, especially those where simplicity and low overhead are priorities, IoT devices may communicate directly over standard transport layer protocols like TCP or UDP. Data is transmitted as raw packets without the additional structure and overhead of a dedicated application layer protocol.

Proprietary Communication Protocols: Some IoT systems, particularly those developed for specific industrial or proprietary applications, may use custom or proprietary communication protocols that are not standardized or widely recognized as application layer protocols. These protocols are often optimized for the specific needs of the application.

Low-Level Communication: In certain scenarios, IoT devices communicate at a lower, more hardware-specific level, bypassing the traditional application layer entirely. This can be common in applications where devices are highly resource-constrained or where real-time communication is critical.

Custom Communication Logic: IoT developers may implement custom communication logic without adhering to a specific application layer protocol. This approach allows for flexibility in designing the communication patterns and data formats to suit the unique requirements of the IoT application.

Limited Data Exchange: In cases where IoT devices primarily collect and transmit simple sensor data or telemetry, the need for complex application layer protocols may be minimal. The focus is on efficient and reliable data transfer rather than standardized application layer interactions.

It's important to note that while some IoT systems may not explicitly use application layer protocols, they still rely on lower-level transport layer protocols (e.g., TCP, UDP) to handle basic communication functions like data routing, reliability, and addressing. Additionally, the absence of an application layer protocol may imply that data interpretation and processing are performed directly at the destination, such as within a cloud service or server, without relying on intermediary application layer logic.

The choice of whether to use an application layer protocol or not depends on the specific requirements and constraints of the IoT application, including factors like device capabilities, data complexity, security, and interoperability with other systems.

Z-Wave

Z-Wave is a wireless communication protocol specifically designed for home automation and Internet of Things (IoT) applications. It's a popular choice for creating smart homes and building automation systems due to its reliability, low power consumption, and scalability. Here's a detailed overview of the Z-Wave protocol in IoT:

Define: Z-Wave is a proprietary wireless communication protocol developed by Sigma Designs (now Silicon Labs).

It operates in the sub-1 GHz frequency band, which offers better range and wall-penetration capabilities compared to some other wireless protocols. Z-Wave is optimized for low power consumption, making it suitable for battery-powered IoT devices.

Topology: Z-Wave networks typically use a mesh topology, where devices (nodes) communicate with each other via hopping through intermediate nodes.

This mesh network topology enhances range and reliability as messages can find multiple paths to their destination.

Communication: Z-Wave uses a low-power, low-data-rate communication scheme.

It operates in the ISM (Industrial, Scientific, and Medical) radio bands and uses a GFSK (Gaussian Frequency Shift Keying) modulation scheme.

Devices communicate using a master-slave model, with one controller (master) managing multiple end devices (slaves).

Interoperability: Z-Wave Alliance, a consortium of companies, manages the Z-Wave standard to ensure interoperability among various Z-Wave devices.

Z-Wave devices from different manufacturers can work together within the same network, promoting a wide selection of compatible devices.

Security: Z-Wave has built-in security features, including AES-128 encryption for secure communication between devices.

It also supports secure key exchange during device inclusion, preventing unauthorized access to the network.

Range: Z-Wave's sub-1 GHz frequency range allows for longer communication ranges compared to higher-frequency protocols like Wi-Fi or Bluetooth.

The actual range can vary depending on environmental factors and the specific Z-Wave hardware used but can typically cover a home or building.

Device Types: Z-Wave supports various types of devices, including sensors, switches, dimmers, locks, thermostats, and more.

It offers a wide range of application possibilities, such as lighting control, climate management, security systems, and energy management.

Controller Options: Z-Wave networks are typically controlled by a Z-Wave hub or gateway, which can be managed through smartphone apps or web interfaces.

Users can remotely control and automate their Z-Wave devices through these controllers.

Installation and Inclusion: Adding a new Z-Wave device to a network is known as inclusion. This process typically involves putting the new device into inclusion mode and initiating the inclusion process on the Z-Wave controller.

Advantages:

Z-Wave's low power consumption is well-suited for battery-powered devices.

Its mesh networking ensures robust and reliable communication.

Z-Wave devices can be easily integrated into home automation ecosystems.

Limitations:

Z-Wave is a proprietary protocol, which may limit some users' choices and interoperability compared to open standards like Zigbee.

It operates in specific frequency bands, which can vary by region and may be subject to interference.

In summary, Z-Wave is a wireless communication protocol designed for IoT and home automation applications, known for its reliability, low power consumption, and interoperability among Z-Wave devices. It has gained popularity in the smart home industry due to its ability to create robust and scalable networks of interconnected devices.

Differentiate between WiFi and WiMax

Aspect	Wifi	WiMax
Definition	Wi-Fi is a wireless networking technology that provides short-range, local area network (LAN) connectivity.	WiMax is a wireless broadband technology that offers long-range wireless connectivity for metropolitan and wide area networks (MAN and WAN).
Range	Typically has a shorter range, covering a few hundred feet to a few hundred meters.	Offers a longer range, typically up to several miles or kilometres.
Coverage Area	Suitable for small-scale, local network deployments within homes, offices, and public spaces.	Designed for large-scale network deployments in urban and rural areas, including wide geographic regions.
Frequency Bands	Operates in unlicensed bands (2.4 GHz and 5 GHz) as well as licensed bands in some cases.	Utilizes licensed spectrum in the 2.3 GHz, 2.5 GHz, and 3.5 GHz frequency bands.
Data Transfer Rate	Offers relatively lower data transfer rates, typically up to several Gbps in the latest standards (Wi-Fi 6, 802.11ax).	Provides higher data transfer rates, ranging from Mbps to Gbps, depending on the configuration and version.
Infrastructure	Typically uses access points (APs) and routers for network connectivity.	Requires base stations (BS) or access points (APs) connected to a wired network infrastructure.
Network Topology	Works well for creating local wireless networks with a star or mesh topology.	Supports the creation of larger, point-to-multipoint networks suitable for urban or rural deployments.
Use Cases	Commonly used for home and office networks, public hotspots, and IoT applications.	Used for providing wireless broadband internet access, backhaul for cellular networks, and last-mile connectivity in underserved areas.

Exercise

Exercise 1 – MCQ

1. Which type of protocol is commonly associated with Wireless Sensor Networks (WSN)?

a) EPC Gen2

b) ISO 14443

c) IEEE 802.15.4

d) Bluetooth

2. In which context are M2M (Machine-to-Machine) protocols frequently employed?

a) Real-time location tracking

b) Contactless payment systems

c) Supply chain management

d) Proximity cards

Exercise 2 – True/False

1. IoT standardization is essential for ensuring that IoT devices can communicate and work together smoothly, regardless of their manufacturers.
2. IoT standardization primarily focuses on creating unique, customized protocols for each IoT application to maximize flexibility.

Exercise 3 – Fill in the blanks

1. AMQP, which stands for Advanced Message Queuing Protocol, is favoured in Machine-to-Machine communication for its lightweight and efficient ____________ capabilities.
2. IoT standardization is crucial to ensure that IoT devices can communicate and work together smoothly, promoting ____________ and consistency across various applications and manufacturers.

Exercise 4 – Match case

Match the correct protocol with its corresponding technology or application:

1. IEEE 802.11
2. IEEE 802.15.4
3. AMQP (Advanced Message Queuing Protocol)
4. IoT Standardization

Technology or application:

a) Wi-Fi
b) Wireless Sensor Networks (WSN)
c) Machine-to-Machine (M2M) Communication
d) Interoperability and Consistency across IoT

Exercise 5 – One word answer

1. WSN stands for?
2. M2M stands for?

Exercise 6 – Small answer

1. What is the primary goal of standardization?
2. Name some WSM protocols.

Exercise 7 – Long answer

1. Explain the significance of "M2M" protocols in the context of the Internet of Things (IoT) and provide an example of an application where M2M communication is essential.
2. Describe the role of IoT standardization in ensuring the success and widespread adoption of Internet of Things technologies.

Answer:

Exercise 1.

1. c) IEEE 802.15.4
2. c) Supply chain management

Exercise 2.

1. True
2. False

Exercise 3.

1. message queuing
2. interoperability

Exercise 4.

1. IEEE 802.11
2. IEEE 802.15.4 – b)
3. AMQP (Advanced Message Queuing Protocol)– c)
4. IoT Standardization – d)

Exercise 5.

1. Wireless Sensor Network
2. Machine-to-Machine

Previous Year Questions

1. Explain IoT technologies: RFID and NFC What is the difference. (SPPU B.Tech. 2022)

2. Explain Wireless Sensor Network in IoT paradigm (Mumbai University B.Tech. 2017)
3. Write a note on importance of networking protocol LoWIPv6 in IoT context. (Uttar Pradesh university B.Tech. 2021-22)
4. List layers of IoT protocol. (SPPU B.Tech. 2022)
5. What is wireless sensor network? (SPPU B.Tech. 2017)
6. Differentiate between IoT and M2M (SPPU B.Tech. 2017)
7. What are the different layers of IoT protocols? Explain functions of all the layers. (SPPU B.Tech. 2017)
8. What are the issues with IoT Standardization. (SPPU B.Tech. 2017)
9. Define M2M communication. (Uttar Pradesh university B.Tech. 2021-22)
10. What is requirement of IoT protocol standardization? (Uttar Pradesh university B.Tech. 2021-22)
11. Explain with example. (Uttar Pradesh university B.Tech. 2018-19)
12. Explain the concepts and terminology of RFID Application (Uttar Pradesh university B.Tech. 2018-19)
13. Explain CoAP messaging format. (SPPU B.Tech. 2019)
14. What are various components of RFID? Explain any two. (SPPU B.Tech. 2019)
15. How it is related to IoT? (SPPU B.Tech. h 2017)
16. How it is related to IoT? (SPPU B.Tech. 2017)

a) IPv6
b) MQTT
c) CoAP
d) XMPP (IGNOU MCA 2022)

17. Explain IPv6 packet format in detail. (SPPU B.Tech. 2019)
18. Write a note on importance of networking protocol LoWIPv6 in IoT context. (Mumbai University B.Tech. _2017)
19. Write a detail note on NFC and its use in IoT applications. (Mumbai University B.Tech. 2017)
20. What impact could IPv6 have on IoT? Explain. (RTU B.Tech. 2022)
21. What is COAP? (Anna University MTech 2018)
22. Write the salient features of M2M protocol. (Anna University MTech 2018)
23. Differentiate between WiFi and WiMax. (SPPU B.Tech. 2017)

ONLINE RESOURCES

Link: https://forms.gle/bHZaBznyeVigJj5P7

QR Code:

Link: https://www.youtube.com/playlist?list=PLzlh_31VWEFqkqJqc7cYrF0P8fssxMzvK

QR Code:

Chapter 6: IoT Data and Analytics

Data Collection and Management

Data collection and management are pivotal in our data-centric world. They provide the basis for informed decision-making, shape research and innovation, and enable businesses to understand their customers better. Here's a concise look at their significance, methods, challenges, and future trends.

Significance of Data Collection:

Informed Decision-Making: Data collection is the cornerstone of informed decision-making in various domains, from business strategies to public policies.

Performance Evaluation: Organizations use data collection to assess their performance, track progress, and pinpoint areas for improvement.

Research and Discovery: Data collection drives scientific research and knowledge advancement across disciplines.

Customer Understanding: In business, data collection helps tailor products and services by understanding customer behaviour and preferences

Methods of Data Collection:

Surveys and Questionnaires: Structured surveys gather opinions, preferences, and demographic data.

Observations: Systematic recording of events or behaviours in scientific research and quality control.

Sensors and IoT Devices: Sensors and IoT devices capture data from the physical world for various applications.

Social Media and Web Data: User-generated content on the internet offers insights for market research and sentiment analysis.

Interviews: Direct communication with individuals or groups for qualitative data collection.

Significance of Data Management:

Data Quality: Effective data management ensures data accuracy, completeness, and consistency.

Data Storage: Secure and efficient data storage solutions are essential for data preservation and accessibility.

Data Integration: Data integration combines disparate data sources for unified analysis and reporting.

Data Governance: Establishing policies and standards for ethical data usage, privacy, and security.

Data Analysis: Data management includes preparing and organizing data for analysis.

Challenges in Data Collection and Management:

Data Privacy and Security: Protecting data from breaches and ensuring privacy is a top concern.

Data Volume and Variety: Managing the vast and diverse data generated today is a challenge.

Data Integration: Integrating data from various sources with differing formats can be complex.

Data Quality Assurance: Ensuring data accuracy and consistency is an ongoing effort.

Regulatory Compliance: Organizations must navigate complex data protection regulations.

The Future of Data Collection and Management:

AI and Automation: AI and automation will enhance data management processes.

Edge Computing: Edge computing will enable real-time data processing closer to data sources.

Blockchain Technology: Blockchain will enhance data security and traceability.

Data Ethics: Ethical considerations in data handling will continue to evolve.

Data Collaboration: More data-sharing initiatives and collaborations between organizations will foster innovation and knowledge sharing.

In conclusion, data collection and management are fundamental for informed decisions, innovation, and addressing complex challenges. Responsible data handling is key to unlocking their potential in shaping our future.

Data Analytics and Machine Learning

In today's data-driven world, the convergence of data analytics and machine learning has revolutionized the way we harness information to gain insights, make predictions, and drive innovation. This article explores the symbiotic relationship between data analytics and machine learning, their significance, methodologies, real-world applications, and the promising future they hold.

Significance:

Data Analytics: Understand past and present data to inform decisions.

Machine Learning: Predict future outcomes using data-driven algorithms.

Methodologies:

Data Preparation: Clean and preprocess data for accuracy.

Descriptive Analytics: Summarize historical data for insights.

Predictive Analytics: Use machine learning to forecast future trends.

Prescriptive Analytics: Recommend actions for optimization.
Applications:
Healthcare: Disease prediction and personalized treatment.
Finance: Algorithmic trading and fraud detection.
Retail: Customer segmentation and inventory management.
Manufacturing: Predictive maintenance and quality control.
Marketing: Customer behaviour analysis and targeted ads.
Challenges:
Data Quality: Ensure data accuracy.
Interpretability: Address "black box" machine learning models.
Data Privacy: Protect sensitive data.
Scalability: Efficiently handle large datasets.
Bias and Fairness: Mitigate bias in models.
Future Trends:
Explainable AI for transparency.
Automated Machine Learning (AutoML) for broader accessibility.
Edge AI for real-time processing.
Ethical AI with a focus on fairness.
Expansion of applications across industries.
In conclusion, data analytics and machine learning continue to drive innovation, improve decision-making, and shape our data-centric future.

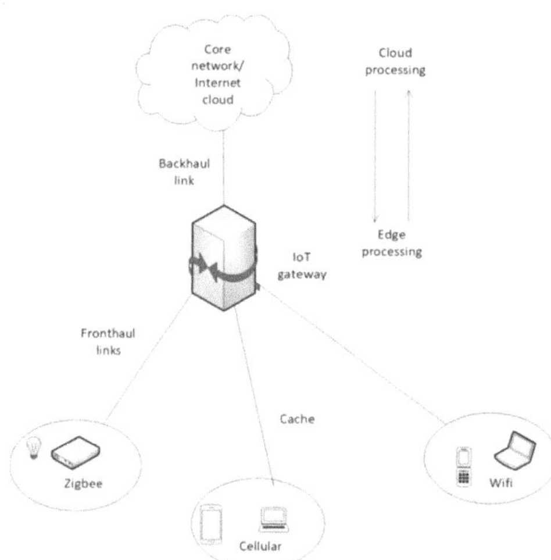

Real-time Monitoring and Decision-Making

The advent of the Internet of Things (IoT) has ushered in a new era of real-time data connectivity, revolutionizing how organizations monitor and make instant decisions. Here's a concise overview of its significance, applications, challenges, and future prospects:
Significance:
Immediate Insights: Real-time data provides instant operational insights.
Proactive Issue Resolution: Anomalies can be detected and addressed in real-time, preventing problems.
Optimized Efficiency: Processes are optimized promptly, resulting in cost savings.
Enhanced Safety: Real-time monitoring enhances safety through early warning systems.
Applications:
Manufacturing: IoT sensors reduce downtime and prevent equipment breakdowns.
Energy Management: Smart grids optimize energy distribution and consumption.
Healthcare: Wearable devices enable remote patient monitoring and intervention.
Transportation: Real-time traffic data enhances navigation and safety.
Environmental Monitoring: IoT aids in pollution control and disaster management.
Retail: Real-time analytics optimize inventory and personalize marketing.

Challenges:

Data Volume and Velocity: Handling large real-time data streams can be resource-intensive.

Data Quality: Ensuring data accuracy and reliability is essential.

Latency: Reducing processing and decision-making delays is critical.

Scalability: IoT deployments require robust infrastructure.

Security: Protecting real-time data from cyber threats is paramount.

In conclusion, real-time monitoring and Decision Making in IoT data and analytics is transformative, offering immediate insights, proactive decisions, and efficiency gains across industries, with a promising future as technology advances.

IoT Data Management and Compute Stack

Design Considerations:

Scalability: Design the stack to accommodate a growing number of IoT devices and data volume. Ensure that it can scale horizontally to meet increasing demands.

Data Ingestion: Choose efficient data ingestion mechanisms that can handle various data formats and protocols. Consider real-time and batch data ingestion methods.

Data Processing: Implement data processing pipelines that clean, filter, and transform raw data. Handle data normalization and schema evolution gracefully.

Edge Computing: Leverage edge computing for real-time data processing to reduce latency and bandwidth usage. Define what processing tasks should be performed at the edge versus in the cloud.

Data Storage: Select appropriate storage solutions based on data structure and access patterns. Consider databases (SQL or NoSQL), data lakes, and cloud-based storage.

Data Analytics: Design analytics modules to extract valuable insights from IoT data. Consider machine learning models for predictive analytics.

Data Security: Implement robust security measures, including data encryption, access controls, and authentication, to protect IoT data from unauthorized access and cyber threats.

Data Privacy: Comply with data privacy regulations (e.g., GDPR) and implement privacy-enhancing technologies (PETs) to safeguard sensitive data.

Device Management: Integrate device management capabilities for remote monitoring, configuration, and firmware updates of IoT devices.

Orchestration: Create data orchestration workflows to manage data flow between different components of the stack effectively.

Integration: Develop APIs and connectors for seamless integration with other systems, applications, and third-party services.

Data-Related Problems:

Data Volume Overload: As the number of IoT devices grows, the stack may struggle to handle the increasing data volume, leading to performance issues and data loss.

Data Quality: IoT data can be noisy and inconsistent. Inaccurate or missing data can lead to flawed analytics and decisions.

Latency: Delayed data processing or transmission can result in missed opportunities for real-time decision-making, affecting critical applications like predictive maintenance.

Security Vulnerabilities: Weak security measures can expose IoT data to unauthorized access, data breaches, and cyberattacks.

Interoperability: Incompatibility between IoT devices, protocols, or data formats can hinder data exchange and integration.

Data Storage Costs: Storing vast amounts of IoT data can become costly. Inefficient data storage practices can strain the budget.

Compliance and Legal Issues: Failing to adhere to data privacy regulations can lead to legal consequences and reputational damage.

Data Governance: Lack of clear data ownership, management policies, and data lifecycle management can result in data chaos and compliance issues.

Solutions and Best Practices for Data related problems:

Data Compression and Aggregation: Use data compression techniques and aggregation to reduce data volume and improve efficiency.

Data Quality Assurance: Implement data validation, cleansing, and error-handling mechanisms to ensure data quality.

Edge Intelligence: Leverage edge computing for immediate data processing and filtering to reduce latency.

Data Encryption: Encrypt data in transit and at rest to safeguard it from unauthorized access.

Standardization: Adopt standardized IoT protocols and data formats to enhance interoperability.

Cost Optimization: Implement data retention policies and tiered storage solutions to manage storage costs.

Privacy by Design: Incorporate privacy considerations into the stack's design from the outset.

Data Governance Framework: Establish clear data governance practices and assign responsibilities for data management.

Data synchronization techniques in the Internet of Things (IoT)

Data synchronization techniques in the Internet of Things (IoT) involve the process of ensuring that data collected from various IoT devices and sensors are consistently and accurately updated across different parts of the IoT ecosystem, including edge devices, cloud servers, databases, and user interfaces. Effective data synchronization is crucial for maintaining data integrity, real-time insights, and seamless operation of IoT applications. Here are several data synchronization techniques commonly used in IoT:

Time-Stamped Data: Time-stamping data is fundamental for synchronization in IoT. Each data point collected by IoT devices is tagged with a timestamp indicating when the data was captured. This timestamp helps ensure that data from various sources can be correctly ordered and synchronized.

Batch Processing: In batch processing, data from multiple IoT devices is collected and stored locally on the edge device until a predetermined condition is met, such as a specific time interval or a certain amount of data being accumulated. Once the condition is met, the data is sent in a batch to the central server for processing and synchronization.

Real-Time Data Streams:Real-time data synchronization involves the continuous streaming of data from IoT devices to centralized servers or databases as soon as it is generated. Technologies like MQTT and Apache Kafka are commonly used for real-time data streaming, ensuring minimal latency and near-instant synchronization.

Edge Computing: Edge computing involves processing data locally on IoT devices or edge servers, reducing the need for data to travel to a central server for processing and synchronization. Edge devices can process and aggregate data before sending only relevant information to the cloud, reducing network congestion and latency.

Caching and Buffering: Caching and buffering techniques store data temporarily on edge devices or gateways before transmitting it to the cloud. This helps manage network traffic and ensures data synchronization even in intermittent connectivity scenarios.

Data Deduplication: Data deduplication techniques identify and eliminate redundant data to reduce the amount of data transferred during synchronization. This optimization helps conserve bandwidth and storage space.

Conflict Resolution:In situations where multiple IoT devices or users may update the same data simultaneously, conflict resolution mechanisms are necessary to determine which version of the data should be considered authoritative. Common methods include last-write-wins or timestamp-based resolution.

Checkpoints and Checksums:Checkpoints and checksums are used to verify data integrity during synchronization. Devices or servers can exchange checksums or hashes of data to confirm that data has not been corrupted during transmission.

Data Compression: Data compression techniques reduce the size of data before transmission, reducing bandwidth requirements and synchronization times. Common compression algorithms include gzip and brotli.

Data Partitioning: For large-scale IoT deployments, data partitioning techniques divide data into smaller, manageable subsets. Each subset is then synchronized independently, improving parallelism and scalability.

Data Replication:Data replication involves maintaining copies of data across multiple locations or servers. It ensures data availability, fault tolerance, and load balancing. However, synchronization mechanisms are required to keep replicas consistent.

Synchronization Protocols: Various synchronization protocols, such as the Constrained Application Protocol (CoAP) and the Advanced Message Queuing Protocol (AMQP), are used to facilitate communication and synchronization between IoT devices and servers.

Conflict Detection and Resolution Algorithms: Complex IoT systems may require advanced conflict detection and resolution algorithms that consider various factors when resolving data conflicts, such as data freshness, priority, or user-defined rules.

Synchronization Frequency and Policies: Define synchronization policies and frequency based on the specific IoT application's requirements. Some applications may require real-time synchronization, while others can tolerate periodic updates

Monitoring and Alerts: Implement monitoring and alerting systems to detect synchronization failures or anomalies, ensuring timely intervention in case of issues.

Effective data synchronization techniques in IoT applications depend on the specific use case, network conditions, and scalability requirements. Designing a synchronization strategy that aligns with these factors is essential for reliable and efficient IoT data management.

Data collection and analysis approach of M2M

Machine-to-Machine (M2M) communication involves the exchange of data between devices and systems without human intervention. The data collection and analysis approach in M2M typically follow these steps:

Data Generation: M2M starts with data generation, where sensors or devices collect information from the physical world. This data can include various types, such as temperature readings, GPS coordinates, machine status, or any other relevant measurements.

Data Transmission: Once collected, the data is transmitted from the source device to a central repository or another device for further processing. Data transmission can occur over wired or wireless networks, depending on the application and the communication capabilities of the devices involved.

Data Aggregation: In many M2M systems, data from multiple sources is aggregated to provide a comprehensive view of a specific process or environment. Aggregation helps in consolidating information for analysis.

Data Storage: Data collected in M2M scenarios is typically stored in databases or data storage systems. The choice of storage depends on factors like data volume, speed of data arrival, and data retention requirements.

Data Analysis: This is a critical step in M2M communication. Data analysis involves processing the collected data to extract meaningful insights or trigger specific actions. Various analytical techniques are applied, such as statistical analysis, machine learning algorithms, and predictive modelling.

Real-time Analysis

Some M2M applications require real-time analysis, where data is processed as soon as it arrives. For example, in industrial automation, real-time analysis can detect anomalies in manufacturing processes and trigger immediate corrective actions.

Batch Analysis: In other cases, data is collected over a period and analysed in batches. This is common in scenarios where historical data analysis is essential for long-term optimization and decision-making.

Action Triggering: Based on the results of data analysis, M2M systems can trigger actions or decisions. For instance, if a temperature sensor detects a reading outside the acceptable range, it can automatically signal a cooling system to activate.

Reporting and Visualization: M2M systems often include reporting and visualization tools to present data insights to users or administrators. Dashboards and reports provide a user-friendly interface for monitoring and decision-making.

Feedback Loop: In some M2M applications, the results of data analysis and actions taken can be used to fine-tune the behaviour of devices or processes, creating a feedback loop for continuous improvement.

Security and Privacy: Throughout the data collection and analysis process, security measures are crucial to protect data from unauthorized access or tampering. Encryption, authentication, and access controls are commonly used to ensure data security.

Scalability and Optimization: As the number of connected devices grows, M2M systems must be scalable to handle increased data volume and processing demands. Optimization techniques are employed to ensure efficient use of resources.

M2M communication is fundamental in various domains, including industrial automation, healthcare, agriculture, transportation, and smart cities. The approach to data collection and analysis in M2M systems varies dependinspecific application's requirements and objectives, but the core principles of data generation, transmission, analysis,and action remain consistent.

Data collection and analysis approach of WSN

Wireless Sensor Networks (WSNs) are networks of interconnected sensor nodes that collect data from their surroundings and transmit it to a central or sink node for analysis and further processing. The data collection and analysis approach in WSNs involves several key steps:

Sensor Deployment: Sensor nodes are strategically deployed in the target environment or area of interest. The placement of these nodes should consider factors such as coverage, node density, and the specific data to be collected.

Data Sensing: Each sensor node is equipped with one or more sensors to capture data from the environment. These sensors can measure various parameters like temperature, humidity, light, sound, or specific chemical concentrations, depending on the application.

Data Aggregation: In many WSNs, data from multiple sensor nodes is aggregated locally before being transmitted to a central node. This local aggregation helps reduce data redundancy and save energy by sending summarized information rather than raw sensor readings.

Data Transmission: Sensor nodes communicate with each other and with a central sink node using wireless communication protocols, such as Zigbee, Wi-Fi, or Bluetooth. Data is transmitted from the source nodes to the sink node via multi-hop routing or direct communication, depending on the network topology.

Data Reception: The sink node receives data from multiple sensor nodes. It acts as a gateway between the WSN and external systems, such as a data analysis server or a user interface.

Data Storage: Data received by the sink node may be stored locally or forwarded to a data storage server for long-term retention and historical analysis. The choice of storage depends on the application's requirements.

Data Analysis: Data analysis involves processing the collected data to extract meaningful information or insights. Various techniques may be applied, including statistical analysis, machine learning, and data mining. The analysis can be real-time or batch processing, depending on the application's needs.

Event Detection: WSNs often focus on detecting specific events or anomalies. For example, in environmental monitoring, an event might be the detection of a sudden temperature change or an increase in air pollution.

Pattern Recognition: In some cases, WSNs analyse data to recognize patterns or trends. For instance, in agriculture, WSNs can identify patterns in soil moisture levels to optimize irrigation.

Decision Making: Based on the results of data analysis, decisions or actions can be triggered. For example, in home automation, a WSN can adjust the heating or cooling system based on temperature readings.

Reporting and Visualization: The results of data analysis can be presented to users or administrators through dashboards, reports, or user interfaces, allowing them to monitor and make informed decisions.

Energy Management: Since sensor nodes are typically battery-powered, energy efficiency is critical. Techniques such as duty cycling (putting nodes to sleep to conserve energy) and data aggregation are used to extend node battery life.

Security and Privacy: Ensuring data security and privacy is essential in WSNs, as the transmitted data may be sensitive. Encryption, authentication, and access control measures are implemented to protect data.

The data collection and analysis approach in WSNs is tailored to the specific application, and the design of the network and data processing algorithms will vary accordingly. WSNs find applications in various domains, including environmental monitoring, healthcare, industrial automation, and smart cities, where they play a crucial role in data-driven decision-making and automation.

Real-Time Location Systems (RTLS) in Healthcare IoT

Real-Time Location Systems (RTLS) play a crucial role in healthcare systems when integrated with IoT (Internet of Things) technologies. RTLS is a solution used to track and manage the real-time location of people, assets, and equipment within a healthcare facility. It relies on various technologies like RFID (Radio-Frequency Identification), GPS (Global Positioning System), Bluetooth Low Energy (BLE), Wi-Fi, and sensors to provide accurate and up-to-date information about the whereabouts of objects or individuals. Here's an explanation of how RTLS functions within the context of healthcare IoT:

Asset Tracking: RTLS in healthcare helps in the real-time tracking of critical assets such as medical equipment (e.g., infusion pumps, defibrillators), medication carts, wheelchairs, and even expensive diagnostic devices. This ensures that these assets are readily available when needed, reducing delays and improving overall operational efficiency.

Personnel Tracking: In healthcare, it's essential to know the location of healthcare professionals, patients, and visitors. RTLS can provide insights into the real-time movements of personnel, helping to optimize staffing levels, enhance security, and improve patient care by ensuring prompt response times.

Patient Safety: RTLS systems are used to improve patient safety. For example, they can alert staff when a patient with dementia or Alzheimer's disease wanders into restricted areas or outside the facility. It's also beneficial for tracking newborns in maternity wards and ensuring they remain within secure areas.

Workflow Optimization: RTLS can optimize workflows within a healthcare facility. By tracking the movement of patients and healthcare providers, it can identify bottlenecks and inefficiencies in processes, allowing for adjustments to improve patient flow and reduce wait times.

Infection Control: Infection control is critical in healthcare settings. RTLS can help track the movement of medical equipment and ensure that items are properly sanitized between uses. It can also aid in contact tracing during disease outbreaks.

Temperature Monitoring: In the healthcare supply chain, RTLS can be used to monitor the temperature of sensitive medications and vaccines during storage and transportation. Alerts can be triggered if temperature thresholds are exceeded, helping to maintain the integrity of medical supplies.

Emergency Response: During emergencies, such as fires or natural disasters, RTLS can help locate individuals within a healthcare facility quickly. This is vital for ensuring everyone's safety and organizing effective evacuations.

Data Integration: RTLS data can be integrated with other healthcare systems, such as electronic health records (EHRs), nurse call systems, and inventory management software. This integration provides a comprehensive view of operations and enhances decision-making.

Privacy and Compliance: Healthcare RTLS systems must adhere to strict privacy regulations and compliance standards, such as the Health Insurance Portability and Accountability Act (HIPAA) in the United States. Patient and staff privacy and data security are of paramount importance.

In summary, Real-Time Location Systems (RTLS) integrated with IoT technologies offer healthcare providers a powerful tool for improving operational efficiency, enhancing patient safety, and optimizing resource allocation. They provide real-time insights into the location and movement of assets, personnel, and patients within healthcare facilities, enabling better decision-making and ultimately improving the quality of care.

Collect data in structural health monitoring system

Collecting data in a Structural Health Monitoring (SHM) system involves using various sensors and data acquisition techniques to monitor the condition and behaviour of a structure over time. Here's a step-by-step guide on how to collect data in an SHM system:

Define Objectives and Requirements:

Clearly define the objectives of your SHM system. What specific parameters or characteristics of the structure are you monitoring? What are the critical aspects to be assessed, such as vibrations, temperature, strain, or corrosion?

Select Appropriate Sensors:

Choose sensors that are suitable for monitoring the parameters of interest. Common sensors in SHM include:

Accelerometers for measuring vibrations and motion.

Strain gauges to measure structural deformation and stress.

Temperature sensors to monitor thermal conditions.

Displacement sensors (e.g., LVDT or laser displacement sensors).

Ultrasonic sensors for crack detection.

Corrosion sensors to detect corrosion in metal structures.

Ensure that the sensors are compatible with the structural materials and conditions.

Sensor Placement and Installation:

Carefully plan and install sensors at strategic locations on the structure. The location and number of sensors will depend on the specific monitoring objectives and the structural configuration.

Follow best practices for sensor installation, including proper attachment, calibration, and protection from environmental factors.

Data Acquisition System:

Employ a data acquisition system (DAS) to collect data from the sensors. The DAS typically includes analog-to-digital converters (ADCs) to convert Analog sensor signals into digital data.

Ensure that the DAS is compatible with the sensors and can sample data at an appropriate frequency.

Data Storage:

Establish a data storage system to store the collected data. This can include on-site storage devices, cloud-based storage, or a combination of both.

Implement data compression and archiving strategies to manage the volume of data generated over time.

Real-Time Monitoring:

For real-time monitoring and immediate response to critical events, set up a real-time data streaming and analysis system. This can involve edge computing or cloud-based solutions to process and analyse data in real-time.

Communication:

Implement a communication infrastructure to transmit data from the sensors to the data storage and monitoring systems. This can involve wired (Ethernet, RS-485) or wireless (Wi-Fi, cellular) communication methods.

Data Analysis and Interpretation:

Develop algorithms and software tools to analyse the collected data. This includes detecting anomalies, identifying patterns, and assessing the structural health.

Set up thresholds and alert mechanisms to trigger notifications when abnormal conditions are detected

Visualization and Reporting:
Create a user-friendly interface for visualizing and reporting the SHM data. This can include dashboards, graphs, and reports that provide insights into the structural condition.
Maintenance and Calibration:
Regularly maintain and calibrate the sensors and data acquisition system to ensure accurate and reliable data collection.
Data Security and Privacy:
Implement security measures to protect the collected data from unauthorized access and ensure compliance with privacy regulations.
Data Retention:
Define data retention policies to manage the storage of historical data, considering the need for long-term analysis and compliance requirements.
By following these steps, you can establish an effective data collection process in your Structural Health Monitoring system, enabling you to monitor the condition of structures, detect issues early, and make informed decisions regarding maintenance and safety.

Data Enrichment and consolidation

Data enrichment and consolidation are important processes in the context of the Internet of Things (IoT) that help improve the quality and usefulness of data collected from various devices and sensors. These processes involve refining, enhancing, and organizing raw IoT data to make it more valuable and actionable for analysis, decision-making, and application development. Here's an overview of both concepts:

Data Enrichment: Data enrichment in IoT involves enhancing raw data with additional information or context to make it more meaningful and useful. This enrichment can include:

Metadata Addition: Adding metadata such as timestamps, geolocation, device identifiers, and data source information to provide context to the data points.

Data Annotation: Annotating data with descriptive labels, tags, or categories to make it easier to understand and classify.

External Data Integration: Combining IoT data with external data sources, such as weather data, traffic data, or demographic data, to provide additional context and insights.

Normalization: Converting data from different devices or sensors into a common format or unit of measurement for consistency and compatibility.

Data enrichment helps IoT data become more informative, making it easier for analytics algorithms and applications to extract valuable insights and support decision-making.

Data Consolidation: Data consolidation in IoT involves aggregating, organizing, and centralizing data from multiple sources or devices into a unified dataset. This process has several objectives:

Reducing Redundancy: Eliminating duplicate or redundant data points to optimize storage and processing.

Data Integration: Combining data from various IoT devices, sensors, or platforms into a single, coherent dataset.

Data Quality Improvement: Identifying and handling missing, inconsistent, or erroneous data to ensure data quality.

Time-Series Alignment: Aligning data collected at different time intervals or from various sources to enable meaningful time-series analysis.

Data Storage: Storing consolidated data in a structured format, such as a database or data warehouse, for easy access and retrieval.

Data consolidation is essential for enabling efficient data analysis, reporting, and application development in IoT environments, as it provides a unified and consistent view of the data across the ecosystem.

Together, data enrichment and consolidation contribute to the overall data management strategy in IoT, making the data more valuable, reliable, and accessible for various use cases, including predictive maintenance, anomaly detection, real-time monitoring, and business intelligence. These processes are often part of larger data processing pipelines and are crucial for extracting actionable insights and deriving business value from IoT data.

Big Data

Big data refers to large and complex datasets that are too massive to be effectively processed, managed, and analysed using traditional data processing tools and methods. These datasets are characterized by their volume, velocity, variety, and sometimes veracity. Here's what each of these characteristics means:

Volume: Big data typically involves extremely large amounts of data. This can range from terabytes to petabytes and beyond. The sheer quantity of data is one of the defining features of big data.

Velocity: Data in big data environments is generated, collected, and processed at high speeds. This can include real-time data streaming from various sources like sensors, social media, and web logs. The rapid rate of data generation requires efficient processing and analysis.
Variety: Big data is diverse in nature. It includes structured data (e.g., databases and spreadsheets), unstructured data (e.g., text, images, videos), and semi-structured data (e.g., XML or JSON files). This variety makes it challenging to store, process, and analyse using traditional methods.
Veracity: Veracity refers to the trustworthiness or reliability of the data. Big data often includes data from various sources, some of which may be incomplete, inconsistent, or inaccurate. Managing and ensuring data quality is a significant challenge in big data environments.
In addition to these "Vs," some discussions also include other characteristics like "variability" and "value." Variability refers to the inconsistency in the data flow, while value emphasizes the importance of deriving meaningful insights and value from big data. The goal of working with big data is to extract valuable insights, make informed decisions, and gain a competitive advantage. To achieve this, organizations use various technologies and approaches, including distributed computing frameworks like Hadoop, NoSQL databases, data lakes, machine learning, and advanced analytics.
Examples of big data applications span various industries, including finance (fraud detection), healthcare (patient data analysis), retail (customer behaviour analysis), manufacturing (predictive maintenance), and more. The ability to harness and analyse big data has become increasingly vital in today's data-driven world, as it offers opportunities for innovation, improved decision-making, and better understanding of complex phenomena.

Relation of Big Data and IoT

Big Data and IoT (Internet of Things) are closely intertwined, and the use of Big Data analytics in IoT can unlock valuable insights from the vast amounts of data generated by IoT devices and sensors. Here's a detailed explanation of how Big Data can be used in IoT:
Data Collection from IoT Devices: IoT devices generate large volumes of data, including sensor readings, device statuses, and environmental conditions. Big Data platforms can collect, store, and manage this data efficiently. This data collection forms the foundation for subsequent analytics.
Real-Time Data Processing: IoT often involves real-time applications, such as industrial automation, smart cities, and healthcare monitoring. Big Data tools like Apache Kafka and Apache Storm can process data streams in real time, allowing for immediate insights and responses to events.
Data Integration: IoT environments consist of diverse devices and sensors that may use different data formats and protocols. Big Data solutions provide data integration capabilities to unify data from various sources, making it accessible for analysis.
Data Storage: Big Data technologies, including distributed file systems like Hadoop HDFS and cloud-based data warehouses, can efficiently store and manage large volumes of IoT data. This storage is scalable to accommodate the growing data requirements of IoT applications.
Data Transformation and Cleaning: IoT data may contain noise, outliers, or missing values. Big Data analytics can preprocess and clean the data, ensuring its quality and reliability for subsequent analysis.
Complex Event Processing (CEP): Big Data platforms, in combination with CEP engines, enable the detection of complex patterns and events in real-time IoT data streams. This is useful for applications like fraud detection, predictive maintenance, and anomaly detection.
Predictive Analytics: Big Data analytics can be applied to historical IoT data to build predictive models. These models can forecast future events, such as equipment failures, energy consumption, or supply chain disruptions, allowing for proactive actions.
Machine Learning and AI: Big Data enables the application of machine learning and AI algorithms to IoT data. This can lead to advanced analytics, including predictive maintenance, demand forecasting, recommendation engines, and image or speech recognition in IoT applications.
Data Visualization and Dashboards: Big Data tools can create interactive dashboards and visualizations that provide meaningful insights to end-users. These visual representations help stakeholders understand IoT data and make informed decisions.
Scalability: Both Big Data and IoT solutions are designed for scalability. As the number of IoT devices and data volume increases, Big Data technologies can scale horizontally to handle the load without compromising performance.
Cost Efficiency: By using distributed storage and processing, Big Data solutions can be cost-effective for handling large IoT datasets compared to traditional databases. This makes it financially feasible to analyse vast amounts of IoT data.

Optimizing Operations: Big Data analytics can help organizations optimize their IoT operations by identifying inefficiencies, bottlenecks, and opportunities for improvement. For example, in manufacturing, it can optimize production schedules based on real-time data.

Security and Anomaly Detection: Big Data analytics can enhance IoT security by detecting unusual patterns or suspicious activities in IoT data. It can identify security breaches or potential cyberattacks and trigger immediate responses.

In summary, Big Data analytics in IoT empowers organizations to extract valuable insights, improve operational efficiency, enhance decision-making, and gain a competitive edge. It enables IoT applications to move beyond simple data collection to advanced analytics and intelligence, making IoT a transformative force across industries.

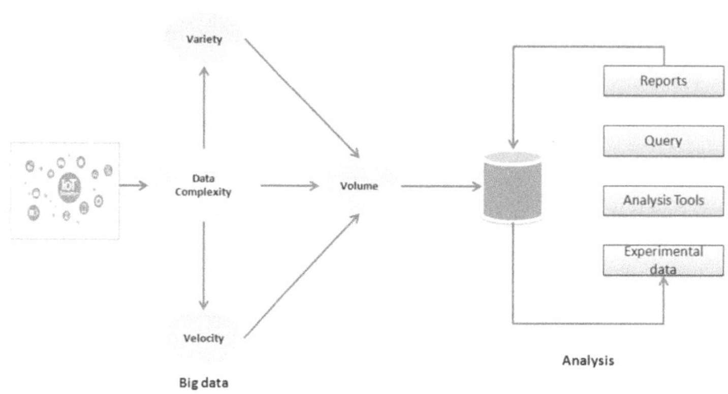

Data visualization and Dashboards

Data visualization and dashboards play a crucial role in IoT (Internet of Things) by providing a visual representation of complex data collected from IoT devices and systems.

Data visualization: It refers to the graphical representation of data to help users understand complex datasets more easily and make informed decisions. In the context of the Internet of Things (IoT), data visualization plays a vital role in transforming the massive amounts of data generated by IoT devices into meaningful insights that can drive actionable outcomes. Here's an explanation of data visualization and its importance in IoT:

What is Data Visualization?

Data visualization involves the use of charts, graphs, maps, dashboards, and other visual elements to present data in a visually comprehensible format. It simplifies complex datasets, making it easier for humans to identify patterns, trends, anomalies, and relationships within the data.

Importance of Data Visualization in IoT:

Enhanced Understanding: IoT generates data from various sensors and devices across diverse domains, such as manufacturing, healthcare, agriculture, and smart cities. Data visualization helps users, including non-technical stakeholders, understand this data without requiring in-depth technical knowledge.

Real-Time Insights: Many IoT applications demand real-time monitoring and decision-making. Data visualization tools can provide instant insights into sensor data, enabling rapid responses to changing conditions or anomalies.

Data Correlation: IoT often involves multiple data sources and sensors. Data visualization allows users to correlate data from different sources, which can reveal insights that may not be apparent when looking at individual datasets.

Anomaly Detection: Visualizations can highlight unusual patterns or deviations in IoT data. Detecting anomalies promptly is critical in applications like predictive maintenance, where it can prevent costly equipment failures.

Predictive Analytics: Data visualizations can facilitate the presentation of predictive analytics results, helping users understand forecasts, trends, and predictive models derived from IoT data.

Decision Support: IoT data often informs critical decision-making processes. Visualizations provide decision-makers with clear, data-driven insights to make informed choices about resource allocation, process optimization, and more.

Efficiency and Productivity: In industrial settings, visualizing production data can improve efficiency and productivity by identifying bottlenecks, optimizing workflows, and reducing downtime.

Customization: Data visualization tools allow users to customize dashboards and reports to match their specific requirements and preferences, ensuring that the most relevant information is readily accessible.

Remote Monitoring: IoT systems often involve remote monitoring of assets and processes. Data visualization platforms enable stakeholders to access and interpret data from anywhere, facilitating remote decision-making.

Communication: Effective data visualization enhances communication within organizations by presenting data in a format that is easily understandable to different teams and stakeholders, fostering collaboration and shared insights.

User Engagement: Visual representations of data are more engaging and memorable than raw numbers or text. This can lead to better retention of information and more effective communication of insights.

Types of IoT Data Visualizations:

IoT data can be visualized in various ways, including time series plots, heatmaps, scatter plots, bar charts, pie charts, geographical maps, and more. The choice of visualization type depends on the nature of the data and the insights required.

In summary, data visualization is a crucial component of IoT systems as it transforms raw sensor data into actionable insights. It enhances understanding, facilitates real-time monitoring, aids in decision-making, and improves efficiency across various IoT applications and industries. Effective data visualization empowers organizations to harness the full potential of IoT data for better-informed decision-making and optimized operations.

Network Function Virtualization (NFV)

Network Function Virtualization (NFV) is a key concept in modern networking, and while it is not exclusive to IoT, it plays a crucial role in supporting IoT deployments. NFV is a network architecture framework that aims to virtualize and abstract network functions traditionally performed by dedicated hardware appliances, transforming them into software-based services that can run on standard IT hardware, servers, and virtual machines. Here's a detailed explanation of Network Function Virtualization in the context of IoT:

Traditional Network Infrastructure: In traditional network architectures, various network functions are executed on specialized, purpose-built hardware devices. For example, functions like routing, load balancing, firewalling, and intrusion detection were performed by dedicated physical appliances.

Challenges in Traditional Networks for IoT: In IoT environments, especially in scenarios with a large number of devices, traditional network infrastructure may face scalability and flexibility challenges. Deploying and maintaining dedicated hardware for each network function can be expensive and inflexible.

NFV Principles: NFV proposes the virtualization of network functions using software-based implementations. These virtualized functions can run on commodity hardware, reducing the need for expensive, proprietary appliances.

Key Components of NFV in IoT:

Virtual Network Functions (VNFs): VNFs are software-based instances of network functions, such as firewalls, load balancers, or intrusion detection systems. In IoT, VNFs can include functions like data filtering, protocol translation, and security services.

NFV Infrastructure (NFVI): NFVI consists of the physical hardware (servers, storage, and networking) and the virtualization layer that manages and orchestrates the VNFs. It provides the resources necessary to run VNFs efficiently.

NFV Management and Orchestration (MANO): MANO is responsible for the lifecycle management of VNFs. It includes functions like VNF onboarding, scaling, orchestration, and monitoring. MANO ensures that VNFs are deployed, scaled, and maintained as needed

Virtualization Layer: The virtualization layer, often based on technologies like hypervisors or containerization (e.g., Docker), abstracts the underlying hardware and enables the execution of multiple VNFs on the same physical infrastructure.

Benefits of NFV in IoT:

Scalability: NFV allows for flexible scaling of network functions to accommodate the increasing number of IoT devices and changing network traffic patterns.

Cost Reduction: By replacing dedicated hardware with virtualized network functions, NFV can reduce capital and operational costs associated with IoT network infrastructure.

Flexibility and Agility: NFV enables rapid deployment and modification of network functions, making it easier to adapt to changing IoT requirements.

Resource Optimization: Resources in NFV can be dynamically allocated to VNFs based on demand, optimizing resource utilization.

Elasticity: NFV systems can automatically scale up or down in response to fluctuations in IoT device activity, ensuring efficient resource allocation.

Centralized Management: With NFV, network functions can be centrally managed and orchestrated, simplifying network operations and troubleshooting.

Use Cases in IoT: NFV in IoT can be applied to a variety of use cases, including:

IoT security: Virtualized security functions like firewalls and intrusion detection systems.

IoT data processing: Virtualized data filtering and processing functions.

IoT connectivity: Virtualized routing and network optimization functions.

In conclusion, Network Function Virtualization (NFV) is a critical technology for optimizing network infrastructure in IoT deployments. It allows for the flexible and cost-effective deployment of network functions, making it easier to scale and manage IoT networks efficiently and adapt to changing requirements. NFV enhances the agility, scalability, and resource optimization of IoT network infrastructure.

IoT Dashboards:

IoT dashboards are user interfaces that display visual representations of IoT data and system status.

They can be web-based or mobile applications accessible to users, including operators, technicians, and decision-makers. **1.Components of IoT Dashboards:**

Widgets and Charts: Dashboards feature various widgets and charts, such as gauges, graphs, heatmaps, and pie charts, to represent IoT data.

Customization: Users can often customize dashboards to display the specific data and visualizations they require.

Alerts and Notifications: Dashboards may include alert mechanisms to notify users when predefined conditions or thresholds are met.

User Access Control: Role-based access control ensures that users see only the data relevant to their responsibilities.

Integration: IoT dashboards can integrate with other systems, databases, and APIs to fetch and display data from various sources.

Use Cases for IoT Dashboards:

Industrial IoT (IIoT): Dashboards in manufacturing monitor equipment, track production metrics, and optimize processes.

Smart Cities: Dashboards help city planners monitor traffic, environmental data, and utilities to improve urban living.

Agriculture: Farmers use dashboards to monitor soil conditions, weather, and crop health for precision farming.

Healthcare: IoT dashboards facilitate remote patient monitoring and provide healthcare professionals with real-time patient data.

Energy Management: Dashboards help businesses and homes optimize energy consumption by visualizing usage patterns.

Environmental Monitoring: Environmental agencies use dashboards to track air quality, water quality, and weather conditions.

Data generation from IoT (Internet of Things) and M2M (Machine-to-Machine) devices

Data generation from IoT (Internet of Things) and M2M (Machine-to-Machine) devices is a fundamental aspect of these technologies, and it involves the collection and transmission of data from various sensors and devices to centralized systems for analysis and decision-making. Here's a description of the data generation process from IoT and M2M devices:

Sensor Inputs: IoT and M2M devices are equipped with a variety of sensors, such as temperature sensors, humidity sensors, GPS receivers, accelerometers, cameras, and more. These sensors continuously collect data from their surroundings or monitor the device's internal conditions.

Data Sampling: The sensors sample data at predefined intervals or in response to specific events. For example, a temperature sensor in a smart thermostat might sample temperature data every minute, while a motion sensor in a security camera might trigger data collection when motion is detected.

Data Types: The data generated by IoT and M2M devices can be of various types, including:

Numerical Data: This includes measurements like temperature, pressure, humidity, and voltage levels.

Binary Data: This represents simple on/off or true/false states, often used for binary sensors like door/window open/close sensors.

Image and VideoData: Cameras on IoT devices capture images or videos, which can be used for surveillance, image recognition, or video streaming applications.

Location Data: GPS-enabled devices generate location data in the form of latitude and longitude coordinates.

Text or Sensor Metadata: Some sensors may provide additional textual information or metadata about the data they collect, such as device IDs, timestamps, or sensor-specific information.

Data Transmission: Once collected, the data is typically transmitted to a central server or cloud platform using various communication protocols. Common protocols for data transmission in IoT and M2M systems include MQTT, HTTP/HTTPS, CoAP, and LoRaWAN, depending on the application and network requirements.

Data Aggregation: In many cases, data from multiple IoT and M2M devices are aggregated to provide a more comprehensive view of a system or environment. This aggregation can happen at the device level or within intermediate gateways before reaching the central server.

Data Storage: Data generated by IoT and M2M devices is often stored in databases or data lakes for historical analysis, reporting, and long-term storage. Depending on the volume, velocity, and variety of data, different storage solutions may be employed, such as relational databases, NoSQL databases, or distributed file systems.
Data Processing and Analysis: After storage, the data can be processed and analysed to extract valuable insights, detect anomalies, and make informed decisions. This may involve machine learning algorithms, statistical analysis, or real-time data processing.
Data Visualization: The results of data analysis are often presented in a visual format, such as graphs, charts, dashboards, or notifications, to make it easier for users to understand and act upon the information.
Action and Control: Depending on the application, IoT and M2M systems can trigger actions or control devices based on the data analysis. For example, a smart thermostat can adjust the temperature based on occupancy and user preferences.
Security and Privacy: Data generated by IoT and M2M devices must be secured during transmission and storage to protect against unauthorized access and breaches of privacy. Encryption, authentication, and access control mechanisms are crucial for data security.

Exercise

Exercise 1 – MCQ

1. What is the primary goal of data collection in the context of IoT?
a) To maximize data volume at all times.
b) To collect data without any filtering or preprocessing.
c) To gather relevant data that informs decision-making and addresses specific objectives.
d) To collect data only for regulatory compliance.
2. In IoT, what does "real-time monitoring" refer to?
a) Collecting data and processing it at any time during the day.
b) Continuously tracking and analysing data as it is generated, with minimal delay.
c) Storing data for future analysis and making decisions later.
d)Monitoring data once a day to reduce computational costs.

Exercise 2 – True/False

1. Data collection in IoT should prioritize gathering as much data as possible, regardless of its relevance or purpose.
2. The primary purpose of using machine learning in IoT data analytics is to completely replace human decision-making.

Exercise 3 – Fill in the blanks

1. Effective data collection in IoT involves gathering __________ data that serves specific objectives and informs decision-making.
2. Real-time monitoring in IoT refers to continuously tracking and analysing data as it is generated, with ________ delay.

Exercise 4 – Match case

Match the following terms with their descriptions:
1. Data Collection and Management
2. Data Analytics and Machine Learning
3. Real-time Monitoring and Decision-Making
Descriptions:
a) Gathering relevant data that serves specific objectives and informs decision-making.
b) Continuously tracking and analysing data as it is generated, with minimal delay.
c) Using machine learning to uncover hidden patterns and insights from large datasets.

Exercise 5 – One word answer

1. What is the main purpose of using machine learning in IoT data analytics?
2. What does "real-time monitoring" in IoT emphasize?

Exercise 6 – Small answer

1. What is the significance of Real-time Monitoring and Decision-Making?
2. Name the methods of data collection.

Exercise 7 – Long answer

1. Explain the significance of data collection in IoT and why it should prioritize gathering relevant data. Provide examples of relevant data in specific IoT applications.

2. Describe the role of machine learning in IoT data analytics and provide examples of how it can uncover hidden patterns in large datasets. Explain the potential benefits of using machine learning in IoT applications.

Answer:

Exercise 1.

1. c) To gather relevant data that informs decision-making and addresses specific objectives.
2. b) Continuously tracking and analysing data as it is generated, with minimal delay.

Exercise 2.

1. False
2. False

Exercise 3.

1. relevant
2. minimal

Exercise 4.

1. Data Collection and Management – a)
2. Data Analytics and Machine Learning- c)
3. Real-time Monitoring and Decision-Making – b)

Exercise 5

1. Insights
2. imeliness

Previous Year Questions

1. Data synchronization techniques in the Internet of Things (IoT) (SPPU B.Tech. 2017)
2. How do data collection and analysis approaches differ in M2M and IoT? (SPPU B.Tech. 2018)
3. What is data enrichment and consolidation? (Uttar Pradesh University B.Tech. 2021- 22)
4. Compare IoT and M2M services (SPPU B.Tech. 2019)
5. How do data collection and analysis approaches differ in M2M and IoT?(RTU B.Tech. 2017)
6. How to collect data in structural health monitoring system?(RTU B.Tech. 2017)
7. Explain Data visualization and its importance in IoT. (Uttar Pradesh university B.Tech. 2018-19)
8. How Big Data can be used in IoT? Explain in detail. (Uttar Pradesh university B.Tech. 2018-19)
9. Describe data generation from IoT/ M2M devices.(SPPU B.Tech.2018)
10. How to collect data in structural health monitoring system? (SPPU B.Tech. 2017)
11. What is big-data and why we are using big-data in IoT? (SPPU B.Tech. 2017)

ONLINE RESOURCES

Link: https://forms.gle/kPG94eiXyrhckGtd7

QR Code:

Link: https://www.youtube.com/playlist?list=PLzlh_31VWEFopZ1sbBBP36lhGhE5YtSEx

QR Code :

Chapter 7: IoT Security and Privacy

Threats and Vulnerabilities

The Internet of Things (IoT) has ushered in an era of convenience and connectivity, but it also introduces significant security and privacy challenges. In this, we'll explore the primary threats and vulnerabilities associated with IoT security and privacy, emphasizing the importance of vigilance for individuals, organizations, and governments.

Device Vulnerabilities:

Inadequate Security Measures: Due to cost constraints or rushed development, many IoT devices lack robust security features.

Outdated Firmware: The absence of regular security updates or patches leaves devices vulnerable to exploits.

Weak Authentication and Authorization:

Default Credentials: Manufacturers sometimes ship devices with default usernames and passwords, making them susceptible to attacks.

Lack of Multi-Factor Authentication: Many IoT devices lack multi-factor authentication, simplifying unauthorized access.

Insecure Communication:

Unencrypted Data: Some IoT devices transmit data without encryption, exposing it to eavesdropping and interception.

Inadequate Protocols: Weak or outdated communication protocols can be exploited by attackers.

Physical Attacks:

Physical Tampering: Attackers can tamper with IoT devices, installing malicious hardware or intercepting communication cables.

Device Theft: Stolen devices may expose sensitive data if not adequately secured.

Distributed Denial of Service (DDoS) Attacks:

Botnet Vulnerability: IoT devices can be compromised to create botnets, launching massive DDoS attacks on other targets.

Privacy Concerns:

Data Collection and Sharing: IoT devices often gather extensive personal data, raising concerns about privacy breaches and unauthorized data sharing.

Geolocation Tracking: Location data from IoT devices can be misused for unauthorized tracking.

Supply Chain Vulnerabilities:

Counterfeit Devices: Counterfeit or compromised IoT devices may infiltrate the supply chain, posing security risks.

Third-Party Services: Relying on third-party services for device functionalities can introduce vulnerabilities if those services are compromised.

Lack of Regulation and Standards:

Fragmented Standards: Absence of unified IoT security standards leads to inconsistent security practices across devices.

Limited Regulation: The regulatory landscape for IoT security and privacy is evolving but lacks comprehensive oversight in many regions.

Insider Threats:

Unauthorized Access: Employees or individuals with access to IoT systems may misuse privileges for malicious purposes.

Data Leakage: Insider threats can result in sensitive data leakage or theft.

Human Error:

Misconfigurations: Human errors like misconfiguring device settings or security protocols can create vulnerabilities.

Security Measures and Best Practices

As the Internet of Things (IoT) continues to proliferate, ensuring the security and privacy of connected devices and systems becomes increasingly vital. In this article, we will explore essential security measures and best practices to safeguard IoT environments, mitigate vulnerabilities, and protect sensitive data while maintaining user privacy.

Device Authentication:

Strong Authentication: Implement robust authentication mechanisms, such as complex passwords, biometrics, or device certificates, to verify the identity of users and devices.

Multi-Factor Authentication (MFA): Encourage the use of MFA to add an extra layer of security by requiring multiple forms of identification.

Regular Software Updates:

Firmware Updates: Provide regular firmware and software updates to patch known vulnerabilities and enhance security.

Automatic Updates: Enable automatic updates to ensure that devices receive critical security patches promptly.

Data Encryption:

End-to-End Encryption: Encrypt data both in transit and at rest to protect it from unauthorized access or interception.

Secure Protocols: Employ secure communication protocols such as HTTPS and MQTT with TLS/SSL to safeguard data during transmission.

Network Security:

Firewalls: Implement firewalls to control incoming and outgoing traffic, effectively restricting unauthorized access.

Network Segmentation: Isolate IoT devices on separate network segments to minimize potential attack vectors and limit lateral movement.

Access Control:

Least Privilege Principle: Limit user and device access to only the necessary resources and functions to reduce the attack surface.

Role-Based Access Control (RBAC): Assign roles and permissions based on user responsibilities to ensure appropriate access.

Secure Development Practices:

Security by Design: Embed security into the IoT device development lifecycle from the initial design stages.

Security Testing: Regularly conduct security assessments, penetration testing, and code reviews to identify and address vulnerabilities.

Privacy Protection:

Data Minimization: Collect only the data required for device functionality and the user experience to minimize privacy risks.

Transparent Data Usage: Clearly communicate data collection, processing, and sharing practices to users, ensuring transparency.

Physical Security:

Tamper Detection: Implement tamper detection mechanisms to identify and respond to physical tampering attempts.

Device Identification: Label and secure devices to prevent unauthorized physical access.

Incident Response Plan:

Plan Development: Establish an incident response plan outlining procedures to address security breaches or vulnerabilities promptly.

Employee Training: Ensure that employees are trained to respond effectively to security incidents.

Compliance with Regulations:

Stay Informed: Stay current with privacy and security regulations relevant to your region and industry.

Compliance Audits: Regularly conduct compliance audits to verify adherence to regulations such as GDPR, HIPAA, or industry-specific standards.

Data Encryption in Transit and at Rest:

Utilize encryption protocols to secure data during transmission between IoT devices and cloud platforms.

Implement encryption mechanisms to protect data stored both on IoT devices and in data centers.

Secure Supply Chain Management:

Verify the security of IoT components and software throughout the supply chain.

Implement stringent security measures during manufacturing, shipping, and deployment to prevent tampering or compromise.

Monitoring and Intrusion Detection:

Continuously monitor IoT networks and devices for unusual or suspicious activities.

Deploy intrusion detection systems to detect and respond to potential threats in real time.

User Education and Awareness:

Educate users about IoT security risks and best practices, such as regularly updating passwords and recognizing phishing attempts.

Provide resources and guidelines to promote safe IoT usage and foster security awareness.

Non-Repudiation:

Digital Signatures: Digital signatures provide non-repudiation by associating a message or action with a specific user or device. This means that the sender cannot deny sending the message, and the recipient can verify its authenticity.

Audit Trails: Maintaining detailed audit trails of all actions and communications within an IoT system can provide evidence of who initiated specific actions, aiding in non-repudiation.

Availability:

Redundancy and Failover: Ensuring high availability involves implementing redundancy and failover mechanisms. Redundant servers, backup power sources, and load balancing can help maintain system availability in the face of failures.

Distributed Architectures: Distributing IoT services and resources across multiple locations or cloud regions can improve availability and fault tolerance.

Denial-of-Service (DoS) Protection: Implementing DoS protection measures, such as rate limiting and traffic filtering, can help mitigate attacks that seek to disrupt availability.

Implementing these security measures and best practices is essential to safeguard IoT environments, protect against threats, and uphold user privacy. In the ever-evolving IoT landscape, a proactive security approach is crucial to establish trust and confidence among users and stakeholders.

Privacy Concerns and Regulations

The widespread adoption of Internet of Things (IoT) devices has raised significant privacy concerns and prompted the development of regulatory frameworks to address these issues. In this, we will explore the primary privacy concerns associated with IoT and the relevant regulations aimed at safeguarding individuals' privacy and data.

Privacy Concerns in IoT:

Data Collection and Usage: IoT devices often gather extensive amounts of personal data, including location, behaviour patterns, and preferences, leading to concerns about how this data is utilized and shared.

Data Ownership: Ownership of data generated by IoT devices is often ambiguous, creating uncertainty about who has control over this sensitive information.

Data Security: Inadequate security measures on IoT devices can result in data breaches, exposing personal information to malicious actors.

User Consent: Users may not have a clear understanding of the extent of data collection by IoT devices or the purposes for which their data is being used, raising concerns about informed consent.

Data Retention: IoT companies may retain user data for extended periods, prompting concerns about the implications of long-term data storage.

Profiling and Targeted Advertising: The data collected by IoT devices can be used to create detailed user profiles, enabling targeted advertising and potentially infringing on user privacy.

Relevant Regulations and Frameworks:

General Data Protection Regulation (GDPR): GDPR is a comprehensive European Union regulation governing data protection and privacy, imposing strict rules on the collection, processing, and storage of personal data.

GDPR applies to IoT devices and services handling personal data, ensuring users have greater control over their data and understand how it is used.

California Consumer Privacy Act (CCPA):

CCPA is a state-level privacy law in California, USA, granting consumers the right to know what personal information is collected about them and request its deletion.

IoT companies operating in California must comply with CCPA regulations if they meet specific criteria.

Cybersecurity ImprovementActs: Various countries have enacted cybersecurity improvement acts that mandate companies, including IoT manufacturers, adhere to security standards and promptly report data breaches.

IoT Security Certification Schemes: Some regions and industry bodies have introduced certification schemes for IoT devices, ensuring they meet specific security and privacy standards.

International Privacy Frameworks: Organizations like the Asia-Pacific Economic Cooperation (APEC) have developed privacy frameworks to facilitate cross-border data flows while safeguarding privacy.

Self-Regulatory Initiatives: Industry associations and IoT consortia have established self-regulatory codes of conduct and best practices to address privacy concerns.

Best Practices for Privacy in IoT:

To navigate the evolving landscape of IoT privacy concerns and regulations, consider implementing these best practices:

Privacy by Design: Embed privacy considerations into the design and development of IoT devices and services from the beginning.

Clear Privacy Policies: Provide transparent and easily accessible privacy policies that inform users about data collection, usage, and retention.
User Consent: Ensure users are informed and explicitly consent to data collection and usage.
Data Minimization: Collect only the data necessary for the intended purpose and minimize data retention.
Security Measures: Implement robust security measures to protect user data from unauthorized access or breaches.
Data Ownership: Clarify data ownership and provide users with control over their data.
Regular Audits and Compliance: Conduct routine privacy audits to ensure compliance with applicable regulations and frameworks.
User Education: Educate users about privacy risks and best practices for safely using IoT devices.
Balancing the potential benefits of IoT with privacy concerns requires a proactive approach that respects user rights and complies with privacy regulations. As the IoT landscape evolves, staying informed about privacy regulations and adhering to best practices is crucial for maintaining trust among users and fostering responsible IoT development and deployment.

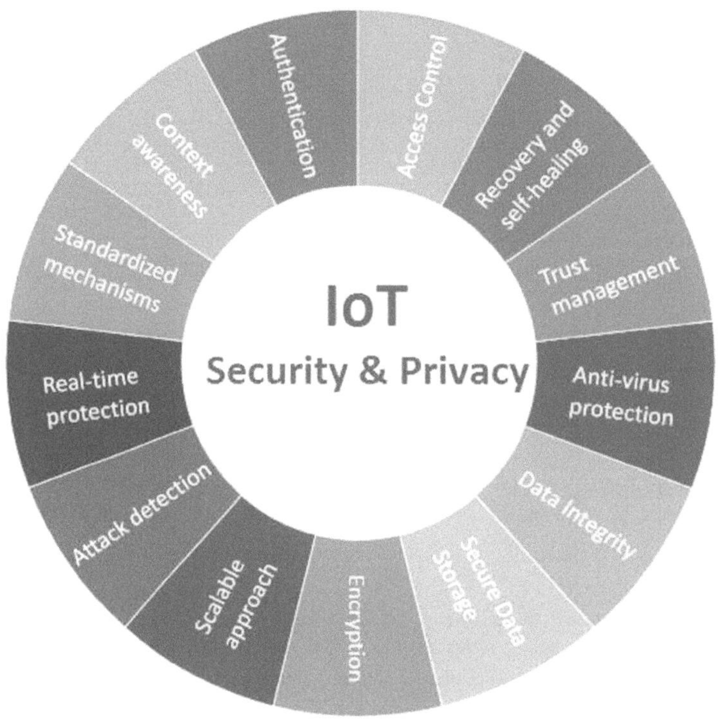

Security model in Internet of Things

Security is a paramount concern in the Internet of Things (IoT) due to the proliferation of interconnected devices and the sensitive data they often handle. Various security models and approaches have been developed to address the unique challenges of IoT security. Here are several security models in IoT, along with explanations:
Perimeter Security Model:
Description: In this model, security is focused on establishing a strong perimeter defense around IoT networks. It aims to keep unauthorized users and devices from gaining access to the network.
Features: Firewalls, intrusion detection systems (IDS), intrusion prevention systems (IPS), and network segmentation are commonly used to create a secure perimeter.
Limitations: Perimeter security alone may not be sufficient, as threats can also originate from within the network.
Device Authentication Model:
Description: This model emphasizes the authentication of IoT devices before they are allowed to connect to the network. It ensures that only trusted devices can participate.
Features: Digital certificates, secure boot processes, and cryptographic authentication mechanisms are used to verify device identity.
Limitations: Device authentication does not protect against compromised devices that were initially trusted.

Data Encryption Model:
Description: Data encryption is used to protect data both in transit and at rest. This model ensures that even if data is intercepted, it remains unreadable without the proper decryption key.
Features: Secure communication protocols like TLS/SSL, IPsec, and AES encryption are employed to secure data.
Limitations: Encryption adds computational overhead and can be complex to manage at scale.
Access Control Model:
Description: Access control mechanisms are employed to restrict access to IoT devices and data. It defines who can access what and under what conditions.
Features: Role-based access control (RBAC), attribute-based access control (ABAC), and fine-grained access policies are used to define and enforce access rules.
Limitations: Effective access control requires a thorough understanding of IoT device roles and dependencies.
Trust Model:
Description: Trust models establish trust levels for devices, users, and entities within the IoT ecosystem. Devices are considered trusted or untrusted based on various factors.
Features: Trust can be based on device behaviour, reputation, manufacturer reputation, or a combination of these factors.
Limitations: Trust models require continuous monitoring and updating as trustworthiness can change over time.
Blockchain-Based Security Model:
Description: Blockchain technology is used to create a tamper-proof and decentralized ledger of IoT device transactions and data. This ensures data integrity and immutability.
Features: Smart contracts, distributed ledgers, and consensus algorithms provide security in a decentralized manner.
Limitations: Blockchain can be resource-intensive and may not be suitable for all IoT applications.
Security by Design Model:
Description: This model promotes security as an integral part of the IoT device and system development process. Security is considered from the initial design phase.
Features: Threat modelling, security requirements, and secure coding practices are implemented during the device's development lifecycle.
Limitations: Retrofitting security into existing devices can be challenging, and not all developers prioritize security by design.
Behavioural Analytics Model:
Description: Behavioural analytics focuses on monitoring and analysing the behaviour of devices and users within the IoT network. Deviations from expected behaviour trigger alerts.
Features: Machine learning algorithms and anomaly detection techniques are used to identify suspicious behaviour.
Limitations: Behavioural analytics may generate false positives and require continuous training and tuning.
Firmware and Patch Management Model:
Description: Ensures that IoT devices are regularly updated with security patches and firmware updates to mitigate vulnerabilities.
Features: Centralized management systems are used to distribute updates and monitor the patch status of devices.
Limitations: Managing updates in large-scale IoT deployments can be complex, and some devices may not be updated if not properly maintained.
Physical Security Model:
Description: Physical security measures protect IoT devices from physical tampering, theft, and unauthorized access.
Features: Physical locks, tamper-evident packaging, and secure housing are used to protect devices.
Limitations: Physical security measures may not prevent all types of attacks and require regular maintenance.
Supply Chain Security Model:
Description: Focuses on securing the entire supply chain of IoT devices, from manufacturing to deployment, to prevent tampering or malicious components.
Features: Supply chain audits, secure manufacturing practices, and trusted supply chain partners are employed.
Limitations: Supply chain security requires collaboration across multiple organizations and may add cost and complexity.
Incident Response and Recovery Model:
Description: Defines procedures for detecting, responding to, and recovering from security incidents in IoT environments.

Features: Incident response plans, backup and recovery strategies, and communication protocols are established.
Limitations: The effectiveness of incident response relies on timely detection and well-prepared response teams.
These security models can be used in combination to create comprehensive IoT security strategies tailored to the specific needs and risks of a given IoT deployment. Additionally, ongoing monitoring and adaptation to evolving threats are essential to maintaining a robust IoT security posture.

Layered Attacker Models:

In the realm of cybersecurity and IoT security, attacker models are used to define potential threats and adversaries. A layered attacker model considers different levels or layers of attackers based on their capabilities, resources, and objectives. These models help security practitioners and researchers to better understand and mitigate potential security risks.

Here's an overview of a layered attacker model:

Basic Layer (Layer 1):

Description: This is the lowest level of attackers, often referred to as "script kiddies" or opportunistic attackers. They have limited technical skills and resources and are typically looking for easy targets.

Objectives: Simple attacks like scanning for vulnerable devices, exploiting known vulnerabilities, or launching basic attacks like DDoS (Distributed Denial of Service) attacks.

Intermediate Layer (Layer 2):

Description: Intermediate attackers possess moderate technical skills and resources. They are more capable and motivated than basic attackers.

Objectives: Conducting more sophisticated attacks such as targeted malware attacks, social engineering, and stealing data for financial gain or competitive advantage.

Advanced Layer (Layer 3):

Description: Advanced attackers are highly skilled and well-resourced. They often have specific goals and are capable of launching sophisticated and persistent attacks.

Objectives: Carrying out advanced persistent threats (APTs), state-sponsored espionage, intellectual property theft, or other highly targeted and complex attacks.

Nation-State Layer (Layer 4):

Description: At this highest layer, attackers represent nation-states or highly organized and well-funded groups. They have significant technical capabilities and resources.

Objectives: Conducting cyber warfare, large-scale espionage, or attacks on critical infrastructure with potentially devastating consequences.

By considering these layered attacker models, organizations and security experts can tailor their security strategies to defend against threats at various levels. Different layers may require different approaches to detection, prevention, and mitigation. It's essential to recognize that the threat landscape is dynamic, and attackers may evolve from one layer to another as they gain skills and resources. Therefore, continuous monitoring and adaptation of security measures are crucial in IoT security and cybersecurity in general.

Challenges for Secure IoT

Securing the Internet of Things (IoT) poses a multitude of challenges due to the complex and interconnected nature of IoT systems. Addressing these challenges is essential to protect IoT devices, data, and the overall ecosystem. Here are some of the key challenges for securing IoT:

Diversity of Devices: IoT encompasses a wide range of devices, from simple sensors to complex industrial machinery. Ensuring security across this diversity can be challenging, as each device may have unique vulnerabilities.

Limited Computing Resources: Many IoT devices are resource-constrained in terms of processing power, memory, and storage. Implementing robust security measures on such devices can be difficult.

Firmware and Software Updates: IoT devices often require frequent updates to patch vulnerabilities and improve security. However, ensuring that all devices receive timely updates can be a logistical challenge.

Authentication and Access Control: Proper authentication and access control mechanisms are crucial to prevent unauthorized access to IoT devices. Managing credentials securely can be complex.

Data Encryption: Protecting data both in transit and at rest is essential. IoT devices may not always have the computational capacity to handle encryption efficiently.

Network Security: IoT devices often communicate over wireless or public networks, making them vulnerable to eavesdropping and man-in-the-middle attacks. Ensuring network security is critical.

Device Identity Management: Managing and securing device identities (e.g., certificates) is crucial to verify the authenticity of devices in an IoT network.

Privacy Concerns: IoT devices collect and transmit data, raising privacy concerns for individuals. Implementing privacy protections and adhering to regulations like GDPR is challenging.
IoT Ecosystem Complexity: IoT systems often involve multiple components, including devices, gateways, cloud services, and mobile apps. Securing the entire ecosystem is a complex task.
Vendor-Specific Protocols: Different IoT vendors may use proprietary communication protocols, making it challenging to achieve interoperability and security.
Physical Security: Many IoT devices are deployed in uncontrolled environments where physical security can't be guaranteed. This can make devices vulnerable to tampering.
Supply Chain Security: Ensuring the security of IoT devices throughout their supply chain is essential to prevent malicious components from entering the ecosystem.
Regulatory Compliance: IoT projects may need to comply with various regulations and standards, which can be complex and demanding.
Lack of Security Awareness: Many IoT developers and manufacturers may not prioritize security, leading to the creation of vulnerable devices.
Legacy Systems: Retrofitting security into existing IoT systems and legacy devices can be challenging due to compatibility issues and constraints.
Distributed Denial of Service (DDoS) Attacks: IoT devices have been used in large-scale DDoS attacks, highlighting the need for security against such threats.
Addressing these challenges requires a multi-faceted approach involving device-level security, network security, encryption, access control, secure development practices, and ongoing monitoring and updates. Collaboration among stakeholders, including device manufacturers, service providers, and regulatory bodies, is essential to create a secure IoT ecosystem. Additionally, IoT security should be a consideration from the early stages of IoT system design and development.

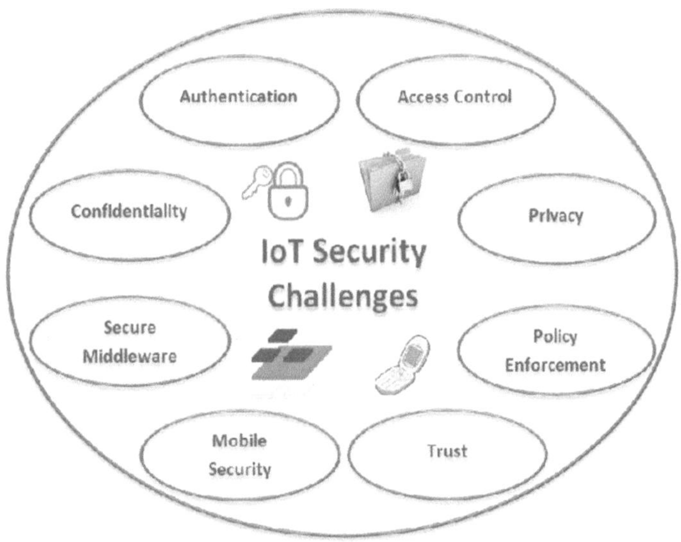

Threat Modelling

Threat modelling is a systematic approach to identifying and mitigating security threats and vulnerabilities in a software system or an application. It's a proactive process that helps software developers and security teams anticipate potential threats and implement appropriate security controls to protect against them. Here's an overview of threat modelling:
Define the Scope: Begin by defining the scope of your threat modelling exercise. Identify the software system, application, or component you want to analyse.
Create a Diagram: Develop a visual representation of the system, often in the form of a data flow diagram (DFD) or architectural diagram. This diagram should illustrate the various components, data flows, and interactions within the system.
Identify Assets: Determine the assets within the system that need protection. These can include sensitive data, user accounts, software components, and hardware devices.

Enumerate Threats: Brainstorm and list potential threats and vulnerabilities that could compromise the security of the system. Threats may come from various sources, such as external attackers, malicious insiders, or system failures.

Assess Risks: Evaluate the risks associated with each identified threat. Assess the likelihood of the threat occurring and the potential impact it could have on the system.

Prioritize Threats: Prioritize the threats based on their risk level. Focus on the threats that pose the highest risk to the system's security.

Mitigation Strategies: Develop mitigation strategies for each high-priority threat. These strategies may include implementing security controls, changing the system design, or enhancing user authentication and access controls.

Documentation: Document the threat model, including the identified threats, risk assessments, and mitigation strategies. This documentation serves as a reference for development and security teams.

Review and Iterate: Review the threat model with stakeholders, including developers, security experts, and system architects. Gather feedback and refine the model as needed.

Implementation and Testing: Implement the security controls and mitigation measures identified in the threat model. Thoroughly test the system to ensure that the security measures are effective.

Monitoring and Maintenance: Continuously monitor the system for new threats and vulnerabilities. Update the threat model as the system evolves and new risks emerge. Implement patches and updates as necessary.

Benefits of Threat Modelling:

Early Detection: Threat modelling helps identify security issues at an early stage of development, reducing the cost and effort required to fix them.

Improved Security: By systematically addressing security threats, organizations can strengthen their software and system security, reducing the risk of data breaches and other security incidents.

Risk Prioritization: Threat modelling allows organizations to prioritize security investments by focusing on the most critical threats.

Compliance: Many security standards and regulations require threat modelling as part of the security assessment process.

Communication: Threat modelling promotes communication among development, security, and business teams, ensuring that everyone understands the security requirements and risks.

Threat modelling is a proactive approach to security that should be integrated into the software development lifecycle. It helps organizations build more secure systems, protect sensitive data, and respond effectively to evolving security threats.

Security model for IoT Light weight cryptography

Lightweight cryptography is a critical component of the security model for IoT (Internet of Things) devices, particularly for resource-constrained devices with limited processing power, memory, and energy resources. Lightweight cryptography focuses on providing strong security with minimal computational overhead. Here's an overview of the security model for IoT with lightweight cryptography:

Device Authentication: Lightweight cryptographic algorithms are used to establish device identities and verify the authenticity of IoT devices during the authentication process. For example, lightweight digital signatures or lightweight public-key cryptography can be employed for device authentication.

Secure Communication: Lightweight cryptographic protocols are used to secure communication between IoT devices and with backend servers or gateways. Protocols like DTLS (Datagram Transport Layer Security) or lightweight versions of TLS/SSL (Transport Layer Security/Secure Sockets Layer) are suitable for securing data in transit.

Data Encryption: Lightweight encryption algorithms are used to protect data both in transit and at rest on resource-constrained IoT devices. Stream ciphers or lightweight block ciphers can be applied to encrypt data efficiently.

Message Integrity: Lightweight cryptographic hash functions and message authentication codes (MACs) are used to ensure the integrity of messages exchanged between IoT devices. These mechanisms help detect any unauthorized tampering with data during transmission.

Key Management: Secure key management is crucial in IoT systems. Lightweight cryptographic algorithms are employed for key exchange and management. Protocols like ECDH (Elliptic Curve Diffie-Hellman) with lightweight elliptic curves can be used for efficient key exchange.

Resource Efficiency: Lightweight cryptography is designed to minimize computational and memory resource requirements, making it suitable for IoT devices with limited resources. Algorithms and protocols are optimized to reduce energy consumption and processing overhead.

Resistance to Attacks: Lightweight cryptographic algorithms are designed to resist common cryptographic attacks, such as brute-force attacks, side-channel attacks, and replay attacks. Techniques like constant-time implementations and masking can be employed to enhance security.

Scalability: The security model should be scalable to accommodate a growing number of IoT devices while maintaining efficient cryptographic operations.

Regulatory Compliance: IoT systems using lightweight cryptography should adhere to relevant security standards and regulations, ensuring compliance with industry-specific requirements.

Continuous Updates: The security model should be adaptable to evolving threats. Regular updates and patches may be necessary to address newly discovered vulnerabilities.

Integration with IoT Protocols: Lightweight cryptographic algorithms and protocols should seamlessly integrate with IoT-specific communication protocols like MQTT or CoAP (Constrained Application Protocol).

Privacy Considerations: The security model should account for privacy concerns, allowing for data anonymization and user consent mechanisms as required by privacy regulations.

By incorporating lightweight cryptography into the security model, IoT devices can achieve strong security without overburdening their limited resources. Security should be considered throughout the IoT device lifecycle, from design and development to deployment and ongoing management, to ensure robust protection against emerging threats.

Exercise

Exercise 1 – MCQ

1. What is a common security threat in IoT devices?
a) Over-encryption
b) Firmware updates
c) Unauthorized access
d) Data compression

2. Which of the following is a recommended security measure for IoT devices?
a) Disabling all security features
b) Regularly updating firmware and software
c) Sharing device credentials openly
d) Using weak passwords

Exercise 2 – True/False

1. Unauthorized access is a common security threat in IoT devices.
2. Regularly updating firmware and software is a recommended security measure for IoT devices.

Exercise 3 – Fill in the blanks

1. One of the key privacy concerns associated with IoT is unauthorized data ________ and ________.
2. One of the recommended security measures for IoT devices is regularly updating ________ and ________.

Exercise 4 – One word answer

1. What is a common security threat in IoT devices?
2. What is a recommended security measure for IoT devices?

Exercise 5 – Small answer

1. What are the best practises for Privacy in IoT?
2. What is a recommended security practice for IoT devices?

Exercise 6 – Long answer

1. Explain why unauthorized access is a significant security threat in IoT devices.
2. Describe the importance of regularly updating firmware and software in IoT devices. Explain how this practice enhances security and mitigates vulnerabilities.

Answer:

Exercise 1.

1. c) Unauthorized access
2. b) Regularly updating firmware and software

Exercise 2.

1. True
2. True

Exercise 3.

1. collection; usage

2. firmware; software
Exercise 4.
1. Unauthorized
2. Updating

Previous Year Questions

1. What are the challenges for securing IoT. (SPPU B.Tech. 2018)
2. Write a detail note on secured communication in IoT applications for data transfer and its importance. (Mumbai University B.Tech. 2017)
3. What is threat analysis in Internet of Things? Explain detail threat analysis. (SPPU 2017)
4. Why security required in IoT? Explain in detail various security model in Internet of Things. (SPPU 2017)
5. What is Internet of Things security tomography? Explain in detail layered attacker mode? (SPPU 2017)
6. Why security required in IoT? Explain detail various security in Internet of Things. (Uttar Pradesh university B.Tech. 2018-19)
7. What is threat analysis in Internet of Things? Explain detail threat analysis. (Uttar Pradesh university B.Tech. 2018-19)

ONLINE RESOURCES

Link: https://forms.gle/RHLJQP5S5w6Q7xG7A

QR Code :

Link: https://www.youtube.com/playlist?list=PLzlh_31VWEFqwQXwmArQJ7GY7XfNxcNFX

QR Code :

Chapter 8: IoT Development and Prototyping

Prototyping Tools and Platforms

Prototyping is a critical phase in the development of Internet of Things (IoT) projects, enabling developers to design and test both hardware and software components before full-scale production. To facilitate this process, a variety of prototyping tools and platforms are available. In this article, we will explore some popular options for creating IoT prototypes.

Arduino:

Description: Arduino is a well-known open-source hardware and software platform offering a wide range of microcontroller boards, sensors, and shields for building IoT prototypes.

Key Features: User-friendly, extensive community support, a vast library of pre-built code, and compatibility with various sensors and actuators.

Raspberry Pi:

Description: Raspberry Pi is a versatile, credit card-sized single-board computer suitable for prototyping IoT applications, with multiple models available.

Key Features: Powerful, supports multiple programming languages, and provides GPIO pins for hardware interfacing.

ESP8266 and ESP32:

Description: These low-cost, Wi-Fi-enabled microcontrollers are popular choices for IoT prototyping. The ESP8266 is known for simplicity, while the ESP32 is a series of low-cost, low-power system-on-a-chip (SoC) microcontrollers with integrated Wi-Fi and Bluetooth capabilities. It's highly suitable for IoT applications requiring wireless connectivity.

Key Features: Cost-effective, wireless connectivity, and suitable for battery-powered applications.

Particle:

Description: Particle offers a range of IoT development boards and a cloud platform that simplifies device management, cloud integration, and over-the-air updates.

Key Features: Cloud-based development, scalable infrastructure, and a user-friendly interface.

Tinker card:

Description: Tinker card is an online platform that allows users to create IoT prototypes in a virtual environment, particularly useful for beginners and educational purposes.

Key Features: Web-based, drag-and-drop components, and simulation capabilities.

Node-RED:

Description: Node-RED is a flow-based development tool for IoT applications, streamlining the connection of devices, APIs, and online services.

Key Features: Visual programming, extensive library of nodes, and integration with various IoT platforms.

Thing Worx:

Description: Thing Worx, by PTC, is a comprehensive IoT platform offering tools for IoT application development, including prototyping, connectivity, and analytics.

Key Features: End-to-end IoT platform, rapid application development, and industrial-grade capabilities.

Blynk:

Description: Blynk is a mobile app builder for IoT projects, enabling users to create smartphone interfaces for controlling and monitoring IoT devices.

Key Features: User-friendly app builder, cloud connectivity, and support for popular IoT hardware.

Autodesk Fusion 360:

Description: Fusion 360 is a 3D CAD/CAM tool suitable for IoT hardware design and prototyping, offering a range of tools for 3D modelling and simulation.

Key Features: 3D design, simulation, and collaboration capabilities.

Microsoft Azure IoT Central:

Description: Azure IoT Central is a fully managed IoT Software as a Service (SaaS) platform by Microsoft, providing tools for device connectivity, management, and analytics.

Key Features: Cloud-based, scalable, and integrated with Azure services.

Cloud bit/Little bits:

Description: Cloud bit is part of the little bit's platform, which offers modular electronic building blocks that snap together magnetically. Cloud bit is designed to connect little bits creations to the internet and cloud services.

Key Features: Modular Building Blocks, Internet Connectivity, Cloud Integration, Wireless Communication, Programming Options etc.

Selecting the appropriate prototyping tool or platform for your IoT project depends on factors such as your expertise, project requirements, and budget. These tools and platforms offer diverse options to assist you in effectively designing, developing, and testing IoT prototypes, expediting the path from concept to production-ready devices.

Programming for IoT

Programming for the Internet of Things (IoT) involves the development of software to enable IoT devices to collect, transmit, process, and act upon data. IoT programming encompasses a wide array of programming languages, platforms, and frameworks, all tailored to meet the unique requirements of IoT applications. In this article, we'll delve into the fundamental aspects of programming for IoT.

Choice of Programming Languages:

Several programming languages are commonly employed in IoT development, each with its own set of strengths and weaknesses:

C/C++: These languages are popular choices for programming IoT devices due to their low-level system access and efficiency, making them well-suited for resource-constrained environments.

Python: Python is often utilized for IoT applications that demand rapid development and prototyping. It boasts extensive libraries and strong community support.

Java: Java is favoured for IoT applications running on edge gateways or more powerful devices. It offers platform independence and robust support for object-oriented programming.

JavaScript: JavaScript is prevalent in web-based IoT applications and interfaces, serving both frontend and backend development.

Node.js: Node.js, a JavaScript runtime, is well-suited for server-side IoT applications and real-time data processing.

IoT Platforms and Frameworks:

IoT development can benefit from various platforms and frameworks that provide tools and services aimed at simplifying the development process:

Arduino: Arduino offers an integrated development environment (IDE) and a diverse range of libraries for programming IoT devices. It enjoys popularity among beginners and hobbyists.

Raspberry Pi: Raspberry Pi, often programmed in Python or C/C++, stands as a versatile platform for creating IoT applications, especially those demanding more computational power.

Platform-specific SDKs: Many IoT device manufacturers furnish software development kits (SDKs) tailored to their hardware, streamlining the programming process.

IoT Platforms: Cloud-based IoT platforms like Microsoft Azure IoT, AWS IoT, and Google Cloud IoT Core offer comprehensive services for device management, data storage, and analytics.

Communication Protocols:

IoT devices communicate with each other and the cloud via various communication protocols:

MQTT (Message Queuing Telemetry Transport): MQTT stands as a lightweight and efficient protocol for IoT device-to-device and device-to-cloud communication.

HTTP/HTTPS: Frequently utilized for web-based IoT applications, enabling data exchange over the internet.

CoAP (Constrained Application Protocol): Designed for resource-constrained IoT devices, CoAP simplifies communication in low-power, low-bandwidth environments.

Security Considerations:

Security assumes paramount importance in IoT programming due to the potential risks associated with data breaches and device vulnerabilities:

Data Encryption: Implementation of end-to-end encryption safeguards data both during transit and at rest.

Authentication: Robust authentication mechanisms ensure that only authorized devices can access IoT networks.

Access Control: Access control measures restrict device and user access to sensitive resources.

Firmware Updates: Regular firmware updates are vital to patch security vulnerabilities and maintain device security.

Data Management and Analytics:

IoT programming often involves the collection and processing of substantial data volumes generated by devices. Key considerations include:

Data Storage: Deciding where and how data will be stored, whether locally on devices, in the cloud, or on edge gateways.

Data Processing: Developing algorithms and scripts to process and analyze IoT data to extract valuable insights.
Real-time Processing: For applications necessitating real-time responses, mechanisms for immediate data processing and decision-making are crucial.
Programming for IoT necessitates a multidisciplinary approach, blending expertise in hardware, software, networking, and security. As IoT technology continues to evolve, IoT programming will play a pivotal role in shaping the future of smart cities, industries, healthcare, and more, offering innovative solutions to complex challenges.

Arduino Programming for IoT

Arduino is a versatile open-source platform that has gained popularity for IoT (Internet of Things) development due to its ease of use and extensive community support.

8.3.1 Key features of Arduino

Microcontroller: Arduino boards are equipped with microcontrollers (typically AT mega series) that provide processing power for your projects.
GPIO Pins: Arduino boards feature a set of General-Purpose Input/Output (GPIO) pins that can be used to connect and control various sensors, LEDs, motors, and other external components.
Analog Pins: Arduino has Analog input pins for reading Analog signals from sensors like light sensors, temperature sensors, and potentiometers.
PWM (Pulse Width Modulation): Arduino provides PWM pins, allowing you to simulate Analog output by controlling the duty cycle of the signal. This is useful for dimming LEDs and controlling motor speed.
Analog-to-Digital Conversion (ADC): Arduino has built-in ADC capabilities that enable it to convert Analog sensor readings into digital values for processing.
Programming Environment: Arduino uses a simplified programming environment based on C/C++. The Arduino IDE (Integrated Development Environment) provides an easy-to-use interface for writing, compiling, and uploading code to Arduino boards.
Libraries: Arduino has a vast library ecosystem that simplifies complex tasks. These libraries provide pre-written code for various functions, sensors, and communication protocols.
Community Support: Arduino has a large and active community of developers and enthusiasts who share knowledge, offer support, and contribute to the development of libraries and projects.
Variety of Boards: Arduino offers a range of boards, each with its own specifications and capabilities. Common models include Arduino Uno, Arduino Nano, and Arduino Mega, suitable for different project requirements.
Versatile Power Options: Arduino boards can be powered through USB, batteries, or external power supplies, making them adaptable to various power sources.
Easy Hardware Connections: Arduino boards are designed with standard pin layouts, making it simple to connect sensors and components without the need for soldering.
Open Source: Arduino is open-source hardware and software, allowing users to modify and share designs freely. This fosters innovation and collaboration.
Low-Cost: Arduino boards are affordable and widely available, making them an excellent choice for educational and hobbyist projects.
Cross-Platform Compatibility: The Arduino IDE is available for Windows, macOS, and Linux, ensuring compatibility with most computer systems.
Real-Time Interaction: Arduino can interact with the physical world in real time, making it suitable for applications such as robotics, home automation, and IoT.
Custom Shields: Arduino shields are expansion boards that can be stacked onto the main Arduino board, adding specific functionalities like Wi-Fi, GPS, and motor control.
Diverse Applications: Arduino is used in a wide range of applications, including robotics, home automation, IoT, wearable technology, and educational projects.
These features collectively make Arduino a versatile and accessible platform for electronics and embedded systems development, making it a popular choice for both beginners and experienced developers.

Arduino programming for IoT:

Accessibility: Arduino's user-friendly development environment and simple programming language make it accessible to both beginners and experienced developers. This accessibility is particularly valuable for IoT enthusiasts who may not have extensive coding experience.
Hardware Compatibility: Arduino boards come with a range of input and output pins, enabling seamless integration with various sensors, actuators, and communication modules commonly used in IoT projects. This compatibility simplifies the creation of IoT prototypes and applications.

Arduino IDE: The Arduino Integrated Development Environment (IDE) is a straightforward platform for writing, compiling, and uploading code to Arduino boards. It employs a simplified version of the C/C++ programming language, making it easy for users to get started.

Extensive Library Support: The Arduino community has developed an extensive library of pre-written code and libraries. These libraries cover a wide range of functions, including connecting to Wi-Fi networks, handling sensor data, and controlling actuators. This vast resource library accelerates IoT project development

IoT Connectivity: Arduino boards can connect to the internet and other devices through various communication modules such as Wi-Fi, Ethernet, Bluetooth, and LoRa. This capability is essential for IoT applications, enabling data exchange with cloud services and other IoT devices.

Sensor Integration: Arduino supports a wide array of sensors, including temperature, humidity, motion, and environmental sensors. These sensors can be easily integrated into IoT projects, allowing for data collection and monitoring.

Rapid Prototyping: Arduino excels in prototyping IoT applications. Its quick development cycle and ease of use allow developers to rapidly create and test IoT solutions before scaling to production-ready hardware.

Strong Community: The Arduino community is active and collaborative, with numerous forums, tutorials, and resources available online. This community support facilitates problem-solving, knowledge-sharing, and learning.

Scalability Considerations: While Arduino is an excellent choice for prototyping and small-scale IoT projects, it may not be suitable for large-scale deployments due to hardware limitations. However, it serves as an invaluable starting point for proof-of-concept development.

In summary, Arduino programming is a versatile and accessible approach for IoT development. Its user-friendly environment, hardware compatibility, library support, and community resources make it an attractive choice for IoT enthusiasts and hobbyists exploring the possibilities of IoT technology.

Raspberry Pi Programming for IoT

Raspberry Pi is a versatile and cost-effective single-board computer that is widely used for IoT (Internet of Things) projects and applications.

Key Features of Raspberry Pi boards:

CPU and Processing Power: Raspberry Pi boards are equipped with a CPU that ranges from single-core to quad-core, depending on the model. The CPU architecture varies between ARM-based processors, providing processing power suitable for a wide range of applications.

RAM (Random Access Memory):

Raspberry Pi models typically come with varying amounts of RAM, ranging from 256MB to 8GB. Sufficient RAM is essential for multitasking and running applications smoothly.

GPIO (General-Purpose Input/Output) Pins: GPIO pins allow users to connect external sensors, actuators, and other hardware components to the Raspberry Pi. GPIO pins are programmable and can be controlled through software, making them central to IoT and hardware projects.

USB Ports: Raspberry Pi boards feature multiple USB ports, which are useful for connecting peripherals like keyboards, mice, Wi-Fi dongles, and external storage devices.

HDMI Output: Raspberry Pi provides HDMI output for connecting to monitors and TVs, supporting both Full HD and 4K resolutions. This feature makes Raspberry Pi suitable for media playback and digital signage applications.

Audio Output: Raspberry Pi boards have a 3.5mm audio jack for connecting headphones or speakers. Some models also support digital audio via HDMI.

Ethernet Port: Many Raspberry Pi models include an Ethernet port for wired network connectivity. This is useful for projects requiring a stable and high-speed internet connection.

Wireless Connectivity: Some Raspberry Pi models come with built-in Wi-Fi and Bluetooth capabilities, eliminating the need for external dongles. Wireless connectivity enhances IoT projects and simplifies network access.

Storage Options: Raspberry Pi boards use microSD cards as the primary storage medium for the operating system and data. Some models support USB-connected storage devices for additional storage capacity.

Camera and Display Ports: Raspberry Pi includes camera and display ports for connecting official Raspberry Pi Camera Modules and touchscreen displays. These ports enable projects involving photography, video streaming, and interactive displays.

Power Supply: Raspberry Pi boards are powered via a micro-USB port or a USB-C port, depending on the model.The power supply voltage and current requirements vary among models.

Operating System Compatibility: Raspberry Pi supports various operating systems, including Raspberry Pi OS (formerly Raspbian), Linux distributions, and even Windows 10 IoT Core. This flexibility allows developers to choose the OS that best suits their project requirements.

Expansion Headers: Some Raspberry Pi models feature additional expansion headers, such as the Camera Serial Interface (CSI) and Display Serial Interface (DSI), for connecting compatible accessories.

GPIO Header: The GPIO header includes pins for digital input and output, analog input, power, and ground. It facilitates the connection of sensors, displays, and other hardware components for DIY projects.

Official Accessories: Raspberry Pi offers a range of official accessories, including camera modules, touchscreen displays, power supplies, and cases, designed to enhance the functionality and versatility of the board.

Community and Support: Raspberry Pi boasts a large and active community of developers and enthusiasts who provide extensive online resources, forums, tutorials, and support.

Raspberry Pi's diverse features and capabilities make it a versatile platform for a wide range of projects, from IoT applications and robotics to media centres and educational tools. The choice of a specific Raspberry Pi model depends on the project's requirements and desired performance.

Brief overview of Raspberry Pi programming for IoT:

Affordable and Compact: Raspberry Pi is an affordable and compact computing platform that is suitable for a wide range of IoT applications. It offers a variety of models with different capabilities to suit specific project requirements.

Linux-Based OS: Raspberry Pi runs on a Linux-based operating system (e.g., Raspbian), which provides a familiar and robust environment for software development. Developers can use Python, C/C++, and other programming languages for IoT applications.

GPIO Pins: One of the standout features of Raspberry Pi for IoT is its General-Purpose Input/Output (GPIO) pins. These pins allow developers to connect sensors, actuators, and other hardware components directly to the Raspberry Pi for data input and output.

Connectivity Options: Raspberry Pi can connect to the internet and other devices through various methods, including Ethernet, Wi-Fi, and Bluetooth. This connectivity is essential for IoT projects to exchange data with the cloud or other IoT devices.

Extensive Community Support: The Raspberry Pi community is vast and active, with a wealth of online resources, forums, tutorials, and projects available. This community support facilitates learning and problem-solving for IoT enthusiasts and developers.

Pre-installed Software: Raspberry Pi comes with pre-installed software and tools that are beneficial for IoT development. For example, it includes Python and libraries for GPIO control and accessing sensors.

Multimedia Capabilities: In addition to IoT, Raspberry Pi's multimedia capabilities make it suitable for projects involving media playback, cameras, and image processing, expanding its versatility.

IoT Prototyping: Raspberry Pi is an excellent platform for prototyping IoT solutions. Developers can quickly create and test IoT prototypes before moving to production-grade hardware.

Real-Time Interaction: With its GPIO pins and powerful processing capabilities, Raspberry Pi can interact with sensors and actuators in real time, making it suitable for projects requiring timely data collection and response.

Customization and Flexibility: Raspberry Pi offers flexibility in hardware and software customization, allowing developers to tailor IoT solutions to their specific needs and requirements.

Education and Learning: Raspberry Pi is a valuable educational tool for teaching and learning about IoT, programming, and computer science. It is used in schools, workshops, and online courses to introduce students to IoT concepts.

In conclusion, Raspberry Pi programming for IoT offers a versatile and accessible platform for creating IoT projects. Its affordability, compact size, GPIO pins, and robust community support make it an ideal choice for both beginners and experienced developers looking to explore the world of IoT and build innovative IoT applications.

Building Your Own IoT Device

Creating your own Internet of Things (IoT) device can be a rewarding and educational experience. IoT devices are designed to collect, process, and transmit data, allowing them to interact with the physical world and communicate with other devices or cloud services. Below are the steps to guide you in building your custom IoT device:

Define Your IoT Device's Purpose: Begin by identifying the specific problem or task your IoT device will address. Consider what data it needs to collect, how it will process this data, and what actions it should take based on the information.

Choose Hardware Components: Select the hardware components that suit your project's requirements. Common components include microcontrollers (e.g., Arduino, Raspberry Pi), sensors (e.g., temperature, humidity, motion), actuators (e.g., motors, relays), and power sources (e.g., batteries or USB power).
Assemble Hardware: Connect and assemble the chosen components, ensuring they are wired correctly. Follow data sheets, pin diagrams, and tutorials for proper connections.
Develop Firmware or Software: Write the code (firmware or software) that will run on your IoT device. Depending on your hardware, you may use programming languages like C/C++, Python, JavaScript, or others. Your code should handle data collection, processing, and communication.
Implement Data Communication: Decide how your IoT device will communicate with the outside world. Common communication methods include Wi-Fi, Ethernet, Bluetooth, Zigbee, LoRa, or cellular networks. Choose the one that best suits your project's connectivity needs.
Set Up Data Storage: Determine where you want to store the data collected by your IoT device. Options include local storage on the device, cloud-based storage services (e.g., AWS, Azure, Google Cloud), or a dedicated server.
Ensure Data Security: Implement security measures to protect the data your IoT device collects and transmits. This may include encryption, authentication, and access control to prevent unauthorized access to your device and data.
Develop User Interfaces (Optional): Depending on your project, you may need to create user interfaces, such as web or mobile apps, to interact with your IoT device and visualize its data.
Power Management: Consider power consumption and management to ensure your IoT device can run efficiently and for extended periods if needed. Implement sleep modes and power-saving strategies.
Test and Debug: Test your IoT device thoroughly to ensure it functions as expected. Debug any issues and refine your code or hardware as necessary.
Deployment: If your IoT device is meant for a specific location or use case, deploy it in the appropriate environment. Ensure its installed securely and has reliable power sources.
Monitor and Maintain: Continuously monitor your IoT device's performance and data to identify any anomalies or issues. Regular maintenance and updates may be required to keep it running smoothly.
Scale and Expand: If your project is successful, consider scaling it by adding more devices or expanding its capabilities based on user feedback and evolving requirements.

Building your own IoT device is a hands-on learning experience that allows you to explore various aspects of hardware and software development, data management, and connectivity. It's important to document your project, share your findings, and engage with the IoT maker community for support and inspiration. With creativity and dedication, you can bring your IoT ideas to life and contribute to the growing world of interconnected devices.

IoT Hardware - Arduino, Raspberry Pi, ESP32, Cloud bit/Little bits

IoT hardware encompasses a wide range of devices and platforms that enable the connection of physical objects to the internet. The hardware you choose depends on your specific IoT project requirements. Here's an overview of some popular IoT hardware platforms you mentioned:

Arduino:

Description: Arduino is an open-source hardware and software platform that offers a variety of microcontroller boards for building IoT devices. It's known for its simplicity and versatility.
Use Cases: Arduino is suitable for a wide range of IoT projects, from simple sensor monitoring to home automation and robotics.

Raspberry Pi:

Description: Raspberry Pi is a credit card-sized single-board computer that can run various operating systems. It provides more processing power and capabilities compared to microcontrollers like Arduino.
Use Cases: Raspberry Pi is ideal for IoT projects that require computing power, multimedia capabilities, and running full-fledged applications. It's commonly used in home automation, media centers, and edge computing.

ESP32:

Description: ESP32 is a series of low-cost, low-power system-on-a-chip (SoC) microcontrollers with integrated Wi-Fi and Bluetooth capabilities. It's highly suitable for IoT applications requiring wireless connectivity.
Use Cases: ESP32 is often used in IoT projects that involve sensor data collection, remote monitoring, and control due to its wireless communication capabilities.

Cloud bit/Little bits:

Description: Cloud bit is part of the little bit's platform, which offers modular electronic building blocks that snap together magnetically. Cloud bit is designed to connect little bits creations to the internet and cloud services.
Use Cases: Little bits and Cloud bit are excellent for educational IoT projects and prototyping where simplicity and ease of use are essential. They are great for teaching electronics and IoT concepts to beginners.

Each of these hardware platforms has its strengths and is suitable for specific IoT applications. When selecting IoT hardware, consider factors like processing power, connectivity options, power consumption, ease of use, and compatibility with your project's goals. Additionally, take into account the community support, libraries, and resources available for each platform to streamline your development process.

Particle Photon

The Particle Photon is a popular development board designed for creating your own IoT (Internet of Things) devices. It's part of the Particle platform, which provides a set of hardware and software tools to simplify IoT development. Here are some key features and aspects of the Particle Photon in the context of creating your own IoT device:

Microcontroller: The Particle Photon is equipped with a powerful microcontroller, which is based on the ARM Cortex-M3 architecture. This microcontroller provides the processing power needed for IoT applications.

Wi-Fi Connectivity: One of the standout features of the Particle Photon is its built-in Wi-Fi module. This allows your IoT device to connect to Wi-Fi networks and communicate with other devices and cloud services over the internet.

Cloud Integration: Particle offers a cloud platform that seamlessly integrates with the Particle Photon. This cloud platform allows you to remotely manage and control your IoT devices, receive data from them, and send commands to them.

Development Environment: Particle provides a user-friendly development environment based on the Arduino programming language. You can write code for your IoT device using the Particle Web IDE or Particle Workbench, which is an extension for Visual Studio Code.

IoT Features: The Particle Photon includes features tailored for IoT development, such as over-the-air (OTA) firmware updates, which allow you to update your device's software remotely.

Particle Libraries: The Particle platform offers a wide range of libraries and resources for common IoT tasks, making it easier to add sensors, actuators, and other components to your IoT device.

Community and Support: Particle has an active community of developers and provides support through forums, documentation, and tutorials, making it accessible to both beginners and experienced makers.

Scalability: Particle supports device fleet management, making it suitable for scaling up your IoT project to include multiple devices.

Prototyping: The Particle Photon is ideal for prototyping IoT projects due to its ease of use and quick development cycle.

Open Source: Particle hardware and software are open source, allowing you to customize and extend the platform to suit your specific project requirements.

Overall, the Particle Photon is a versatile and user-friendly IoT development board that simplifies the process of creating your own IoT devices. It's particularly well-suited for projects that require Wi-Fi connectivity and cloud integration, making it a popular choice among IoT enthusiasts and developers.

Beagle bone Black

The Beagle Bone Black is a single-board computer (SBC) that is widely used for various embedded computing and Internet of Things (IoT) applications. Here are some key features and aspects of the Beagle Bone Black:

Microprocessor: The Beagle Bone Black is powered by an ARM Cortex-A8 processor, providing sufficient processing power for a range of embedded applications.

I/O Ports: It offers a variety of I/O pins, including digital I/O, Analog inputs, PWM outputs, UART, SPI, and I2C interfaces. These pins make it versatile for connecting to a wide range of sensors, actuators, and external devices.

Memory: It typically comes with 512MB of DDR3 RAM, which is sufficient for many embedded projects. It also has built-in eMMC storage for the operating system and data storage.

Connectivity: The Beagle Bone Black has built-in Ethernet connectivity, making it suitable for networking and IoT applications. Some models also come with onboard Wi-Fi and Bluetooth options.

Operating System: It supports various Linux distributions, including Debian and Ubuntu. These operating systems offer a familiar development environment for programmers.

Expansion Capes: The Beagle Bone Black supports expansion capes (add-on boards) that can extend its functionality. Capes are available for tasks such as motor control, LCD displays, and more.

USB Ports: It includes USB host and USB client ports, which can be used for connecting peripherals, external storage, or even connecting the Beagle Bone Black to a host computer.

HDMI Output: It features an HDMI output port, allowing you to connect it to a monitor or TV for display purposes.

Community and Documentation: The Beagle Bone community is active and provides extensive documentation, tutorials, and support for users. This community-driven aspect can be helpful for both beginners and experienced developers.
Open Source: The Beagle Bone Black hardware and software are open source, encouraging customization and adaptation for specific projects.
Low Cost: Compared to some other SBCs, the Beagle Bone Black offers a reasonable price point, making it accessible for hobbyists, makers, and small-scale IoT projects.
Industrial Applications: Its reliability and robustness make it suitable for industrial applications and automation tasks.
The Beagle Bone Black is known for its versatility and flexibility, making it a popular choice for a wide range of projects, including robotics, home automation, IoT gateways, and embedded systems development. Its rich I/O options, coupled with an active community and extensive documentation, make it a valuable tool for both prototyping and production-level projects.
IoT Software - languages for programming IoT hardware for middleware applications and API development, for making front ends, REST and JSON-LD
IoT software development encompasses various aspects, including programming IoT hardware, creating middleware applications, developing APIs, designing front ends, and utilizing technologies like REST and JSON-LD. Here, we'll delve into each of these aspects in detail:
Programming IoT Hardware:
IoT devices often require firmware or software to control sensors, actuators, and communication with other devices or the cloud. Common programming languages and platforms for IoT hardware include:
C/C++: These languages are commonly used for low-level programming of microcontrollers like Arduino or ESP8266/ESP32. They offer fine-grained control over hardware resources.
Micro Python: Micro Python allows you to program microcontrollers using a Python-like language. It simplifies IoT development by providing a high-level language.
JavaScript (Node.js): Node.js can be used for IoT development on platforms like Raspberry Pi or Beagle Bone. It's suitable for web-based IoT applications.
Python: Python is widely used for IoT programming, especially for Raspberry Pi-based projects. Libraries like GPIO Zero simplify hardware control.
Middleware Applications:
Middleware acts as an intermediary layer between IoT devices and the application layer. It handles communication, data processing, and device management. Common languages for middleware development include:
Java: Java is suitable for building robust middleware applications. It offers features like multi-threading and extensive libraries for networking and data processing.
Python: Python's simplicity and versatility make it a popular choice for developing middleware. Libraries like Flask and Django can be used for building RESTful APIs.
Node.js: Node.js is well-suited for real-time applications and can be used to build lightweight middleware for IoT systems.
API Development:
APIs (Application Programming Interfaces) are essential for communication between IoT devices, middleware, and front-end applications. REST (Representational State Transfer) is a common architectural style for designing APIs, and JSON-LD (JavaScript Object Notation for Linked Data) can enhance data interchange. Common languages for API development include:
Python: Python is often used with frameworks like Flask or Django to create RESTful APIs. The json module simplifies JSON data handling.
JavaScript (Node.js): Node.js is suitable for building APIs, and libraries like Express.js make it easy to create RESTful endpoints.
Java: Java's robustness makes it suitable for developing RESTful APIs. Frameworks like Spring Boot can streamline API development.
Front-End Development:
Front-end development involves creating user interfaces (UIs) for IoT applications. Web technologies are commonly used for this purpose, and languages include:
HTML/CSS/JavaScript: These are the core technologies for web-based front-end development. Frameworks like React, Angular, or Vue.js are popular choices for building interactive IoT dashboards.
Python (Django, Flask): Python can be used for server-side rendering of front-end templates in web applications.

JavaScript (Electron): Electron allows you to build cross-platform desktop applications using web technologies, making it suitable for IoT desktop applications.

In summary, IoT software development requires a mix of programming languages and technologies, depending on the specific aspects of your IoT project. Hardware programming languages, middleware development languages, API development languages, and front-end development technologies all play crucial roles in building a comprehensive IoT solution. The choice of language and technology depends on factors like the type of hardware, application requirements, and the skillset of the development team.

A comparison of IoT boards and platforms in terms of computing

Aspect	Raspberry Pi 4 y	Arduino Uno	ESP8266	AWS IoT Core
CPU	Quad-core Cortex-A72, CPU @ 1.5GHz	8-bit ATmega328P, MCU @ 16MHz	Single-core Tensilica, LX106 CPU @ 80MHz	Cloud-based
RAM	2GB, 4GB, or 8GB	2KB SRAM	160KB SRAM	Varies by instance
Storage	MicroSD card slot	Flash (32KB)	External SPI Flash	Cloud-based
GPU	Broadcom Video Core VI	None	None	None
Networking	Gigabit Ethernet	None	Wi-Fi	Cloud-based
Operating System	Raspberry Pi OS	Arduino IDE	Custom Firmware	N/A

List of available wireless communications boards available in Raspberry Pi

Raspberry Pi, a popular single-board computer, can be equipped with various wireless communication modules or boards to enable wireless connectivity for different purposes. Here are some of the available wireless communication boards and modules that you can use with Raspberry Pi:

Raspberry Pi WiFi and Bluetooth Modules:

Raspberry Pi 3 and later models come with built-in WiFi and Bluetooth capabilities. No additional hardware is required to use these features.

USB WiFi Adapters:

Various USB WiFi adapters are compatible with Raspberry Pi. These adapters can provide improved WiFi performance, extended range, or support for specific WiFi standards.

USB Bluetooth Dongles:

If you need additional Bluetooth capabilities or compatibility with specific Bluetooth profiles, you can use USB Bluetooth dongles with your Raspberry Pi.

Raspberry Pi Zero W:

The Raspberry Pi Zero W is a compact and affordable version of the Raspberry Pi that includes built-in WiFi and Bluetooth.

Raspberry Pi 4G/3G HATs:

HATs (Hardware Attached on Top) are add-on boards for Raspberry Pi. Some HATs are designed to provide 3G or 4G cellular connectivity to your Raspberry Pi.

LoRaWAN HATs:

LoRaWAN HATs enable long-range, low-power wireless communication for IoT applications. They are compatible with Raspberry Pi and can be used for remote sensor and data transmission.

Zigbee and Z-Wave HATs:

Zigbee and Z-Wave are popular wireless protocols for home automation and IoT. HATs are available to add Zigbee or Z-Wave capabilities to your Raspberry Pi for smart home projects.

GSM/GPRS Modules:

Raspberry Pi can be paired with GSM/GPRS modules to enable cellular connectivity. This is useful for applications that require remote data transmission.

GPS Modules:

GPS modules can be connected to Raspberry Pi to enable location tracking and geolocation functionality for various projects.

IR (Infrared) Receivers and Transmitters:

Raspberry Pi can be equipped with IR receivers and transmitters to enable infrared communication for remote control and automation.

Raspberry Pi Pico Wireless Options:

The Raspberry Pi Pico, a microcontroller board, can be used with various wireless modules like ESP8266 and ESP32 to add WiFi and Bluetooth capabilities.

Camera Modules:

While not strictly wireless communication, Raspberry Pi camera modules can capture images and videos wirelessly and transmit them to other devices or cloud services over WiFi or Ethernet.

Exercise

Exercise 1 – MCQ

1. Which programming language is often used for rapid development and prototyping in IoT applications?
a) C/C++
b) Python
c) JavaScript
d) Java

2.Which of the following is an open-source hardware and software platform commonly used for building IoT prototypes?
a) Node-RED
b) Raspberry Pi
c) Microsoft Azure IoT Central
d) Particle

Exercise 2 – True/False

1. Raspberry Pi is an open-source hardware and software platform commonly used for building IoT prototypes.
2. Python is often chosen for IoT applications that require rapid development and prototyping due to its extensive libraries and community support.

Exercise 3 – Fill in the blanks

1. In the process of building your own IoT device, you should start by defining the device's _________ and objectives.
2. An essential aspect of IoT device development is testing and ____________ to ensure it functions as expected.

Exercise 4 – Match case

Match the following terms with their descriptions:
1. Prototyping Tools and Platforms
2. Programming for IoT
3. Building Your Own IoT Device

Descriptions:
a) Visual tool for developing IoT prototypes.
b) Choosing the appropriate programming language for IoT projects.
c) Defining the device's purpose and objectives.

Exercise 5 – One word answer

1. What is Node-RED primarily used for in IoT development?
2. What is the first step in building your own IoT device?

Exercise 6 – Small answer

1. Name one example of a visual tool used for developing IoT prototypes.
2. What is one essential aspect of IoT device development that involves identifying and resolving issues?

Exercise 7 – Long answer

1. Explain the importance of selecting the appropriate programming language for IoT projects. Provide examples of programming languages suitable for different IoT applications.
2. Describe the key steps involved in building your own IoT device, from conceptualization to deployment. Provide examples or use cases to illustrate the importance of each step.

Answer:

Exercise 1.
1. b) Python
2. b) Raspberry Pi

Exercise 2.
1. True
2. True

Exercise 3.
1. purpose
2. debugging

Exercise 4. Q
1. Prototyping Tools and Platforms – a)
2. Programming for IoT– b)
3. Building Your Own IoT Device– c)
Exercise 5.
1. Visualization
2. Purpose

Previous Year Questions

1. Write a short note on Arduino programming for IoT.(SPPU B.Tech. 2017)
2. Write a short note on Raspberry Pi programming for IoT. (Mumbai University B.Tech._2017)
3. Explain in detail steps involved in Prototype design of IoT. (Mumbai University B.Tech._2019)
4. List and explain various features of Raspberry Pi board. (Mumbai University 2018)
5. What is Raspberry Pi? Explain 4 features of it. (SPPU B.Tech. 2012)
6. Explain in detail Arduino and sensor and interfacing for it. (RTU. B.Tech.2019)
7. Define Arduino? (SPPU B.Tech. 2022)
8. Differentiate between Raspberry Pi and desktop computer. (Uttar Pradesh university B.Tech. 2018-19)
9. Explain the following computing components used in laboratories of IoT. (Mumbai University 2018)
a)Arduino
b)Raspberry Pi (IGNOU MCA 2022)
10. Write a short note on Raspberry Pi programming for IoT Write a short note to give abstract view of Internet of Things. (Mumbai University B.Tech._2017)
11. What instruction set architecture is used in Raspberry Pi?(RTU B.Tech. 2017)
12. Explain fundamental components of IoT? How can IoT benefit the health care industry? Explain. (RTU B.Tech. 2022)
13. Define Arduino? (RTU B.Tech. 2022)
14. List available wireless communications boards available in Raspberry Pi? (RTU B.Tech. 2022)
15. Differentiate between Arduino and Raspberry Pi? (RTU B.Tech. 2022)

ONLINE RESOURCES
Link: https://forms.gle/Qm4aUYyWXVmBRSHc6

QR Code :
Link: https://www.youtube.com/playlist?list=PLzlh_31VWEFoLEfKNQcB07CaDP2qYX-Bc

QR Code:

Chapter 9: IoT and the Future

Emerging Trends and Technologies

The Internet of Things (IoT) is continuously evolving, reshaping the way we live, work, and engage with the world. As we move forward, numerous emerging trends and technologies are influencing the IoT landscape, offering exciting opportunities and challenges for businesses, industries, and individuals.

Edge Computing:

IoT (Internet of Things) and edge computing are two transformative technologies that, when combined, hold immense promise for the future. Here's an exploration of the role of IoT in the future of edge computing:

IoT and Edge Computing: A Synergistic Partnership

IoT devices have proliferated across various domains, from smart homes and cities to industrial automation and healthcare. These devices generate vast amounts of data, often requiring real-time processing and low-latency responses. This is where edge computing comes into play.

Real-time Decision-Making: One of the most significant advantages of combining IoT and edge computing is the ability to make real-time decisions at the edge of the network. Instead of sending all IoT data to centralized cloud servers for processing, edge computing devices, such as gateways or edge servers, can analyze data locally. This reduces latency and enables faster responses, which is critical for applications like autonomous vehicles, industrial automation, and remote healthcare monitoring.

Bandwidth Efficiency: Transmitting large volumes of IoT data to the cloud can strain network bandwidth and incur high data transfer costs. Edge computing allows IoT devices to filter and preprocess data locally, sending only relevant or summarized information to the cloud. This not only conserves bandwidth but also reduces cloud service costs.

Enhanced Security and Privacy: Edge computing can bolster security and privacy in IoT systems. By processing sensitive data locally, IoT devices can minimize exposure to potential threats associated with transmitting data over the internet. Additionally, edge devices can implement security measures like encryption and access control more effectively.

Scalability and Resilience: Edge computing can improve the scalability and resilience of IoT systems. By distributing processing tasks across a network of edge devices, organizations can handle a larger number of IoT devices without overburdening a centralized cloud infrastructure. Edge nodes can also continue to operate locally even if the connection to the cloud is lost, ensuring uninterrupted service.

Customization and Adaptability: Edge computing allows for customized data processing and analytics tailored to specific IoT use cases. Organizations can develop and deploy edge applications that address their unique requirements, ensuring optimal performance and adaptability to changing conditions.

The Future of IoT in Edge Computing

As IoT continues to evolve, several trends and developments can be expected in the integration of IoT with edge computing:

Edge AI and Machine Learning: Edge devices will increasingly incorporate AI and machine learning capabilities to enable advanced data analytics at the edge. This will lead to more autonomous and intelligent IoT systems capable of making complex decisions locally.

Edge-to-Cloud Orchestration: IoT systems will become more sophisticated in managing the orchestration of tasks between edge devices and the cloud. Hybrid architectures will seamlessly balance processing workloads to optimize performance and resource utilization.

Industry-Specific Solutions: Edge computing will give rise to industry-specific IoT solutions. For example, in manufacturing, edge devices will enable predictive maintenance, while in healthcare, they will support real-time patient monitoring and diagnostics.

5G Connectivity: The rollout of 5G networks will further enhance the capabilities of IoT and edge computing. Ultra-low latency and high-speedconnections will enable new applications and use cases that demand instantaneous data processing.

Standardization and Interoperability: As the IoT and edge computing ecosystems grow, there will be a push for standardization and interoperability to ensure devices, protocols, and platforms can seamlessly work together. This will promote greater innovation and adoption.

The future of IoT in edge computing is incredibly promising. This synergy enables faster, more efficient, and more secure data processing and decision-making, paving the way for transformative applications in various industries. As these technologies continue to advance, we can expect to see increasingly intelligent, responsive, and adaptable IoT systems that will shape the way we live and work.

5G Networks:

IoT and Future in 5G Networks. IoT (Internet of Things) and 5G networks are converging to shape the future of connectivity and technology. This partnership promises:
Enhanced Connectivity: 5G's high speed and low latency enable real-time communication for IoT devices, benefiting applications like autonomous vehicles and smart cities.
Massive IoT: 5G supports massive IoT deployments, allowing billions of devices to connect simultaneously, opening doors to applications in various industries.
Edge Computing: 5G's low latency facilitates real-time data processing at the network edge, enhancing IoT data privacy, security, and efficiency.
Industry 4.0: IoT and 5G transform manufacturing with precise coordination, predictive maintenance, and efficiency gains.
Smart Cities: IoT and 5G empower smart cities with data-driven decision-making, improving sustainability and citizen services.
Healthcare Revolution: Telemedicine and remote patient monitoring thrive with 5G, improving healthcare access and outcomes.
AR and VR: AR and VR applications benefit from 5G's high bandwidth and low latency, enabling immersive experiences in gaming, education, and more.
Energy Efficiency: Both IoT and 5G prioritize energy efficiency, crucial as IoT deployments scale.
Security and Privacy: Robust security measures protect data and devices in the growing IoT-5G ecosystem.
Environmental Monitoring: IoT sensors and 5G networks aid in real-time environmental monitoring and disaster management.
This convergence will lead to innovative applications, improved user experiences, and a more connected, intelligent world. **3.AI and Machine Learning:**
IoT and Future in AI and Machine Learning. The future of IoT in AI and machine learning is poised to transform industries and automation.
Enhanced Data Analytics: AI and machine learning will extract insights from IoT data, improving predictive analytics and decision-making.
Predictive Maintenance: AI will forecast equipment maintenance needs, reducing downtime and costs.
Autonomous Device: AI will power self-driving cars, drones, and autonomous machinery.
Personalized Experiences: IoT devices will offer tailored experiences in smart homes and wearables.
Natural Language Processing: IoT devices will better understand and respond to voice commands.
Edge AI: Devices will run AI locally, enhancing privacy and reducing latency.
Energy Efficiency: AI will optimize energy usage in IoT, benefitting smart grids.
Healthcare Revolution: Remote monitoring and AI diagnosis will transform healthcare.
Industry 4.0: AI-driven automation will optimize manufacturing.
Environmental Impact: IoT and AI will monitor and manage environmental data.
Security: AI will enhance IoT security with real-time threat detection.
Transportation and Logistics: IoT and AI will optimize transportation and logistics with smart routing and autonomous vehicles.
Blockchain for Security:
Certainly, here are some key points about the future of IoT and blockchain for security:
Immutable Data: Blockchain's tamper-proof ledger ensures that IoT data remains unchanged, enhancing data integrity and trustworthiness.
Secure Device Identity: Blockchain enables the creation of unique, unforgeable identities for IoT devices, preventing unauthorized access.
Decentralized Security: Blockchain's decentralized nature eliminates single points of failure, making IoT systems more resilient against cyberattacks.
Smart Contracts: IoT devices can execute smart contracts on the blockchain, automating actions based on predefined conditions securely.
Data Ownership: Blockchain allows users to have more control over their IoT data and who accesses it, enhancing privacy.
Supply Chain Security: Blockchain can be used to track and secure the supply chain, ensuring the authenticity of products and components.
Interoperability: Blockchain standards will improve interoperability between IoT devices from different manufacturers, enhancing security and compatibility.
Zero Trust Security: Blockchain's trust less model ensures that devices and users are authenticated before gaining access to IoT networks.

Data Encryption: IoT data can be encrypted and stored on the blockchain, protecting it from unauthorized access.
Audit Trails: Blockchain maintains a transparent and immutable record of all IoT transactions and interactions, facilitating auditing and compliance.
The integration of IoT and blockchain promises to address security concerns and build trust in IoT ecosystems, making them more resilient and secure.
IoT in Healthcare: Certainly, here are some key points about the future of IoT in healthcare:
Remote Monitoring: IoT enables continuous monitoring of patients' vital signs, chronic conditions, and medication adherence from the comfort of their homes.
Telemedicine: IoT facilitates virtual doctor-patient consultations, increasing healthcare access and reducing the need for in-person visits.
Wearable Health Devices: Wearables, like smartwatches and fitness trackers, monitor users' health, providing real-time data for wellness and early disease detection.
Predictive Analytics: IoT data, combined with AI, allows healthcare providers to predict disease outbreaks, patient deterioration, and treatment outcomes.
Drug Management: Smart pill dispensers and medication trackers improve medication management and reduce errors.
Patient Records: IoT streamlines the management of electronic health records (EHRs), making them easily accessible and secure.
Surgical Assistance: IoT assists surgeons with real-time data during procedures, enhancing precision and safety.
Supply Chain Efficiency: IoT monitors the supply chain for pharmaceuticals, vaccines, and medical equipment, ensuring timely delivery and quality control.
Emergency Response: Wearable panic buttons and IoT-connected emergency devices enhance rapid response in emergencies.
Health and Wellness Apps: IoT-powered mobile apps offer personalized health advice, fitness plans, and mental health support.
Aging Population: IoT helps address the needs of aging populations by providing remote care and safety monitoring.
Patient Engagement: IoT devices encouragepatients to actively participate in their healthcare, leading to better outcomes.
Sustainability and Green IoT:
Certainly, here are some key points about the future of IoT in sustainable and green IoT:
Environmental Monitoring: IoT sensors track air and water quality, climate data, and wildlife patterns to inform conservation efforts.
Smart Agriculture: IoT optimizes farmingpractices, reducing water and pesticide usage while increasing crop yields.
Energy Efficiency: IoT systems manage and optimize energy consumption in buildings, industries, and transportation, reducing carbon footprints.
Waste Management: IoT-based smart bins and waste tracking systems improve waste collection efficiency and recycling rates.
Renewable Energy: IoT enhances the performance and maintenance of solar panels and wind turbines, promoting clean energy adoption.
Green Supply Chains: IoT sensors track and reduce emissions in supply chains, promoting sustainable sourcing and logistics.
Electric Mobility: IoT-enabled electric vehicles and charging stations reduce greenhouse gas emissions in transportation.
Water Conservation: IoT helps monitor and manage water resources, reducing wastage and ensuring sustainable water use.
Ecosystem Preservation: IoT aids in protecting ecosystems by monitoring biodiversity and habitat conditions.
Circular Economy: IoT systems facilitate the tracking and recycling of materials, promoting a circular economy.
Sustainable Cities: IoT technologies make cities more sustainable with smart transportation, waste management, and energy solutions
Consumer Awareness: IoT devices provide consumers with real-time information on their environmental impact, encouraging sustainable choices.
The future of sustainable and greenIoT is one where technology plays a pivotal role in preserving the environment and mitigating climate change. These developments aim to createa more sustainable and eco-friendlier world.
Quantum IoT:

Certainly, here are some key points about the future of Quantum IoT:

Quantum-Secure Encryption: Quantum IoT will employ quantum-resistant encryption to safeguard data against quantum attacks, ensuring data privacy and security.

Ultra-Sensitive Sensors: Quantum sensors will offer unprecedented sensitivity for IoT applications, allowing for precise measurements in fields like healthcare, environmental monitoring, and defence.

Quantum Key Distribution (QKD): Quantum IoT will utilize QKD for ultra-secure communication, protecting sensitive data exchanged between devices.

Quantum Machine Learning: Quantum algorithms will accelerate machine learning tasks, enabling IoT devices to process and analyse data faster and more efficiently.

Complex Simulations: Quantum computing will enable IoT to perform complex simulations for predictive analytics and optimization in fields like finance and logistics.

Network Scalability: Quantum IoT networks will be scalable and capable of handling a massive number of devices, making them suitable for the expanding IoT ecosystem.

Quantum Sensors in Healthcare: Quantum IoT sensors will revolutionize healthcare with ultra-precise diagnostics, remote patient monitoring, and drug discovery.

Quantum Internet: The development of a quantum internet will enable secure and instant communication between IoT devices across vast distances.

Enhanced Environmental Monitoring: Quantum IoT will provide highly accurate environmental data, aiding in climate research, disaster prediction, and natural resource management.

Quantum-Assisted AI: Quantum IoT will leverage quantum-assisted machine learning for advanced analytics, enabling more intelligent and responsive IoT applications.

In the future, Quantum IoT will bring quantum computing's capabilities to the world of connected devices, offering enhanced security, data processing, and sensing capabilities across various industries.

IoT Interoperability:

Certainly, here are some key points about the future of IoT interoperability:

Standardized Protocols: Future IoT devices will increasingly adopt standardized communication protocols to ensure seamless interaction with other devices and platforms.

IoT Platforms: Universal IoT platforms will emerge, enabling cross-device and cross-vendor compatibility, simplifying device integration for users.

Edge Computing: Edge computing will play a crucial role in IoT interoperability by enabling devices to process data locally, reducing the reliance on centralized cloud services.

API Integration: Robust Application Programming Interfaces (APIs) will be developed to facilitate interoperability between IoT devices and software applications.

IoT Gateways: IoT gateways will act as intermediaries, translating data and protocols between different devices and ecosystems.

Device Profiles: Standardized device profiles and metadata will help IoT systems identify and understand connected devices, promoting compatibility.

Blockchain for Trust: Blockchain technology will be used to establish trust and transparency in IoT ecosystems, ensuring data integrity and secure interactions.

Cross-Industry Standards: Industries will collaborate on cross-industry IoT standards to create interoperable solutions, particularly in areas like smart cities and healthcare.

IoT Testbeds: Research and development in IoT testbeds will drive innovation and provide real-world testing environments for interoperable solutions.

Regulatory Support: Governments and regulatory bodies will promote IoT interoperability through policies and guidelines, fostering a more connected and efficient world.

Interoperability is crucial for realizing the full potential of IoT, as it allows devices and systems to work together seamlessly, enabling more comprehensive and efficient solutions.

Edge AI:

Certainly, here are some key points about the future of IoT in Edge AI:

Real-time Processing: Edge AI enables IoT devices to process data locally, reducing latency and allowing for real-time decision-making.

Efficient Data Usage: Edge AI filters and analyses data at the source, sending only relevant information to the cloud, reducing bandwidth and storage requirements.

Enhanced Privacy: Edge AI preserves data privacy by processing sensitive information on the device itself, minimizing the need for data to be sent over the internet.

Improved Security: Local processing through Edge AI can enhance device security by reducing exposure to **external threats and vulnerabilities.**
Autonomous Devices: IoT devices equipped with Edge AI can make autonomous decisions, reducing the need for constant human intervention.
Low-power Processing: Edge AI algorithms are designed to be power-efficient, extending the battery life of IoT devices.
Customized AI Models: Edge AI allows for the development of customized AI models tailored to specific IoT applications and use cases.
Reduced Cloud Dependence: Edge AI reduces the dependency on centralized cloud services, making IoT systems more resilient and reliable.
Edge AI Ecosystem: An ecosystem of AI algorithms, hardware accelerators, and development tools will support the growth of Edge AI in IoT.
AI at the Edge: Edge AI will empower IoT devices with capabilities like image recognition, natural language processing, and predictive analytics, opening up new possibilities for applications.
In the future, Edge AI will be a driving force behind the evolution of IoT, enabling smarter, more responsive, and more efficient connected devices and systems.
Human Augmentation:
Certainly, here are some key points about the future of IoT in human augmentation:
Wearable Devices: IoT-enabled wearable devices will enhance human capabilities by providing real-time data on health, performance, and environmental factors.
Health Monitoring: IoT will play a crucial role in remote health monitoring, allowing for continuous tracking of vital signs and chronic conditions.
Assistive Technologies: IoT-powered assistive devices willimprove the quality of life for individuals with disabilities, enabling greater independence and mobility.
Biometric Authentication: IoT devices will integrate biometric authentication methods like facial recognition and fingerprint scanning for enhanced security and convenience.
Prosthetics and Exoskeletons: IoT sensors and actuators will enhance the functionality of prosthetic limbs and exoskeletons, providing better mobility and control.
Neurotechnology: IoT-based neurotechnology devices will assist in brain-computer interfaces, enabling direct communication between the human brain and machines.
Augmented Reality: IoT will enable augmented reality (AR) devices that overlay digital information onto the physical world, enhancing perception and knowledge.
Human-Machine Collaboration: IoT will facilitate seamless collaboration between humans and machines, enabling tasks that require a combination of human and artificial intelligence.
Customization: IoT will allow for the customization of augmentation technologies to meet individual needs and preferences.
Ethical Considerations: As human augmentation technologies advance, ethical concerns related to privacy, consent, and fairness will need to be addressed.
In the future, IoT will be integral to the development and deployment of human augmentation technologies, offering a wide range of benefits for healthcare, accessibility, and human-computer interaction.

Ethical and Social Implications

The Internet of Things (IoT) has ushered in a new era of connectivity, reshaping the way we interact with technology and the world. While IoT offers numerous benefits, it also raises a host of ethical and social implications that necessitate careful consideration as this technology continues to expand. Below, we outline key ethical and social concerns associated with IoT:
Privacy Concerns: IoT devices amass vast amounts of data about individuals, their behaviours, and their surroundings, including sensitive personal information. The risk of misuse or unauthorized access to this data is a significant privacy concern. Balancing data collection for valuable purposes with safeguarding individual privacy is a pivotal ethical challenge.
Data Security: IoT devices often present security vulnerabilities, making them attractive targets for cyberattacks. Compromised IoT devices can result in severe consequences, ranging from breaches of personal information to disruptions in critical infrastructure. Ensuring robust security measures and encryption protocols is imperative to mitigate these risks.
Ownership and Control of Data: The ownership and control of data generated by IoT devices are complex ethical issues. Users may not fully comprehend the extent to which their data is collected, stored, and shared by IoT devices

and the organizations behind them. Ensuring transparency and granting users control over their data are essential for ethical IoT deployments.

Bias and Discrimination: IoT systems often rely on algorithms and machine learning to make decisions and predictions based on data. If these algorithms are trained on biased or incomplete data, they can perpetuate or exacerbate existing societal biases, leading to unfair or discriminatory outcomes. Ensuring fairness and inclusivity in IoT systems is a pressing concern.

Digital Divide: The widespread adoption of IoT technology can exacerbate existing social inequalities. Not everyone has equal access to the internet or can afford IoT devices, potentially leaving marginalized communities at a disadvantage. Bridging the digital divide is an ethical imperative to ensure equitable access to the benefits of IoT.

Job Displacement and Economic Impact: The automation and efficiency gains brought by IoT can lead to job displacement in certain industries. Preparing the workforce for these changes and considering the economic implications of job loss are vital for addressing the societal impact of IoT.

Environmental Impact: The proliferation of IoT devices and the data centres supporting them have environmental consequences. The manufacturing, disposal, and energy consumption associated with IoT hardware can contribute to environmental degradation. Sustainable practices in IoT development and operation are essential.

Ethical Design and Development: Ethical considerations should be integrated into the design and development of IoT systems from the outset. This includes contemplating the potential for harm, prioritizing user consent and autonomy, and addressing issues related to data ethics, transparency, and accountability.

Regulatory Frameworks: Governments and regulatory bodies must establish clear and robust frameworks to govern IoT technology. These frameworks should address privacy, security, data ownership, and other ethical concerns while allowing for innovation and growth in the IoT sector.

Public Awareness and Education: Raising public awareness about the ethical and social implications of IoT is crucial. Users should be educated about the data their devices collect, how it's used, and how to protect their privacy. Education can empower individuals to make informed choices about IoT adoption.

In conclusion, while IoT has the potential to bring about significant advancements in various aspects of our lives, it also presents ethical and social challenges that require thoughtful consideration and proactive solutions. Striking a balance between the benefits of IoT and its ethical and social implications is essential for harnessing this technology's potential for the greater good of society.

Predictions for the IoT Landscape

The Internet of Things (IoT) has rapidly evolved since its inception, and it continues to exert a profound influence on various facets of life. Looking ahead, several predictions can be made about the future of IoT and its transformative impact on different sectors:

Anticipating the Surge in IoT Devices: The IoT ecosystem is poised for substantial growth, with billions of new devices projected to join IoT networks in the near future. This expansion will be driven by increased adoption across homes, industries, agriculture, healthcare, and smart cities.

5G's IoT Revolution: The deployment of 5G networks will significantly expedite the adoption of IoT. With its high-speed, low-latency connectivity, 5G will enable smoother and more responsive IoT applications, spanning from autonomous vehicles to augmented reality.

Edge Computing as the New Norm for IoT: Edge computing, which allows data processing to take place closer to the data source, will become a standard practice in IoT deployments. This will reduce latency, minimize data transfer costs, and enhance real-time decision-making, particularly for mission-critical applications.

AI and IoT Synergy: IoT devices will increasingly incorporate artificial intelligence (AI) and machine learning algorithms for data analysis. This integration will result in smarter and more autonomous IoT systems capable of making real-time decisions and predictions.

Blockchain's Role in Reinforcing IoT Security: Blockchain technology will play an expanding role in enhancing IoT security. It will be used to establish secure, tamper-proof ledgers for device authentication and data integrity, bolstering the overall trustworthiness of IoT networks.

Transforming Healthcare with IoT: IoT will revolutionize healthcare through wearable devices, remote monitoring, and smart healthcare systems. Patients will gain access to continuous, real-time health data, leading to improved disease management and better medical outcomes.

Smart Cities Redefined by IoT Advancements: The concept of smart cities will continue to evolve, with IoT serving as its foundation. Smart city initiatives will prioritize infrastructure optimization, enhanced public services, reduced energy consumption, and overall improved quality of life for urban dwellers.

IoT for Sustainability: IoT will play a pivotal role in sustainability endeavours. IoT technologies will facilitate smart grid management, efficient resource utilization, and environmentally-conscious practices in agriculture, contributing to a more environmentally friendly planet.

The Crucial Role of IoT in Industry 4.0: Industry 4.0, characterized by smart factories and industrial automation, will rely extensively on IoT. Manufacturers will employ IoT devices to optimize efficiency, reduce downtime, and implement predictive maintenance.

Privacy and Security in IoT: The growth of IoT will keep data privacy and security concerns at the forefront. Striking a balance between data collection and user privacy will remain an ongoing challenge, necessitating robust regulations and best practices.

Ethical Challenges on the Horizon for IoT: Ethical concerns regarding data usage, algorithmic bias, and equitable access to IoT benefits will gain more prominence. Ethical design and governance will be essential for responsible IoT development.

Personalization Through IoT: IoT will enable increased personalization and customization across various aspects of life, including shopping and entertainment, as devices gather data to tailor services to individual preferences.

In conclusion, the future of IoT holds immense promise, with the potential to drive transformative changes across numerous domains. While IoT will usher in significant advancements, it will also raise important challenges related to privacy, security, ethics, and regulation. Successful IoT implementations will require a thoughtful approach to address these issues while harnessing the technology's potential for the betterment of society and industry.

Business Model in IoT

A business model in IoT defines how an organization creates, delivers, and captures value through its IoT-related products, services, and solutions. IoT business models typically focus on the following key elements:

Value Proposition: Identify the unique value that IoT can offer to customers. This could include improved operational efficiency, cost savings, enhanced customer experiences, predictive maintenance, or data-driven insights.

Customer Segments: Define the target customer segments that will benefit most from the IoT solution. IoT can have applications across various industries, from healthcare and agriculture to manufacturing and smart cities.

Revenue Streams: Determine the sources of revenue generated from IoT offerings. Common revenue streams in IoT include subscription models, pay-per-use pricing, licensing fees, hardware sales, and data monetization.

Key Partnerships: Identify key partners, such as device manufacturers, connectivity providers, data analytics companies, and software developers, that are crucial for the success of the IoT ecosystem.

Channels: Establish distribution and communication channels to reach target customers effectively. This may involve partnerships with system integrators, resellers, or direct sales channels.

Key Activities: Outline the core activities required to deliver and support IoT solutions. This includes device provisioning, data management, analytics, security, and customer support.

Cost Structure: Calculate the costs associated with IoT implementation, including hardware production, software development, connectivity, data storage, security measures, and ongoing maintenance.

Customer Relationships: Define the nature of customer relationships, such as whether they are transactional, contractual, or ongoing. For IoT, maintaining customer trust and ensuring data privacy are critical aspects of customer relationships.

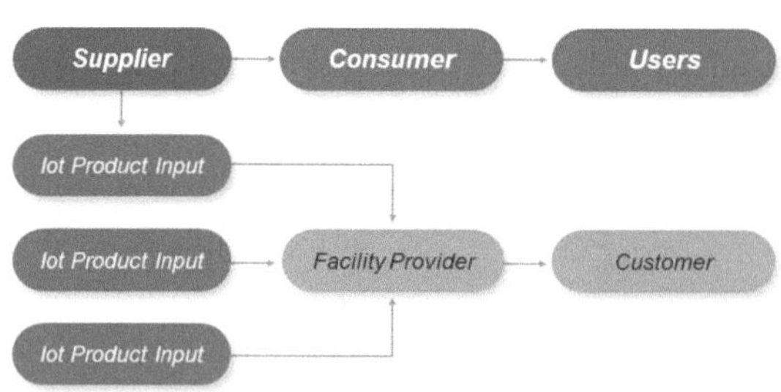

Business Innovation in IoT

Business innovation in IoT involves leveraging IoT technologies to create new business models, disrupt existing industries, and gain a competitive advantage. Here are several ways organizations can innovate using IoT:

New Products and Services: Develop innovative IoT-based products and services that cater to unmet needs or pain points in the market. For example, wearable healt**h devices that monitor vital signs and provide real-time health insights.**

Data Monetization: Explore opportunities to collect, aggregate, and analyse IoT data and then monetize it by selling insights, analytics, or benchmarking reports to other businesses or stakeholders.
Predictive Maintenance: Use IoT data and predictive analytics to offer maintenance-as-a-service, enabling organizations to proactively service equipment, reduce downtime, and lower maintenance costs.
Subscription Models: Introduce subscription-based models for IoT services, allowing customers to access and benefit from IoT solutions without the upfront cost of hardware or software.
Cross-Industry Collaboration: Partner with other organizations, including those outside your industry, to create innovative IoT solutions that address broader market needs. For instance, combining IoT data from agriculture and weather sensors to optimize crop management.
Data-Driven Insights: Develop platforms and tools that enable businesses to derive actionable insights from IoT-generated data, facilitating better decision-making and process optimization.
Smart Ecosystems: Create smart ecosystems where multiple devices and services work together seamlessly. Examples include smart homes, smart cities, and connected healthcare systems.
Sustainability Initiatives: Leverage IoT to enhance sustainability efforts by optimizing resource consumption, reducing waste, and promoting eco-friendly practices.
Blockchain and IoT Integration: Explore the integration of blockchain technology with IoT to enhance security, transparency, and trust in data exchange and transactions.
Edge Computing: Embrace edge computing to process IoT data closer to the data source, reducing latency and enabling real-time decision-making in IoT applications.
Business model innovation in IoT requires organizations to rethink their value proposition and revenue generation strategies, while business innovation involves embracing technological advancements and new approaches to gain a competitive edge in the IoT landscape. Successful IoT innovation often involves a combination of creative thinking, strategic partnerships, and a deep understanding of customer needs and market dynamics.

Exercise

Exercise 1 – MCQ

1. What is one of the primary ethical concerns associated with IoT, particularly concerning data privacy?
a) Insufficient data collection
b) Data accuracy
c) Data sharing without user consent
d) Data redundancy
2. Which technology is gaining prominence in IoT deployments by allowing data processing to occur closer to the source, reducing latency and improving real-time decision-making?
a) 4G networks
b) Edge computing
c) Bluetooth technology
d) Quantum computing

Exercise 2 – True/False

1. Edge computing in IoT allows data processing to occur closer to the source, reducing latency and improving real-time decision-making.
2. One of the primary ethical concerns associated with IoT is data sharing without user consent, which can compromise data privacy.

Exercise 3 – Fill in the blanks

1. In the context of IoT predictions, the rapid growth of _________ is expected to drive transformative changes across various sectors.
2. Ethical and social implications in the IoT landscape highlight the need for responsible __________ and governance to address issues such as data privacy and algorithmic bias.
3. _______ allows data processing closer to the data source, reducing latency and improving real-time decision-making in IoT applications.

Exercise 4 – Match case

Match the following terms with their descriptions:
1. Quantum computing
2. Edge computing
3. Data privacy
Descriptions:

a) Ethical and social concerns in IoT often centre around issues like data sharing, surveillance, and user consent.
b) This technology is poised to revolutionize IoT security by solving complex problems and enhancing encryption methods.
3. _______ allows data processing closer to the data source, reducing latency and improving real-time decision-making in IoT applications.

Exercise 5 – One word answer

1. Full Form of OCF?
2. Full Form of CHIP?

Exercise 6 – Small answer

1. What is ethical and social implications?
2. What is Edge Computing?

Exercise 7 – Long answer

1. Discuss two emerging trends and technologies in the IoT landscape and how they are impacting industries or daily life.
2. Explain the ethical and social implications of IoT, particularly in the context of data privacy and security. How can these concerns be addressed?

Answer:

Exercise 1.
1. c) Data sharing without user consent
2. b)Edge computing

Exercise 2.
1. True
2. True

Exercise 3.
1. IoT devices
2. design

Exercise 4.
1. Quantum computing – b)
2. Edge computing – a)
3. Data privacy – c)

Exercise 5.
1. Open Connectivity Foundation (OCF)
2. CHIP (Connected Home over IP)

Previous Year Questions

1. Explain in detail business model and business innovation in internet of Things. (SPPU B.Tech. 2017)
2. Explain in detail Business process in IoT. (SPPU B.Tech. 2017)
3. Write in detail business model scenario for Internet of Things. (Uttar Pradesh university B.Tech. 2018-19)

ONLINE RESOURCES

Link: https://forms.gle/RMye9SkAwJV4PaPw9

QR Code:

Link: https://www.youtube.com/playlist?list=PLzlh_31VWEForeolPBY26bOTo6IHpRYLU

QR Code:

Chapter 10: IoT Billing Solutions

Population Models

In the context of IoT billing, population models involve the segmentation of users or devices based on specific criteria. These criteria may include factors such as the number of connected devices, data usage, or the specific services utilized. By categorizing users or devices into distinct populations, IoT service providers can tailor their billing strategies to accommodate the diverse needs of their customer base.

Types of Population Models:

Device-based Population: This model centres on IoT billing determined by the number of devices connected to the network. Different billing tiers or plans may be offered, each permitting a certain number of devices to be connected. This model suits businesses looking to charge based on the number of devices or sensors in use.

Data-based Population: IoT billing can also revolve around data usage, where users are billed based on the volume of data transmitted or received by their devices. Data-based population models are commonly applied in scenarios where data consumption varies widely.

Service-based Population: For IoT services that offer varying features or service levels, a service-based population model may be employed. Customers can select a service package that aligns with their specific requirements, and billing is determined by the chosen package.

Benefits of Population Models in IoT Billing:

Flexibility: Population models offer flexibility to IoT service providers and customers alike. Providers can design a variety of billing plans to cater to distinct customer segments, while customers can select the plan that best suits their individual needs.

Granular Billing: Population models enable more granular billing, allowing for precise tracking of usage and costs. This granularity is particularly important when managing a diverse range of IoT devices and services.

Fairness: Population models contribute to billing fairness. Customers pay for the specific resources they utilize, and providers can offer diverse plans to accommodate varying budgets and requirements.

Scalability: As IoT deployments expand, population models can seamlessly scale. Providers can readily adapt their billing strategies to accommodate a growing number of devices and users.

Challenges of Population Models in IoT Billing:

Complexity: Implementing population-based billing systems can be complex, particularly when managing diverse IoT ecosystems with various device types and data usage patterns.

Customer Education: IoT service providers must educate their customers about the different billing models and assist them in selecting the most suitable plan. Effective communication and support are essential in this regard.

Data Accuracy: Precise tracking of device counts, data usage, and service levels is crucial for successful population-based billing. Any inaccuracies can lead to billing disputes.

In conclusion, population models represent a crucial element of IoT billing solutions, empowering businesses to tailor their billing strategies to accommodate the diverse needs of their customer base. These models offer flexibility, fairness, and scalability, but they also present challenges related to complexity and customer education. In an evolving IoT landscape, effective billing solutions will continue to play a pivotal role for businesses seeking to monetize their IoT services.

Information Cascades

Within the domain of IoT (Internet of Things) billing solutions, the concept of "information cascades" holds significant relevance in the context of decision-making processes and customer interactions. Information cascades occur when individuals base their decisions on the actions or choices of others, rather than relying solely on their private information. In the context of IoT billing, it is imperative to understand how information cascades can influence pricing strategies and service adoption. Let's explore the concept of information cascades in IoT billing solutions:

Decision-Making in IoT Billing:

IoT billing necessitates individuals and organizations to make informed choices regarding pricing plans, service levels, and usage limits that align with their specific requirements. These decisions often take into account factors such as cost considerations, data demands, and expectations regarding service quality.

The Role of Information Cascades:

Information cascades manifest when an individual's decision-making process is influenced by observing the decisions made by those who came before them, rather than relying on their personal information or preferences.

Essentially, individuals tend to conform to the choices of others, believing that the collective wisdom of previous decisions is more reliable than their own knowledge.

Cascades in IoT Billing Scenarios:

In the context of IoT billing solutions, information cascades can manifest in various ways:

Plan Adoption: When presented with a multitude of IoT billing plans, customers may take note of the choices made by their peers or competitors. If a particular plan gains popularity among similar users or businesses, others may opt for it, assuming it to be the most suitable option.

Device Selection: In scenarios where IoT services offer multiple device options, individuals or organizations might choose devices based on the preferences of industry leaders or early adopters. This can result in a cascade effect where specific devices gain favour.

Pricing Changes: In instances where IoT service providers modify pricing structures or introduce new features, customers may assess these changes by considering the reactions and choices of their counterparts in the industry.

Implications of Information Cascades:

Comprehending the dynamics of information cascades in IoT billing carries substantial implications:

Market Influence: Information cascades can exert a significant influence on market dynamics. A popular billing plan or device can quickly gain traction, leading to shifts in market share and demand.

Pricing Strategies: IoT service providers can strategically leverage information cascades by positioning particular plans or services as popular choices, thereby encouraging others to follow suit.

Risk of Herding: While information cascades can be beneficial, they can also give rise to herding behavior, where individuals make decisions solely based on what others are doing, without thoroughly evaluating their own needs.

Balancing Individual Needs and Collective Wisdom:

Achieving a balance between individual needs and the impact of information cascades is crucial in IoT billing solutions. Customers should be encouraged to make informed decisions based on their specific requirements, while also benefiting from the collective insights derived from others' choices.

In conclusion, information cascades in IoT billing solutions illustrate how social influence and collective decision-making can affect pricing strategies, plan selection, and device adoption. IoT service providers should be cognizant of these dynamics and utilize them strategically to enhance customer experiences, all while ensuring that individual needs remain a paramount consideration in the decision-making process.

Network Effects

The phenomenon of network effects holds profound significance in the domain of IoT (Internet of Things) billing solutions. These effects elucidate how the value of a product or service amplifies with the growing number of users or connected devices. In the context of IoT billing, network effects exert a substantial influence on pricing strategies, customer adoption, and the overall success of IoT services. Let's delve into how network effects shape IoT billing solutions:

Increased Data and Device Volume: As the IoT network expands, encompassing more devices and users, the volume of data generated and exchanged also experiences exponential growth. Network effects within IoT billing solutions harness this surge in data to create added value. Service providers can introduce tiered pricing plans that hinge on data usage, motivating users to connect additional devices or generate more data, thereby leading to increased revenue.

Economies of Scale: IoT billing solutions often reap the benefits of economies of scale. As the user base expands, providers can distribute the costs associated with infrastructure and operations across a larger customer pool. This can culminate in more competitive pricing, rendering IoT services more appealing to potential customers and stimulating further adoption.

Enhanced Service Offerings: Network effects can fuel the innovation and development of new and enhanced IoT services. As more devices and users join the network, providers are incentivized to innovate and introduce additional features or functionalities. This, in turn, can attract a larger user base, fostering a self-reinforcing cycle of value augmentation.

Competitive Advantage: IoT service providers that achieve critical mass in terms of users and devices can solidify a substantial competitive advantage. Customers tend to gravitate toward providers with extensive user bases, as this often translates into a more comprehensive ecosystem, better support, and more robust IoT services.

Interoperability and Compatibility: Network effects stimulate standardization and compatibility within IoT ecosystems. When numerous users and devices coexist on the same network, there is a heightened impetus for manufacturers to ensure that their devices and services are interoperable. This simplifies the user experience and can expedite adoption.

Cross-Selling and Upselling: Providers with a sizeable user base can effectively engage in cross-selling and upselling of supplementary services or complementary products. For instance, an IoT billing solution provider might extend its offerings to include analytics tools or security services, capitalizing on the trust and familiarity established with existing customers.

Data Insights and Monetization: A larger user base generates a wealth of data, which holds substantial value for insights and monetization. Providers can collate and analyse data from diverse sources to deliver data-driven services, such as predictive maintenance or consumer behaviour analysis.

Challenges and Considerations: Despite the numerous advantages, network effects within IoT billing solutions bring forth their share of challenges. Privacy concerns, data security, and the potential for vendor lock-in necessitate vigilant management to uphold trust and safeguard user interests.

In conclusion, network effects stand as a driving force in the landscape of IoT billing. They instigate a virtuous cycle in which the growth in the number of devices and users augments the value of IoT services, fostering increased adoption and revenue. Providers and businesses in the IoT sphere must adeptly leverage these effects to formulate competitive pricing strategies, stimulate customer adoption, and maintain a pioneering position in the swiftly evolving IoT industry.

Network Dynamics

Network dynamics play a pivotal role in the realm of IoT (Internet of Things) billing solutions. As IoT ecosystems continue to expand and evolve, the intricacies of network dynamics significantly influence how billing strategies are formulated, adapted, and optimized. In this context, let's explore the key aspects of network dynamics within IoT billing solutions:

Device Proliferation and Connectivity: The dynamics of IoT networks are shaped by the continuous proliferation of devices and their connectivity. IoT billing solutions must accommodate the ever-growing number of devices, each generating data and requiring billing consideration. Network dynamics dictate that billing systems be scalable to handle the influx of new devices seamlessly.

Real-Time Data Streams: IoT networks generate vast streams of real-time data. Network dynamics require billing solutions to process and analyse this data swiftly. Providers must be able to capture and monetize data usage in real time, as many IoT applications rely on instant decision-making based on data insights.

Dynamic Pricing Models: Network dynamics introduce variability in data usage patterns. IoT billing solutions must support dynamic pricing models that can adapt to fluctuating data consumption, peak usage times, and seasonal variations. Such flexibility ensures fairness and competitiveness in the market.

Service-Level Agreements (SLAs): IoT services often involve SLAs that specify performance levels and quality of service. Network dynamics affect service delivery, and billing solutions must align with SLAs to accurately bill customers based on the agreed-upon service parameters.

Data Security and Privacy: The dynamic nature of IoT networks introduces challenges related to data security and privacy. Billing solutions must comply with evolving regulations and standards to protect sensitive customer data, ensuring that network dynamics do not compromise security measures.

Partner Ecosystems: IoT ecosystems thrive on collaborations and partnerships. Network dynamics extend beyond individual providers to encompass a web of interconnected service providers and platforms. Billing solutions must account for multi-party settlements and revenue sharing, reflecting the dynamics of these partnerships.

Predictive Analytics: To adapt to network dynamics effectively, IoT billing solutions increasingly leverage predictive analytics. These tools anticipate usage patterns, network congestion, and potential billing discrepancies, enabling providers to proactively address issues and optimize their billing strategies.

Scalability and Performance: The dynamic nature of IoT networks demands scalability and high performance from billing solutions. Providers must be prepared to handle sudden surges in device connections and data traffic without compromising the quality of service.

Customer Engagement: Network dynamics also affect customer behaviour and expectations. IoT billing solutions must support customer engagement strategies that align with dynamic pricing, enabling providers to communicate effectively with customers regarding usage, costs, and value-added services.

Regulatory Compliance:

Network dynamics often lead to changes in regulatory requirements. Billing solutions must remain adaptable to evolving regulations to ensure compliance while maintaining business agility.

In conclusion, network dynamics are a central factor in shaping IoT billing solutions. To thrive in the dynamic IoT landscape, providers must adopt flexible, scalable, and data-driven billing strategies that align with the evolving needs of their customers and the intricacies of IoT network dynamics. The ability to navigate these dynamics effectively is pivotal in ensuring the success and sustainability of IoT billing solutions.

Exercise

Exercise 1 – MCQ

1. Which of the following best defines population models in IoT billing solutions?
a) Models for predicting weather patterns in IoT networks.
b) Segmentation of users or devices based on specific criteria for tailored billing strategies.
c) Models for analysing the growth of IoT-related patents.
d) Predictive models for IoT device failure rates.
2. What is a key outcome of network effects and dynamics in IoT billing solutions?
a) Reduced need for scalability and adaptability.
b) Static pricing models that don't change with user behaviour.
c)Increased value of IoT services with growing user and device connections.
d) Limited impact on customer engagement strategies.

Exercise 2 – True/False

1. Population models in IoT billing solutions involve segmenting users or devices based on specific criteria to customize billing strategies.
2. Network effects and dynamics in IoT billing solutions generally result in a reduction of the value of IoT services as more users and devices connect to the network.

Exercise 3 – Fill in the blanks

1. Effective IoT billing solutions are essential for monetizing IoT services and ensuring fair _______________ for customers.
2. IoT billing solutions must be able to adapt to the dynamic nature of IoT networks, supporting real-time data processing and scalable ____________.

Exercise 4 – Match case

Match the following terms with their descriptions:
1. Pricing Models
2. Scalability
3. Revenue Generation
Descriptions:
a) This aspect of IoT billing solutions involves adapting to the growth of IoT ecosystems and the increasing number of connected devices.
b) IoT billing solutions aim to optimize this by offering flexible plans that suit different customer needs.
c) Successful IoT billing solutions are essential for ensuring profitability and sustainability in IoT businesses.

Exercise 5 – One word answer

1. What does scalability address in IoT billing solutions?
2. What do IoT billing solutions aim to optimize for providers?

Exercise 6 – Small answer

1. What is the primary goal of IoT billing solutions?
2. Why is scalability important in IoT billing solutions?

Exercise 7 – Long answer

1. Explain the role of pricing models in IoT billing solutions and how they can be customized to meet diverse customer needs.
2. Discuss the challenges associated with real-time data processing in IoT billing solutions and how these challenges can be addressed to ensure efficient billing processes.

Answer:

Exercise 1.

1. b) Segmentation of users or devices based on specific criteria for tailored billing strategies.
2. c) Increased value of IoT services with growing user and device connections.

Exercise 2.

1. True
2. False

Exercise 3.

1. pricing and revenue generation
2. infrastructure and performance

Exercise 4.

1. Pricing Models - b)
2. Scalability – a)
3. Revenue Generation– c)

Exercise 5.

1. Growth
2. Profitability.

ONLINE RESOURCES

Link: https://forms.gle/rBoJFXFQxchJJxFb9

QR Code:

Link: https://www.youtube.com/playlist?list=PLzlh_31VWEFqLft1LJ3uzXcAU-b9yOqd8

QR Code:

Chapter 11: IoT In Cloud

Why IoT and Cloud are a natural fit?

IoT (Internet of Things) and cloud computing are considered a natural fit for several compelling reasons:

Scalability: IoT deployments can involve a massive number of devices, sensors, and data streams. Cloud computing platforms are inherently scalable, allowing IoT solutions to easily accommodate growth without significant infrastructure changes. Whether you have ten or ten million devices, cloud resources can be provisioned as needed.

Flexibility: IoT deployments often require diverse computing resources for data processing, analytics, and storage. Cloud platforms offer a wide range of services and tools, allowing IoT developers to choose and customize the resources that best fit their specific requirements. This flexibility supports a broad spectrum of IoT use cases.

Data Storage: IoT devices generate vast amounts of data. Storing and managing this data on local servers can be impractical and costly. Cloud-based storage solutions provide the capacity and durability needed to handle IoT data efficiently, with options for real-time access and retrieval.

Data Processing: IoT data often needs to be processed in real-time to extract meaningful insights, trigger actions, or make decisions. Cloud platforms offer powerful computing capabilities and data processing services that can analyse incoming IoT data streams and provide valuable results.

Global Reach: IoT solutions are often deployed across geographical regions. Cloud providers operate data centres worldwide, ensuring low-latency access to IoT services and data regardless of the device's location. This global reach is essential for applications such as fleet management or asset tracking.

Security: Cloud providers invest heavily in security measures, making it easier for IoT developers to implement robust security practices. IoT devices can benefit from cloud-based identity management, authentication, encryption, and access control mechanisms to protect data and devices.

Remote Management: Cloud platforms enable remote management of IoT devices, allowing developers to update firmware, change configurations, and monitor device health without physical access. This is crucial for maintaining large-scale IoT deployments.

Cost Efficiency: Cloud services often follow a pay-as-you-go pricing model, which can be cost-effective for IoT projects. Organizations can avoid large upfront infrastructure investments and only pay for the resources they use, helping to manage costs.

Elasticity: IoT traffic can be highly variable, with peaks and valleys in data generation. Cloud resources can be easily scaled up or down to match demand, ensuring efficient resource utilization and cost savings during idle periods.

Integration with Other Technologies: Cloud platforms offer a rich ecosystem of services, including machine learning, artificial intelligence, big data analytics, and databases. IoT data can be seamlessly integrated with these services to unlock additional value and insights.

Rapid Development and Prototyping: Cloud platforms provide IoT developers with tools, SDKs, and pre-built services that accelerate development and prototyping. This speeds up time-to-market for IoT solutions.

Redundancy and Reliability: Cloud providers offer redundancy and failover mechanisms that enhance the reliability of IoT solutions. In case of hardware failures or other issues, services can automatically switch to backup resources.

Overall, the combination of IoT and cloud computing allows organizations to leverage the power of the cloud to manage, analyse, and derive insights from IoT data while also benefiting from the scalability, flexibility, and cost-effectiveness that cloud platforms offer. This synergy makes IoT and cloud computing a natural and powerful combination for a wide range of applications and industries.

Cloud Platform Selection

Comparison of Major Cloud Providers

Three major cloud providers, often referred to as the "big three," are Amazon Web Services (AWS), Microsoft Azure, and Google Cloud Platform (GCP). These providers offer a wide range of cloud servicesand have a significant presence in the cloud computing industry. Below is a comparison of these major cloud providers in various aspects:

Market Share and Presence:

AWS: AWS is the market leader in cloud services, with a significant share of the global cloud market. It has a broad and established customer base across various industries.

Azure: Microsoft Azure is the second-largest cloud provider and is known for its strong presence in the enterprise market. It has a global network of data centres.

GCP: Google Cloud Platform, while growing rapidly, holds a smaller market share compared to AWS and Azure. It is known for its expertise in data analytics and machine learning.

Service Offerings:
AWS: AWS offers a comprehensive set of cloud services, including computing, storage, databases, machine learning, IoT, and more. It has a vast marketplace for third-party solutions.
Azure: Microsoft Azure provides a wide range of services, including those for Windows-based workloads, AI and machine learning, IoT, and extensive integration with Microsoft products.
GCP: Google Cloud is known for its strengths in data analytics, machine learning, and containerization technologies. It also offers a variety of cloud services.
Global Reach:
AWS: AWS has a global presence with data centres in multiple regions around the world, making it one of the most geographically diverse cloud providers.
Azure: Microsoft Azure also has a global network of data centres in many regions, with a strong focus on compliance and regulatory requirements.
GCP: Google Cloud has data centres in several regions but is expanding its global footprint. It is known for its network infrastructure and global edge locations.
Hybrid Cloud and On-Premises Integration:
AWS: AWS offers hybrid cloud solutions, such as AWS Outposts and AWS Hybrid, for integrating on-premises environments with the cloud.
Azure: Azure provides Azure Stack for hybrid cloud deployments, enabling consistent management and development across on-premises and cloud environments.
GCP: Google Cloud's Anthos allows hybrid and multi-cloud deployments, providing consistency across on-premises and cloud environments.
Pricing and Cost Management:
AWS: AWS offers various pricing models, including pay-as-you-go, reserved instances, and spot instances. AWS Cost Explorer helps users manage expenses.
Azure: Azure provides flexible pricing options, including reserved instances and pay-as-you-go. Azure Cost Management helps users monitor and optimize costs.
GCP: Google Cloud offers competitive pricing with sustained use discounts. It also provides tools like Cost Management to analyse and control costs.
AI and Machine Learning:
AWS: AWS offers a wide range of AI and ML services, including Amazon Sage Maker for building and training models.
Azure: Azure has Azure Machine Learning and integration with popular AI frameworks like TensorFlow and PyTorch.
GCP: Google Cloud is known for its expertise in AI and ML, with services like AI Platform and TensorFlow.
IoT Services:
AWS: AWS IoT provides a suite of services for IoT device management, data processing, and analytics.
Azure: Azure IoT offers IoT Hub, IoT Central, and a range of tools for IoT device management and data processing.
GCP: Google Cloud IoT Core provides device management and data ingestion for IoT applications.
Databases:
AWS: AWS offers various database options, including Amazon RDS, DynamoDB, and Redshift for data warehousing.
Azure: Azure provides Azure SQL Database, Cosmos DB, and SQL Data Warehouse, among others.
GCP: Google Cloud offers Cloud SQL, Firestore, and Bigtable for various database needs.
It's important to note that the cloud computing landscape is dynamic, and these providers continuously expand their services and geographic presence. When choosing a cloud provider, organizations should consider their specific requirements, existing technology stack, budget, and long-term strategy.

Choosing the Right Cloud Platform for IoT

Choosing the right cloud platform for IoT (Internet of Things) is a critical decision that can significantly impact the success of your IoT project. Here are some key factors to consider when making this choice:
IoT Requirements: Start by clearly defining your IoT project's requirements. What type of IoT devices will you use? What data will you collect? What are your scalability and performance needs? Understanding your project's specifics is essential.
Device Compatibility: Ensure that the cloud platform supports the communication protocols and standards required by your IoT devices. Common IoT protocols include MQTT, CoAP, and HTTP.

Data Processing and Analytics: Evaluate the cloud platform's capabilities for data processing and analytics. Can it handle real-time data streams, perform data transformations, and support machine learning and predictive analytics if needed?
Scalability and Performance: Assess the platform's ability to scale horizontally to accommodate a growing number of IoT devices and data streams. Look for load balancing, auto-scaling, and low-latency data processing.
Security: Security is paramount in IoT. Check the platform's security features, including data encryption in transit and at rest, access control, identity management, and compliance certifications (e.g., GDPR, HIPAA).
Device Management: Consider how easy it is to onboard, manage, and monitor IoT devices on the platform. Features like remote device management, firmware updates, and device health monitoring are crucial.
Cost and Pricing Model: Understand the pricing structure of the cloud platform. Different providers offer various pricing models, such as pay-as-you-go, reserved instances, or consumption-based pricing. Calculate the expected costs for your IoT project.
Integration Capabilities: Evaluate the ease of integrating the cloud platform with other systems, applications, and services that are part of your IoT ecosystem. Robust integration capabilities can streamline your workflows.
Developer Support and Resources: Consider the availability of developer resources, documentation, SDKs, and community support. A strong developer ecosystem can accelerate development and troubleshooting.
Geographic Presence: If your IoT project has a global reach, check the cloud provider's data center locations and edge computing capabilities. Proximity to IoT devices can reduce latency.
Compliance and Regulations: Ensure that the cloud platform complies with relevant industry-specific regulations and data privacy laws. Some platforms offer compliance certifications to simplify regulatory adherence.
Reliability and Redundancy: Look for features that ensure high availability and redundancy. Consider disaster recovery options to minimize downtime in case of failures.
Use Case Suitability: Different cloud providers may excel in specific use cases. Consider which provider aligns best with your industry or application. For example, Google Cloud may be a strong choice for data analytics, while Azure may be well-suited for Microsoft-centric environments.
Vendor Lock-In: Be mindful of potential vendor lock-in. Consider whether you want the flexibility to switch cloud providers in the future or if you're comfortable with the selected provider's ecosystem.
Cost Optimization: Implement cost management strategies, such as monitoring and optimizing resource usage, to control IoT project expenses over time.
Proof of Concept (PoC): Consider running a proof of concept or pilot project on the cloud platform to assess its suitability for your specific IoT use case before committing to a full-scale deployment.
Long-Term Strategy: Think about your long-term strategy for the IoT project. Consider how the cloud platform aligns with your organization's growth and technology roadmap.
Ultimately, the right cloud platform for your IoT project will depend on your specific requirements, budget, and strategic goals. It's often beneficial to engage with cloud providers directly, conduct thorough testing and evaluation, and consult with experts if needed to make an informed decision. Additionally, keep in mind that the cloud computing landscape evolves, so periodically reassess your choice to ensure it still aligns with your project's needs.

Mobile Cloud Computing

"Mobile Cloud Computing" (MCC) and "Cloud of Things" (CoT) are two important concepts that, when combined, enable powerful and connected mobile applications and services. Let's explore both concepts in more detail:

Mobile Cloud Computing (MCC):

Mobile Cloud Computing (MCC) is a paradigm that combines mobile computing and cloud computing to provide various services and resources to mobile devices over the internet. MCC extends the capabilities of mobile devices by offloading computation, storage, and data processing to cloud servers. Here are key aspects of MCC:
Resource Offloading: MCC allows resource-intensive tasks, such as data processing, complex computations, and storage, to be performed on powerful cloud servers rather than on limited mobile devices. This offloading improves the performance and efficiency of mobile applications.
Data Synchronization: Mobile apps can seamlessly synchronize data with cloud storage, ensuring that data is accessible from any device and remains consistent across multiple platforms.
Scalability: Cloud resources can be easily scaled up or down to accommodate fluctuating demand from mobile users. This ensures that mobile appscan handle high traffic loads without performance degradation.
Cost Efficiency: MCC can be cost-effective as it reduces the need for powerful hardware on mobile devices. Users can benefit from advanced features without the need for expensive hardware upgrades.

Real-time Collaboration: Cloud services facilitate real-time collaboration among mobile users by providing shared data and synchronization capabilities. This is essential for applications like collaborative document editing or multiplayer gaming.

Cross-Platform Compatibility: Cloud services enable cross-platform development, allowing mobile apps to run on various operating systems and devices.

Cloud of Things (CoT) Architecture

Cloud of Things (CoT) is an architectural concept that extends the Internet of Things (IoT) by integrating IoT devices, sensors, and data with cloud computing resources. CoT enhances IoT applications by enabling data processing, analysis, and storage in the cloud. Here are key elements of the CoT architecture:

IoT Devices: These are physical devices, sensors, and actuators that collect data from the environment or interact with it. IoT devices may include smart sensors, wearables, and connected appliances.

Edge Devices: Some data processing and analytics can occur at the edge of the network (near the IoT devices) to reduce latency and improve real-time decision-making. Edge computing devices act as intermediaries between IoT devices and the cloud.

Connectivity: IoT devices and edge devices use various communication protocols (e.g., Wi-Fi, Bluetooth, LoRa, cellular) to transmit data to the cloud or edge computing resources.

Cloud Infrastructure: The cloud provides scalable computing and storage resources for processing and storing vast amounts of IoT data. Cloud services offer data analytics, machine learning, and data visualization tools for extracting insights.

Security and Privacy: CoT architectures prioritize security measures to protect IoT data from unauthorized access, breaches, and tampering. Encryption, access controls,and authentication mechanisms are essential components.

Data Integration and Analysis: Data from IoT devices is collected, integrated, and analyzed in the cloud. Advanced analytics and machine learning algorithms can provide valuable insights, trigger alerts, and automate actions based on the data.

Scalability and Elasticity: Cloud resources can scale horizontally and vertically to accommodate the growing volume of IoT data and support dynamic workloads.

APIs and Integration: Cloud services often offer APIs that enable developers to integrate IoT data and functionality into applications, dashboards, and other systems.

When MCC and CoT are combined, mobile devices can access and interact with IoT devices, sensors, and data stored in the cloud. This integration enables mobile apps to offer real-time monitoring, control, and data-driven insights for IoT applications. Whether in healthcare, smart homes, transportation, or industrial settings, MCC and CoT together open up new possibilities for connected and intelligent mobile applications.

Security in Cloud Computing

Identity and Access Management (IAM): Use strong authentication and access control mechanisms to manage user and application access to cloud resources. Implement multi-factor authentication (MFA) for added security.

Data Encryption:

Encrypt data at rest using encryption keys managed by the cloud provider or customer-controlled keys.

Encrypt data in transit using secure protocols like TLS/SSL.

Network Security:

Configure network security groups, firewalls, and virtual private networks (VPNs) to protect cloud networks.

Implement distributed denial of service (DDoS) protection to defend against attacks.

Compliance and Certifications:

Choose a cloud provider that complies with industry-specific regulations and holds relevant certifications.

Understand the shared responsibility model for security, which outlines responsibilities between the cloud provider and the customer.

Security Services:

Leverage built-in security services provided by the cloud provider, such as AWS Security Hub, Azure Security Centre, and Google Cloud Security Command Centre.

Incident Response and Forensics:

Establish an incident response plan and conduct regular security audits and testing.

Implement forensic capabilities to investigate and mitigate security incidents.

Resource Monitoring and Logging:

Monitor cloud resources for suspicious activity and configure logs to capture security-related events.

Use security information and event management (SIEM) tools to analyze logs.

DevOps:

Integrate security into the DevOps pipeline by implementing security testing, code reviews, and automated vulnerability scanning.

Backup and Disaster Recovery:

Implement backup and disaster recovery strategies to ensure data availability in case of failures or attacks.

Security Training and Awareness:

Educate cloud users and administrators about security best practices and potential threats.

Security in both IoT and cloud environments is an ongoing process that requires regular assessment, updates, and adaptation to evolving threats. It's essential to stay informed about emerging security vulnerabilities and practices to maintain a strong security posture. Additionally, consider engaging with security experts and conducting security assessments or audits to identify and address vulnerabilities.

The Hierarchy of Edge, Fog and Cloud computing

Edge, Fog, and Cloud computing are three distinct layers in the hierarchy of computing infrastructure, each serving specific purposes in the realm of distributed computing. Here's an overview of this hierarchy:

Edge Computing:

Definition: Edge computing brings computational resources closer to the data source or "edge" of the network. It involves processing data locally on devices or at the edge of the network, typically in close proximity to the data source.

Characteristics:

Low Latency: Edge computing reduces data round-trip time, minimizing latency for real-time applications.

Data Localization: Data is processed and stored locally, reducing the need for extensive data transfers.

Edge Devices: Edge devices can range from IoT sensors to edge servers.

Real-Time Processing: Suitable for applications requiring immediate decision-making, such as autonomous vehicles **and** industrial automation.

Limited Resources: Edge devices often have constrained computational and storage resources.

Use Cases: Edge computing is applied in scenarios like autonomous vehicles, industrial IoT, real-time monitoring, and robotics.

Fog Computing:

Definition: Fog computing extends the concept of edge computing by creating a hierarchical architecture that includes intermediary nodes or "fog nodes" between the edge and the cloud. These fog nodes perform processing tasks closer to the edge devices while also connecting to cloud resources.

Characteristics:

Hierarchical: Fog nodes create a multi-tiered architecture between the edge and the cloud.

Resource Augmentation: Fog nodes can provide additional computational and storage resources for edge devices.

Data Aggregation: Data from multiple edge devices can be aggregated and processed at fog nodes.

Interconnectivity: Fog nodes can communicate with each other and with the cloud for more comprehensive dataanalysis.

Use Cases: Fog computing is employed in applications such as smart cities, healthcare, and video surveillance, where data needs to be aggregated and processed before reaching the cloud.

Cloud Computing:

Definition: Cloud computing involves centralized data storage, processing, and management in remote data centers or the "cloud." Users access cloud services and resources over the internet.

Characteristics:

Scalability: Cloud resources can be easily scaled up or down to meet changing demands.

Ubiquitous Access: Cloud services are accessible from anywhere with an internet connection.

Data Centralization: Data is stored and processed in centralized data centers.

Elasticity: Resources are provisioned dynamically, optimizing resource utilization.

Vast Computational Power: Cloud providers offer a wide range of computational resources and services.

Use Cases: Cloud computing serves a broad range of applications, including web hosting, data storage, software as a service (SaaS), and big data analytics.

Hierarchy and Collaboration:

Edge, fog, and cloud computing are not mutually exclusive but rather exist in a hierarchical structure. Edge devices collect data and perform initial processing. Fog nodes enhance processing capabilities and facilitate data aggregation. Cloud resources provide extensive storage and computational power for in-depth analysis and long-term data storage.

Collaboration between these layers is crucial for optimizing system performance and efficiency. Data can flow seamlessly from edge devices to fog nodes for preprocessing, and then to the cloud for advanced analytics and storage. This hierarchy allows organizations to balance computational needs, latency requirements, and resource constraints across various applications and use cases.

Scalability and High Availability

Scaling IoT Solutions in the Cloud: Scaling IoT (Internet of Things) solutions in the cloud is essential to accommodate the growing number of devices and data generated by IoT deployments. Here are key strategies and considerations for scaling IoT solutions in the cloud:

Use a Cloud-Native Architecture: Design your IoT solution with cloud-native principles in mind. Leverage cloud services and microservices architecture to ensure scalability, flexibility, and resilience.

Auto-Scaling: Configure auto-scaling rules to automatically adjust computing resources based on demand. This ensures that your IoT infrastructure can handle varying workloads without manual intervention.

Load Balancing: Implement load balancers to evenly distribute incoming traffic across multiple instances or resources. Load balancing helps distribute the workload efficiently and improves fault tolerance.

Message Queues and Event Brokers: Utilize message queues and event brokers, such as AWS IoT Core, Azure IoT Hub, or Google Cloud Pub/Sub, to decouple IoT devices from backend services. These services can handle the communication and data routing, allowing for horizontal scaling of processing resources.

Serverless Computing: Consider using serverless computing platforms, like AWS Lambda, Azure Functions, or Google Cloud Functions, to execute code in response to IoT events. Serverless architectures automatically scale based on event triggers.

Database Scaling: Choose a database solution that can scale horizontally, such as NoSQL databases or distributed databases like Amazon DynamoDB, Azure Cosmos DB, or Google Cloud Bigtable. These databases can handle massive amounts of IoT data.

Edge Computing: Implement edge computing for data processing closer to the IoT devices. Edge devices can pre-process data, reducing the load on the central cloud infrastructure.

Content Delivery Networks (CDNs): Use CDNs to distribute content and reduce latency for IoT applications. CDNs cache content at edge locations, improving data delivery to end-users.

Caching and In-Memory Data Stores: Implement caching mechanisms and in-memory data stores to reduce database load and improve response times for frequently accessed IoT data.

Data Partitioning: Divide your IoT data into smaller partitions or shards, distributing the data across multiple storage instances. This approach can improve data retrieval and processing performance.

Optimize Communication Protocols: Choose efficient communication protocols between IoT devices and the cloud. Lightweight protocols like MQTT or CoAP reduce bandwidth usage and improve scalability.

Monitoring and Analytics: Implement real-time monitoring and analytics to identify performance bottlenecks and optimize resource allocation. Services like AWS CloudWatch, Azure Monitor, or Google Cloud Monitoring can help.

Cost Optimization: Continuously review and optimize resource utilization to control costs while scaling. Leverage cloud cost management tools to monitor and manage expenses.

Security at Scale: Ensure that security measures, including authentication, access control, and encryption, are implemented at scale as your IoT solution grows.

Global Scaling: If your IoT deployment spans multiple geographic regions, choose cloud providers with global reach to minimize latency and ensure high availability.

Testing and Performance Tuning: Conduct load testing and performance tuning exercises to identify and address potential bottlenecks before they impact the production environment.

Documentation and Best Practices: Document your scaling strategies and best practices for your IoT solution to ensure that all team members understand how to manage and scale the infrastructure effectively. Scaling IoT solutions in the cloud requires careful planning, monitoring, and ongoing optimization. By following these strategies and staying proactive, you can ensure that your IoT infrastructure can grow to meet the demands of your application while maintaining performance and reliability.

Ensuring High Availability and Redundancy

Ensuring high availability (HA) and redundancy in IoT solutions hosted in the cloud is crucial to maintain uninterrupted operation, minimize downtime, and provide a reliable user experience. Here are key strategies and considerations for achieving high availability and redundancy in IoT deployments in the cloud:

Multi-Region Deployment: Deploy IoT resources in multiple geographic regions provided by your cloud provider to ensure redundancy across data centres. This minimizes the impact of regional outages or failures.

Load Balancing: Implement load balancers to distribute traffic evenly across redundant instances or resources. This ensures that no single instance is overwhelmed and improves fault tolerance.
Data Replication: Replicate IoT data across multiple data centres or regions to ensure data availability even in the event of a failure. Use database replication, object storage replication, or distributed data stores.
Hot Standby Resources: Maintain hot standby resources that are ready to take over in case of a failure. This includes standby servers, databases, and IoT device communication endpoints.
Failover Mechanisms: Implement automated failover mechanisms that can redirect traffic or services to healthy resources when failures are detected. Use health checks and monitoring to trigger failovers.
Multi-Cloud Strategy: Consider using a multi-cloud strategy, where you deploy critical components across multiple cloud providers. This provides redundancy beyond a single cloud platform.
Distributed Architecture: Design your IoT architecture to be distributed and loosely coupled. Decoupling components reduces the impact of failures in one part of the system on the rest of the system.
Edge Computing: Utilize edge computing devices and gateways for local data processing and decision-making. This can reduce the reliance on a centralized cloud infrastructure and improve responsiveness.
Backup Data Centres: Maintain backup data centres or disaster recovery sites that can be activated in case of a major outage. Regularly test failover procedures to ensure they work as expected.
Redundant Connectivity: Ensure redundant internet connectivity for IoT devices and cloud resources. Use multiple internet service providers (ISPs) or network links to minimize connectivity downtime.
Global Content Delivery Networks (CDNs): Leverage CDNs with global points of presence to serve content, such as firmware updates or configuration files, from the nearest edge location, reducing latency and improving availability.
Monitoring and Alerts: Implement robust monitoring solutions that continuously check the health and performance of IoT resources. Configure alerts and notifications to respond quickly to issues.
Regular Backups: Perform regular backups of IoT device configurations, data, and application states. Store backups securely and test data restoration procedures.
Redundant Power and Infrastructure: Ensure that data centres hosting IoT resources have redundant power supplies, cooling systems, and network infrastructure to reduce the risk of facility-related failures.
Security Measures: Maintain security measures at scale. This includes access controls, authentication, encryption, and security patches to protect redundant resources.
Documentation and Runbooks: Document HA and redundancy strategies, as well as detailed runbooks for responding to failures. Ensure that team members are trained in disaster recovery procedures.
Regular Testing: Conduct regular disaster recovery drills and failover tests to validate the effectiveness **of your** HA and redundancy solutions.
High availability and redundancy planning should be an integral part of your IoT in the cloud architecture from the beginning. It's essential to continually monitor and update your HA strategies as your IoT deployment evolves to ensure it remains resilient and reliable.

Integration with Other Services

Integrating IoT Data with Machine Learning: Integrating IoT data with machine learning (ML) is a powerful way to extract valuable insights, make predictions, and automate decision-making in IoT applications. This integration enables you to harness the data generated by IoT devices to improve operational efficiency, optimize processes, and create intelligent IoT systems. Here's how you can effectively integrate IoT data with machine learning:
Data Collection and Ingestion: Gather and ingest IoT data into a central repository or data lake in the cloud. Ensure that the data is clean, well-structured, and timestamped.
Data Preprocessing: Prepare IoT data for ML by performing data preprocessing tasks such as cleaning, filtering, and handling missing values. Data should be in a format suitable for analysis.
Feature Engineering: Create relevant features from IoT data that can serve as input to ML models. Feature engineering may involve aggregation, transformation, or extraction of meaningful information.
Data Labelling (Supervised Learning): In supervised learning scenarios, label the data to create a training dataset. The labels represent the target variable that the ML model aims to predict.
Choosing ML Algorithms: Select ML algorithms that are well-suited to your IoT use case. Common algorithms for IoT applications include regression, classification, time series forecasting, clustering, and anomaly detection.
Model Training: Train ML models using the labeled training dataset. Depending on the complexity of your problem, you may use traditional ML algorithms or deep learning models.
Real-Time Inference: Deploy ML models to make real-time predictions or classifications based on incoming IoT data. This is often done using inference engines or serverless computing platforms.

Batch Processing: For some IoT use cases, batch processing of historical data may be necessary to retrain models periodically for better accuracy. Schedule batch processing jobs as needed.
Model Evaluation and Monitoring: Continuously evaluate model performance using validation datasets and monitoring tools. Re-train models as necessary to adapt to changing data patterns.
Integration with IoT Devices: Integrate ML models with IoT devices or IoT edge devices if low-latency processing is required at the edge. This allows devices to make local decisions based on ML insights.
Feedback Loop: Implement a feedback loop to capture outcomes and feedback from ML predictions. Use this feedback to continuously improve model accuracy.
Security and Data Privacy: Implement security measures to protect ML models, data, and communications between IoT devices and the ML infrastructure. Ensure compliance with data privacy regulations.
Scalability: Design the ML infrastructure to be scalable so that it can handle increased data volumes and growing numbers of IoT devices without performance degradation.
Visualization and Reporting: Create dashboards and reports to visualize ML insights and results. Make these insights accessible to stakeholders for decision-making.
Use Case Examples: Consider specific use cases for IoT and ML integration, such as predictive maintenance, anomaly detection, demand forecasting, recommendation systems, and image/object recognition.
Iterative Improvement: Continuously iterate on your ML models and integration as you collect more IoT data and gain insights. ML is an ongoing process of improvement.
Documentation and Knowledge Sharing: Document the entire process, from data collection to model deployment, and share knowledge within your team to ensure transparency and collaboration.

Integrating IoT data with machine learning allows you to uncover hidden patterns, optimize operations, and drive innovation in various industries, including manufacturing, healthcare, agriculture, smart cities, and more. By effectively combining the power of IoT and ML, you can make your IoT applications smarter, more efficient, and more capable of meeting the demands of the modern world.

IoT and Big Data Analytics

IoT (Internet of Things) and big data analytics are tightly interconnected, and their synergy has the potential to bring about significant advancements in various industries. Here's how IoT and big data analytics work together and some key considerations:
Data Generation from IoT Devices: IoT devices, such as sensors, cameras, and smart appliances, generate vast amounts of data continuously. This data includes sensor readings, location information, device status, and more.
Data Ingestion and Storage: IoT data is ingested into cloud-based or on-premises data storage solutions. These data lakes or databases are designed to handle massive volumes of incoming data.
Real-Time Data Processing: Real-time data processing systems are used to analyse data streams from IoT devices as they are generated. This enables immediate responses, such as triggering alerts or making real-time decisions.
Data Transformation and Preparation: Raw IoT data often needs to be cleaned, transformed, and enriched to be suitable for analysis. This may involve filtering noise, aggregating data, or joining it with other datasets.
Advanced Analytics: Big data analytics techniques, including machine learning, artificial intelligence, and statistical analysis, are applied to IoT data to extract insights, detect patterns, and make predictions.
Anomaly Detection: IoT data is analysed to identify anomalies or unusual patterns that may indicate device malfunctions, security breaches, or other issues. Anomaly detection can help prevent failures and mitigate risks.
Predictive Maintenance: IoT and big data analytics can be used for predictive maintenance. By analysing historical data, models can predict when equipment is likely to fail, allowing for timely maintenance to prevent costly downtime.
Asset Tracking and Optimization: In industries like logistics and manufacturing, IoT sensors can track the location and condition of assets, and big data analytics can optimize routes, schedules, and resource allocation.
Energy Efficiency: IoT devices can monitor energy consumption in buildings, factories, and vehicles. Analytics can identify opportunities for energy savings and reduce costs.
Healthcare and Remote Monitoring:
Bash code- IoT-enabled medical devices and wearables collect patient data, **which** can be analyzed to monitor health conditions, predict health events, and **enable** remote patient monitoring.
Environmental Monitoring:
Sql code -IoT sensors **are** deployed **for** environmental monitoring, measuring parameters **like** air quality, water quality, **and** temperature. Analytics help assess environmental conditions **and** detect pollution events.
Data Visualization:
Css code - Data visualization tools are used to create dashboards and reports that make IoT data and analytics results accessible and actionable to users and stakeholders.

Scalability:
Kotlin code - The scalability of big **data** analytics platforms is essential to handle the growing volume and velocity of IoT **data as** deployments expand.
Security and Privacy:
Css code- Robust security measures must be in place to protect sensitive IoT data and analytics results from unauthorized access and cyber threats.
Regulatory Compliance:
kotlin code- Depending on the industry, IoT and big **data** analytics solutions must adhere to specific regulations and **data** privacy laws, such **as** GDPR or HIPAA.
IoT and big data analytics create a symbiotic relationship where the IoT generates the data, and big data analytics extracts valuable insights from that data. This synergy is driving innovation in industries such as manufacturing, healthcare, transportation, agriculture, and smart cities, enabling organizations to make data-driven decisions, optimize operations, and enhance customer experiences.

IoT and Business Applications

Internet of Things (IoT) technology has found applications across various industries, enabling businesses to improve operations, enhance customer experiences, and create new revenue streams. Here are five IoT business applications in different sectors:
Smart Manufacturing and Industry 4.0:
In manufacturing, IoT sensors and devices are used to monitor equipment, track inventory, and optimize production processes. Businesses can implement predictive maintenance solutions to reduce downtime by detecting equipment failures before they occur. IoT-driven automation and robotics also improve efficiency and product quality.
Connected Healthcare:
IoT is transforming the healthcare industry by enabling remote patient monitoring, wearable health devices, and smart medical equipment. These applications enhance patient care by collecting real-time health data, allowing for early intervention, and reducing hospital readmissions. For example, IoT-enabled devices can monitor vital signs and send alerts to healthcare providers or family members in case of anomalies.
Smart Retail and Inventory Management:
Retailers use IoT to enhance the shopping experience and optimize inventory management. IoT sensors track customer behaviour, monitor foot traffic, and gather data on product interactions. This data helps retailers personalize marketing, improve store layouts, and manage inventory more efficiently. Smart shelves and RFID tags streamline inventory tracking and reduce stockouts.
Fleet Management and Logistics:
In the transportation and logistics industry, IoT is used for real-time tracking of vehicles, shipments, and goods. Businesses can optimize routes, improve delivery accuracy, and reduce fuel consumption. IoT sensors also monitor vehicle health, enabling predictive maintenance and reducing vehicle downtime.
Smart Cities and Public Services:
IoT technologies are deployed in smart city initiatives to improve urban living. Examples include smart streetlights that adjust brightness based on traffic and weather conditions, waste management systems that optimize trash collection schedules, and environmental sensors that monitor air quality and noise levels. These applications enhance sustainability, reduce costs, and improve the quality of life for residents.
These are just a few examples of how IoT is transforming businesses across various sectors. IoT's ability to collect, transmit, and analyse data in real time is driving innovation and creating opportunities for businesses to gain a competitive edge by offering new services, improving operational efficiency, and enhancing customer satisfaction. As IoT technology continues to evolve, it is expected to unlock even more possibilities for businesses in the future.

Cost Management

Optimizing Cloud Costs for IoT

Optimizing cloud costs for IoT (Internet of Things) deployments is crucial for maintaining the efficiency and sustainability of your IoT project. Cloud services can become expensive if not managed effectively. Here are strategies to help you optimize cloud costs for IoT:
Right size Resources: Choose the appropriate instance types and sizes for your IoT workloads. Don't overprovision resources. Use cloud provider tools to analyse usage patterns and right size accordingly.
Auto-Scaling: Implement auto-scaling for IoT workloads. Set up policies to automatically add or remove resources based on demand, reducing costs during periods of low usage.
Use Reserved Instances or Savings Plans: Commit to long-term usage by purchasing reserved instances or savings plans from your cloud provider. This can significantly reduce the cost of compute resources.

Spot Instances or Preemptible VMs: Consider using spot instances (AWS) or preemptible VMs (Google Cloud) for non-critical workloads. These instances are cost-effective but may be terminated if resources are needed elsewhere.

Data Lifecycle Management: Define data retention policies for IoT data. Delete or archive data that is no longer needed, as storage costs can accumulate over time.

Cost Monitoring and Alerts: Set up cost monitoring and alerts to track spending in real-time. Receive notifications when costs exceed predefined thresholds, allowing you to take corrective action promptly.

Resource Tagging: Use resource tagging to categorize IoT-related resources. This helps you identify and allocate costs accurately and manage resources effectively.

Idle Resource Termination: Automatically shut down or terminate idle IoT devices or resources when they are not in use, such as during non-business hours.

Storage Optimization: Optimize storage costs by using the appropriate storage class (e.g., standard, cold, archive) based on data access patterns. Delete redundant or obsolete data regularly.

Data Compression and Encryption: Implement data compression and encryption techniques to reduce storage and transmission costs while ensuring data security.

Data Aggregation and Filtering: Aggregate IoT data before storing or analysing it. Reduce the volume of data by filtering out unnecessary or redundant information at the device level or at the edge.

Use Edge Computing: Process data at the edge, closer to IoT devices, to reduce data transfer costs and latency. Send only relevant insights or aggregated data to the cloud.

Serverless Architectures: Consider serverless computing for event-driven IoT applications. Serverless platforms automatically scale and charge based on actual usage.

Data Tiers and Archiving: Implement data tiering and archival policies to move less frequently accessed IoT data to lower-cost storage solutions like cold storage or object archiving.

Evaluate Third-Party Solutions: Explore third-party solutions and IoT platforms that offer cost optimization features and analytics to help you manage expenses more effectively.

Continuous Review and Optimization: Regularly review and optimize your cloud infrastructure and spending. Technology and usage patterns evolve, so your optimization strategies should evolve with them.

Educate and Train Teams: Ensure that your teams are aware of cost optimization best practices and tools. Regular training can help them make informed decisions.

Cost optimization for IoT in the cloud is an ongoing process that requires vigilance and adaptability. By implementing these strategies and regularly reviewing your cloud usage and costs, you can maximize the value of your IoT deployment while keeping expenses in check.

Cost Modelling and Analysis

Cost modelling and analysis are essential processes for managing expenses effectively, making informed decisions, and optimizing resource allocation in various domains, including cloud computing, IoT, and business operations. Here are key steps and considerations for cost modelling and analysis:

Define Objectives and Scope: Clearly define the objectives of your cost modelling and analysis efforts. Determine what specific aspects or areas you want to analyse and improve.

Data Collection: Gather comprehensive data related to your objectives. This data may include financial records, usage metrics, resource consumption, and other relevant information. In the context of cloud computing or IoT, collect data on resource provisioning, usage patterns, and associated costs.

Categorize Costs: Categorize costs into different groups or categories to make analysis more manageable. Common categories include operational costs, capital expenditures (CapEx), variable costs, fixed costs, and direct/indirect costs.

Build Cost Models: Create cost models that represent the relationships between various cost factors and variables. Thesemodels may be simple spreadsheets or complex mathematical models, depending on the complexity of your analysis.

Allocate Costs: Allocate costs to specific activities, projects, departments, or resources as accurately as possible. Allocation methods may include direct allocation, activity-based costing (ABC), or cost drivers.

Analyse Historical Data: Analyse historical cost data to identify trends, patterns, and anomalies. Historical analysis can help you understand cost behaviour and make future predictions.

Forecast Future Costs: Use historical data and relevant assumptions to forecast future costs. This is especially important for budgeting, capacity planning, and long-term financial planning.

Identify Cost Drivers: Identify the factors that drive costs within your organization or project. For example, in cloud computing, cost drivers may include resource usage, data transfer, storage, and software licenses.

Cost Variance Analysis: Conduct cost variance analysis to compare actual costs against budgeted or forecasted costs. Identify and investigate significant variances to understand the reasons behind cost fluctuations.

Cost Optimization Strategies: Develop cost optimization strategies based on your analysis. These strategies may involve reducing unnecessary expenses, renegotiating contracts, optimizing resource usage, or adopting new technologies.

Scenario Analysis: Perform scenario analysis to assess the impact of different cost scenarios and decisions. Evaluate "what-if" scenarios to make informed choices.

Cost-Benefit Analysis: Conduct cost-benefit analyses to determine the return on investment (ROI) for various projects or initiatives. Compare the expected benefits against the associated costs.

Stakeholder Communication: Communicate cost analysis findings and recommendations to relevant stakeholders, such as executives, project managers, and finance teams. Ensure that decision-makers understand the implications of cost analysis.

Continuous Monitoring and Improvement: Establish a process for continuous cost monitoring and improvement. Regularly review and update your cost models and strategies to adapt to changing circumstances.

Tools and Software: Utilize cost analysis tools and software, such as spreadsheets, financial management software, and specialized cloud cost management platforms, to streamline the analysis process.

Documentation: Document your cost modelling and analysis methodologies, assumptions, and results. Proper documentation ensures transparency and helps in knowledge sharing within your organization.

Cost modelling and analysis are ongoing processes that require regular updates and adjustments as circumstances change. By implementing these steps and incorporating cost analysis into your decision-making processes, you can effectively manage costs, optimize resource allocation, and make informed financial decisions in various domains.

Challenges and Pitfalls

Common Challenges in IoT Projects

IoT (Internet of Things) projects offer numerous benefits, but they also come with a set of common challenges that organizations must address to ensure successful implementation. Here are some of the most prevalent challenges in IoT projects:

Security Concerns: Security is a significant challenge in IoT due to the vast number of devices connected to the internet. Devices can be vulnerable to hacking, and data transmitted between devices and the cloud can be intercepted. Ensuring robust security measures, including encryption, authentication, and access control, is crucial.

Data Privacy: IoT devices collect and transmit a vast amount of data, often including sensitive information. Ensuring compliance with data privacy regulations (e.g., GDPR, HIPAA) while collecting, storing, and processing data is a complex challenge.

Interoperability: IoT ecosystems often comprise devices from different manufacturers, using various communication protocols and standards. Ensuring seamless interoperability and data exchange between devices can be challenging.

Scalability: As IoT deployments grow, managing the scalability of the infrastructure, including cloud resources, networking, and device management, becomes increasingly complex.

Connectivity Issues: IoT devices rely on network connectivity, and network outages or limitations in remote or hostile environments can disrupt operations. Ensuring reliable connectivity is critical.

Power Management: Many IoT devices are battery-powered or have limited power sources. Managing power consumption to extend battery life and reduce the need for frequent maintenance is a significant challenge.

Device Management: Handling a large number of IoT devices, including onboarding, configuration, monitoring, and firmware updates, can be resource-intensive and complex.

Data Management: The volume, velocity, and variety of data generated by IoT devices can overwhelm traditional data management systems. Handling, storing, and processing IoT data efficiently is a challenge.

Cost Management: IoT projects can incur significant costs, including device procurement, connectivity fees, cloud services, and maintenance. Controlling costs while ensuring effective deployment is a balancing act.

Regulatory Compliance: Different industries and regions have specific regulations and standards that must be adhered to in IoT deployments. Ensuring compliance with these requirements can be complex and time-consuming.

Lack of Standardization: The lack of standardized protocols, communication standards, and device management frameworks in the IoT space can lead to compatibility and integration challenges.

Data Analytics and Insights: Extracting meaningful insights from the massive amounts of IoT data can be challenging. Organizationsmust invest in analytics tools and expertise to turn data into actionable information.

Data Quality: Ensuring the accuracy and reliability of data collected from IoT devices, especially in harsh or dynamic environments, can be a significant challenge.

Environmental Considerations: IoT devices deployed in harsh environments, such as industrial settings or outdoor locations, may face challenges related to temperature extremes, humidity, and physical wear and tear.

Change Management: Implementing IoT often requires a cultural shift within organizations. Ensuring that employees are trained and comfortable with new technologies and workflows is essential.

Successful IoT projects require careful planning, expertise, and ongoing management to address these challenges effectively. Organizations that proactively address these issues are better positioned to harness the benefits of IoT and overcome potential obstacles.

How to Avoid IoT Pitfalls

Avoiding pitfalls in IoT projects hosted in the cloud is crucial for ensuring the success and reliability of your deployment. Here are key strategies to help you avoid common pitfalls in IoT in the cloud:

Clearly Define Objectives and Use Cases:

Pitfall: Lack of clear objectives and use cases can lead to unfocused projects and ineffective IoT implementations.

Solution: Begin by defining your project's goals, use cases, and expected outcomes. Ensure alignment with your organization's broader strategic objectives.

Choose the Right Cloud Platform:

Pitfall: Selecting the wrong cloud provider or platform can lead to compatibility issues, vendor lock-in, or limited scalability.

Solution: Conduct a thorough evaluation of cloud providers based on your specific IoT requirements, such as device support, scalability, and data processing capabilities.

Plan for Scalability from the Start:

Pitfall: Neglecting scalability can result in performance bottlenecks and increased costs as your IoT deployment grows.

Solution: Design your IoT architecture with scalability in mind. Use cloud-native services that can automatically scale with increased demand.

Prioritize Security:

Pitfall: Inadequate security measures can expose IoT devices and data to cyber threats and breaches.

Solution: Implement robust security practices, including device authentication, data encryption, accesscontrols, andregular security audits. Follow industry best practices for IoT security.

Effective Data Management:

Pitfall: Mishandling of IoT data can lead to data quality issues, storage inefficiencies, and difficulties in deriving meaningful insights.

Solution: Develop a data management strategy that includes data cleansing, normalization, storageoptimization, andtimely data archiving to maintain data quality and cost-effectiveness.

Optimize Costs:

Pitfall: Ignoring cost optimization can result in budget overruns and reduced ROI.

Solution: Continuously monitor and optimize cloud costs. Implement cost control measures such asresource rightsizing, use of reserved instances, and efficient data storage practices.

Proper Device Management:

Pitfall: Neglecting device management can lead to difficulties in onboarding, monitoring, and maintaining IoT devices.

Solution: Implement a robust device management system to provision, configure, monitor, and update IoT devices remotely.

Data Governance and Compliance:

Pitfall: Overlooking data governance and regulatory compliance can result in legal and compliance issues.

Solution: Establish clear data governance policies, adhere to data protection regulations, and ensure data privacy and consent management are part of your IoT solution.

Regular Monitoring and Maintenance:

Pitfall: Failing to monitor and maintain IoT devices and cloud resources can result in unexpected failures and downtime.

Solution: Implement continuous monitoring, automated alerts, and regular maintenance to proactively address issues before they impact operations.

User Training and Change Management:

Pitfall: Neglecting to train users and address the cultural and organizational changes that IoT introduces can lead to resistance and underutilization of IoT capabilities.

Solution: Invest in user training and change management initiatives to ensure that employees are comfortable with IoT technologies and embrace new workflows.

Backup and Disaster Recovery:
Pitfall: Not having a robust backup and disaster recovery plan can result in data loss and extended downtime in the event of a catastrophe.
Solution: Implement regular data backups and disaster recovery procedures to ensure data availability and business continuity.
By proactively addressing these pitfalls and incorporating these solutions into your IoT in the cloud strategy, you can enhance the success, security, and efficiency of your IoT deployment.

Xively Cloud for IoT

Xively, formerly known as Cosm and Pachube, was an IoT platform and cloud service that allowed organizations to connect, manage, and collect data from IoT devices and applications. Xively provided a range of tools and services to simplify IoT development, data ingestion, device management, and application integration.
Key features of Xively Cloud for IoT included:
Device Connectivity: Xively supported a wide range of IoT devices, sensors, and communication protocols, making it easier to connect and collect data from various types of devices.
Data Management: The platform allowed users to ingest, store, and manage IoT data efficiently. It provided data analytics and visualization tools to derive insights from the collected data.
Device Management: Xively offered device management capabilities, including remote configuration, firmware updates, and monitoring, to ensure the health and performance of IoT devices.
Security: Security was a priority, with features like device authentication, data encryption, and access control to protect IoT data and devices.
Scalability: Xively was designed to scale to accommodate a growing number of IoT devices and data, making it suitable for both small-scale and large-scale IoT deployments.
Integration: The platform supported integration with other cloud services, APIs, and third-party applications, enabling users to build comprehensive IoT solutions.
It'sworth noting that Xively was acquired by Google's parent company, Alphabet Inc., and was later discontinued. Existing Xively customers were transitioned to other IoT platforms.
If you have a specific question or need information related to Xively Cloud for IoT or its successor services, please provide more details, and I'll do my best to assist you further.

Amazon Web Services for IoT

Amazon Web Services (AWS) offers a comprehensive suite of services and tools for building, managing, and scaling IoT (Internet of Things) applications and solutions. AWS IoT provides a robust platform to connect, manage, and analyze IoT device data securely. Here are some key components and services of AWS for IoT:
AWS IoT Core: AWS IoT Core is a managed cloud service that allows you to connect and manage IoT devices at scale. It provides secure and reliable communication between devices and the cloud using MQTT or HTTP.
Device Management: AWS IoT Device Management helps you onboard, organize, monitor, and remotely manage IoT devices. You can update device firmware, configure device parameters, and track device health.
Security & Identity: AWS IoT offers robust security features, including device authentication and authorization, data encryption, and fine-grained access control. AWS Identity and Access Management (IAM) can be used to manage access to IoT resources.
Message Broker: The AWS IoT message broker enables devices to publish messages and subscribe to topics. It supports message routing, filtering, and transformation, allowing you to process and route data efficiently.
Rules Engine: AWS IoT Rules Engine allows you to define rules for processing incoming data from IoT devices. You can route data to other AWS services, perform data transformations, or trigger actions based on rule matches.
Device Shadows: Device Shadows provide a virtual representation of physical IoT devices. They allow you to synchronize and maintain the desired state of a device even when it's offline or unreachable.
Analytics: AWS IoT Analytics enables you to preprocess, store, and analyse IoT data at scale. You can gain insights into device behaviour, trends, and anomalies using AWS services like Amazon Kinesis, Amazon Redshift, and Amazon Quick Sight.
Greengrass: AWS IoT Greengrass extends IoT capabilities to the edge, allowing devices to run AWS Lambda functions locally. This is useful for real-time edge processing and decision-making.
Integration with AWS Services: AWS IoT seamlessly integrates with other AWS services, such as AWS Lambda, Amazon S3, Amazon DynamoDB, and Amazon Machine Learning, enabling you to build end-to-end IoT solutions.
Device SDKs: AWS provides device SDKs for popular programming languages, making it easier to develop applications for IoT devices that connect to AWS IoT Core.
IoT Events: AWS IoT Events helps you detect andrespond to IoT events and anomalies in real time, allowing you to automate actions and trigger alerts.

IoT Things Graph: IoT Things Graph is a service that enables you to build IoT applications visually by connecting devices and services using a drag-and-drop interface.

Free RTOS: AWS offers Free RTOS, an open-source real-time operating system for microcontrollers, which simplifies IoT device development.

IoT Site Wise: AWS IoT Site Wise is designed for industrial IoT, helping you collect, structure, and analyse industrial data from sensors and equipment.

AWS IoT is a versatile platform suitable for various IoT use cases, including smart home applications, industrial automation, agriculture, healthcare, and more. It provides the scalability, security, and flexibility needed to develop and deploy IoT solutions on a global scale.

RESTful Web Service

A RESTful web service is a type of web service that adheres to the principles and constraints of Representational State Transfer (REST) architecture. REST is an architectural style for designing networked applications, and it is often used in the context of web services to create scalable and interoperable systems. Here are the key characteristics and concepts of RESTful web services:

Resource-Based: In REST, resources are the central abstractions. Resources are identified by URIs (Uniform Resource Identifiers), such as URLs (Uniform Resource Locators). Each resource is a conceptual mapping to a set of data.

Stateless: RESTful web services are inherently stateless, which means that each request from a client to the server must contain all the information needed to understand and process the request. There should be no session state stored on the server between requests.

HTTP Methods: RESTful services use standard HTTP methods to perform operations on resources. The primary HTTP methods used in REST are:

GET: Retrieve resource data.

POST: Create a new resource.

PUT: Update an existing resource.

DELETE: Remove a resource.

PATCH: Partially update a resource.

Uniform Interface: REST encourages a uniform and consistent interface, which simplifies client-server interactions. The uniform interface consists of a limited set of well-defined methods and the use of URIs to identify resources.

Representation: Resources can have multiple representations, such as JSON, XML, or HTML. Clients interact with resources by requesting or modifying representations of those resources.

Statelessness: RESTful services are stateless, meaning that each request from a client to the server must contain all the information needed to understand and process the request. There is no session state stored on the server between requests.

Client-Server Architecture: REST follows a client-server architecture, where the client and server are separate entities that communicate over a network. This separation promotes scalability and flexibility.

Layered System: REST allows for the use of intermediaries, such as proxy servers and load balancers, which can enhance system scalability, performance, and security.

Resource Hierarchy: Resources can be organized in a hierarchical structure. For example, a RESTful API for a blogging platform might have resources like "/blog", "/blog/post", and "/blog/post/comment".

Stateless Communication: Each request from a client to a server must contain all the information needed to understand and process the request. There should be no session state stored on the server between requests.

RESTful web services are widely used for building APIs and web services because of their simplicity, scalability, and compatibility with the HTTP protocol. They are commonly used in web and mobile applications to facilitate communication between clients and servers. When designing and implementing RESTful web services, adherence to the principles of REST helps create systems that are easy to understand, maintain, and extend.

GRPC and SOAP are two different communication protocols used in the context of IoT (Internet of Things) in the cloud. Each has its own set of advantages and use cases. Let's explore how these protocols relate to IoT in the cloud:

GRPC (Google Remote Procedure Call):

Overview: GRPC is a high-performance, open-source RPC (Remote Procedure Call) framework developed by Google. It uses Protocol Buffers (protobufs) for serialization and HTTP/2 for transport, making it efficient and suitable for various use cases, includingIoT.

IoT in Cloud: GRPC is well-suited for IoT in the cloud because it offers efficient and lightweight communication between IoT devices and cloud services. It can be used for real-time data streaming, device management, and control in IoT applications.

Benefits: Somebenefits of using GRPC in IoT cloud applications include high performance, efficient data serialization, bi-directional streaming, and supportfor multiple programming languages.

SOAP (Simple Object Access Protocol):

Overview: SOAP is a protocol used for exchanging structured information in the implementation of web services. It uses XML for message formatting and can be transported over various protocols, including HTTP, SMTP, and more.

IoT in Cloud: SOAP has been used in IoT applications in the past, but it is less common in modern IoT implementations. It can still be employed for IoT in the cloud when legacy systems or specific requirements necessitate its use.

Benefits: SOAP provides a well-defined and standardized way of structuring messages and handling security through features like WS-Security. However, it can be considered more heavyweight compared to GRPC.

When choosing between GRPC and SOAP for IoT in the cloud, consider the following factors:

Performance: GRPC is typically more lightweight and offers better performance due to its use of binary serialization and HTTP/2 transport, making it a suitable choice for real-time IoT applications.

Interoperability: SOAP has better support for interoperability with different platforms and programming languages because it is based on XML and has established standards. GRPC, while providing support for multiple languages, may require additional work for some platforms.

Legacy Systems: If you have existing systems that rely on SOAP or have specific requirements that SOAP addresses well (e.g., WS-Security), you might choose SOAP for compatibility reasons.

In conclusion, both GRPC and SOAP can be used in IoT cloud applications, but GRPC is often favoured for its performance and efficiency, especially in modern IoT deployments. SOAP may still be relevant for specific use cases and legacy systems where its features are necessary or preferred. The choice between them depends on your specific project requirements and constraints

Advance techniques in cloud computing -IOT

Advanced techniques in cloud computing for IoT (Internet of Things) have emerged to address the unique challenges posed by IoT applications, including massive data volumes, low-latency requirements, and the need for efficient resource management. Here are some advanced techniques and technologies used in cloud computing for IoT:

Edge Computing and Fog Computing: Edge computing and fog computing bring computation and data storage closer to IoT devices, reducing latency and bandwidth usage. They enable real-time processing of IoT data at the network edge or within the IoT device itself. This approach is crucial for applications that require immediate responses, such as autonomous vehicles and industrial automation.

Serverless Computing: Serverless computing platforms, like AWS Lambda and Azure Functions, allow developers to run code in response to IoT events without managing servers. This approach is highly scalable and cost-effective, as you only pay for the computing resources used during execution.

Containerization and Orchestration: Containers (e.g., Docker) and container orchestration platforms (e.g., Kubernetes) are used to package IoT applications and their dependencies. This ensures consistent deployment across cloud environments, simplifies scaling, and enhances resource utilization.

Machine Learning and AI at the Edge: Running machine learning models and AI algorithms at the edge of the network allows IoT devices to make intelligent decisions without relying solely on cloud processing. This reduces latency and bandwidth consumption while enabling real-time insights and actions.

Blockchain for IoT Security: Blockchain technology is used to enhance the security and trustworthiness of IoT data. It provides a tamper-resistant ledger for recording device transactions and can be used to secure IoT device identity and data integrity.

5G and Low-Latency Networks: The rollout of 5G networks significantly improves IoT connectivity by offering lower latency and higher bandwidth. This enables real-time communication between IoT devices and cloud resources.

Multi-Cloud and Hybrid Cloud Strategies: Organizations are increasingly adopting multi-cloud and hybrid cloud approaches for IoT. This ensures redundancy, fault tolerance, and flexibility by distributing IoT workloads across multiple cloud providers or combining on-premises infrastructure with public and private clouds.

Security and Privacy Enhancements: Advanced encryption, access control mechanisms, and security analytics tools are used to protect IoT data and devices from cyber threats. Privacy-preserving techniques, such as differential privacy, are employed to handle sensitive data while respecting user privacy.

IoT Data Management and Analytics: Advanced data management and analytics platforms are used to process, store, and analyse massive volumes of IoT data. Techniques like stream processing, complex event processing (CEP), and data lakes are employed to derive valuable insights from IoT data streams.

Autoscaling and Resource Optimization: IoT applications often experience variable workloads. Advanced cloud platforms use autoscaling and resource optimization algorithms to dynamically allocate and de-allocate resources based on demand, reducing costs and ensuring consistent performance.

DevOps and Continuous Integration/Continuous Deployment (CI/CD): DevOps practices and CI/CD pipelines are employed to automate the deployment, monitoring, and management of IoT applications, ensuring rapid development and updates while maintaining reliability.

These advanced techniques in cloud computing for IoT are continually evolving to meet the evolving demands of IoT applications, which vary across industries and use cases. Implementing the right combination of these techniques depends on the specific requirements and constraints of your IoT project.

Cloud Convergence: The Cloud and IoT in your Home

Cloud convergence refers to the integration and synergy between cloud computing and the Internet of Things (IoT) within your home environment. It involves the seamless connection of various IoT devices and sensors to cloud services, enabling enhanced functionality, automation, and control of smart home devices and data. Here's how cloud convergence impacts your home IoT ecosystem:

Data Aggregation and Storage: IoT devices in your home, such as smart thermostats, security cameras, and voice assistants, generate large amounts of data. Cloud convergence allows this data to be aggregated and securely stored in the cloud. Cloud storage provides ample space for historical data, which can be valuable for analytics, insights, and monitoring.

Remote Access and Control: With cloud convergence, you can remotely access and control your IoT devices from anywhere with an internet connection. For instance, you can adjust your thermostat, check security camera feeds, or control smart lights using a mobile app or a web portal, even when you're not at home.

Scalability and Flexibility: Cloud services offer scalability, allowing you to easily add new IoT devices to your home network. Whether you're adding smart appliances, sensors, or entertainment systems, the cloud can accommodate these additions without the need for extensive on-premises infrastructure upgrades.

Automation and Intelligence: Cloud convergence enables the implementation of automation and intelligent routines in your smart home. Cloud-based platforms can analyse IoT data to make intelligent decisions, such as adjusting thermostat settings based on your preferences and weather forecasts or triggering security alerts when suspicious activity is detected.

Interoperability: Cloud convergence can bridge the gap between different IoT ecosystems and device manufacturers. Cloud platforms often support multiple communication protocols and device integrations, allowing you to mix and match devices from various brands and create a unified smart home experience.

Voice and AI Integration: Cloud-based voice assistants, such as Amazon Alexa, Google Assistant, or Apple Siri, are examples of how cloud convergence enhances IoT in the home. These voice-controlled platforms leverage cloud resources for natural language processing and AI capabilities, enabling voice commands for controlling smart devices and answering questions.

Security and Privacy: Cloud convergence also addresses security and privacy concerns. Cloud providers invest heavily in security measures, including encryption, access control, and threat detection. Additionally, user data privacy is a focus, with options for controlling data sharing and access permissions.

Analytics and Insights: Cloud platforms offer analytics and data processing capabilities that can provide valuable insights into your home's energy usage, device performance, and user behavior. This data-driven approach can lead to more efficient resource management and cost savings.

Software Updates and Maintenance: IoT device manufacturers can push software updates and patches through the cloud, ensuring that your devices remain up to date and secure without requiring manual intervention.

Energy Efficiency: Cloud convergence can contributeto energy efficiency in your home. By analyzing data from various sensors and devices, the cloud can optimize heating, cooling, lighting, and other systems to reduce energy consumption.

In summary, cloud convergence in the context of IoT in your home empowers you to create a connected, intelligent, and efficient living environment. It leverages cloud resources to enhance the functionality and capabilities of your IoT devices, offering convenience, automation, and security. However, it's essential to consider data privacy and security aspects when integrating cloud services into your smart home ecosystem.

The IOT and cloud in your Automobile

The integration of IoT (Internet of Things) and cloud computing in automobiles has transformed the automotive industry, offering a wide range of benefits, including improved safety, efficiency, and convenience. Here's how IoT and the cloud are reshaping automobiles:

Telematics and Connectivity: IoT-enabled devices and sensors are embedded in vehicles, allowing them to connect to the internet and communicate with cloud platforms. Cloud connectivity enables features such as remote diagnostics, over-the-air (OTA) software updates, and real-time monitoring of vehicle health.

Remote Vehicle Management: Car manufacturers and owners can remotely monitor and manage various vehicle functions through cloud-basedapplications. Features like remote start, lock/unlock, climate control, and vehicle tracking are accessible via mobile apps or web interfaces.

Predictive Maintenance: IoT sensors collect data on vehicle performance and health, which is sent to the cloud for analysis. Machine learning algorithms in the cloud can predict maintenance needs and alert drivers or service centres before problems occur, reducing downtime and repair costs.

Enhanced Safety: IoT sensors in cars can provide real-time data on road conditions, traffic, and potential hazards to cloud-based systems. Cloud platforms can then analyse this data and provide drivers with alerts and assistance, enhancing safety.

Navigation and Traffic Management: Cloud-based navigation systems receive real-time traffic and map data, helping drivers find optimal routes and avoid congestion. IoT sensors on vehicles can contribute to crowd-sourced traffic information, improving the accuracy of traffic updates.

Infotainment and Connectivity: IoT enables in-car infotainment systems to connect to the cloud, providing access to streaming services, apps, and over-the-air updates for entertainment systems.

Fleet Management: For businesses with vehicle fleets, IoT and cloud solutions offer real-time tracking, route optimization, and vehicle health monitoring. Fleet managers can access data on fuel consumption, driver behaviour, and maintenance needs to optimize operations and reduce costs.

Data Analytics and Personalization: Cloud platforms collect data from IoT sensors and user interactions, enabling car manufacturers to analyse user behaviour and preferences.

This data can be used to personalize in-car experiences, offer targeted services, and improve user satisfaction.

Security and Anti-Theft: IoT sensors and cloud-based security systems can help track stolen vehicles, disable engines remotely, and provide real-time location updates to law enforcement.

Environmental Impact: Cloud-connected vehicles can contribute to environmental sustainability by providing data on fuel efficiency and emissions.

This data can be used to encourage eco-friendly driving habits and reduce a vehicle's carbon footprint.

Driver Assistance Systems (ADAS): IoT sensors and cloud-based AI systems support advanced driver assistance systems, such as adaptive cruise control, lane-keeping assist, and autonomous emergency braking, improving overall vehicle safety.

Data Privacy and Security: Protecting the privacy and security of driver and vehicle data is paramount. Robust security measures, including encryption, access controls, and authentication, are implemented to safeguard sensitive information.

In summary, the integration of IoT and cloud computing in automobiles is ushering in a new era of connected and intelligent vehicles. These technologies are enhancing vehicle safety, maintenance, efficiency, and user experience, while also contributing to the development of autonomous and environmentally friendly transportation solutions. However, it's essential to address cybersecurity and data privacy challenges to ensure the responsible deployment of these technologies in the automotive industry.

PERSONAL: IoT in Healthcare

IoT (Internet of Things) in healthcare, when combined with cloud computing, has the potential to revolutionize patient care, improve medical outcomes, and enhance operational efficiency in the healthcare industry. Here are some key ways IoT and the cloud are transforming healthcare on a personal level:

Remote Patient Monitoring: IoT devices such as wearables (e.g., smartwatches, fitness trackers), medical sensors, and implantable devices can continuously monitor vital signs, glucose levels, medication adherence, and other health metrics.

Data from these devices is securely transmitted to the cloud, where it can be accessed by healthcare providers and analyzed in real-time. Remote monitoring allows for early detection of health issues, reducing the need for frequent hospital visits and improving the quality of care for patients with chronic conditions.

Telemedicine and Telehealth: The combination of IoT and cloud enables telemedicine services, where patients can consult with healthcare professionals remotely through video conferencing and receive medical advice.

IoT devices can be used to capture and transmit patient data during telehealth consultations, providing valuable information to healthcare providers for diagnosis and treatment planning.

Medication Management: Smart medication dispensers and pill bottles with IoT capabilities help patients adhere to their prescribed medication schedules. These devices can send reminders to patients, track medication usage, and notify healthcare providers or caregivers if doses are missed.

Wearable Health Devices: Wearable IoT devices, such as smartwatches and fitness trackers, can monitor physical activity, sleep patterns, and overall health. Data collected by wearables is often synced to the cloud, allowing users and healthcare professionals to track and analyse health trends over time.

Fall Detection and Emergency Response: IoT sensors and wearables can detect falls or sudden health emergencies, automatically sending alerts to healthcare providers or emergency responders. Cloud-based systems can provide real-time location data to ensure timely assistance.

Chronic Disease Management: IoT-enabled devices and cloud-based platforms facilitate personalized care plans for patients with chronic diseases like diabetes, hypertension, and asthma. Continuous monitoring and data analysis help healthcare providers adjust treatment plans and provide timely interventions.

Data Analytics and Predictive Healthcare: Cloud computing enables the storage and analysis of vast amounts of healthcare data, including patient records, medical images, and IoT-generated data. Machine learning and AI algorithms can identify patterns and predict health issues, supporting early intervention and preventive care.

Security and Privacy: In healthcare, data security and patient privacy are paramount. IoT devices and cloud platforms implement robust security measures, including encryption and access controls, to protect patient data from unauthorized access and breaches.

Cost Reduction and Efficiency: IoT and cloud technologies help healthcare organizations streamline operations by reducing paperwork, minimizing errors, and optimizing resource allocation.

Remote monitoring and telemedicine can lead to cost savings and improved resource utilization.

Patient Empowerment: IoT devices and cloud-connected health applications empower patients to take a more active role in managing their health by providing access to real-time health data and educational resources.

In summary, IoT in healthcare, coupled with cloud computing, is enhancing the patient experience by providing personalized, efficient, and data-driven care. It enables healthcare providers to make more informed decisions, improves patient outcomes, and ultimately leads to a more connected and proactive approach to healthcare management. However, ensuring the security and privacy of patient data remains a top priority in the deployment of these technologies in the healthcare sector.

Cloud of Things: Grid/SOA and Cloud Computing

Cloud of Things" (CoT) is a concept that combines the Internet of Things (IoT) with cloud computing to create a more integrated and scalable ecosystem. Within CoT, there are various approaches and technologies, including Service-Oriented Architecture (SOA) and Grid Computing, that play essential roles in achieving the goals of a connected and efficient IoT ecosystem. Here's how SOA and Grid Computing relate to CoT and cloud computing:

Service-Oriented Architecture (SOA):

Overview: SOA is an architectural approach that promotes the design of software components as services. These services can be loosely coupled, self-contained, and independent of the underlying technology. SOA is based on the concept of providing services that can be accessed and used by other applications over a network.

Role in CoT: SOA is a fundamental concept in CoT because it allows IoT devices and cloud services to interact seamlessly. In CoT, IoT devices are often seen as service providers, offering data and functionality as services, while cloud services act as consumers or orchestrators of these services.

Benefits: SOA provides interoperability and flexibility in CoT. IoT devices can expose their capabilities as services, and cloud-based applications can consume these services, enabling dynamic and scalable interactions. It promotes a modular and extensible approach to building CoT solutions.

Grid Computing:

Overview: Grid Computing is a distributed computing paradigm that leverages the computational resources of multiple interconnected computers to solve complex problems or perform large-scale data processing. It focuses on sharing and coordinating resources across a network.

Role in CoT: Grid Computing can be applied to CoT to efficiently process and analyze the massive amounts of data generated by IoT devices. Grid systems can distribute computing tasks across cloud resources, including servers, data centres, and edge devices, to handle data-intensive operations **such as real-time analytics and machine learning on IoT** data.

Benefits: Grid Computing enhances the scalability and performance of CoT applications. It allows the cloud infrastructure to scale dynamically to accommodate varying workloads, ensuring that IoT data processing remains efficient and responsive.

Cloud Computing:

Overview: Cloud computing provides on-demand access to a shared pool of computing resources (such as servers, storage, and databases) over the internet. It includes various service models like Infrastructure as a Service (IaaS), Platform as a Service (PaaS), and Software as a Service (SaaS).

Role in CoT: Cloud computing is the backbone of CoT, serving as the central platform for storing, processing, and analysing IoT data. It provides the necessary infrastructure and services to support the scalability, reliability, and accessibility of CoT applications.

Benefits: Cloud computing offers the flexibility to deploy and manage CoT solutions across different cloud service models. It enables cost-effective scaling, data storage, security, and access control, making it a vital component of CoT architecture.

In summary, the concept of "Cloud of Things" (CoT) represents the convergence of IoT and cloud computing, with Service-Oriented Architecture (SOA) facilitating interoperability and Grid Computing optimizing data processing. Cloud computing, on the other hand, serves as the foundational platform that supports CoT by providing the necessary infrastructure and services. These technologies work together to create a more connected, scalable, and efficient IoT ecosystem.

Cloud Middleware, Cloud Standards and Cloud Providers and Systems

Cloud middleware and cloud standards are critical components of cloud computing that help ensure interoperability, portability, and efficiency in cloud-based systems. Cloud providers and systems adhere to these standards and leverage middleware to offer robust cloud services. Let's explore these concepts further:

Cloud Middleware: Cloud middleware refers to software that acts as an intermediary layer between the cloud infrastructure (hardware and software resources) and cloud applications or services. It provides a set of services and functionalities that facilitate communication, data management, and integration within a cloud environment. Some key aspects of cloud middleware include:

Integration: Cloud middleware helps integrate different cloud services, applications, and data sources, allowing them to work together seamlessly. It often supports various communication protocols, data formats, and APIs.

Security: Middleware plays a crucial role in enforcing security measures such as authentication, authorization, encryption, and identity management in a cloud environment.

Scaling and Load Balancing: It assists in scaling applications horizontally or vertically by managing resource allocation and load balancing across multiple cloud instances.

Data Management: Middleware can handle data storage, retrieval, and synchronization across distributed cloud resources. This is especially important for data-intensive applications.

Orchestration: Cloud middleware often includes orchestration tools that automate workflows and processes, allowing for efficient resource provisioning and management.

Monitoring and Management: It provides tools for monitoring the health and performance of cloud applications and infrastructure components, helping with troubleshooting and optimization.

Messaging and Communication: Middleware supports message queuing, event-driven communication, and publish-subscribe patterns, enabling real-time data exchange between cloud components.

Cloud Standards: Cloud standards are a set of guidelines, specifications, and best practices that ensure consistency, interoperability, and portability across different cloud providers and systems. These standards help organizations avoid vendor lock-in and provide a level of assurance regarding data security and compliance. Some important cloud standards include:

OpenStack: An open-source cloud computing platform that provides a set of APIs for managing cloud resources. OpenStack allows organizations to build private and public clouds while avoiding vendor-specific solutions.

Cloud Computing Reference Architecture (CCRA): Developed by the National Institute of Standards and Technology (NIST), CCRA defines a conceptual framework for cloud computing, providing a common terminology and understanding of cloud concepts.

Cloud Security Alliance (CSA): CSA offers a set of best practices and guidelines for ensuring security in cloud environments. Their Cloud Controls Matrix (CCM) is a widely used tool for assessing and addressing cloud security risks.

Cloud Data Management Interface (CDMI): A standard for managing data in the cloud, CDMI defines how data is stored, accessed, and transferred between cloud systems.

OAuth: Awidely adopted authorization framework used for securing cloud API access and enabling Single Sign-On (SSO) across cloud applications.

ISO/IEC 27001: An international standard for information security management systems, including cloud-based systems. Compliance with this standard assures customers of robust security practices.

Service-Level Agreements (SLAs): While not a technical standard, SLAs define the terms, availability, and performance commitments offered by cloud providers. They are essential for service quality and accountability.

Cloud Providers and Systems: Cloud providers are organizations that offer cloud computing services and infrastructure. These providers build and manage the underlying cloud systems based on industry standards and middleware technologies. Some well-known cloud providers include:

Amazon Web Services (AWS): A leading cloud provider offering a wide range of cloud services, including computing, storage, databases, and AI/ML.
Microsoft Azure: Microsoft's cloud platform, providing services such as virtual machines, Azure Kubernetes Service (AKS), and Azure Functions.
Google Cloud Platform (GCP): Google's cloud offering, which includes services like Google Compute Engine, Google Kubernetes Engine (GKE), and Big Query.
IBM Cloud: IBM's cloud services encompass a variety of offerings, including IBM Cloud Virtual Servers and IBM Watson.
Oracle Cloud: Oracle provides cloud services for database management, applications, and infrastructure, including Oracle Cloud Infrastructure (OCI).
Alibaba Cloud: A major cloud provider in Asia, Alibaba Cloud offers services like Elastic Compute Service (ECS) and Alibaba Cloud Object Storage Service (OSS).
These cloud providers adhere to cloud standards and leverage cloud middleware to deliver reliable, scalable, and secure cloud computing solutions to businesses and organizations worldwide. Users can choose a provider based on their specific requirements, such as application needs, budget, and geographical presence.

IoT in Cloud: Interfacing IoT device with Cloud

Interfacing an IoT device with the cloud is a fundamental aspect of IoT (Internet of Things) architecture. This connection allows IoT devices to transmit data to cloud platforms for storage, analysis, and remote management. Here are the key steps and considerations for interfacing an IoT device with the cloud:
Choose the Right Cloud Platform: Begin by selecting a cloud platform that suits your IoT project's requirements. Popular cloud providers for IoT include Amazon Web Services (AWS), Microsoft Azure, Google Cloud Platform (GCP), IBM Cloud, and others. Consider factors such as scalability, security, cost, and the availability of IoT-specific services when choosing a cloud platform.
Select Appropriate IoT Protocols: IoT devices communicate with cloud services using various protocols, such as MQTT, HTTP, CoAP, and AMQP. Choose the protocol that best fits your device's capabilities and your cloud platform's supported protocols.
Device Integration: IoT devices need to be equipped with the necessary hardware and software to connect to the internet. This may include Wi-Fi or cellular connectivity modules and IoT-focused software libraries.
Security Measures: Implement robust security practices to protect the IoT device and the data it transmits. Use secure communication protocols, device authentication, encryption, and access controls.
Data Ingestion: Create an endpoint on your cloud platform for data ingestion. This endpoint should accept data from the IoT device and securely transmit it to the cloud.
Data Serialization and Payload Format: Data from IoT devices is typically serialized and formatted into a standardized payload, such as JSON or Protocol Buffers (protobufs), before transmission to the cloud. Ensure that your device and cloud service can serialize and deserialize data in the same format.
Message Queues and Brokers: Insome cases, message brokers or message queuing services (e.g., AWS IoT Core, Azure IoT Hub, MQTT brokers) can facilitate reliable and asynchronous communication between the device and cloud.
Authentication and Authorization: Implement strong authentication mechanisms to verify the identity of the IoT device when connecting to the cloud. Use access controls and policies to restrict device access to specific cloud resources.
Data Storage and Database: Cloud platforms offer data storage solutions, such as databases or data lakes, for storing IoT data. Design your data storage schema and strategy to accommodate the volume and structure of IoT data.
Real-time Processing and Analytics: Leverage cloud services for real-time data processing and analytics. Services like AWS Lambda, Azure Stream Analytics, or Google Cloud Dataflow can analyse incoming data for immediate insights or trigger actions based on predefined rules.
Monitoring and Management: Implement monitoring and management tools to track the health and status of IoT devices. Cloud platforms often provide dashboards and services for device management, troubleshooting, and software updates.
Scalability and Redundancy: Design your IoT system to be scalable and fault-tolerant. Ensure that it can handle a growing number of devices and maintain high availability.
Cost Optimization: Keep an eye on cloud costs, especially as your IoT deployment scales. Cloud providers offer tools to monitor and optimize resource usage, helping you control expenses.

Compliance and Privacy: Depending on your application, you may need to comply with industry-specific regulations (e.g., HIPAA for healthcare, GDPR for data privacy). Ensure that your IoT device and cloud infrastructure meet these requirements.
Testing and Validation: Thoroughly test the IoT device's communication with the cloud platform to ensure data is transmitted accurately and securely. Conduct load testing to assess performance under various conditions.
Interfacing IoT devices with the cloud is a crucial step in harnessing the power of IoT for data-driven insights, automation, and remote management. It enables organizations to collect, process, and act on IoT data efficiently, driving innovation and improved decision-making.

Design cloud based IoT systems

Designing cloud-based IoT systems requires careful planning and consideration of various components and technologies. These systems enable the collection, processing, storage, andanalysis of data from IoT devices in the cloud. Here's a step-by-step guide to designing a cloud-based IoT system:
Define the Objectives and Use Cases: Clearly define the objectives of your IoT system and identify specific use cases. Understand what data you need to collect, how it will be processed, and the desired outcomes.
Choose the Right Cloud Platform: Select a cloud platform that aligns with your project's requirements. Consider factors like scalability, security, pricing, and IoT-specific services. Popular options include AWS, Azure, GCP, and IBM Cloud.
Identify IoT Devices and Sensors: Determine the types of IoT devices and sensors needed for your project. Consider the communication protocols (e.g., Wi-Fi, Bluetooth, LoRaWAN) and the data they will generate.
Connectivity and Data Ingestion: Implement secure and reliable connectivity between IoT devices and the cloud. Use MQTT, HTTP, or other IoT protocols to transmit data to the cloud. Set up endpoints or message brokers for data ingestion.
Security Measures: Implement strong security measures, including device authentication, encryption, and access controls. Protect against common IoT security threats like unauthorized access and data breaches.
Data Serialization and Payload Format: Standardize the format in which IoT data is serialized and transmitted. Common formats include JSON, Protocol Buffers (protobufs), or XML.
Edge Computing (Optional): Consider implementing edge computing devices or gateways to preprocess and filter IoT data before sending it to the cloud. This reduces latency and bandwidth usage.
Data Storage: Set up data storage solutions in the cloud, such as databases (SQL or NoSQL) or data lakes, to store incoming IoT data. Design the schema to accommodate the structure and volume of the data.
Real-time Processing and Analytics: Leverage cloud services for real-time data processing and analytics. Use services like AWS Lambda, Azure Stream Analytics, or Google Cloud Dataflow for immediate insights and actions.
Batch Processing (Optional): Implement batch processing workflows for in-depth analysis of historical IoT data. Use services like AWS Glue, Azure Data Factory, or Google Data prep for data transformation.
Monitoring and Alerts: Set up monitoring and alerting systems to track the health and performance of IoT devices and cloud resources. This includes monitoring device status, data transmission, and cloud service availability.
Device Management: Implement device management capabilities for remote configuration, software updates, and troubleshooting of IoT devices.
Scalability and Redundancy: Design the system to be scalable and fault-tolerant. Ensure that it can handle a growing number of devices and maintain high availability.
API Integration: Create APIs that allow external applications, dashboards, or third-party services to access and interact with IoT data and functionalities.
Cost Optimization: Continuously monitor and optimize cloud resource usage to control costs. Use cloud cost management tools and practices to stay within budget.
Compliance and Privacy: Ensure that your IoT system complies with industry-specific regulations and data privacy laws (e.g., GDPR, HIPAA) if applicable.
Testing and Validation: Thoroughly test the end-to-end functionality of your IoT system. Conduct testing for data accuracy, security, scalability, and performance under different scenarios.
Documentation and Training: Document the system architecture, configurations, and processes. Provide training to personnel responsible for managing and maintaining the IoT system.
Deployment and Maintenance: Deploy the IoT system in a production environment and continuously monitor, maintain, and update it as needed.
Designing a cloud-based IoT system requires a multidisciplinary approach that encompasses hardware, software, networking, security, and data management. By following these steps and best practices, you can create a robust and scalable IoT system that effectively leverages cloud resources for data-driven insights and automation.

Exercise

Exercise 1 – MCQ

1. Which technology plays a crucial role in connecting IoT devices to cloud services for data processing and management?
a) RFID
b) Blockchain
c) MQTT
d) NFC
2. In the context of IoT and cloud computing, what does "Edge Computing" refer to?
a) Computing resources located in the cloud data centers.
b) Data processing that occurs on IoT devices or gateways before data is sent to the cloud
c) A type of cloud service for IoT device management
d) Encryption technique used for IoT data transmission

Exercise 2 – True/False

1. Cloud-based IoT systems can offer scalability advantages, allowing organizations to easily handle a growing number of IoT devices and data.
2. IoT devices typically perform all data processing and analytics tasks locally without the need for cloud resources.

Exercise 3 – Fill in the blanks

1. In IoT systems, ___________ refers to the process of transmitting data from IoT devices to cloud platforms for further processing and analysis.
2. Cloud computing enables the ___________ and storage of large volumes of IoT data, making it accessible for real-time analytics and insights.

Exercise 4 – One word answer

1. AWS stands for?
2. GCP stands for?

Exercise 5 – Small answer

1. What is the primary purpose of MQTT in IoT cloud communication?
2. Name one key security measure that should be implemented to protect IoT devices when interfacing with the cloud.

Exercise 6 – Long answer

1. Explain the concept of "Edge Computing" in the context of IoT and cloud systems. Provide examples of scenarios where edge computing is beneficial and how it contributes to overall system efficiency.
2. Describe the typical steps involved in designing a cloud-based IoT system, from defining objectives to deployment. Highlight the key considerations at each stage of the design process and the importance of addressing security and scalability.

Answer:

Exercise 1.
1. c) MQTT
2. b) Data processing that occurs on IoT devices or gateways before data is sent to the cloud

Exercise 2.
1. True
2. False

Exercise 3.
1. Data Ingestion
2. Processing

Exercise 4.
1. Amazon Web Services
2. Google Cloud Platform

Previous Year Question

1. Explain IoT cloud-based data collection, storage and computing services. (SPPU B.Tech. 2017)

ONLINE RESOURCES

Link: https://forms.gle/DYEDVzgaj7NR8h1b7

QR Code:

Link : https://www.youtube.com/playlist?list=PLzlh_31VWEFqYKxnsTBPQ_fAXsP2an0uz

QR Code :

Chapter 12: Web Of Things

What is Web of Things?

The Web of Things (WoT) is a concept and technological framework that extends the Internet of Things (IoT) by integrating IoT devices and objects into the World Wide Web. It aims to create a seamless and standardized way for IoT devices to communicate and interact with web-based applications and services, using web technologies and protocols. Essentially, WoT enables IoT devices to have web addresses, making them accessible and controllable through web browsers and applications, thus bridging the gap between the physical world of devices and the digital realm of the internet. This integration enhances interoperability, accessibility, and ease of use for IoT devices, ultimately leading to more efficient and user-friendly IoT ecosystems.

Web technologies play a significant role in enabling the integration of Internet of Things (IoT) devices into the World Wide Web (Web of Things or WoT). Here are some key web technologies commonly used in IoT:

HTTP (Hypertext Transfer Protocol): HTTP is the foundation of the World Wide Web and is often used to facilitate communication between IoT devices and web servers. It enables devices to send and receive data over the internet.

RESTful APIs (Representational State Transfer): REST is an architectural style that uses HTTP requests to perform CRUD (Create, Read, Update, Delete) operations on IoT device resources. RESTful APIs provide a standardized way to interact with IoT devices through the web.

WebSocket: WebSocket is a communication protocol that enables full-duplex, bidirectional communication between IoT devices and web servers. It's often used for real-time data exchange and control.

MQTT (Message Queuing Telemetry Transport): MQTT is a lightweight publish-subscribe messaging protocol commonly used in IoT for efficient and low-latency communication between devices and servers.

CoAP (Constrained Application Protocol): CoAP is a lightweight protocol designed for resource-constrained devices in IoT. It is similar to HTTP but optimized for low-power, low-bandwidth devices.

HTTP/2: This is an updated version of HTTP that provides faster and more efficient data transfer. It can be beneficial in IoT scenarios with bandwidth constraints.

WebSocket over MQTT: Combining WebSocket and MQTT, this approach allows for real-time, bidirectional communication while maintaining the lightweight characteristics of MQTT.

WebRTC (Web Real-Time Communication): WebRTC is used for browser-based real-time communication, making it suitable for IoT applications that require audio, video, or peer-to-peer data transfer.

JSON (JavaScript Object Notation) and XML (extensible Markup Language): These data formats are often used to structure and exchange data between IoT devices and web services due to their lightweight and human-readable nature.

HTTPS (Hypertext Transfer Protocol Secure): For secure communication, IoT devices and web services use HTTPS, which encrypts data exchanged over HTTP, ensuring data privacy and security.

OAuth: OAuth is a protocol for secure authorization. It is used to grant limited access to IoT devices and applications, ensuring secure and controlled access to resources.

OpenID Connect: OpenID Connect is an identity layer built on top of OAuth 2.0. It is used for authentication, allowing IoT devices to verify the identity of users or other devices securely.

These web technologies form the foundation for connecting and interacting with IoT devices over the internet, enabling seamless integration into the Web of Things.

Common types of web applications used in IoT

Web applications play a crucial role in interacting with and managing Internet of Things (IoT) devices and data. These applications provide user-friendly interfaces for monitoring, controlling, and analysing IoT devices and their data.

IoT Dashboards: These web applications offer real-time visualizations of IoT data, allowing users to monitor device status, sensor readings, and other relevant information. Dashboards often include charts, graphs, and customizable widgets for data presentation.

Device Management Portals: Device management portals enable users to register, configure, and manage IoT devices remotely. They provide functionalities like firmware updates, device provisioning, and access control.

Home Automation Apps: Smart home applications control IoT devices within a household. Users can manage smart lights, thermostats, security cameras, and other connected devices through a single interface.

Industrial Control Systems: In industrial IoT (IIoT), web applications are used for supervisory control and data acquisition (SCADA) systems. They help monitor and control manufacturing processes, machinery, and industrial equipment.

Environmental Monitoring: These applications collect data from various IoT sensors to monitor environmental conditions such as air quality, temperature, humidity, and pollution levels. They are often used in smart cities and agriculture.

Healthcare and Wearable Apps: IoT web applications in healthcare facilitate remote patient monitoring, collect health data from wearables, and provide insights to medical professionals and patients.

Smart Agriculture Platforms: These applications help farmers manage their agricultural operations by monitoring soil conditions, weather forecasts, crop health, and irrigation systems.

Fleet Management Software: Used in logistics and transportation, fleet management applications track and optimize the performance of vehicles, monitor fuel efficiency, and provide route planning.

Energy Management Solutions: These applications help users control and monitor energy consumption in homes, buildings, and industries, contributing to energy efficiency.

Smart City Solutions: Smart city applications connect and manage various IoT systems, including traffic management, waste management, public safety, and utilities, to improve urban living.

Retail and Inventory Management: IoT applications in retail monitor inventory levels, track goods in real-time, and provide insights into customer behaviour to enhance shopping experiences.

Environmental Conservation: These applications collect data from IoT sensors to monitor wildlife, ecosystems, and environmental changes for conservation efforts.

Asset Tracking: Asset tracking applications utilize IoT devices to monitor the location and condition of valuable assets, such as vehicles, equipment, and containers.

Security and Surveillance: IoT-based security applications use cameras, sensors, and access control devices to enhance security and surveillance systems, enabling real-time monitoring and alerts.

Smart Building Management: These applications control and optimize building systems, including HVAC, lighting, and access control, to improve energy efficiency and occupant comfort.

These web applications are essential for harnessing the power of IoT, making data accessible and actionable, and enhancing user experiences in various domains. They enable users to interact with IoT devices and systems efficiently and make informed decisions based on real-time data.

Web of Things (WOT) Architecture

The Unified Multitenant Web of Things (WOT) Architecture is a conceptual framework designed to accommodate multiple tenants or users within a single, shared IoT ecosystem. This architecture is particularly relevant in scenarios where different organizations, individuals, or entities need to coexist and collaborate while sharing the same IoT infrastructure. Here, we'll explain the Unified Multitenant WOT Architecture in detail:

Multitenancy in IoT:

Tenants: In the context of IoT, tenants refer to different organizations, users, or entities that share a common IoT infrastructure. Each tenant has its own set of IoT devices, data, and applications.

Core Components:

IoT Devices: These are the physical devices that collect data and perform actions in the physical world. Each tenant has its own set of IoT devices.

IoT Gateways: Gateways facilitate communication between IoT devices and the cloud or central server. In a unified multitenant architecture, gateways are typically shared but can isolate data based on tenant.

Cloud Infrastructure: The central cloud infrastructure hosts the core IoT services, including data storage, processing, and application logic. It must support multitenancy, allowing data and services to be segregated by tenant.

Tenant Isolation:

Data Segregation: Data from each tenant's IoT devices should be stored in separate, isolated data repositories within the cloud infrastructure. This ensures data privacy and security.

Authentication and Authorization**: Robust authentication and authorization mechanisms are crucial to ensure that tenants can only access their own data and devices.

API Management:

APIs for Tenants: The cloud infrastructure provides APIs (Application Programming Interfaces) that are exposed to tenants, allowing them to interact with their IoT devices and data.

API Gateway: An API gateway manages and secures access to these APIs, ensuring that tenants can access only their own resources.

Tenant Management:

Tenant Onboarding: The architecture should support the onboarding of new tenants, allowing them to register their devices, set up access controls, and configure their IoT applications.

Resource Allocation: The system should allocate appropriate resources (such as storage, processing capacity, and bandwidth) to each tenant based on their needs and subscription levels.

Application Layer:

IoT Applications: Tenants can develop their own IoT applications or use existing ones to interact with their devices and data.

Customization: The architecture should support customization and branding of IoT applications to reflect each tenant's unique requirements and preferences.

Monitoring and Analytics:

Tenant-Specific Insights: Each tenant should have access to analytics and insights based on their own IoT data. The architecture should support customized analytics dashboards for each tenant.

Overall System Monitoring: The central cloud infrastructure should also have tools for monitoring the health and performance of the entire system.

Scalability and Performance:

Elastic Scaling: The architecture should be designed for scalability, allowing the system to accommodate a growing number of tenants and IoT devices without compromising performance.

Resource Optimization: It should optimize resource usage to ensure efficient utilization of computing, storage, and network resources.

Compliance and Security:

Data Privacy: Compliance with data privacy regulations is crucial. Each tenant's data must be handled in accordance with applicable laws.

Security Measures: Robust security measures, including encryption, access controls, and intrusion detection, should be in place to protect tenant data and the overall system.

The Unified Multitenant WOT Architecture aims to provide a shared yet secure and isolated IoT ecosystem, allowing multiple tenants to harness the benefits of IoT while maintaining control over their own data and devices. It addresses the challenges of multitenancy in the context of IoT, enabling collaboration and resource sharing while safeguarding data and privacy.

Web of Things

Two Pillars of the Web

The "Two Pillars of the Web" typically refer to two foundational technologies and principles that underpin the World Wide Web. These pillars are:

HTML (Hypertext Markup Language):

HTML is a markup language used to create the structure and content of web pages. It provides the essential building blocks for web documents, allowing creators to define headings, paragraphs, lists, links, images, and other elements.

HTML is a semantically structured language that uses tags to describe the purpose and hierarchy of content on a web page. It provides a standardized way for browsers to render web content.

HTML documents are viewed in web browsers, and the structure defined in HTML is critical for the presentation and accessibility of web content.

HTTP (Hypertext Transfer Protocol):

HTTP is a protocol used for transferring data over the World Wide Web. It defines the rules and conventions for requesting and delivering web resources, such as HTML documents, images, videos, and other media.

HTTP operates as a client-server protocol, where web browsers (clients) request web content from web servers. The server responds to these requests with the requested resources.

HTTP is designed around the concept of stateless, request-response communication. Each HTTP request from a client is independent of previous requests, and each response is self-contained.

The combination of HTML and HTTP forms the foundation of the web's structure and communication. HTML defines how content is structured, and HTTP governs how that content is requested and delivered.

Together, HTML and HTTP are the fundamental building blocks of the World Wide Web, enabling the creation, presentation, and dissemination of information and resources across the internet. These two pillars have evolved over time, with new versions and technologies (e.g., HTML5, HTTP/2, HTTP/3) continually improving the capabilities and performance of the web.

Architecture Standardization for WoT

Standardization is crucial in the development of the Web of Things (WoT) to ensure interoperability, security, and scalability across diverse IoT devices and platforms. Several organizations and standardization bodies are actively working on defining WoT architectures and protocols. Below are some key architectural standardization efforts for the Web of Things:

W3C WoT Architecture:

The World Wide Web Consortium (W3C) has initiated standardization efforts for the Web of Things. The W3C Web of Things Interest Group is actively working on defining the architecture and specifications for WoT.
The W3C WoT Architecture document outlines key components, including Things, WoT Servient, and the Scripting API, to describe how WoT devices and applications interact over the web.

OneM2M: OneM2M is a global standards initiative focused on M2M (Machine-to-Machine) and IoT interoperability. It aims to provide a common service layer for IoT devices and applications. OneM2M's architecture includes standard interfaces and protocols for IoT device management, data communication, and security.

O-MI/O-DF: Open Messaging Interface (O-MI) and Open Data Format (O-DF) are standards developed by the Open Group for IoT data interoperability. O-MI defines a protocol for real-time data exchange, while O-DF provides a format for describing data models and structures.

IoTivity and AllJoyn: These are open-source projects that have been adopted by the Open Connectivity Foundation (OCF) to provide a standard framework for IoT device discovery and communication. They define an architecture for device-to-device communication and interoperability, allowing IoT devices to discover and communicate with each other seamlessly.

ETSI SmartM2M: The European Telecommunications Standards Institute (ETSI) has developed the Smart Machine-to-Machine (SmartM2M) standard for IoT device management, data exchange, and security. It provides a framework for managing IoT devices, including device registration, security, and data collection.

Fiware IoT Architecture: Fiware is an open-source platform for building smart applications in various domains, including smart cities and Industry 4.0. Fiware's architecture defines a set of generic enablers (GEs) and context information management (CIM) for IoT applications.

Hyperledger Aries: Hyperledger Aries is an open-source project under the Linux Foundation focused on digital identity management and verifiable credentials, which are critical aspects of WoT security and privacy.

Edge Computing Standards: In addition to cloud-based architectures, edge computing is becoming increasingly important in WoT. Standards related to edge computing, such as the Open Edge Computing (OEC) framework, are relevant to WoT architectures as they define how IoT data can be processed and managed at the edge.

These standardization efforts aim to provide a common framework for developing, connecting, and managing IoT devices and applications in a secure and interoperable manner. The adoption of these standards is crucial for the growth and maturity of the Web of Things.

Platform Middleware for WoT

Platform middleware for the Web of Things (WoT) plays a pivotal role in enabling interoperability, communication, and seamless integration of IoT devices and applications across diverse platforms. This middleware serves as a bridge between the physical IoT devices and the application layer, providing essential services for device discovery, data communication, security, and management. Here are some key aspects of platform middleware for WoT:

Device Discovery: Middleware facilitates the discovery of IoT devices on the network. It provides mechanisms for applications to identify and connect to available devices.

Protocol Bridging: WoT middleware often supports multiple communication protocols (e.g., MQTT, CoAP, HTTP) to ensure that IoT devices can communicate with applications using their preferred protocol.

Data Serialization and Transformation: Middleware can convert and standardize data formats to ensure that data from different devices is represented consistently and can be easily consumed by applications.

Security and Authentication: Middleware enforces security measures such as device authentication, access control, and data encryption to protect IoT devices and data from unauthorized access and attacks.

Data Aggregation and Preprocessing: Some middleware solutions offer data aggregation and preprocessing capabilities, allowing data from multiple devices to be combined or transformed before being sent to the application layer.

Pub/Sub and Event Handling: Middleware often supports publish/subscribe (pub/sub) mechanisms and event-driven communication, enabling real-time data updates and event handling.

Device Management: Middleware provides tools and interfaces for managing IoT devices, including device registration, configuration, and software updates.

Interoperability: WoT middleware strives to ensure interoperability by adhering to standardized protocols and data models, allowing devices from different vendors to work seamlessly together.

Edge Computing Integration: In edge-centric WoT architectures, middleware may include components for edge computing, enabling data processing and analytics to occur closer to IoT devices for reduced latency.

Scalability and Load Balancing: Middleware solutions are designed to handle large-scale WoT deployments by providing load balancing and scalability features.

Standardization and APIs: Middleware may provide standardized APIs and libraries that developers can use to interact with IoT devices, making it easier to develop WoT applications.

Logging and Monitoring: Middleware often includes logging and monitoring capabilities to track device status, data flows, and application interactions for troubleshooting and optimization.

Open Source and Vendor Solutions: WoT middleware solutions can be open-source projects or commercial products offered by vendors. The choice depends on the specific requirements and preferences of the IoT project.

Examples of WoT middleware solutions include Eclipse IoT, Node-RED, Kaa, and commercial offerings from cloud providers like AWS IoT Core and Azure IoT Hub.

In summary, platform middleware for the Web of Things plays a critical role in enabling the seamless integration of IoT devices and applications by providing essential services such as discovery, communication, security, and management. It serves as a bridge between the physical IoT world and the digital application layer, facilitating the creation of innovative and interoperable WoT solutions.

Unified Multitier WoT Architecture

The Unified Multitier WoT Architecture is a conceptual framework that combines the principles of the Web of Things (WoT) with a multitier architecture to create a structured and scalable approach for building WoT applications. This architecture aims to provide a clear separation of concerns and the flexibility to accommodate the diverse requirements of WoT applications. Here's an overview of the key components and layers of the Unified Multitier WoT Architecture:

Perception Layer: The Perception Layer represents the physical world of IoT devices and sensors. It includes all the sensors, actuators, and devices that collect data from the environment. Devices in this layer communicate using various IoT protocols, such as MQTT, CoAP, or HTTP.

Network Layer: The Network Layer is responsible for connecting the devices in the Perception Layer to the rest of the architecture. It handles data transmission and routing. This layer includes gateways, routers, and communication protocols that ensure reliable and secure data transfer.

Access Layer: The Access Layer provides an interface for applications and users to interact with the WoT devices. It exposes a standardized API that allows access to device data and functionalities. This layer may include authentication and authorization mechanisms to ensure secure access.

Processing Layer: The Processing Layer is where data processing, aggregation, and transformation take place. It includes services for data normalization, filtering, and enrichment. Real-time processing and analytics may occur in this layer to extract insights from the data.

Logic Layer: The Logic Layer hosts the business logic and rules for WoT applications. It defines how devices should behave based on incoming data and user interactions. It includes scripting engines, rule engines, and decision-making components.

Application Layer: The Application Layer represents the user-facing part of the WoT system. It includes web and mobile applications, dashboards, and user interfaces. Users interact with WoT devices and access data through applications built on top of this layer.

Data Storage Layer: The Data Storage Layer is responsible for storing historical data, configuration settings, and metadata related to WoT devices and applications. Databases, data lakes, and storage systems are part of this layer.

Management and Orchestration Layer: The Management and Orchestration Layer handles device management, provisioning, and orchestration of WoT services. It ensures that devices are registered, configured, and maintained correctly.

Security Layer: Security is a cross-cutting concern that spans all layers of the architecture. The Security Layer includes mechanisms for securing data in transit and at rest, access control, and threat mitigation.

Cloud Services and Edge Computing (Optional): Depending on the deployment, cloud services and edge computing resources may be integrated into the architecture to provide scalability and data processing capabilities.

The Unified Multitier WoT Architecture promotes a modular and scalable approach to building WoT applications. It allows for flexibility in choosing components and technologies that best suit the specific requirements of an IoT project. This architecture emphasizes the importance of standardized APIs, security, and data processing to create robust and interoperable WoT solutions.

WoT Portals and Business Intelligence.

WoT Portals and Business Intelligence (BI) play significant roles in enhancing the accessibility, usability, and value of IoT data for businesses and decision-makers. Here's how WoT Portals and BI are related and their importance:

WoT Portals:

WoT Portals are web-based interfaces or platforms that serve as the user-facing entry points to access and interact with IoT devices and data within a WoT ecosystem. These portals are designed to provide users, including both technical and non-technical personnel, with easy and intuitive access to IoT information. Key features and aspects of WoT Portals include:

Device Management: Users can register, configure, and manage IoT devices through the portal. This includes tasks likeadding new devices, setting up device parameters, and updating firmware.
Real-time Monitoring: Users can monitor the real-time status and data from IoT devices. Dashboards and visualizations provide insights into the current state of devices and the environment.
Remote Control: Some WoT Portals allow users to remotely control IoT devices, such as turning on/off lights, adjusting thermostats, or triggering actions.
Data Visualization: WoT Portals often include interactive charts, graphs, and maps to help users understand and analyse IoT data. Visualization tools make it easier to identify trends and anomalies.
Alerts and Notifications: Users can set up alerts and notifications based on predefined rules and thresholds. This feature enables timely responses to critical events.
User Authentication and Access Control: Security is a priority in WoT Portals. User authentication and access control mechanisms ensure that only authorized individuals can access and control IoT devices and data.
Cross-Platform Compatibility: WoT Portals are designed to work on various devices and platforms, including desktop computers, tablets, and smartphones.
Business Intelligence (BI):
Business Intelligence refers to the technologies, processes, and tools used to collect, analyse, and present data to support business decision-making. In the context of WoT, BI adds a layer of data analysis and insights to the raw IoT data. Key aspects of BI in WoT include:
Data Integration: BI tools integrate data from multiple IoT sources, including WoT Portals, databases, and external data, to create a comprehensive view of the IoT landscape.
Data Analysis: BI tools perform various types of data analysis, including descriptive, diagnostic, predictive, and prescriptive analytics, to extract valuable insights from IoT data.
Reporting and Dashboards: BI solutions generate reports, dashboards, and visualizations that summarize IoT data in a format that is easy to understand. These reports help businesses track performance and make informed decisions.
Data Mining and Machine Learning: BI tools may employ data mining and machine learning algorithms to discover patterns, trends, and anomalies in IoTdata, enabling proactive decision-making.
Predictive Maintenance: BI can help predict when IoT devices are likely to fail or require maintenance based on historical data, reducing downtime and operational costs.
Cost Optimization: BI aids in optimizing IoT-related expenses by identifying inefficiencies, underutilized resources, and opportunities for improvement.
Integration of WoT Portals and BI: The integration of WoT Portals and BI solutions enables organizations to harness the full potential of their IoT data. WoT Portals provide real-time access to device data and control, while BI tools add the capability to analyse historical data, generate actionable insights, and support strategic decision-making. Together, they enable businesses to improve efficiency, reduce costs, enhance product offerings, and gain a competitive advantage in the IoT landscape.

RFID Multi-Tier WoT Architecture

RFID (Radio-Frequency Identification) Multi-Tier Web of Things (WoT) Architecture is a system architecture that combines RFID technology with the principles of the Web of Things to create a scalable and interoperable framework for tracking and managing objects in the physical world. This architecture allows for efficient data collection, processing, and integration into IoT systems. Here's a detailed explanation of the key components and layers of the RFID Multi-Tier WoT Architecture:

RFID Hardware Layer:

RFID Tags: These are physical devices attached to objects to uniquely identify them. Each RFID tag contains a unique identifier (such as an EPC - Electronic Product Code) that can be read wirelessly.
RFID Readers: These devices communicate with RFID tags using radio-frequency signals and retrieve data from the tags.
Antennas: Antennas are used to transmit and receive RFID signals between readers and tags.

RFID Middleware Layer:

Data Acquisition: RFID readers capture data from RFID tags. This layer collects data from multiple readers.
Data Filtering and Cleansing: Raw RFID data may contain errors or duplicates. The middleware layer filters and cleanses the data to ensure accuracy.
Data Transformation: Data from RFID tags may be in a proprietary format. The middleware converts it into a standardized format (e.g., EPCglobal).
Event Processing: This layer handles real-time processing of RFID data, including event detection and triggering of actions based on predefined rules.

Edge Computing: In some cases, event processing and initial data analysis occur at the edge, near the RFID readers, to reduce latency.

Data Management Layer:

Data Storage: Processed RFID data is stored in databases or data lakes for historical analysis and future reference.

Data Security: Security measures are implemented to protect RFID data during storage and transmission.

Data Access and APIs: This layer provides APIs for authorized users and applications to access and retrieve RFID data.

Communication Layer:

RFID Data Communication: Data from RFID readers is transmitted to the middleware and data management layers using communication protocols such as MQTT, CoAP, or HTTP.

Integration with IoT Platforms: RFID data can be integrated into larger IoT platforms and systems using standardized communication protocols and APIs.

Web of Things (WoT) Layer:

Web Integration: RFID data is exposed as web resources or services, making it accessible via HTTP and RESTful APIs.

Semantic Web: Semantic technologies like RDF (Resource Description Framework) can be used to add context and meaning to RFID data, allowing for easier integration with other IoT devices and services.

Discovery and Interoperability: The WoT layer enables the discovery of RFID data sources and promotes interoperability by adhering to WoT principles.

Application Layer:

Web and Mobile Applications: Applications and user interfaces are developed to visualize, analyze, and interact with RFID data. Users can access this layer through web browsers or mobile apps.

Integration with Business Processes: RFID data can be integrated into business processes such as inventory management, supply chain optimization, and asset tracking.

Security Layer:

Access Control: Access to RFID data and system resources is controlled and restricted based on user roles and permissions.

Data Encryption: RFID data is encrypted during transmission and storage to ensure its confidentiality and integrity.

Authentication and Authorization: Users and devices are authenticated before accessing RFID data, and their permissions are determined based on their roles.

In summary, the RFID Multi-Tier WoT Architecture integrates RFID technology with the principles of the Web of Things to create a scalable and interoperable framework for tracking and managing objects in the physical world. It encompasses layers for data acquisition, processing, storage, communication, web integration, and application development, all while ensuring security and adherence to WoT and semantic web principles. This architecture is particularly valuable in industries like logistics, supply chain management, and asset tracking.

Exercise

Exercise 1 – MCQ

1. What is the primary purpose of a WoT Portal in the context of the Web of Things (WoT)?
a) Analysing historical IoT data
b) Providing a user-friendly interface for IoT device control and monitoring
c) Integrating data from external sources
d) Securing IoT devices from cyber threats

2. Which aspect of Business Intelligence (BI) is particularly valuable in the context of IoT data analysis?
a) Real-time data collection
b) Predictive maintenance
c) Device registration
d) Data transmission protocols

Exercise 2 – True/False

1. WoT focuses on creating a standardized framework for seamlessly connecting and interacting with IoT devices using web technologies.

2. WoT Portals primarily serve as backend systems for IoT device management and do not offer user-friendly interfaces for controlling and monitoring IoT devices.

Exercise 3 – Fill in the blanks

1. In the Web of Things (WoT), WoT Portals serve as user-facing interfaces for ________________ and interacting with IoT devices.
2. Business Intelligence (BI) tools enhance IoT data analysis by providing insights through data integration, analysis, and visualization, supporting informed ________________ and strategic decision-making.

Exercise 4 – One word answer

1. WoT stands for?
2. Name two pillars of Web.

Exercise 5 – Small answer

1. What is the primary goal of the Web of Things (WoT) architecture?
2. Name one key benefit of integrating Business Intelligence (BI) with IoT data analysis.

Exercise 6 – Long answer

1. Explain the concept of WoT Portals in the context of the Web of Things (WoT). How do these portals enhance user interactions with IoT devices?
2. Describe the typical steps involved in implementing predictive maintenance using Business Intelligence (BI) in an IoT ecosystem. Provide examples of how this approach can benefit industries like manufacturing or transportation.

Answer:

Exercise 1.
1. b) Providing a user-friendly interface for IoT device control and monitoring
2. b) Predictive maintenance

Exercise 2.
1. True
2. False

Exercise 3.
1. controlling, monitoring, and accessing data from
2. decision-making

Exercise 4.
1. Web of Things
2. HTML and HTTP

Previous Year Questions

1. Define Web of Things and explain two pillars of the web. (SPPU B.Tech. 2019)
2. Explain Unified Multitier WOT Architecture in details. (SPPU B.Tech. 2019)
3. Explain the concept of web of things and Cloud of thing. (Mumbai University B.Tech. 2019)
4. Explain RFID multitier WOT Architecture in details. (SPPU B.Tech.2018)

ONLINE RESOURCES

Link: https://forms.gle/TKDAQztmJrSvDQaL9

QR Code:

Link: https://www.youtube.com/playlist?list=PLzlh_31VWEFrmWlp5I9HndEsrkDvP9HtQ

QR Code:

Miscellaneous Topics

Mashup and its role in IoT

A mashup is a term that originated in the world of web development and refers to a web application or digital service that combines data, content, or functionality from multiple sources to create a new, integrated, and often more valuable application. Mashups are designed to provide a seamless user experience by bringing together information or services that were originally isolated or distributed across different websites or systems. They can be thought of as a "mashing up" of data and services to create something new and useful.

In the context of the Internet of Things (IoT) environment, mashups play a crucial role in integrating and enhancing the capabilities of IoT systems. Here's a detailed explanation of their role in IoT:

Data Integration: IoT ecosystems generate vast amounts of data from various sensors, devices, and systems. This data is often siloed in different formats and locations. Mashups can be used to integrate and aggregate this data from diverse sources, making it accessible and useful for decision-making and analytics.

Interoperability: IoT devices and systems often use different communication protocols and standards. Mashups can act as intermediaries or translators, enabling different devices and platforms to communicate and work together seamlessly. This promotes interoperability and ensures that data from different IoT sources can be combined effectively.

Visualization: Mashups can create intuitive and informative dashboards or user interfaces that display IoT data in a user-friendly manner. Visualization tools can provide real-time insights into IoT data, making it easier for users to understand and act upon the information.

Automation: IoT mashups can automate actions based on predefined conditions. For example, if a temperature sensor detects a critical temperature threshold in a warehouse, a mashup could trigger an alert to the facility manager or adjust the thermostat settings automatically.

Customization: IoT mashups allow users to tailor IoT applications to their specific needs. Users can combine data and services to create custom solutions that address their unique requirements, whether it's for home automation, industrial processes, healthcare, or other IoT applications.

Enhanced Functionality: By combining data and services from various sources, mashups can enhance the functionality of IoT applications. For instance, an IoT application for smart agriculture could combine weather data, soil moisture readings, and crop growth information to provide farmers with recommendations for irrigation and fertilization.

Scalability: As IoT ecosystems grow, mashups provide a scalable approach to managing and utilizing the increasing volume of data and devices. They can adapt to changing requirements and accommodate new data sources and devices.

Security: Mashups can also play a role in IoT security by aggregating data from various security sensors and devices and providing real-time alerts and actions in response to security threats.

Energy Efficiency: In energy management applications, mashups can combine data from IoT sensors that monitor energy consumption with weather forecasts and occupancy patterns to optimize heating, cooling, and lighting systems for energy efficiency.

Cost Reduction: By leveraging existing data and services, mashups can help reduce development costs and time-to-market for new IoT applications, as developers can build on top of existing APIs and data sources.

In summary, mashups in the IoT environment serve as powerful tools for data integration, interoperability, customization, and automation. They enhance the overall functionality and value of IoT ecosystems by enabling users to make sense of data from diverse sources and create tailored solutions to address specific IoT challenges and opportunities.

Multiagent system in IoT

A Multiagent System (MAS) in Internet of Things (IoT) refers to a network of intelligent software agents that work together to manage, control, and optimize various aspects of an IoT ecosystem. These agents are autonomous, goal-driven entities that can interact with each other and with IoT devices to make decisions, perform tasks, and adapt to changing conditions. The goal of a multiagent system in IoT is to enhance the efficiency, responsiveness, and intelligence of the overall IoT environment. Here are the key components and concepts of a Multiagent System in IoT:

Agents: Agents are the fundamental building blocks of a MAS in IoT. Each agent is a software entity with its own set of capabilities, knowledge, and goals. In the context of IoT, agents can represent various entities such as IoT devices, applications, users, or even third-party services. These agents are responsible for collecting and processing data, making decisions, and taking actions within the IoT ecosystem.

Autonomy: Agents in a multiagent system are autonomous, meaning they can operate independently and make decisions without human intervention. They have the ability to perceive their environment, reason about it, and take actions based on their goals and the information available to them.

Communication: Agents in a MAS can communicate with each other to exchange information, coordinate activities, and collaborate on tasks. In the context of IoT, this communication can occur through various communication protocols and standards, allowing agents to interact with IoT devices and other agents effectively.

Coordination: Coordination mechanisms are essential in a multiagent system to ensure that agents work together efficiently and avoid conflicts. In IoT, agents may need to coordinate their actions to manage resources, optimize energy consumption, or respond to changing conditions in a coordinated manner.

Knowledge Sharing: Agents in a MAS can share their knowledge and expertise with other agents. In the context of IoT, this can involve sharing sensor data, analytics results, or insights about the environment. Knowledge sharing enables agents to make more informed decisions and collectively enhance the intelligence of the IoT ecosystem.

Adaptation: Agents in a MAS can adapt to changing conditions and requirements. In IoT, this is crucial for responding to dynamic factors such as sensor failures, network disruptions, or changes in user preferences. Adaptive agents can reconfigure themselves and adjust their behaviour to maintain system performance and reliability.

Resource Management: Multiagent systems can be used to manage and optimize IoT resources efficiently. For example, agents can allocate computing resources, network bandwidth, or energy resources to IoT devices based on demand and priority.

Security and Privacy: Agents in a MAS must address security and privacy concerns in the IoT environment. They can enforce access control, authentication, and encryption measures to protect sensitive IoT data and ensure the integrity and confidentiality of communications.

Scalability: Multiagent systems are designed to be scalable, allowing them to accommodate a growing number of agents and IoT devices as the IoT ecosystem expands. Scalability ensures that the system can handle increased data volume and complexity.

Decision Making: Agents in a multiagent system use decision-making algorithms and heuristics to make choices and take actions that align with their goals and objectives. These decisions can involve resource allocation, task scheduling, and response to events or anomalies.

In summary, a Multiagent System in the Internet of Things is a framework that leverages intelligent software agents to enhance the management, coordination, and optimization of IoT ecosystems. These agents work together to improve efficiency, adaptability, and intelligence within the IoT environment, making it more responsive to changing conditions and user needs.

Horizontal and vertical approaches

In the context of the Internet of Things (IoT), the concepts of "horizontal" and "vertical" refer to two different approaches or dimensions of IoT implementation and deployment. These terms are used to describe the scope and focus of IoT solutions. Let's explore each concept in detail:

Horizontal IoT:

Scope: Horizontal IoT solutions are characterized by their broad and cross-industry application. They are designed to address common challenges and provide generic capabilities that can be used across various domains and industries.

Common Features: Horizontal IoT solutions often include foundational technologies and services that are applicable across different use cases. These may include connectivity, device management, data analytics, security, and communication protocols.

Interoperability: Interoperability is a key aspect of horizontal IoT. These solutions are designed to work with a wide range of devices and applications, regardless of the specific industry or vertical they belong to.

Examples: Horizontal IoT solutions can include general-purpose IoT platforms like AWS IoT, Microsoft Azure IoT, or Google Cloud IoT Core, which offer a suite of services applicable to various industries. They can also encompass communication protocols like MQTT or CoAP, which are widely used across different IoT applications.

Benefits: Horizontal IoT solutions promote standardization and interoperability, which can lead to reduced development costs, faster deployment, and easier integration of IoT technologies across different industries.

Vertical IoT:

Scope: Vertical IoT solutions, on the other hand, are tailored to address specific industry or application domains. They are designed to meet the unique requirements, challenges, and use cases of a particular vertical market.

Customization: Vertical IoT solutions are often customized to cater to the specific needs of industries such as healthcare, agriculture, manufacturing, transportation, or smart cities. They may include industry-specific protocols, data models, and analytics algorithms.

Industry Expertise: Vertical IoT solutions typically require a deep understanding of the intricacies of a particular industry, including its regulatory compliance, operational workflows, and domain-specific challenges.
Examples: In healthcare, a vertical IoT solution might involve remote patient monitoring devices and healthcare-specific analytics platforms. In agriculture, it could be precision farming solutions that optimize irrigation and crop management. Each of these solutions is tailored to the specific requirements of its respective industry.
Benefits: Vertical IoT solutions offer industry-specific optimizations and can provide greater value by addressing unique challenges effectively. They often lead to innovations that are more closely aligned with the needs of a particular industry.
In practice, many IoT ecosystems may incorporate both horizontal and vertical elements. For example, a horizontal IoT platform might provide the foundational connectivity and device management capabilities, while industry-specific applications and analytics are built on top of it to address vertical requirements.
The choice between a horizontal or vertical IoT approach depends on the specific goals and context of an IoT project. Organizations may opt for horizontal solutions when they seek broad compatibility and interoperability across diverse industries. In contrast, vertical solutions are chosen when they aim to address the specialized needs of a specific vertical market and deliver tailored IoT solutions that cater to those needs effectively.

SCADA

Integration of IoT and SCADA in Industrial Settings: Enhancing Monitoring and Control"

SCADA (Supervisory Control and Data Acquisition) is not inherently a topic of the Internet of Things (IoT), but it can be related and integrated with IoT technologies in certain contexts. Let's break down the relationship between SCADA and IoT:
SCADA is a control system architecture that is typically used in industrial and critical infrastructure settings. It's designed for real-time monitoring, control, and data acquisition of industrial processes and systems.
SCADA systems are traditionally centralized and use proprietary communication protocols to connect to sensors, actuators, and other devices in industrial environments.
SCADA systems are known for their reliability, real-time capabilities, and ability to manage complex industrial processes. They are commonly used in applications like manufacturing, energy production, water treatment, and transportation.
Supervisory Control and Data Acquisition (SCADA) systems consist of several key blocks or components that work together to enable the monitoring, control, and data acquisition of industrial processes. These blocks can vary in complexity depending on the specific SCADA system and application, but the following are the fundamental components commonly found in SCADA systems:
Human-Machine Interface (HMI): The HMI block provides a graphical user interface (GUI) for operators and engineers to interact with the SCADA system. It includes screens, displays, and controls that allow users to monitor real-time data, view process status, and issue control commands.
Data Acquisition System (DAS): The DAS block is responsible for collecting data from various sensors, instruments, and devices located throughout the industrial process. This data is then transmitted to the SCADA system for processing and analysis.
Remote Terminal Units (RTUs) or Programmable Logic Controllers (PLCs): RTUs or PLCs serve as intermediary devices that interface with sensors and actuators in the field. They collect data, execute control logic, and transmit information to the SCADA system. RTUs and PLCs are critical for real-time control and data acquisition.
Communication Infrastructure: SCADA systems rely on a robust communication infrastructure to transmit data between field devices, RTUs/PLCs, and the central SCADA server. This infrastructure includes wired (e.g., Ethernet, serial communication) and wireless (e.g., radio, cellular) technologies.
Control Servers: Control servers host the core software and logic responsible for supervisory control and process automation. These servers receive data from RTUs/PLCs, process it, execute control strategies, and send control commands back to the field devices.
Historian Database: The historian database block stores historical data collected over time. This data is crucial for trend analysis, reporting, and performance optimization. It provides a historical record of process variables and events.
Alarm and Event Management: This block handles alarms, alerts, and events generated by the SCADA system. It notifies operators of abnormal conditions or critical events, allowing them to take timely actions.
Security and Authentication: Security is a crucial component of SCADA systems. This block includes authentication, access control, and encryption mechanisms to protect the system from unauthorized access and cyber threats.

Data Presentation and Visualization: SCADA systems provide various tools and components for data visualization, including trend charts, graphs, and reports. These help operators and engineers interpret data and make informed decisions.

Redundancy and Failover: To ensure high availability and reliability, many SCADA systems incorporate redundancy and failover mechanisms. This ensures that the system can continue operating even in the event of hardware or network failures.

Configuration and Programming Tools: These tools allow engineers and administrators to configure and program the SCADA system, define control logic, set up alarms, and manage system parameters.

Remote Access and Mobile Apps: In modern SCADA systems, remote access capabilities and mobile applications enable operators and engineers to monitor and control processes from remote locations using smartphones or tablets.

These blocks work together to provide comprehensive monitoring and control capabilities in SCADA systems, making them invaluable tools for managing and optimizing industrial processes in various industries, including manufacturing, energy, water treatment, and transportation.

IoT: IoT, on the other hand, is a broader concept that involves connecting various physical objects and devices to the internet to collect and exchange data. IoT encompasses a wide range of use cases, from consumer devices like smart thermostats and wearables to industrial applications like asset tracking and predictive maintenance.

IoT often leverages standard internet protocols and cloud-based services to connect devices, enabling data analytics, remote monitoring, and control.

Unlike SCADA, IoT is not limited to industrial settings and is often associated with consumer applications and the digitization of everyday objects.

Integration of SCADA and IoT:

While SCADA and IoT are distinct concepts, they can be integrated in certain scenarios, particularly in modernizing and enhancing industrial automation and control systems. Here's how they can intersect:

Data Integration: IoT sensors and devices can be integrated into existing SCADA systems to provide additional data sources for monitoring and control. This allows organizations to collect more data, including environmental data, equipment health, and energy consumption, which can be valuable for optimizing industrial processes.

Remote Monitoring: IoT can enable remote monitoring of industrial processes and assets, which can be useful for maintenance personnel and managers. This extends the reach of traditional SCADA systems.

Cloud-Based Analytics: IoT data can be sent to cloud-based platforms for advanced analytics, predictive maintenance, and historical data analysis, augmenting the capabilities of SCADA systems.

Scalability: IoT technologies can provide a more scalable and cost-effective solution for expanding the reach of monitoring and control systems to new areas or facilities.

Cybersecurity: Integrating IoT into SCADA systems can introduce new cybersecurity challenges, as IoT devices are often more vulnerable. Ensuring the security of both IoT and SCADA components is essential.

In summary, while SCADA and IoT are distinct concepts, they can complement each other in industrial settings by extending monitoring and control capabilities, providing additional data sources, and enabling advanced analytics. The integration of IoT with SCADA is part of the broader trend of Industry 4.0, which focuses on the digital transformation of industrial processes.

The ETSI M2M Architecture

The ETSI (European Telecommunications Standards Institute) M2M (Machine-to-Machine) architecture is designed to provide a framework for enabling communication between machines, devices, and applications in the context of IoT (Internet of Things). ETSI M2M architecture defines a set of key elements that work together to facilitate M2M communications and services. Here are the key elements of the ETSI M2M architecture:

M2M Devices: These are the physical devices or sensors that collect data, monitor the environment, or perform specific tasks. M2M devices are equipped with sensors, actuators, communication modules, and processing capabilities.

M2M Gateway: The M2M gateway serves as an intermediary between M2M devices and the core network or the internet. It is responsible for aggregating data from multiple devices, performing local processing, and transmitting the data to the M2M Service Layer.

M2M Device Management: Device management functions are crucial for provisioning, configuring, monitoring, and maintaining M2M devices. This element ensures that devices are properly registered, updated, and controlled throughout their lifecycle.

M2M Service Layer: The M2M Service Layer is a critical component responsible for handling communication between M2M devices and applications. It provides various services such as data storage, data processing, and event handling.

M2M Application Platform: This element represents the platform where M2M applications and services are developed, hosted, and executed. It provides APIs and tools for application developers to create software that interacts with M2M devices and data.
M2M Application: M2M applications are software programs that leverage data from M2M devices to deliver specific services or functionalities. These applications can be diverse, ranging from asset tracking and remote monitoring to smart city services.
Security and Privacy: Security and privacy are essential elements of the ETSI M2M architecture. This includes mechanisms for device authentication, data encryption, access control, and privacy protection to ensure the integrity and confidentiality of data.
M2M Management and Orchestration: This element manages the provisioning, configuration, and coordination of various M2M components and services. It ensures that M2M devices and applications work harmoniously within the architecture.
Interoperability and Standardization: ETSI M2M emphasizes the importance of interoperability and standardization to ensure that different M2M devices and systems can work together seamlessly. Standardized communication protocols and data formats are essential for achieving this goal.
Connectivity: Connectivity elements encompass the network infrastructure and communication protocols used for M2M communication. These may include cellular networks (2G, 3G, 4G, 5G), Wi-Fi, Bluetooth, Zigbee, and other wireless technologies.
Policy and Business Management: This element involves defining policies, business rules, and governance models for managing M2M services. It includes considerations for billing, quality of service, and regulatory compliance.
Location and Context Awareness: M2M devices can often benefit from location and context-awareness. This element ensures that devices can access information about their physical location and adapt their behavior based on contextual factors.
Scalability and Flexibility: The ETSI M2M architecture is designed to be scalable and flexible to accommodate a wide range of use cases and varying numbers of devices. This adaptability is critical for the diverse IoT landscape.
Lifecycle Management: Managing the lifecycle of M2M devices, applications, and services involves tasks such as provisioning, updating, decommissioning, and replacing devices or software components.
The ETSI M2M architecture provides a comprehensive framework for designing, deploying, and managing M2M and IoT solutions. It aims to enable seamless communication, interoperability, and security across a wide array of M2M devices and applications while supporting various industries and use cases.

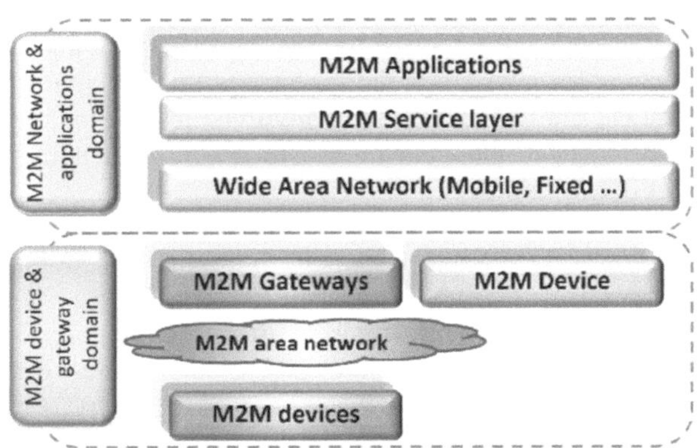

Clustering in IoT

Clustering in the context of the Internet of Things (IoT) refers to the process of grouping or organizing IoT devices into clusters or subsets based on certain criteria or characteristics. These criteria may include device type, functionality, location, communication protocol, or other relevant attributes. Clustering is an important concept in IoT as it helps in the efficient management, communication, and coordination of devices within a network.
The term "clustering principle" in IoT refers to the fundamental principles and objectives behind the process of clustering IoT devices. These principles guide the grouping of devices to achieve specific goals and enhance the overall efficiency and performance of IoT networks. Let's explore the clustering principle in more detail:
Clustering Principle in IoT:

Resource Optimization: One of the primary objectives of clustering in IoT is to optimize the utilization of resources, including energy, bandwidth, and computational power. By grouping devices with similar characteristics or functions, it becomes possible to manage and allocate resources more efficiently within each cluster.
Scalability: IoT networks often consist of a large number of devices, and managing them individually can be challenging. Clustering enables scalability by dividing the network into manageable clusters. This simplifies network management and allows for the addition of new devices without significantly increasing complexity.
Reduced Overhead: Clustering helps in reducing the overhead associated with communication and coordination between devices. Devices within the same cluster can communicate directly with one another, reducing the need for centralized control and minimizing communication delays.
Enhanced Security: Security is a critical concern in IoT, and clustering can enhance security by isolating devices with specific security requirements into separate clusters. This can help contain security breaches and limit the impact of attacks.
Improved Reliability: Clustering can improve the reliability of IoT networks by providing redundancy and fault tolerance within clusters. If one device within a cluster fails, other devices in the same cluster can compensate for the loss of functionality.
Context-Awareness: Clustering can be based on device location or context, enabling context-aware IoT applications. Devices in the same cluster may share similar environmental conditions, making it easier to implement context-aware services.
Load Balancing: Clusters can help distribute workloads and data processing tasks efficiently. By balancing the load among devices within a cluster, it becomes possible to avoid congestion and ensure that devices operate within their capacity limits.
Application-Specific Clusters: In some cases, clustering may be designed to align with specific IoT applications or use cases. For example, in a smart city application, streetlight control devices may be grouped into a lighting cluster, while environmental sensors form a separate cluster for monitoring air quality.
Latency Reduction: Clustering can reduce latency in IoT networks, particularly in real-time or low-latency applications. Devices within the same cluster can communicate more quickly with each other, reducing the time it takes to process data and make decisions.
Energy Efficiency: Clustering can lead to energy-efficient IoT networks. Devices in a cluster can coordinate their sleep and wake cycles to conserve energy, especially in battery-powered IoT devices.
Overall, the clustering principle in IoT is aimed at creating well-organized, efficient, and manageable networks of devices. The specific criteria and algorithms used for clustering may vary depending on the application and network requirements, but the underlying objective is to enhance the performance, reliability, and scalability of IoT systems.

Conceptual Framework of IoT

In the context of IoT (Internet of Things), a conceptual framework refers to a high-level, abstract structure or model that outlines the key components, concepts, and relationships within an IoT system. It provides a conceptual understanding of how IoT works and the various elements involved in creating an IoT ecosystem. This framework helps both practitioners and researchers in the field of IoT to organize their thinking, design IoT solutions, and understand the broader context of IoT technology.
A typical conceptual framework in IoT may include the following key components:
Devices and Sensors: These are the physical objects or nodes in the IoT system that collect data. Devices can range from simple sensors to complex devices with processing capabilities.
Connectivity: This component represents the communication infrastructure that allows IoT devices to transmit data. It encompasses various communication technologies like Wi-Fi, cellular networks, LPWAN (Low-Power Wide-Area Network), and more.
Data Processing and Analytics: IoT generates vast amounts of data. This component involves the processing and analysis of data to extract valuable insights. Techniques like edge computing and cloud-based analytics may be part of this component.
Security and Privacy: Security is a critical consideration in IoT, as devices are often connected to the internet and can be vulnerable to cyber threats. This component focuses on ensuring the confidentiality, integrity, and availability of data and devices.
Applications and Use Cases: IoT is driven by specific applications and use cases. This component represents the various real-world scenarios where IoT technology is applied, such as smart homes, industrial automation, healthcare, and agriculture.
User Interface and Interaction: In many IoT systems, there are user interfaces, whether through mobile apps or web dashboards, that allow users to interact with and control IoT devices or access data.

Standards and Protocols: IoT involves a wide array of standards and protocols for device communication, data exchange, and interoperability. This component ensures that devices and systems can work together seamlessly.

Scalability and Management: IoT systems often need to scale to accommodate a growing number of devices. This component includes mechanisms for device provisioning, management, and scalability.

Ecosystem Partners: IoT ecosystems can involve multiple stakeholders, including device manufacturers, service providers, and application developers. This component accounts for the various participants in the IoT ecosystem.

Regulatory and Ethical Considerations: IoT often operates within a regulatory framework, and ethical considerations like data privacy and consent are crucial. This component addresses compliance and ethical concerns.

A conceptual framework serves as a foundational guide for designing, implementing, and understanding IoT systems. It helps clarify the relationships between different elements, provides a common language for discussing IoT concepts, and aids in problem-solving within the IoT domain.

Role of the Internet of Things for Increased Autonomy and Agility in Collaborative Production Environments

The Internet of Things (IoT) plays a significant role in enhancing autonomy and agility in collaborative production environments, such as manufacturing and supply chain operations. Here's how IoT contributes to these aspects:

Real-Time Data Collection: IoT sensors and devices collect real-time data from various points in the production process, including machinery, inventory, and logistics. This data provides visibility into the status and performance of assets and processes, enabling quick decision-making.

Predictive Maintenance: IoT-enabled predictive maintenance systems use data analytics to predict equipment failures or maintenance needs before they occur. This allows for planned downtime, reducing unplanned disruptions and production delays.

Remote Monitoring and Control: IoT technology enables remote monitoring of equipment and processes. Operators and managers can access real-time data and control machinery from anywhere, improving operational agility and reducing the need for physical presence on the factory floor.

Supply Chain Visibility: IoT extends visibility across the supply chain, allowing organizations to track the movement of raw materials, components, and finished products. This transparency helps in anticipating disruptions, optimizing inventory levels, and ensuring timely deliveries.

Inventory Management: IoT-based inventory management systems provide accurate, real-time information about stock levels. This enables just-in-time inventory practices, reducing carrying costs and ensuring products are available when needed.

Quality Control: IoT sensors can monitor product quality throughout the production process. Any deviations from quality standards can trigger immediate corrective actions, reducing defects and waste.

Adaptive Manufacturing: IoT enables adaptive manufacturing processes where production parameters can be adjusted in real time based on changing conditions or customer demands. This agility allows for efficient customization and rapid response to market changes.

Energy Efficiency: IoT sensors and analytics can optimize energy usage in production facilities. By monitoring energy consumption patterns, organizations can reduce costs and minimize their environmental footprint.

Collaboration and Communication: IoT facilitates communication and collaboration among various stakeholders, including suppliers, manufacturers, and customers. Real-time data sharing enables better coordination, faster issue resolution, and more agile decision-making.

Data Analytics and AI: IoT-generated data can be processed through advanced analytics and artificial intelligence (AI) algorithms. These technologies can identify patterns, trends, and anomalies, providing insights for continuous process improvement and optimization.

Safety and Compliance: IoT sensors and monitoring systems enhance safety in collaborative production environments by detecting unsafe conditions or equipment malfunctions. They also help ensure compliance with regulatory requirements.

Scalability: IoT solutions are scalable, allowing organizations to expand and adapt their IoT deployments as production needs change or as they enter new markets.

Cost Reduction: By optimizing operations, minimizing downtime, reducing waste, and improving efficiency, IoT can lead to significant cost reductions in collaborative production environments.

In summary, the Internet of Things empowers collaborative production environments with increased autonomy and agility by providing real-time data, predictive capabilities, remote monitoring and control, and improved collaboration among stakeholders. These IoT-driven improvements lead to more efficient and responsive production processes, ultimately contributing to better competitiveness and customer satisfaction.

Components and communication media required for making smart building

Creating a smart building involves integrating various components and communication media to enhance efficiency, security, comfort, and sustainability. These components enable the building to collect data, communicate with devices, and automate processes. Here are the key components and communication media required for making a smart building:

Sensors:

Motion Sensors: Detect occupancy in rooms to control lighting and HVAC systems.
Temperature and Humidity Sensors: Monitor environmental conditions for efficient climate control.
Light Sensors: Adjust artificial lighting based on natural light levels.
Occupancy Sensors: Detect the presence of people to optimize lighting, heating, and cooling.
CO2 and Air Quality Sensors: Ensure indoor air quality is within acceptable levels.
Window and Door Sensors: Monitor open/close status for security and energy conservation.
Smoke and Fire Detectors: Enhance safety by detecting potential hazards.
Water Leak Sensors: Detect leaks to prevent water damage.

Actuators:

HVAC Systems: Actuators control heating, ventilation, and air conditioning for temperature regulation.
Smart Lighting: Actuators control lighting systems, adjusting intensity and color.
Automated Blinds: Actuators adjust window coverings for light and temperature control.
Smart Locks: Actuators control door locks for access control.
Irrigation Systems: Actuators manage outdoor watering based on weather and soil conditions.
Fire Suppression Systems: Actuators trigger fire suppression measures in case of emergencies.

Communication Media:

Wi-Fi: Provides wireless connectivity for devices within the building.
Ethernet: Wired connections for stable and high-speed data transfer.
Zigbee and Z-Wave: Low-power, wireless communication protocols for IoT devices.
Bluetooth: Short-range wireless for connecting smartphones and devices.
LoRaWAN: Long-range, low-power network for IoT sensors and devices.
5G: High-speed mobile network for real-time data transfer and connectivity.
Powerline Communication: Data transmission over electrical wiring.

Building Management System (BMS):

A central control system that integrates and manages various building components, such as HVAC, lighting, security, and energy management.

IoT Gateway:

Acts as a bridge between IoT devices and the central control system, allowing them to communicate effectively.

Cloud Platform:

A cloud-based platform that stores and analyses data from sensors, enabling remote monitoring and control.

User Interfaces:

Mobile Apps: Allow users to control and monitor building systems remotely via smartphones or tablets.
Web Interfaces: Web-based dashboards provide real-time data and control options.

Security Systems:

Surveillance Cameras: Monitor and record activities in and around the building.
Access Control Systems: Control entry and exit points through keycards, biometrics, or smartphone apps.
Intrusion Detection Systems: Notify authorities of unauthorized access.

Energy Management Systems:

Monitor and control energy consumption, optimizing usage for cost savings and sustainability.

Data Analytics and Artificial Intelligence (AI):

Analyse data from sensors to make informed decisions, predict maintenance needs, and optimize building performance.

Renewable Energy Sources:

Solar panels, wind turbines, or other renewable sources to generate clean energy for the building.

Energy Storage Systems:

Batteries or energy storage solutions to store excess energy for later use.

By integrating these components and communication media, a smart building can achieve energy efficiency, improve security, enhance comfort, and provide an intelligent environment that adapts to the needs of its occupants while reducing its environmental impact.

IoT Standards and Ecosystems: Building the Foundation for a Connected World

The Internet of Things (IoT) has revolutionized the way we interact with technology and the world around us. It has ushered in an era where everyday objects are equipped with sensors, connectivity, and intelligence, enabling them to collect and exchange data for various applications. However, the seamless functioning of IoT relies heavily on standards and ecosystems that define how devices communicate and work together. In this article, we will delve into the importance of IoT standards and ecosystems and their role in shaping the connected world.

Understanding IoT Standards:

IoT standards are a set of rules and protocols that ensure interoperability, security, and reliability among the myriad of IoT devices and systems. These standards are crucial for enabling devices from different manufacturers to communicate and collaborate effectively. Without such standards, the IoT landscape would be a fragmented and chaotic space, hindering innovation and limiting the potential of IoT technology.

Some key IoT standards include:

Communication Protocols: IoT devices often use various communication protocols, such as MQTT, CoAP, and HTTP, to exchange data with other devices or cloud services. These protocols ensure that data can be **transmitted efficiently and securely across different networks.**

Security Standards: Security is a paramount concern in the IoT ecosystem. Standards like OAuth 2.0, TLS/SSL, and PKI (Public Key Infrastructure) help safeguard data and devices from cyber threats.

Data Standards: Standardizing data formats and structures, such as JSON and XML, ensures that devices can interpret and process data consistently, facilitating data exchange and analytics.

Device Management Standards: These standards define how devices are managed, configured, and updated remotely. MQTT-SN and LwM2M are examples of protocols designed for device management.

13.10.2. Importance of IoT Ecosystems:

IoT ecosystems are the collaborative networks of devices, platforms, and applications that work together to deliver specific services or solutions. These ecosystems play a pivotal role in expanding the reach and impact of IoT technology. Here's why they are crucial:

Interoperability: IoT ecosystems bring together devices from various manufacturers, ensuring that they can work seamlessly with each other. This interoperability simplifies the deployment of IoT solutions and reduces compatibility issues.

Scalability: IoT ecosystems enable the easy integration of new devices and services as needed. This scalability is essential for businesses looking to expand their IoT deployments over time.

Innovation: Ecosystems foster innovation by providing a platform for developers to create new applications and services that leverage existing IoT infrastructure. Open APIs (Application Programming Interfaces) and developer tools encourage creativity and experimentation.

End-to-End Solutions: IoT ecosystems often offer end-to-end solutions, covering device connectivity, data processing, analytics, and user interfaces. This simplifies the implementation of IoT projects, making them more accessible to businesses and consumers.

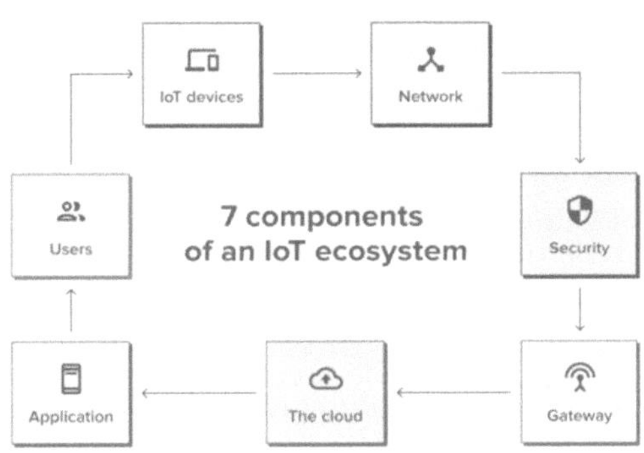

Challenges and Future Trends:

While IoT standards and ecosystems have come a long way in enabling a connected world, several challenges and future trends deserve attention:

Security and Privacy: As IoT adoption grows, security and privacy concerns become more complex. Future standards and ecosystems must prioritize robust security measures and data protection to address these challenges.

Edge Computing: Edge computing, which processes data closer to the source, is gaining prominence. Future IoT ecosystems will likely incorporate edge computing capabilities to reduce latency and enhance real-time decision-making.
5G Connectivity: The rollout of 5G networks is set to revolutionize IoT by providing faster, more reliable connectivity. IoT standards and ecosystems will need to adapt to harness the full potential of 5G technology.
AI and Machine Learning Integration: **Integrating** AI and machine learning into IoT ecosystems will enable devices to make intelligent decisions autonomously. This trend will require standardized data formats and protocols for efficient data exchange.
In conclusion, IoT standards and ecosystems are the backbone of the connected world. They provide the rules and structure necessary for devices to communicate effectively and for ecosystems to flourish. As IoT continues to evolve, the development and adherence to these standards will be essential for realizing the full potential of this transformative technology. While challenges lie ahead, the ongoing development of standards and ecosystems promises to make the IoT landscape more secure, efficient, and innovative for years to come.

ARM

In the context of IoT (Internet of Things), "ARM" typically refers to ARM-based microprocessor architecture or microcontroller units (MCUs) used in IoT devices. ARM is a popular and widely adopted architecture for IoT applications due to its energy efficiency, scalability, and versatility.
Here's what "ARM in IoT" generally means:
ARM Architecture: ARM (Advanced RISC Machine) is a family of microprocessor architectures known for its Reduced Instruction Set Computing (RISC) design. ARM processors are highly energy-efficient, which is crucial for IoT devices that often run on battery power or have limited power sources.
ARM-based MCUs: ARM-based microcontroller units (MCUs) are a common choice for IoT devices. These MCUs, such as those from the Cortex-M series (e.g., Cortex-M0, Cortex-M4), provide a balance of performance and power efficiency, making them suitable for a wide range of IoT applications.
Scalability: ARM offers a range of processor cores, from low-power Cortex-M cores for simple sensors to high-performance Cortex-A cores for more powerful IoT edge devices. This scalability allows IoT manufacturers to choose the ARM core that best matches the processing needs of their specific IoT application.
Compatibility: ARM processors are compatible with various operating systems, development tools, and middleware commonly used in IoT development. This compatibility simplifies the development process and enables seamless integration with IoT ecosystems and cloud platforms.
Ecosystem: ARM has a rich ecosystem of software libraries, development boards, and community support that facilitates the development and deployment of IoT solutions. This ecosystem provides developers with the tools and resources needed to create IoT applications efficiently

Features and advantages are particularly of ARM

Energy Efficiency: IoT devices often run on batteries or have limited power sources. ARM processors' energy-efficient architecture ensures that IoT devices can operate for extended periods without frequent battery replacements or recharging. This is crucial for the longevity and reliability of IoT deployments, especially in remote or inaccessible locations.
Reduced Instruction Set Computing (RISC) Architecture: In the context of IoT, where devices may have limited processing power and memory, ARM's RISC architecture shines. It enables efficient execution of code on resource-constrained devices, making it suitable for IoT applications that require lightweight and responsive processing.
Architecture Variability: IoT encompasses a wide range of applications, from simple sensors to complex edge computing devices. ARM's diverse portfolio of processor cores, including the low-power Cortex-M series and higher-performance Cortex-A series, allows IoT developers to choose the right core for their specific use case. This flexibility is crucial for tailoring IoT solutions to varying performance and power requirements.
Compatibility and Ecosystem: ARM enjoys widespread compatibility with various IoT operating systems, middleware, and development tools. IoT developers benefit from a rich ecosystem of software libraries and tools that simplify application development, device management, and integration with cloud platforms.
Scalability and Customization: IoT deployments often involve a mix of devices with varying processing needs. ARM's scalability allows for a seamless transition from small-scale IoT sensors to more powerful edge devices, all using ARM-based processors. Additionally, ARM's design flexibility enables manufacturers to customize processors for specific IoT applications, optimizing performance and power consumption.
In summary, ARM's energy-efficient, RISC-based architecture, along with its variability, compatibility, scalability, and customization options, makes it exceptionally well-suited for IoT applications. ARM processors provide the foundation for building energy-efficient, reliable, and scalable IoT solutions, which is why they are widely adopted in the IoT ecosystem.

Designing an IoT application

Designing an IoT application using the CC3100 Wi-Fi module to connect a sensor involves several steps. In this example, we'll create a simple IoT application that reads data from a temperature and humidity sensor (DHT22) and sends that data to a cloud service (in this case, we'll use Thing Speak) for visualization and monitoring. Here's a high-level overview of the steps involved:

Components Needed:

CC3100 Wi-Fi module
DHT22 temperature and humidity sensor
Microcontroller (e.g., Arduino, Raspberry Pi)
Power source (e.g., batteries or USB power supply)
Internet connection

Steps to Design the IoT Application:

Set Up Hardware:

Connect the DHT22 sensor to your microcontroller. Typically, the sensor has three pins: VCC (power), GND (ground), and DATA (data signal). Connect these pins to the appropriate pins on your microcontroller.

Connect the CC3100 Wi-Fi module to your microcontroller according to the manufacturer's instructions.

Install Necessary Libraries:

Depending on your microcontroller, you'll need to install the required libraries for the CC3100 module and the DHT22 sensor. For Arduino, you can use libraries like "Adafruit_CC3000" for CC3100 and "DHT sensor library" for DHT22.

Write the Code:

Write the code for your microcontroller to read data from the DHT22 sensor and establish a connection with the CC3100 Wi-Fi module. Here's a simplified example using Arduino:

Code -

```
#include <Adafruit_CC3000.h>
#include <Adafruit_CC3000_Client.h>
#include <DHT.h>

#define WLAN_SSID      "YourWiFiSSID"
#define WLAN_PASS      "YourWiFiPassword"
#define WLAN_SECURITY  WLAN_SEC_WPA2
#define SERVER_IP      "api.thingspeak.com"
#define THINGSPEAK_API_KEY "YourAPIKey"

#define DHT_PIN        2 // Replace with your actual pin number
#define DHT_TYPE       DHT22

Adafruit_CC3000 cc3000;
DHT dht(DHT_PIN, DHT_TYPE);

void setup() {
Serial.begin(115200);
dht.begin();
if (!cc3000.begin()) {
Serial.println("Unable to initialize CC3000");
while (1);
}
Serial.println("CC3000 initialized!");
connectToWiFi();
}

void loop() {
float humidity = dht.readHumidity();
float temperature = dht.readTemperature();

if (isnan(humidity) || isnan(temperature)) {
```

```
Serial.println("Failed to read from DHT sensor!");
return;
}

sendToThingSpeak(temperature, humidity);
delay(60000); // Send data every minute
}

void connectToWiFi() {
Serial.print("Connecting to ");
Serial.println(WLAN_SSID);
cc3000.connectToAP(WLAN_SSID, WLAN_PASS, WLAN_SECURITY);
while (!cc3000.checkConnected()) {
delay(1000);
Serial.print(".");
}
Serial.println("Connected!");
}

void sendToThingSpeak(float temperature, float humidity) {
Adafruit_CC3000_Client client;
if (cc3000.connectTCP(SERVER_IP, 80)) {
client.fastrprint("GET /update?key=");
client.fastrprint(THINGSPEAK_API_KEY);
client.fastrprint("&field1=");
client.fastrprint(temperature);
client.fastrprint("&field2=");
client.fastrprint(humidity);
client.fastrprint("\r\n");
client.close();
}
}
```

Configure Thing Speak:
Sign up for a Thing Speak account and create a new channel.
Note your Thing Speak API key and channel number.
Upload Code to Microcontroller:
Compile the code and upload it to your microcontroller.
Monitor Data:
Access your Thing Speak channel to view and analyse the data sent by your IoT device.
This is a simplified example to get you started with IoT using the CC3100 module and a sensor. Depending on your project's requirements, you can expand upon this by adding more sensors, incorporating data processing logic, and integrating with other IoT platforms or services.

Role of controller service in an IoT system

In an IoT (Internet of Things) system, a controller service plays a crucial role in managing and orchestrating various components and functions of the IoT infrastructure. Its primary functions include:

Device Management: Controller services are responsible for registering, provisioning, and managing IoT devices. This includes device onboarding, configuration, and ensuring that devices are securely connected to the network. It also involves monitoring the status and health of devices.

Data Collection: IoT systems typically involve a wide variety of sensors and devices that collect data from the physical world. The controller service facilitates the collection of data from these devices, ensuring that data is transmitted reliably to the central IoT platform or cloud.

Data Processing: IoT systems often generate vast amounts of data. The controller service may preprocess this data locally on edge devices before sending it to the cloud to reduce bandwidth usage and latency. This can include filtering, aggregation, and basic analytics.

Security and Access Control: Ensuring the security of IoT devices and data is paramount. The controller service enforces security policies, manages device authentication, and ensures that data is transmitted and stored securely. It can also control access to devices and data based on user roles and permissions.
Communication: IoT devices communicate with each other, with edge gateways, and with cloud servers. The controller service manages communication protocols and ensures that devices can communicate effectively. It may also handle message queuing and routing.
Scalability: As the number of IoT devices grows, the controller service needs to scale accordingly. It should be capable of handling a large number of devices and data streams efficiently.
Fault Tolerance: IoT systems must be resilient to failures. The controller service should have mechanisms for detecting and handling failures in devices, network connectivity, or other components. It may implement redundancy and failover strategies.
Configuration Management: IoT devices may require periodic updates, configuration changes, or firmware upgrades. The controller service can push these updates to devices and ensure that they are applied correctly.
Integration with Cloud Services: Many IoT applications leverage cloud services for data storage, analytics, and visualization. The controller service integrates with these cloud services, managing the flow of data between edge devices and the cloud.
Monitoring and Analytics: The controller service often includes monitoring and analytics capabilities to track the performance and health of the IoT system. It can generate alerts and reports based on predefined criteria.
Resource Optimization: IoT devices often have limited resources, such as processing power and battery life. The controller service may optimize resource usage by scheduling tasks, managing power states, and optimizing data transmission.
User Interface: In some cases, the controller service provides a user interface or dashboard for administrators and users to monitor and manage the IoT system. This can include real-time data visualization and device management tools.
Overall, the controller service acts as the central intelligence of an IoT system, coordinating the activities of devices, gateways, and cloud services to ensure that the system functions reliably, securely, and efficiently. Its role is critical in enabling the seamless operation of IoT applications in various domains, from smart cities to industrial automation to healthcare.

IoT cloud-based data collection, storage and computing services

IoT (Internet of Things) cloud-based data collection, storage, and computing services are essential components of IoT ecosystems that enable organizations to manage and derive value from the vast amounts of data generated by IoT devices. Here's an explanation of each of these services:
Data Collection:
Role: Data collection is the process of gathering information from IoT devices, sensors, and other data sources distributed across various locations.
Methods: Data collection can be achieved through various communication protocols, including Wi-Fi, cellular networks, LoRaWAN, Zigbee, MQTT, and more, depending on the specific requirements of the IoT devices and the infrastructure.
Data Ingestion: Collected data is ingested into cloud platforms through APIs, gateways, or direct device-to-cloud communication. It may include structured and unstructured data, such as sensor readings, images, videos, and more.
Real-time and Batch: Data collection can occur in real-time or in batch processes, depending on the use case. Real-time collection is critical for applications that require immediate responses, such as industrial automation or security systems.
Data Storage:
Role: Data storage involves securely storing and managing the massive volumes of IoT data for future retrieval, analysis, and processing.
Cloud-Based Storage: IoT cloud platforms typically offer scalable, cloud-based storage solutions that can handle the high data throughput of IoT devices. This storage may be structured (databases) or unstructured (data lakes).
Data Retention: Organizations must define data retention policies that determine how long data should be stored. Some data may only be needed temporarily, while other data might be retained for historical analysis and compliance.
Security: Data storage services implement robust security measures to protect data, including encryption, access control, and authentication.
Data Computing and Processing:
Role: Data computing and processing services enable organizations to analyse and derive insights from IoT data, transforming it into actionable information.

Data Analytics: Cloud platforms provide tools and services for data analytics, including real-time stream processing, batch processing, and machine learning algorithms.
Complex Event Processing (CEP): CEP engines can analyse streaming IoT data for patterns, anomalies, and trigger alerts or automated actions based on predefined rules.
Scalability: Cloud computing services can scale resources up or down to handle fluctuating data processing demands, ensuring efficient resource utilization.
Integration: Data processing services can integrate with other cloud services, databases, and third-party tools, enabling organizations to build end-to-end IoT solutions.
Together, these three services in an IoT cloud-based ecosystem allow organizations to efficiently manage, analyse, and derive insights from IoT data. This data-driven approach enables improved decision-making, predictive maintenance, optimization of operations, and the development of innovative IoT applications across various industries, including manufacturing, healthcare, agriculture, smart cities, and more.

Convergence of IT and OT

The convergence of Information Technology (IT) and Operational Technology (OT) is a significant trend in the field of technology and industrial processes. IT and OT have traditionally been distinct domains within organizations, each serving different purposes and functions. However, as technology advances and organizations seek greater efficiency and agility, the boundaries between IT and OT are blurring. Here's an overview of the convergence of IT and OT:
Definitions:
IT (Information Technology): IT encompasses the use of computer systems, networks, and software to store, process, transmit, and manage data and information for business operations. It includes technologies like data centres, servers, cloud computing, and enterprise applications.
OT (Operational Technology): OT, on the other hand, focuses on the hardware and software used to control and monitor physical processes and devices in industries such as manufacturing, energy, transportation, and utilities. It includes technologies like industrial control systems (ICS), supervisory control and data acquisition (SCADA) systems, programmable logic controllers (PLCs), and sensors.
Key Aspects of Convergence:
Data Integration: One of the primary drivers of IT-OT convergence is the integration of data from OT systems into IT systems. This allows for a more comprehensive view of operations and better decision-making. Data from sensors and industrial equipment can be collected, processed, and analyzed alongside business data.
Cybersecurity: As IT and OT systems become more interconnected, cybersecurity becomes a critical concern. The convergence necessitates robust security measures to protect against cyber threats that can impact both information systems and industrial processes.
Standardization: Standardization efforts are underway to create common protocols and frameworks that facilitate communication and interoperability between IT and OT systems. This enables smoother integration and data exchange.
Cloud Computing: Cloud technologies are increasingly being used to bridge the gap between IT and OT. Cloud platforms provide scalable and cost-effective solutions for storing and processing the vast amounts of data generated by OT systems.
Benefits of Convergence:
Improved Efficiency: Converging IT and OT allows for better coordination of business processes and industrial operations, leading to increased efficiency and reduced downtime.
Data-Driven Insights: Combining data from both domains provides organizations with valuable insights into their operations, enabling predictive maintenance, optimization, and improved decision-making.
Cost Savings: Integration can lead to cost savings through the consolidation of hardware and software systems and more efficient resource allocation.
Agility: Convergence makes it easier for organizations to adapt to changing market conditions and customer demands.
Challenges:
Cultural Differences: IT and OT teams often have different goals, priorities, and skill sets. Bridging these cultural differences and fostering collaboration can be a challenge.
Security Risks: As mentioned earlier, increased connectivity creates new cybersecurity risks that need to be carefully managed.
Legacy Systems: Many industrial environments still rely on legacy OT systems that may not easily integrate with modern IT solutions. Updating and modernizing these systems can be complex and costly.

In summary, the convergence of IT and OT is driven by the need for organizations to harness the power of data, improve operational efficiency, and stay competitive in a rapidly evolving technological landscape. While it offers numerous benefits, it also presents challenges that require
careful planning and management to ensure a successful integration.

BACnet

BACnet, which stands for "Building Automation and Control Networks," is a widely used communication protocol specifically designed for building automation and control systems (BACS) in the context of IoT (Internet of Things). BACnet is an open standard, allowing different devices and systems from various manufacturers to communicate and work together seamlessly within a building or industrial environment. It defines several layers to enable communication between devices and systems. Here's an explanation of the different layers in the BACnet protocol and their functions:

Physical Layer:

Function: The physical layer deals with the actual hardware connections and electrical characteristics of the communication medium. It specifies the physical aspects of how data is transmitted over various types of media, such as Ethernet, RS-485, and IP networks.

Examples: Ethernet cables, RS-485 wiring, wireless RF connections, and the hardware interfaces that connect devices to these media.

Data Link Layer:

Function: The data link layer is responsible for ensuring reliable point-to-point or multi-point communication between devices on the same network segment. It manages data framing, error detection, and error correction.

Examples: MAC (Media Access Control) addressing, frame formats, and data link protocols like BACnet MS/TP (Master-Slave/Token-Passing) for RS-485 networks.

Network Layer:

Function: The network layer is responsible for routing and addressing messages between devices on different network segments or subnetworks. It ensures that data can be delivered across complex building automation networks.

Examples: IP addressing, routing tables, and routers or gateways that connect different network segments.

Transport Layer:

Function: The transport layer provides end-to-end communication services, including message segmentation, reassembly, and error recovery. It ensures that messages sent from one device are reliably received by another.

Examples: BACnet/IP (over TCP or UDP) for reliable transport and BACnet/UDP (User Datagram Protocol) for connectionless transport.

Application Layer:

Function: The application layer is the highest layer of the BACnet protocol and defines the actual BACnet objects, services, and data models used for building automation and control. It enables devices to exchange information related to lighting, HVAC (Heating, Ventilation, and Air Conditioning), access control, and other building systems.

Examples: BACnet objects like Analog Input, Binary Output, and Multi-state Value, along with services like Read Property, Write Property, and Subscribe COV (Change of Value).

Presentation Layer (Optional):

Function: The presentation layer is optional in BACnet and is responsible for data translation, encryption, and decryption. It provides mechanisms for encoding and decoding data in a way that both communicating devices can understand.

Examples: Data encoding formats like ASN.1 (Abstract Syntax Notation One) and security mechanisms for data protection.

Session Layer (Optional):

Function: Also optional in BACnet, the session layer manages sessions between devices, including the establishment, maintenance, and termination of connections. It is responsible for ensuring that communication sessions are reliable and efficient.

Examples: Session management protocols for BACnet/IP and BACnet/UDP.

The EPC Global Architecture Framework is a set of standards and specifications developed by EPC Global for the use of Electronic Product Code (EPC) in RFID (Radio-Frequency Identification) and IoT (Internet of Things) applications. It provides a standardized approach for identifying and tracking physical objects in the supply chain and various industries. The framework is particularly important for enabling efficient inventory management, supply chain optimization, and visibility of products and assets. Here's an explanation of the key components of the EPC Global Architecture Framework:

EPC (Electronic Product Code)

Function: EPC is a unique identifier assigned to physical objects, products, or assets in RFID and IoT systems. It is akin to a serial number that distinguishes one item from another.

Components:

EPC Identifier (EPC ID): A globally unique number that identifies the product or asset.

EPC Manager: Responsible for managing EPCs and ensuring their uniqueness.

RFID Tags:

Function: RFID tags are physical labels or devices containing EPCs. They are attached to objects or products and can be scanned or read by RFID readers.

Types:

Passive RFID Tags: These tags do not have a built-in power source and rely on energy from RFID readers for operation.

Active RFID Tags: These tags have their own power source (usually a battery) and can transmit data actively to RFID readers.

EPC Network:

Function: The EPC Network is a communication infrastructure that enables the exchange of EPC-related data between RFID readers, middleware, and back-end systems.

Components:

RFID Readers: Devices that read EPCs from RFID tags and communicate with the EPC Network.

Middleware: Software that processes and manages EPC data, acting as an intermediary between readers and back-end systems.

EPCIS (EPC Information Service): A standardized interface for storing and querying EPC-related data, allowing for real-time visibility and traceability

EPC Information Services (EPCIS):

Function: EPCIS provides a standardized way to capture, store, and share EPC-related data, including the history and location of tagged objects.

Components:

Event Capture: Records events like tag reads, shipments, and inventory changes.

Event Repository: Stores event data for later retrieval.

Query and Subscription: Allows users and systems to query the EPCIS for specific information or subscribe to events of interest.

EPC global Network Services:

Function: Network services provide secure and standardized communication between different components of the EPC Global Architecture.

Components:

Discovery Services: Help locate EPC services and resources on the network.

Security Services: Ensure data integrity and confidentiality.

Transport Services: Facilitate data exchange over various communication protocols.

EPCglobal Standards and Specifications:

Function: EPC Global has developed a set of standards and specifications that define how EPC data is captured, managed, and shared. These standards ensure interoperability across different systems and vendors.

In summary, the EPC Global Architecture Framework is a standardized approach to using Electronic Product Codes (EPCs) and RFID technology in IoT applications, particularly in the supply chain and logistics sectors. It provides a structured way to uniquely identify objects, capture data about them, and share that data across a network of devices and systems, leading to improved visibility, traceability, and efficiency in various industries.

Exercise

Exercise 1 – MCQ

1. Which of the following best describes the clustering principle in IoT?

a) It involves grouping IoT devices into clusters based on their geographical location.

b) It refers to the process of organizing data into clusters to improve data analytics.

c) It is a security measure to protect IoT devices from unauthorized access.

d) It focuses on reducing power consumption by allowing some devices to act as intermediaries for others.

2. What is the primary role of ARM in the context of IoT?

a) To provide wireless connectivity for IoT devices.

b) To act as a centralized server for IoT data storage.

c) To design energy-efficient processors for IoT devices.

d) To ensure cybersecurity for IoT networks.

Exercise 2 – True/False

1. The clustering principle in IoT involves grouping IoT devices into clusters to improve network management and reduce communication overhead.
2. Clustering in IoT primarily focuses on maximizing individual device performance without considering power consumption.

Exercise 3 – Fill in the blanks

1. ARM, which stands for Advanced RISC Machines, is known for its energy-efficient _________ and is commonly used in various IoT devices.
2. In the context of IoT, the _________ principle involves grouping IoT devices into clusters to improve network efficiency and reduce communication overhead.

Exercise 4 – One word answer

1. M2M stands for?
2. ARM stands for?

Exercise 5 – Small answer

1. Explain the role of controller service in IoT application?
2. Write the steps to create an IoT application.

Exercise 6 – Long answer

1. Explain the significance of ARM (Advanced RISC Machines) architecture in the context of the Internet of Things (IoT).
2. Describe the concept of clustering in the Internet of Things (IoT) and its role in optimizing network performance and power efficiency.

Answer:

Exercise 1.

1. b) It focuses on reducing power consumption by allowing some devices to act as intermediaries for others.
2. c) To design energy-efficient processors for IoT devices.

Exercise 2.

1. True
2. False

Exercise 3.

1. Design or Architecture
2. Clustering

Exercise 4.

1. Machine to Machine
2. Advanced RISC Machines

Previous Year Questions

1. Explain Mashup. Explain its role in IoT environment (SPPU B.Tech. 2017)
2. Explain Multiagent system. (SPPU B.Tech. 2017)
3. Explain the concept of the Horizontal and verticals in IoT. (SPPU B.Tech. 2018)
4. Explain the key elements of the ETSI M2M architecture. (Mumbai University 2018)
5. How to monitor Air-Pollution? (SPPU B.Tech. 2017)
6. What is SCADA? What are the different blocks of SCADA? (SPPU B.Tech. 2019)
7. Explain in detail clustering principal in Internet of Things. (SPPU B.Tech. 2017
8. What is BACnet? Explain the different layer's function. (Uttar Pradesh B.Tech.2018)
9. Explain EPC Global Architecture frame work. (SPPU 2017)

ONLINE RESOURCES

Link: https://forms.gle/doQ3dnnpQN7jHW3m7

QR Code:

Link : https://www.youtube.com/playlist?list=PLzlh_31VWEFoG6H2vGaMR99wNF_YOhRfM

QR Code:

YouTube Videos Playlists for all Chapters

CHAPTER 1

Link: https://www.youtube.com/playlist?list=PLzlh_31VWEFpGs-g6eWSPm6CsA018uRcy

QR Code:

CHAPTER 2

Link: https://www.youtube.com/playlist?list=PLzlh_31VWEFqI4Wonucrh6Dslm1YirsLo

QR Code:

CHAPTER 3

Link: https://www.youtube.com/playlist?list=PLzlh_31VWEFpjEVisU5V0KuxAM8RfOM9u

QR Code:

CHAPTER 4

Link: https://www.youtube.com/playlist?list=PLzlh_31VWEFruOq6KBh8x2-CcFYWGSq2n

QR Code:

CHAPTER 5

Link: https://www.youtube.com/playlist?list=PLzlh_31VWEFqVAcrQ3I9w5RJO7omQSl4A

QR Code:

CHAPTER 6

Link: https://www.youtube.com/playlist?list=PLzlh_31VWEFr7mBvjm7LKdLYum_6GGBNa

QR Code:

CHAPTER 7

Link: https://www.youtube.com/playlist?list=PLzlh_31VWEFoJPD68Eb4H0V2j4OOKzuZG

QR Code:

CHAPTER 8

Link: https://www.youtube.com/playlist?list=PLzlh_31VWEFrdXlukNKDgBjnhiDluWVMA

QR Code:

CHAPTER 9

Link: https://www.youtube.com/playlist?list=PLzlh_31VWEFpqd_WEWxLhLtVeJcapgAX6

QR Code:

CHAPTER 10

Link: https://www.youtube.com/playlist?list=PLzlh_31VWEFojw_BELcF2tQV18fOwfJiH

QR Code:

CHAPTER 11

Link: https://www.youtube.com/playlist?list=PLzlh_31VWEFo1xerecjGi2vDi_Fl3FAFE

QR Code:

CHAPTER 12

Link: https://www.youtube.com/playlist?list=PLzlh_31VWEFpkbpu8cLC6nZ9jy6x2Ovbx

QR Code:

CHAPTER 13

Link: https://www.youtube.com/playlist?list=PLzlh_31VWEFoG6H2vGaMR99wNF_YOhRfM

QR Code:

IOT Textbook Playlist

Link: https://www.youtube.com/playlist?list=PLzlh_31VWEFr1TM4zHPXnO11rfZ_FvOV-

QR Code: